S0-BRS-605

KEESING'S RESEARCH REPORT

AFRICA INDEPENDENT

A Survey of Political Developments

CHARLES SCRIBNER'S SONS

New York

CARL A. RUDISILL LIBRARY
LENOIR RHYNE COLLEGE

320.9603
Af8
85042
Sept 1973

Copyright © 1972 Keesing's Publications, Ltd.

This book published simultaneously in the
United States of America and in Canada -
Copyright under the Berne Convention

All rights reserved. No part of this book
may be reproduced in any form without the
permission of Charles Scribner's Sons.

A-1.72[c]

Printed in the United States of America
Library of Congress Catalog Card Number 70-162750
SBN 684-12532-3 (trade cloth)
SBN 684-12531-5 (trade paper, SL)

CONTENTS

INTRODUCTION

During the ten years between 1960 and 1970 the rapid emergence of politically independent non-white States from formerly dependent colonies or protectorates in Africa radically changed the map of that continent. The process of "decolonization" generally evolved by agreement between the colonial Powers and the emergent national Governments, without protracted warfare between the two sides, except in the case of Algeria which had the largest number of white settlers among those territories which eventually achieved independence.

The steps taken towards the granting of self-government and consequent full independence are illustrated by the political developments, well before 1960, in the former Gold Coast, now the Republic of Ghana, which have therefore been described here in some detail.

Some of the new States, however, were faced with secessionist tendencies within their own borders — first the Congo, and later Nigeria — which caused lengthy armed conflicts with heavy loss of life. Others were involved in border disputes with their neighbours, but all of these quarrels were settled largely on the basis of the principle that the political frontiers inherited from the colonial era should be maintained — as confirmed in the Charter of the Organization of African Unity.

At the end of the decade it appeared that the newly independent States were facing two major problems:

(a) Confrontation with the white-dominated southern part of Africa led by the Republic of South Africa (the economically most advanced State in Africa), comprising also South West Africa (Namibia), the Portuguese provinces of Angola and Mozambique and the self-styled "Republic of Rhodesia"; and

(*b*) their economic dependence, as developing countries, on the major economies of the developed parts of the world.

Politically, the start of the 1970s shows increasing evidence of a new orientation among many of the leaders of these new African States in regard to the best means of ensuring their survival as independent countries. A growing number of the politicians who fought the battles of the pre-independence era are seeing themselves replaced by new leaders, many of whom have risen from the ranks of Africa's small but growing armed forces.

Acknowledgments

This research report is principally based on the information contained in Keesing's Contemporary Archives and derived from a variety of sources, among which the following publications are the most important:

Times, Daily Telegraph, Financial Times, Guardian (all of London); New York Times, International Herald Tribune, Le Monde (Paris), Neue Zürcher Zeitung, Corriere della Sera (Milan), Cape Times (Cape Town); and bulletins issued by the U.S. Information Service, U.N. Information Centre (London) and African States' Information Departments as well as their Embassies or High Commissions in London.

Some of the statistical information has been obtained from the Africa Institute, Pretoria (South Africa), to whom grateful acknowledgment is made. The compilers of this report are also indebted to the editor and publishers (Macmillan London Limited) of the Statesman's Year-Book 1970–71 for permission to quote the figures for the gross national product.

I. INTER-AFRICAN ORGANIZATIONS

1. THE ORGANIZATION OF AFRICAN UNITY (OAU)

All independent countries in Africa (except South Africa and Rhodesia) as well as the Malagasy Republic and Mauritius are member-States of the Organization of African Unity, established at a conference of African Heads of State and Government in Addis Ababa on May 23–26, 1963.

Charter

Those attending the conference signed a Charter of the OAU, the principal provisions of which are as follows:

Establishment
Art. 1. The High Contracting Parties do by the present Charter establish an Organization to be known as the "Organization of African Unity".

The Organization shall include the continental African States, Madagascar and all the islands surrounding Africa.

Purposes
Art. 2. (1) The Organization shall have the following purposes:

(*a*) To promote the unity and solidarity of the African and Malagasy States;

(*b*) to co-ordinate and intensify their co-operation and efforts to achieve a better life for the peoples of Africa;

(*c*) to defend their sovereignty, their territorial integrity and independence;

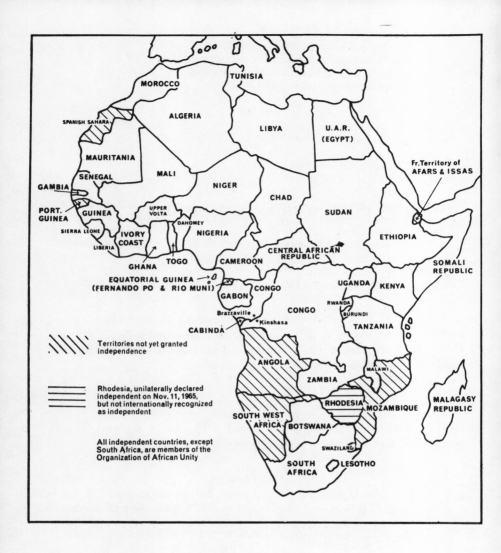

Territories not yet granted independence

Rhodesia, unilaterally declared independent on Nov. 11, 1965, but not internationally recognized as independent

All independent countries, except South Africa, are members of the Organization of African Unity

(*d*) to eradicate all forms of colonialism from Africa; and

(*e*) to promote international co-operation, having due regard to the U.N. Charter and the Universal Declaration of Human Rights.

(2) To these ends, the member-States shall co-ordinate and harmonize their general policies, especially in the following fields:

(*a*) Political and diplomatic co-operation;

(*b*) economic co-operation, including transport and communications;

(c) educational and cultural co-operation;
(d) health, sanitation and nutritional co-operation;
(e) scientific and technical co-operation; and
(f) co-operation for defence and security.

Principles

Art. 3. The member-States, in pursuit of the purposes stated in Article 2, solemnly affirm and declare their adherence to the following principles:

(1) The sovereign equality of all member-States;

(2) non-interference in the internal affairs of States;

(3) respect for the sovereignty and territorial integrity of each member-State and for its inalienable right to independent existence;

(4) peaceful settlement of disputes by negotiation, mediation, conciliation or arbitration;

(5) unreserved condemnation, in all its forms, of political assassination, as well as of subversive activities on the part of neighbouring States or any other States;

(6) absolute dedication to the total emancipation of the African territories which are still dependent;

(7) affirmation of a policy of non-alignment with regard to all blocs.

Institutions

Art. 7. The Organization shall accomplish its purposes through the following principal institutions:

(1) The Assembly of Heads of State and Government;

(2) the Council of Ministers;

(3) the General Secretariat;

(4) the Commission of Mediation, Conciliation and Arbitration.

The Assembly of Heads of State and Government

Art. 8. The Assembly of Heads of State and Government shall be the supreme organ of the Organization. It shall, subject to the provisions of this Charter, discuss matters of common concern to Africa with a view to co-ordinating and harmonizing the general policy of the Organization. It may in addition review the structure, functions and acts of all the organs and any specialized agencies which may be created in accordance with the Charter.

Art. 9. The Assembly shall be composed of the Heads of State or Government, or their duly accredited representatives, and shall meet at least once a year. At the request of any member-State, and upon approval by the majority of the member-States, the Assembly shall meet in extraordinary session.

The Council of Ministers

Art. 12. The Council of Ministers shall consist of Foreign Ministers or such other Ministers as are designated by the Governments of member-States.

The Council of Ministers shall meet at least twice a year. When requested by any member-State and approved by two-thirds of all member-States, it shall meet in extraordinary session.

Art. 13. The Council of Ministers shall be responsible to the Assembly of Heads of State and Government. It shall be entrusted with the responsibility of preparing conferences of the Assembly.

General Secretariat

Art. 16. There shall be an Administrative Secretary-General of the Organization, who shall be appointed by the Assembly of Heads of State and Government on the recommendation of the Council of Ministers. The Administrative Secretary-General shall direct the affairs of the Secretariat.

Commission of Mediation, Conciliation and Arbitration

Art. 19. Member-States pledge to settle all disputes among themselves by peaceful means and, to this end, decide to establish a Commission of Mediation, Conciliation and Arbitration, the composition and the condition of service of which shall be defined by a separate protocol to be approved by the Assembly of Heads of State and Government.

Specialized Commissions

Art. 20. The Assembly shall establish such Specialized Commissions as it may deem necessary, including the following: (1) Economic and Social Commission; (2) Educational and Cultural Commission; (3) Health, Sanitation and Nutrition Commission; (4) Defence Commission; (5) Scientific, Technical and Research Commission.

The conference also appointed a committee of nine members (Algeria, Congo-Léopoldville, Ethiopia, Guinea, Nigeria, Senegal, Tanganyika, Uganda and the U.A.R.) charged with establishing a "Liberation Bureau" in Dar-es-Salaam for the purpose of aiding national liberation movements in their struggle to end the remaining "forms of colonialism" in Africa.

Assemblies of Heads of State and Government

The second Assembly of Heads of State and Government, held in Cairo on July 17–21, 1964, decided *inter alia* (*a*) to make Addis Ababa the seat of the Organization's permanent headquarters; (*b*) to approve a protocol providing for mediation, conciliation, and finally, arbitration in disputes between member-countries, as well as an undertaking by member-States to respect their frontiers as existing at the achievement of independence; and (*c*) to set up two permanent commissions – one of African jurists and another on communications.

The third Assembly of Heads of State and Government, held in Accra on Oct. 21–26, 1965, issued a Declaration on Subversive Activities containing the following main provisions:

(1) The OAU pledged itself to oppose collectively and firmly, by every means at its disposal, every form of subversion conceived, organized or financed by any foreign Power against Africa as a whole or against OAU member-States.

(2) The declaration emphasized that member-States would tolerate neither subversion by one State against another nor the use of their territory for subversive activity directed from outside Africa against another member-State.

(3) All differences between two or more member-States should be settled by bilateral or multilateral consultations, on the basis of a protocol of mediation, conciliation and arbitration as laid down in the OAU Charter, and there should be no reaction against a member-State by means of a radio or press campaign.

(4) Member-States should not give cause for dissension among themselves by fomenting or aggravating racial, religious, linguistic, ethnic or other differences, and should combat all forms of activity of this kind.

(5) In regard to political refugees, the declaration enjoined member-States to observe strictly the principles of international law towards all nationals of member-States; to try to promote through bilateral or multilateral consultations the return of refugees to their home country with the consent both of the refugees themselves and their country of origin; and to continue to guarantee the safety of political refugees from dependent territories and support them in their struggle for the liberation of their countries.

It also adopted a resolution on political refugees which recalled the member-States' pledge to prevent refugees living in their territories from carrying out by any means whatsoever any acts harmful to the interests of member-States; requested all member-States never to allow the refugee question to become a source of disagreement among them; appreciated the assistance given to the refugee programmes of African Governments by the U.N. High Commissioner for Refugees (UNHCR); requested African members of the U.N. Economic and Social Council to seek an increase in African representation on the executive committee of the UNHCR programme on refugees; and requested those member-States which had not already done so to ratify the U.N. convention on refugees and to apply meanwhile the provisions of that convention to refugees in Africa.

The fourth Assembly of Heads of State and Government, held in Addis Ababa on Nov. 5–9, 1966, decided *inter alia* to replace the Liberation

Committee in Dar-es-Salaam by a new committee of 10 members, the executive of which would be placed under the direct control of the OAU Secretariat-General and would be excluded from any initiative of a political nature in its activities.

The fifth Assembly of Heads of State and Government was held in Kinshasa (Congo) on Sept. 11–14, 1967, without Malawi being represented.

The sixth Assembly of Heads of State and Government, attended by representatives of all member-States except Malawi, was held in Algiers on Sept. 13–16, 1968.

A draft resolution on Nigeria, which *inter alia* called on the Biafrans [i.e. the secessionists in Eastern Nigeria then in armed conflict with the Federal Government of Nigeria — see page 110] to abandon their secession and "to co-operate with the Federal authorities with a view to restoring the peace and unity of Nigeria", was adopted by the Assembly by 33 votes to four (Gabon, the Ivory Coast, Tanzania and Zambia — all of whose Governments had recognized Biafra as a sovereign State) with two abstentions (Botswana and Rwanda).

The Assembly was preceded by a meeting of the Liberation Committee, which decided in Algiers on July 20, 1968, (*a*) to give increased aid to the African National Congress (ANC) of South Africa and the *Partido Africano de Independência da Guiné e do Cabo Verde* (PAIGC) while suspending aid to the Pan-Africanist Congress (PAC) of South Africa; and (*b*) to recognize three new African liberation movements — the Liberation Front of the Somali Coast, the Djibouti Liberation Movement, and the Movement for Independence and Self-Determination for the Canary Islands (represented at the meeting by Señor Antonio Cubillo, a lawyer).

The seventh Assembly of Heads of State and Government, held in Addis Ababa on Sept. 6–9, 1969, and attended by all 41 member-States, adopted *inter alia* resolutions on Southern Africa and the civil war in Nigeria.

The Assembly considered a report by its Secretary-General, dealing with the 'struggle against colonialism' in the Portuguese territories, Rhodesia and South Africa and accusing the North Atlantic Treaty

Organization (NATO) of "giving military support to the enemies of our peoples".

U Thant, the U.N. Secretary-General, speaking as the Assembly's guest, deplored the fact that a U.N. declaration on decolonization adopted in 1960 had "very largely failed of fulfilment in Southern Africa". The world's ability to ward off "the grave dangers of violent conflict" arising from the policy of *apartheid* applied in South Africa, depended partly, he said, on "the willingness of some great Powers to take effective measures to turn that country off its present course". The resolution adopted by the Assembly stated *inter alia* that liberation movements recognized by the OAU would be given increased aid and that "member-States should exert every possible effort to have the South African regime — which according to the U.N. Charter has no legal basis — excluded from the United Nations and from other international organizations".

On Nigeria the Assembly adopted, on Sept. 8, with five abstentions (Gabon, the Ivory Coast, Sierra Leone, Tanzania and Zambia) a resolution appealing (*a*) to both parties in the conflict to recognize the unity of Nigeria, to cease all hostilities and to enter into negotiations forthwith; and (*b*) to all foreign Powers and organizations to refrain from all interference.

The Assembly also adopted a Convention on Refugees which confirmed, for the first time in any international instrument, the right of asylum as laid down in a U.N. Declaration issued on Dec. 14, 1967; emphasized the importance of voluntary repatriation; and added that those who returned voluntarily to their countries should in no way be penalized. This Convention would come into force after ratification by one-third of the OAU member-States.

The eighth Assembly of Heads of State and Government, held in Addis Ababa on Sept. 1–3, 1970, was also attended by all 41 member-States.

At this Assembly, (*a*) reconciliation was announced between the Federal Military Government of Nigeria and the Governments of the four member-States (Gabon, the Ivory Coast, Tanzania and Zambia) which had granted diplomatic recognition to the (since defeated) secessionist regime in Biafra; (*b*), on the initiative of the Kenya Government, a resolution was adopted condemning France, Britain and Western Germany for supplying or intending to supply arms to South Africa, and a delegation of four Foreign Ministers (of Algeria, Cameroon, Kenya and Mali) under the leadership of President Kaunda of Zambia was appointed to dissuade Western Governments from supplying arms to South Africa; and (*c*) a resolution was adopted calling upon all suppliers of funds for the building of a large dam at Cabora Bassa (on the Zambesi river) in Mozambique – for which the Portuguese Government had obtained the promise of co-operation from South Africa and firms in several Western countries – to cease their contributions forthwith.

Scientific and Technical Commission

The OAU Scientific and Technical Commission (established under Art. 20 of the OAU Charter) on Jan. 1, 1965, absorbed the Commission for Technical Co-operation in Africa (CTCA), which had been established in Paris in January 1950.

The CTCA had reconstituted itself in Abidjan (Ivory Coast) on Feb. 8–16, 1962, so as to comprise all independent African member-States, ending the full membership of Britain, France and Belgium (which had founded the Commission and were to be invited to participate in the Commission's work at technical level), and excluding Portugal and South Africa.

2. THE COMMON AFRICAN, MALAGASY AND MAURITIAN ORGANIZATION (OCAM)

A Common African and Malagasy Organization, the *Organisation commune africaine et malgache* (OCAM), was established at Nouakchott (Mauritania) on Feb. 12, 1965, by 13 French-speaking African States (Cameroon, Central African Republic, Chad, Congo-Brazzaville, Dahomey, Gabon, Ivory Coast, Madagascar, Mauritania, Niger, Senegal, Togo and Upper Volta), which were later joined by Rwanda. The Congo (Léopoldville – now Kinshasa) was admitted to OCAM on May 26, 1965, and Mauritania withdrew on June 24, 1965.

The new organization superseded the *Union africaine et malgache de coopération économique* (UAMCE) set up in March 1964, which in turn had succeeded the *Union africaine et malgache* (UAM), also known as the "Brazzaville Group" of French-speaking African States, created in Tananarive (Madagascar) in September 1961 by 12 former French territories.

A Charter for OCAM was approved by a conference of leaders of the organization's member-States at Tananarive on June 25–28, 1966.

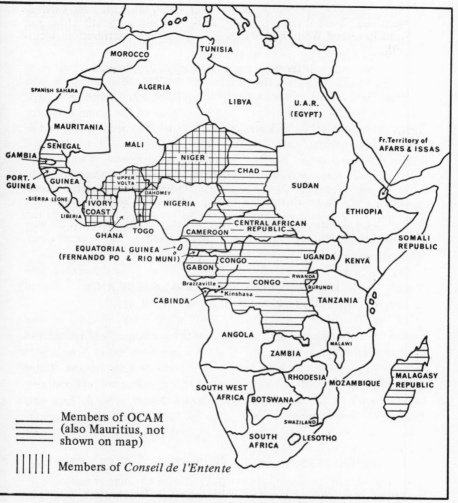

MOROCCO

TUNISIA

SPANISH SAHARA

ALGERIA

LIBYA

U.A.R.
(EGYPT)

MAURITANIA

Fr.Territory of
AFARS & ISSAS

SENEGAL

MALI

GAMBIA

NIGER

PORT.
GUINEA

GUINEA

UPPER
VOLTA

CHAD

SUDAN

·SIERRA LEONE

DAHOMEY

LIBERIA

IVORY
COAST

NIGERIA

ETHIOPIA

GHANA

TOGO

CAMEROON

CENTRAL AFRICAN
REPUBLIC

SOMALI
REPUBLIC

EQUATORIAL GUINEA
(FERNANDO PO & RIO MUNI)

GABON

CONGO

UGANDA

KENYA

Brazzaville

CONGO

RWANDA

BURUNDI

CABINDA

Kinshasa

TANZANIA

ANGOLA

ZAMBIA

MALAWI

MALAGASY
REPUBLIC

RHODESIA

MOZAMBIQUE

SOUTH WEST
AFRICA

BOTSWANA

SWAZILAND

SOUTH
AFRICA

LESOTHO

——— Members of OCAM
≡≡≡ (also Mauritius, not
——— shown on map)

||||| Members of *Conseil de l'Entente*

Defining increased co-operation between member-States as the main object of OCAM, the Charter laid down that any African independent and sovereign State accepting the Charter's provisions could be admitted to the Organization upon application. It provided for three organs of OCAM, as follows:

(*a*) The Conference of the Heads of State and Government as the supreme organ of the Organization, meeting once a year in ordinary session;

9

(*b*) the Council of Ministers consisting of the Foreign Ministers of member-States, meeting once a year in ordinary session, responsible to the Conference, and implementing co-operation between member-States as directed by the Conference;

(*c*) the Administrative General Secretariat, appointed for two years by the Conference upon the proposal of the Council of Ministers, with its seat at Yaoundé (Cameroon) and its mandate being renewable.

At its formation, OCAM was characterized by its first President (M. Ould Daddah of Mauritania) as "an African grouping which has the aim, within the framework of the OAU, of reinforcing co-operation and solidarity among the African States and Madagascar in order to accelerate their development in the political, economic, social, technical and cultural spheres."

Following its first conference at Nouakchott and the second at Tananarive, OCAM held further conferences of the Heads of State of its member-States as follows:

(*a*) At Niamey (Niger) on Jan. 22–23, 1968, when agreement was reached on the setting-up of common markets for sugar and meat, as well as joint institutions for technical co-operation;

(*b*) at Kinshasa on Jan. 27–29, 1969, when it was decided to take action to settle disputes between the two Congo republics and Chad and the Congo (Kinshasa);

(*c*) at Yaoundé on Jan. 28–30, 1970. At this conference it was confirmed that Mauritius had been admitted as a member and that the organization's name had been changed to *Organisation commune africaine, malgache et mauricienne.*

3. CONFERENCES OF EAST AND CENTRAL AFRICAN STATES

Although not joined in a formal organization, the Heads of State and Government of a number of Central and East African States met in conference on various occasions from 1966 onwards.

(*a*) The Nairobi Conference

The Heads of State and members of the Governments of Burundi, both Congos, Ethiopia, Kenya, Malawi, Rwanda, Somalia, the Sudan, Tanzania and Uganda met in Nairobi from March 31 to April 2, 1966.

The joint communiqué issued after the conference dealt mainly with the two questions of Rhodesia and refugees.

Rhodesia. It was agreed that:

(a) each State should exert maximum pressure – diplomatic and otherwise – on the British Government to take effective and decisive measures, including the use of force, against the Smith regime;

(b) the OAU should be asked to continue to seek the most appropriate collective action to be taken by its member-States in an effort to secure a Government based on majority rule in Rhodesia, and also to consider the application of mandatory sanctions under Chapter VII of the U.N. Charter;

(c) an appeal should be made to the African Nationalists of Rhodesia to take action against the rebel regime and to intensify their fight for freedom; and

(d) Zambia should be assisted in every possible way to help her overcome difficulties arising from Rhodesia's UDI.

Refugees. The participants decided that political refugees should be given no Press facilities, aid or military training which could be used against their own countries; that host countries should ensure that such refugees did not settle too close to the borders of their homelands; and that those found working against their home Governments should be expelled.

(b) The "Declaration of Kinshasa"

On the initiative of President Kaunda of Zambia, a conference on "security problems and the interrelation of economic and political liberation in Africa" was held in Kinshasa on Feb. 12–14, 1967, being attended by the leaders of 10 Central African countries, viz., Burundi, the Central African Republic, both Congos, Kenya, Rwanda, the Sudan, Tanzania, Uganda and Zambia.

In a joint communiqué entitled the "Declaration of Kinshasa" and read out by President Mobutu on Feb. 14, the 10 countries:

(1) reaffirmed "their wholehearted support of the Organization of African Unity";

(2) renewed their "support for the OAU's efforts to co-ordinate the liberation movement in Africa" and "firmly called upon all the freedom fighters to unite and work together for the achievement of their independence";

(3) "unreservedly condemned the British Government for its mishandling of the Rhodesian problem and, although supporting the U.N. selective mandatory sanctions, ... reiterated their call for the use of force in accordance with the OAU resolutions as the only effective method of toppling the fascist and racist minority regime in Rhodesia";

(4) "having noted the inherent dangers in the presence of hostile forces in the racist-minority controlled countries bordering on the

Congo (Kinshasa), Brazzaville, Zambia and Tanzania, . . . declared their support for and solidarity with each other in maintaining the security and preserving the sovereignty of their respective countries";

(5) "declared their full support for the Congolese Government in its conflict with the former *Union Minière;*

(6) "declared . . . their solidarity with any other African country which takes similar decisions" and expressed their determination "to oppose any foreign interference – political, economic or otherwise – that may adversely affect such right of national sovereignty".

The conference set up a commission to examine problems of security and another to study economic questions, both to be in continual session.

(*c*) The Kampala Conference

The countries represented at a conference in Kampala (Uganda) on Dec. 15–16, 1967, were Burundi, the Central African Republic, both Congos, Ethiopia, Kenya, Rwanda, Somalia, the Sudan, Tanzania, Uganda and Zambia.

The decisions of the conference were based on recommendations and suggestions of a preparatory Foreign Ministers' meeting held in Lusaka in July 1967. They included an agreement that each of the 12 nations represented would, where possible, buy the manufactures of the others in preference to importing goods from countries outside Africa. The conference also agreed to take positive steps to develop trade and communications in the area, to exchange information on security matters and to conclude bilateral extradition treaties.

(*d*) The Dar-es-Salaam Conference

At the fourth conference, held in Dar-es-Salaam on May 12–15, 1968, and attended by representatives of 14 countries (the 12 represented at Kampala and also Chad and Malawi) as well as the OAU Liberation Committee, a final communiqué expressed concern at the "worsening of the situation in Rhodesia" and the support given to Southern African countries by "certain States", who were called upon to cease all aid to Rhodesia, South Africa and Portugal.

(*e*) The "Lusaka Manifesto"

A conference held in Lusaka (Zambia) on April 14–16, 1969, and attended by representatives of the same 14 countries as the Dar-es-Salaam conference, in its final communiqué rejected the *Fearless* terms for a Rhodesian settlement [see page 180], endorsed NIBMAR ["no independence before majority rule"], condemned the Smith regime for executing "freedom fighters" engaged in guerrilla warfare and called on Britain to take effective measures to "protect the lives and security of its four million African citizens". A paragraph expressing the 14 States' decision to "spurn any dialogue with the minority regimes in Southern Africa" was not endorsed by the Malawi delegation, which asked for time to seek approval from President Banda.

The conference also issued a document known as the "Lusaka Manifesto" on the racial problem in Southern Africa, key passages of which read as follows:

"None of us would claim that within our own States we have achieved that perfect social, economic and political organization which would ensure a reasonable standard of living for all our people and establish individual security against avoidable hardship or miscarriage of justice. On the contrary, we acknowledge that within our own States the struggle towards human brotherhood and unchallenged human dignity is only beginning.

"It is on the basis of our commitment to human equality and human dignity, not on the basis of achieved perfection, that we take our stand of hostility towards the colonialism and racial discrimination which is being practised in southern Africa. . . .

"If commitment to these principles existed among the States holding power in southern Africa, any disagreements we might have about the rate of implementation, or about isolated acts of policy, would be matters affecting only our individual relationships with the States concerned. If these commitments existed, our States would not be justified in the expressed and active hostility towards the regimes of southern Africa such as we have proclaimed and continue to propagate. . . .

"Our objectives in southern Africa stem from our commitment to this principle of human equality. We are not hostile to the administrations of these States because they are manned and controlled by white people. We are hostile to them because they are systems of minority control which exist as a result of, and in pursuance of, doctrines of human inequality. What we are working for is the right of self-determination for the people of those territories. We are working for a rule in those countries which is based on the will of all the people and an acceptance of the equality of every citizen.

"Our stand towards southern Africa involves, thus, a rejection of racialism, not a reversal of the existing racial domination.

"As an aftermath of the present policies it is likely that different groups within these societies will be self-conscious and fearful. The initial political and economic organization may well take account of these fears and this group self-consciousness. But how this is to be done must be a matter exclusively for the peoples of the country concerned, working together. No other nation will have a right to interfere in such affairs. All that the rest of the world has a right to demand is just what we are now asserting – that the arrangements within any State which wishes to be accepted into the community of nations must be based on an acceptance of the principles of human dignity and equality. . . .

"We would prefer to negotiate rather than destroy, to talk rather than kill. We do not advocate violence; we advocate an end to the violence against human dignity which is now being perpetrated by the oppressors of Africa.

"If peaceful progress to emancipation were possible, or if changed circumstances were to make it possible in the future, we would urge our brothers in the resistance movements to use peaceful methods of struggle, even at the cost of some compromise on the timing of change. But while peaceful progress is blocked by the actions of those at present in power in the States of southern Africa, we have no choice but to give to the peoples of those territories all the support of which we are capable in their struggle against their oppressors. . . ."

Dealing specifically with the Republic of South Africa, the Manifesto said:

"The Republic is itself an independent sovereign State and a member of the United Nations. It is more highly developed and richer than any other nation in Africa. On every legal basis its internal affairs are a matter exclusively for the people of South Africa.

"Yet the purpose of law is people, and we assert that the actions of the South African Government are such that the rest of the world has a responsibility to take some action in defence of humanity.

"There is one thing about South African oppression which distinguishes it from other repressive regimes. The *apartheid* policy adopted by the Government, and supported to a greater or lesser extent by almost all its white citizens, is based on a rejection of man's humanity.

"Even if international law is held to exclude active assistance to the South African opponents of *apartheid*, it does not demand that the comfort and support of human and commercial intercourse should be given to a government which rejects the manhood of most of humanity. South Africa should be excluded from the United Nations' agencies and even from the United Nations itself. It should be ostracized by the world community. It should be isolated from world trade patterns and left to be self-sufficient if it can.

"The South African Government cannot be allowed both to reject the very concept of mankind's unity and to benefit by the strength given through friendly international relations."

The Manifesto was approved by the OAU Assembly of Heads of State and Government in Addis Ababa on Sept. 6–10, 1969; welcomed in a resolution adopted by the U.N. General Assembly in November 1969 by 113 votes to two (Portugal and South Africa); and given full support by

President Nixon of the U.S.A. in that part of his statement of Feb. 18, 1970, relating to U.S. policy *vis-à-vis* Africa.

(f) The Khartoum Conference

All the above 14 States except Chad were represented at a conference held in Khartoum on Jan. 26–28, 1970.

At a preparatory meeting of Foreign Ministers of 11 of these countries in Lusaka, Mr. Moto Nkama (Zambian Minister of State for Foreign Affairs) said on Jan. 5 that the response to the Lusaka Manifesto had been disappointing, but that, although Black Africa had no illusions about what the use of force would entail, it had "an inescapable obligation to help the people still under foreign domination" to "fight for their birthright". The meeting *inter alia* condemned Britain for allowing the Rhodesian situation to deteriorate to the extent that Rhodesia could declare herself a Republic.

Mr. R. B. Chidzanja, the Malawian Minister of Agriculture, said afterwards that his Government did not believe in the solutions recommended by the meeting for the transfer of power to black Africans; that it would co-operate with the Portuguese in Mozambique; and that it dissociated itself from the meeting's expression of sympathy with the victims of bombing by Portuguese troops fighting with nationalist guerrillas.

The conference discussed economic perspectives on the basis of reports submitted by various committees on agriculture, trade exchanges, technical co-operation and improvements in transport and communications, as well as bilateral relations among East and Central African countries.

In its final communiqué the conference announced that it had been decided to give substantially increased aid to African liberation movements for their struggle in southern Africa and called for the establishment of a "sanctions committee" to examine the activities of foreign firms and "monopolies" in South Africa, Rhodesia and "territories still under colonial rule".

4. THE EAST AFRICAN COMMUNITY

The East African Community, created under a Treaty for East African Co-operation signed by the Heads of State of Kenya, Uganda and Tanzania on June 6, 1967, was officially inaugurated at Arusha in northern Tanzania on Dec. 1, 1967. All assets and liabilities of the superseded East African Common Services Organization had by then been transferred to the East African Community, and with the entry into force of the Treaty for East African Co-operation new legislation governing the movement of goods between Kenya, Uganda and Tanzania also came into operation.

[The East African Common Services Organization had been created in London in June 1962 to continue the services previously administered by the British East Africa High Commission. The organs of the Organization, in which Kenya, Tanzania and Uganda were equal partners, were (i) the East African Common Services Authority consisting of one elected Minister from each of the three countries; (ii) a Central Legislative Assembly consisting of 12 Ministers, nine members from each country elected by that country's legislature, a Secretary-General and a Legal Secretary.]

Detailed arrangements for the organization of the new Community had been discussed during the months preceding its inauguration by an East African Implementation Committee consisting of ministerial representatives of the three East African countries. Early in September 1967 this committee announced that the East African Posts and Telecommunications Administration – one of the two self-contained Administrations within the East African Common Services Organization – would become a corporation within the East African Community.

The main organs and administrations of the new Community were:

(*a*) The headquarters of the Community in Arusha (Tanzania);

(*b*) the East African Legislative Assembly with nine members from each country, East African Ministers and Deputy Ministers, the Secretary-General of the Community, a Counsel to the Community and a Chairman, superseding the former Central Legislative Assembly of the East African Common Services Organization;

(*c*) a new East African Development Bank with headquarters in Kampala (Uganda);

(*d*) East African Posts and Telecommunications with headquarters in Kampala, instead of Nairobi (Kenya) as hitherto;

(*e*) the Railways Administration with headquarters in Nairobi (unchanged), but the Harbours headquarters to be established in Dar-es-Salaam (Tanzania);

(*f*) the East African Airways Corporation with headquarters in Nairobi.

Statistics for trade among the three East African countries in 1966 and the first half of 1967 showed a constant pattern in that Kenya's trade balance remained favourable and those of Uganda and mainland Tanzania (figures for Zanzibar were not available) adverse.

In 1966 Kenya's exports to Tanzania and Uganda exceeded imports by £17,800,000, while the adverse trade balances of Uganda and Tanzania amounted to £6,000,000 and £12,000,000 respectively. For the first half of 1967 Kenya had a favourable balance of £1,140,000, and Uganda and Tanzania adverse balances of £226,000 and £914,000 respectively.

5. ATTEMPTS AT REGIONAL CO-OPERATION IN CENTRAL AFRICA

A Central African Customs Union (UDEAC), established in Brazzaville on Dec. 8, 1964, came into force on Jan. 1, 1966, between Cameroon and the members of an earlier Equatorial Customs Union embracing the Central African Republic, Chad, the Congo (Brazzaville) and Gabon, with headquarters at Bangui (Central African Republic).

On April 2, 1968, the Presidents of the Central African Republic, Chad and the Congo (Kinshasa) signed in Fort Lamy (Chad) the charter of a newly-established *Union des états de l'Afrique centrale* (UEAC), the creation of which had been decided upon by the three Presidents at Bangui on Feb. 1, 1968.

President Tombalbaye of Chad thereupon declared that the UDEAC was defunct, and President Bokassa of the Central African Republic officially withdrew his country from membership of the UDEAC on April 22, 1968.

Under the UDEAC, a *taxe unique* system had benefited about 100 companies in the five countries, most of which, however, were in Cameroon and Gabon. In order to equalize burdens and benefits under the union, and to compensate its poorer partners (notably the C.A.R. and Chad), a Solidarity Fund had been set up; to this the Congo (Brazzaville) and Gabon each contributed Frs.(CFA) 500,000,000 (then about £726,000), and each of the three other partners Frs.(CFA) 300,000,000 in 1966, while of the total of Frs.(CFA) 1,900,000,000 (about £2,750,000) available, Chad received Frs. 1,175,000,000, the C.A.R. Frs. 665,000,000, the Congo (Brazzaville) Frs. 57,000,000, and Gabon Frs. 2,800,000, but Cameroon as the most industrialized partner received nothing. The trade pattern between the member-States nevertheless remained virtually unchanged, sales of industrial goods to the other partners in 1966 being as follows: Congo (Brazzaville) Frs.(CFA) 3,425,000,000; Cameroon Frs. 646,000,000; the C.A.R. Frs.

546,000,000; Gabon Frs. 110,000,000; and Chad Frs. 12,000,000. The new union thus did not lead to the hoped-for development in the C.A.R. and Chad, and in consequence these two countries had come to an agreement with the Congo (Kinshasa) to form the UEAC.

Cameroon, the Congo (Brazzaville) and Gabon, however, strongly supported the continued existence of the UDEAC, and at a conference held in Brazzaville on Dec. 8, 1968, all its five original members were again represented. President Bokassa announced at this conference that the C.A.R. would leave the UEAC and rejoin the UDEAC; he explicitly declared his letter of April 22, 1968 [see above], to be null and void.

Chad, on the other hand, formally left the UDEAC on Dec. 31, 1968, and the next day imposed Customs duties on goods from UDEAC member-States. The C.A.R. thereupon closed its borders with Chad the same day (Jan. 1, 1969). In mid-February, however, the border was reported to have been re-opened as the result of mediation by the Common African and Malagasy Organization (OCAM).

President Bokassa's decision to leave the UEAC and rejoin the UDEAC greatly aggravated an already existing deterioration in relations between his country and the Congo (Kinshasa).

A public reconciliation, however, between the three Heads of State of the Central African Republic, Chad and the Congo (Kinshasa) took place in Yaoundé on Jan. 10, 1970.

6. OTHER GROUPINGS

Maghreb Permanent Consultative Committee

At a conference held in Tangiers on Nov. 26 and 27, 1964, the Economics Ministers of Algeria, Libya, Morocco and Tunisia decided to establish a permanent joint consultative committee to harmonize economic development plans. The nine-member Maghreb Consultative Committee, which meets every three months, is served by an administrative secretariat and a number of specialized commissions.

Conseil de l'Entente

The *Conseil de l'Entente* was established by Dahomey, Ivory Coast, Niger and Upper Volta at Abidjan (Ivory Coast) on May 29–30, 1959, as the supreme organ of a union which would involve (i) a customs union; (ii)

co-ordination of the four countries' legislation in the spheres of finance, justice, public service, labour, communications and public health; (iii) harmonization of tax legislation; and (iv) the creation of a "Solidarity Fund".

Togo – which had been in a customs union with Dahomey after concluding an agreement on Aug. 20, 1960 – became associated with the *Conseil de l'Entente* in 1966.

The four members of the Council achieved full independence outside the French Community in July 1960 and later signed co-operation agreements with France in economic matters and also in defence in April 1961 – except in the case of Upper Volta which declined to sign a defence agreement.

The Heads of State of the Council's member-States usually meet before each OCAM conference [see page 9] in order to co-ordinate their views.

West African Monetary Union

A West African Monetary Union comprising Dahomey, the Ivory Coast, Mali, Mauritania, Niger, Senegal and Upper Volta was agreed upon in Paris on May 12, 1962. The new Union decided to retain, as a joint currency, the existing CFA franc at the rate of 50 CFA francs = 1 French (new) franc (with CFA standing for *Communauté Financière Africaine*), and with a new joint note-issuing bank. Mali, however, withdrew from this Union on July 1, 1962.

West African Customs Union

A West African Customs Union, the *Union douanière des états d' Afrique occidentale* (UDEAO), established on June 3, 1966, and comprising Dahomey, the Ivory Coast, Mali, Mauritania, Niger, Senegal and Upper Volta, came into force on Dec. 15, 1966.

Organization of Riparian States of the River Senegal

The statute of an Organization of Riparian States of the River Senegal (*Organisation des états riverains du fleuve Sénégal*) was approved on March 24, 1968, by the Heads of State of Guinea, Mali, Mauritania and Senegal.

The agreement provided for four main organs: (i) a Conference of Heads of State meeting at least once a year; (ii) a Council of Ministers, which would act in an executive capacity; (iii) an Interparliamentary Council with consultative functions; and (iv) an Executive Secretariat, with its seat at Dakar (Senegal), which would have under it three general secretariats, respectively for the development of the resources of the Senegal River basin; for planning and development; and for educational, cultural and social matters.

II. ASSOCIATION OF AFRICAN STATES WITH GROUPS
EMBRACING STATES OUTSIDE AFRICA

1. THE COMMONWEALTH

The Commonwealth is an association of independent sovereign States all of which have been, at one time, British territories. It is neither a formal alliance nor a federation of States since there exists no written Commonwealth Constitution and no central Government. Any former British territory, on attaining independence, may seek membership of the Commonwealth; this is granted only by the unanimous consent of the members.

The Head of the Commonwealth is the British Monarch, who is recognized, even by those member-countries which have their own Heads of State, as the symbol of the free association of member-nations of the Commonwealth. In those countries which owe allegiance to her as their Head of State, the Queen is represented by a Governor-General whom she appoints on the recommendation of the country in question.

One of the principal factors binding together the member-nations of the Commonwealth is the use of English Common Law as a basis for most judicial systems.

The members of the Commonwealth in Africa are given in the table below:

Country	Date of Independence	Political Status
Ghana	March 6, 1957	Republic since July 1, 1960
Nigeria	Oct. 1, 1960	Republic since Oct. 1, 1963
Sierra Leone	April 27, 1961	Monarchy
Tanzania	Dec. 9, 1961	Republic since Dec. 9, 1962 (in union with Zanzibar since April 27, 1964)
Uganda	Oct. 9, 1962	Independent Sovereign State on Oct. 9, 1963 Republic (officially) since Sept. 8, 1967
Kenya	Dec. 12, 1963	Republic since Dec. 12, 1964
Malawi	July 6, 1964	Republic since July 6, 1966
Zambia	Oct. 24, 1964	Republic since Oct. 24, 1964
Gambia	Feb. 18, 1965	Republic since April 24, 1970
Botswana	Sept. 30, 1966	Republic since Sept. 30, 1966
Lesotho	Oct. 4, 1966	Monarchy*
Mauritius	March 12, 1968	Monarchy
Swaziland	Sept. 6, 1968	Monarchy*

*These Monarchies are headed by their own Monarchs.

Since the merging of the Colonial Office and the Commonwealth Relations Office in August 1966, to form the Commonwealth Office, the following British Colonies in or around Africa have become the responsibility of this Office:
St. Helena and Dependencies; Seychelles.
Note:
Rhodesia declared its independence unilaterally on Nov. 11, 1965, but is still regarded by Britain, which does not recognize its independent status, as a colony with internal self-government.

Development

An Imperial Conference of 1926, adopting a report by an Inter-Imperial Relations Committee, defined the Dominions and Great Britain as "autonomous communities within the Empire, equal in status, in no way subordinate to one another in any aspect of their domestic or external affairs, though united by a common allegiance to the Crown, and freely associated as members of the British Commonwealth of Nations . . . . Every self-governing member of the Empire is now the master of its destiny. In fact,

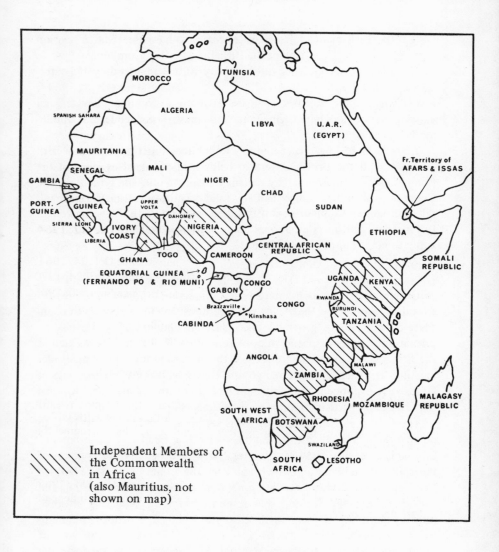

Independent Members of
the Commonwealth
in Africa
(also Mauritius, not
shown on map)

if not always in form, it is subject to no compulsion whatever .... The British Empire is not founded upon negations. It depends essentially, if not formally, on positive ideals. Free institutions are its lifeblood. Free co-operation is its instrument."

The Statute of Westminster of 1931 gave effect to the above definition and offered all former colonies the undisputed right to secede from the Commonwealth. Other provisions of the Statute are:

(1) The Parliament of Westminster ceases to have the right of revision with regard to the legislation of the Parliaments of the Dominions;

(2) a Dominion possesses full authority to make laws possessing extra-territorial validity;

(3) when there are discrepancies between a Dominion law and an existing law of the United Kingdom, this fact shall not render the Dominion law invalid.

After India had been accepted as a Republic within the Commonwealth in 1949, with the British Sovereign being acknowledged as Head of the Commonwealth, the monarchy remained merely a unifying symbol for the Commonwealth; it no longer had any valid constitutional significance, and relations among Commonwealth members were no longer based on constitutional law but on international law, i.e. multilateral treaties which also apply to non-Commonwealth States.

Organs

Questions of common interest to Commonwealth members are discussed at meetings of the Heads of Government of Commonwealth countries. Such meetings generally take place in London. They are held in private and have no special rules of procedure. The agenda is decided at the first session, after which much of the discussion takes place at smaller meetings attended by interested groups. Decisions taken at the meetings of Heads of Government are limited to matters of immediate constitutional importance, in particular, questions of membership.

The Commonwealth Secretariat was set up in London in July 1965 in pursuance of a recommendation made by the Heads of Governments' Conference of July 1964. The Secretariat was to be "a visible symbol of the spirit of co-operation which animates the Commonwealth". Divided into departments dealing with International Affairs, Economic Affairs and Administration, the Secretariat is responsible for disseminating information on questions of common interest; for aiding the various Commonwealth agencies, both official and unofficial, in the promotion of Commonwealth links in all fields; and for preparing and servicing the Heads of Governments' and other Ministerial meetings.

Commonwealth Co-operation

There is co-operation among member-countries of the Commonwealth in many spheres of activity. This takes the form of conferences (economic, educational, scientific, medical, etc.) and of work through specialized agencies.

Commonwealth Citizenship
Under a scheme devised at a meeting of Commonwealth representatives in February 1947, each Commonwealth country recognizes as British subjects (or Commonwealth citizens) both its own citizens and citizens of other Commonwealth countries. Although holders of this common status are not accorded equal rights throughout the Commonwealth, their rights are normally superior to those of aliens.

Economic Co-operation
A system of tariff preferences, known as *Commonwealth Preference*, is in general operation between Commonwealth countries. A lower rate of customs duty, or none at all, is levied on Commonwealth goods, as opposed to the higher rate of duty on imports from foreign countries. (The Republic of Ireland and the Republic of South Africa, as former Commonwealth countries, still enjoy Commonwealth Preference.)

The *Commonwealth Economic Committee*, founded in 1925 as the Imperial Economic Committee, provides economic and statistical information on questions related to Commonwealth production and trade. The Committee is formed by two representatives of each Commonwealth member-country and two members representing the Dependent Territories.

Educational Co-operation
Co-operation in the sphere of education is the concern of the following bodies:

Association of Commonwealth Universities, founded in 1913 as the Universities Bureau of the British Empire;
Commonwealth Education Liaison Committee, founded in 1959;
Commonwealth Education Liaison Unit, founded in 1960;
League for the Exchange of Commonwealth Teachers.

Agriculture and Forestry
The *Commonwealth Agricultural Bureaux* – three Institutes and 11 Bureaux, each concerned with a particular aspect of agricultural science – collect and supply specialized information on agricultural science for research workers. The organization was founded in 1929.
Two bodies concerned with co-operation in the field of forestry are:

Commonwealth Forestry Association, founded in 1921; *Standing Committee on Commonwealth Forestry*, founded in 1923.

Science and Medicine

The following bodies have been set up to aid collaboration between Commonwealth scientists:

Commonwealth Scientific Committee, founded in 1946;
Commonwealth Scientific Liaison Offices, founded in 1948.

The interests and principles of the medical profession are promoted throughout the Commonwealth by the *Commonwealth Medical Association*.

Civil Aviation and Telecommunications

Civil air communications and aeronautical research throughout the Commonwealth are the concern of the following bodies:

Commonwealth Air Transport Council, founded in 1945;
Commonwealth Advisory Aeronautical Research Council, founded in 1946;
Commonwealth Telecommunications Board, formed in 1949, an advisory body on matters related to external telecommunications systems.

Other Commonwealth Organizations

A list of other bodies concerned with various aspects of Commonwealth co-operation is given below.

Commonwealth Committee on Mineral Processing, founded in 1960.
Commonwealth Committee on Mineral Resources and Geology, founded in 1948.
Commonwealth Consultative Space Research Committee, founded in 1960.
Commonwealth Council of Mining and Metallurgical Institutions.
Commonwealth Countries League, a women's organization founded in 1925.
Commonwealth Foundation, founded in 1965 to administer a fund for promoting professional co-operation throughout the Commonwealth.
Commonwealth Institute, founded in 1893 as the Imperial Institute. It functions as an information and education centre.
Commonwealth Parliamentary Association, formed in 1911.
Commonwealth War Graves Commission, founded in 1917.
Federation of Commonwealth Chambers of Commerce, founded in 1911.
Royal Commonwealth Society, to promote understanding among the peoples of the Commonwealth.

26

The Sterling Area

The Sterling Area consists of countries whose currency has a fixed exchange rate with the pound sterling and whose central banks hold most of their gold and dollar reserves in a pool in London, drawing on these reserves as needed.

Its members in Africa are the Commonwealth member-countries, the British dependent territories (except, temporarily, Rhodesia) and South Africa (including South West Africa).

Botswana, Lesotho and Swaziland have been in a monetary and customs union with South Africa since 1910.

2. THE FRENCH COMMUNITY ("Communauté")

Members of the Community: French Republic – including Overseas Departments and Territories, which in Africa are Réunion, the Comoro Islands and the Territory of the Afars and Issas (formerly French Somaliland) – Central African Republic, Chad, Congo (Brazzaville), Gabon, Madagascar, Senegal.

Formation

The French Union, as defined under the 1946 Constitution of the Fourth Republic of France, was reconstituted as the French Community under the new Constitution of the Fifth Republic, published on Sept. 4, 1958.

Section XII of the Constitution deals with the Community. Its most important provisions are the following:

Art. 77. In the Community established by the present Constitution, the member-States enjoy autonomy; they administer themselves and manage their own affairs democratically and freely.

There is only one citizenship in the Community.

All citizens are equal before the law, whatever their origin, their race or religion. They have the same duties.

Art. 78. The competence of the Community comprises foreign policy, defence, currency and common economic and financial policy, as well as policy concerning strategic raw materials.

In addition, it comprises (unless excluded by special agreement) control of justice, higher education, the general organization of external and common transport and telecommunications.

Special agreements may establish other common spheres of competence or regulate the transfer of competences from the Community to one of its members.

Art. 80. The President of the Republic presides over and represents the Community.

The organs of the Community are an Executive Council, a Senate and a Court of Arbitration.

Art. 86. A change in the status of a member-State may be requested either by the Republic or by a resolution of the Legislative Assembly of the State concerned which has been confirmed in a local referendum, the organization and supervision of which is carried out by the organs of the Community. The terms of such a change in status are regulated by an agreement approved by the Parliament of the Republic and the Legislative Assembly concerned.

Under the same conditions a member-State of the Community may become independent. It then ceases to belong to the Community.

Each overseas territory of France was given the choice of: (*a*) becoming a *département* of the French Republic; or (*b*) retaining the territorial status it then enjoyed; or (*c*) entering the French Community as an autonomous unit.

The Central African Republic, Chad, Congo (Brazzaville), Dahomey, Gabon, Ivory Coast, Madagascar, Mauritania, Niger, Senegal, the Sudan and Upper Volta chose to join the Community.

Early in 1960 the Mali Federation (comprising the Republics of Senegal and the Sudan) and Madagascar decided to ask for full independence while retaining membership in the Community. An amendment to the Constitution, enabling member-States to remain in the Community after attaining full independence, was approved by the French National Assembly on May 11, 1960.

The six present members of the Community in Africa gained their independence in June and August of 1960. The five remaining members of the old Community – Dahomey, Ivory Coast, Mauritania, Niger and Upper Volta – chose to leave the Community on attaining independence. [For dates of independence see table below.] [See also *Conseil de l'Entente*, page 18.]

Development of the Community

The character of the French Community was radically altered by the new, independent status of all its members. This was recognized by the French Government which, on May 18, 1961, agreed upon the creation of new governmental machinery for dealing with the relations of France with French-speaking Africa and Madagascar. The new posts of Minister for Co-operation (to deal with technical assistance), Secretary of State for Political Affairs and Secretary-General to the President were created. The function of the latter was to co-ordinate the activities of the President relating to the countries in question. A Council for African and Malagasy Affairs was also created.

The powers exercised by the Community, as laid down in Article 78 of the French Constitution [see above], were transferred to each member-country on its attaining independence. The practical functions of the Community have thus been greatly reduced, and the bond between France and other Community members is now mainly restricted to a co-ordination of foreign policy in certain matters, and to co-operation in the fields of economy and education for which purpose the President of France has

Bilateral Agreements with France			
Country	Independence Agreement signed on	Proclamation of Independence	Co-operation & Mutual Defence Agreements signed on
A. Community Members			
Madagascar	April 2, 1960	June 26, 1960	June 27, 1960
*Mali Federation	April 4, 1960	June 20, 1960	June 22, 1960
Chad	July 12, 1960	Aug. 10, 1960	Aug. 11, 1960 May 1, 1964
Central African Republic	July 12, 1960	Aug. 12, 1960	Aug. 13, 1960
Congo (Brazzaville)	July 12, 1960	Aug. 14, 1960	Aug. 15, 1960
Gabon	July 15, 1960	Aug. 16, 1960	Aug. 17, 1960

*After the secession of Senegal from the Federation of Mali (Aug. 20, 1960) and the subsequent French recognition of Senegal on Sept. 11, 1960, the Republic of Mali declared itself free from all links with France, claiming that the Franco-Malian agreements had been broken by France's recognition of Senegal. Senegal remains within the Community. [See pages 234, 237.]

B. Former Members of the Community		
Dahomey	July 11, 1960	Aug. 1, 1960
Niger	July 11, 1960	Aug. 2, 1960
Upper Volta	July 11, 1960	Aug. 5, 1960
Ivory Coast	July 11, 1960	Aug. 6, 1960
Mauritania	Oct. 19, 1960	Nov. 27, 1960

The Independence agreements signed by these States included no agreements on their continued membership of the Community.

appointed a Secretary-General for the Community and African and Malagasy affairs (at present — March 1971 — M. Jacques Foccart).

Mutual Defence Agreements

Agreements for co-operation between France and the newly-independent States were signed immediately after the various proclamations of independence. These agreements contained important provisions for mutual military aid. The mutual defence agreement between France and the Mali Federation, which may be taken as typical, stated that France and Mali would assist each other in defence matters; Mali would share with France in the defence of the Community and possibly of other African States; a Franco-Malian defence committee would be set up; Mali would obtain military equipment exclusively from France; and Malian nationals would be free to enlist in the French armed forces.

The defence agreements with the Central African Republic, Chad, the Congo Republic and Gabon were supplemented in 1961, when these four States joined to form, with French co-operation, the "Defence Council of Equatorial Africa".

France also has defence agreements with African countries outside the Community, namely Cameroon, Dahomey, Ivory Coast, Mauritania, Niger and Togo.

Although all these defence agreements are still in force, the French military presence in Africa was drastically reduced in the year 1964–65. It was announced on Sept. 29, 1964, that by July 1965 it was intended to reduce the total of French forces in African States and Madagascar to about 6,600 officers and men, from an official total of 27,800 on Oct. 1, 1964. The remaining troops would be regrouped, and there would be four "support points", these being Dakar (Senegal), Abidjan (Ivory Coast), Fort Lamy (Chad) and Diégo-Suarez, Ivato and Antsirabé in Madagascar.

The Franc Zone

The Franc Zone provides for the free movement of currency among its members and a guaranteed franc exchange rate. Its members are France (with its Overseas *Départements* and Territories, except that of the Afars and Issas), Cameroon, the Central African Republic, Chad, Congo (Brazzaville), Dahomey, Gabon, the Ivory Coast, Madagascar, Mali, Mauritania, Niger, Senegal, Togo and Upper Volta.

3. THE ARAB LEAGUE

Members in Africa: Algeria, Libya, Morocco, Sudan, Tunisia, United Arab Republic. (Other members: Iraq, Jordan, Kuwait, Lebanon, Saudi Arabia, South Yemen [now the People's Democratic Republic of Yemen], Syria, Yemen.)

A "League of Arab States" was established by the signing of a "Pact of the Union of Arab States" in Alexandria (Egypt) on March 22, 1945, by representatives of Egypt, Iraq, Lebanon, Saudi Arabia, Syria, Transjordan and Yemen. Later adherents to the pact were Libya (March 28, 1953); the Sudan (Jan. 9, 1956); Tunisia and Morocco (Oct. 1, 1958); Kuwait (July 20, 1961); and Algeria (Aug. 16, 1962).

The provisions of the pact include the following:

It was laid down that "a League of Arab States will be formed by those independent Arab countries who wish to join it"; that it would possess a Council on which all member-States would be on an equal footing; that the Council would organize periodical meetings to improve and strengthen mutual relations, co-ordinate their political programmes with a view to mutual co-operation and "safeguard by every possible means their independence and sovereign rights against all aggression"; that decisions of the Council would be binding on all member-States (disputes between member-States being referred to it for arbitration); that resort to force between member-States in settling disputes was forbidden; and that no State would be permitted to follow a policy prejudicial to the League of Arab States as a whole.

The Arab States would co-operate closely on questions of economics and finance (commercial exchanges, customs duties, currency, agriculture and industry), communications (by land, sea and air), cultural matters, social and hygiene questions and matters relating to nationality, passports and visas, extradition of criminals, etc. For all these questions, commissions of experts would be formed, with a co-ordinating committee to direct their work.

The declaration on Palestine stated *inter alia*: "The Committee considers that Palestine forms an important integral part of the Arab countries and the rights of the Arabs there cannot be infringed without danger to the peace and security of the Arab world."

It was also laid down that the Arab League would study means of collaboration with international organizations; that its permanent headquarters would be in Cairo (though the Council could meet in other cities); that the Council would hold biennial meetings (in March and October); that member-States could withdraw from the League on one year's notice, or be expelled by unanimous vote for not fulfilling their obligations; and that the Pact could be modified by a two-thirds majority vote.

Organization

The League Council is the supreme organ of the Arab League. It is composed of representatives of all the member-States, each of which has one vote, and a representative of the Palestinian Arabs. The Council is responsible for the functioning of the League and the realization of its objectives. It meets in March and September.

The League Council is aided by nine Permanent Committees which deal with Political, Economic, Cultural, Social, Military and Legal Affairs, Information, Health and Communications.

The other organ of the Arab League is the Secretariat, whose main officers are the Secretary-General, three Assistant Secretaries-General, a Military Assistant Secretary and an Economic Assistant Secretary. Among the functions of the Secretary-General are the preparation of a draft budget which he submits to the Council, and the convening of the Council sessions.

Subsidiary Bodies

A considerable number of subsidiary bodies have been set up under the Arab League. The most important of these are:

(1) The Economic Council
Formed in 1950, the Economic Council consists of the Ministers of Economic Affairs of the member-countries.
(2) The Arab Financial Organization
In January 1959 the Economic Council announced the creation of an Arab Development Bank, now known as the Arab Financial Organization.
(3) Council of Arab Economic Unity
A Convention for Economic Unity was signed by Iraq, Jordan, Kuwait, Morocco, Saudi Arabia, Syria, the United Arab Republic and Yemen in June 1957. The Council of Arab Economic Unity came into being seven years later, in June 1964. Its object is, *inter alia*, to reduce internal tariffs, to establish a common external tariff and to bring about the co-ordination of economic policies.
(4) Arab Common Market
An agreement on the creation of an Arab Common Market was signed on Aug. 13, 1964, by representatives of Iraq, Jordan, Kuwait, Syria and the U.A.R.
The agreement provided for (*a*) freedom of movement of persons and of currencies; (*b*) freedom of trade exchanges in local and foreign

products; (c) freedom of residence, work and the pursuit of economic activities; and (d) freedom of transport, transit and the use of airports and harbours. In trade between the five countries there would be a first reduction in customs tariffs of 10 per cent for industrial products and of 20 per cent for agricultural produce, to be followed by similar reductions over the next ten or five years respectively.

The provisions of the agreement were to be implemented within ten years of Jan. 1, 1965, when the Common Market was scheduled to come into operation. Any other member of the Arab League might join the Common Market at any time.

(5) Arab Labour Organization

To co-ordinate labour conditions throughout the Arab world an Arab Labour Organization was set up in 1965.

(6) Joint Defence Council

An Arab Supreme Defence Council, composed of the Foreign and Defence Ministers of countries adhering to the Arab League Collective Security Pact [see below], was set up in 1950 under the terms of that Pact. Its first meeting did not take place until September 1953.

(7) Permanent Military Committee

The formation of a Permanent Military Committee was also provided for in the Collective Security Pact.

(8) Arab Unified Military Command

The establishment of a unified Arab military command was decided at a conference of Arab Heads of State held in Alexandria in September 1964 [see below].

Collective Security Pact

On June 17, 1950, a Collective Security Pact was signed by Egypt, Syria, Lebanon, Saudi Arabia and Yemen. The draft of the pact had been unanimously approved by the Council of the Arab League on April 13, 1950. Subsequent signatories to the Pact were Iraq on Feb. 2, 1951, Jordan on Feb. 16, 1952, Morocco on June 13, 1961, and Libya, Sudan, Algeria, Tunisia and Kuwait on Sept. 10, 1964. The pact came into force on Aug. 24, 1952.

Arab Summit Conferences

Since 1964 Heads of Arab States have repeatedly met in conference to discuss questions of common political interest:

(1) In Cairo on Jan. 13–16, 1964;

(2) in Alexandria on Sept. 5–11, 1964;

(3) in Casablanca on Sept. 13–17, 1965, when the Arab Heads of State signed a "solidarity pact", which was intended to put an end to propaganda attacks by one Arab State against another and to bind the

signatories not to support "subversive movements of any kind" against one another;

(4) in Khartoum on Aug. 29, 1969, when "any reconciliaton with Israel" was rejected, and Saudi Arabia, Kuwait and Libya agreed to resume the production of oil (supplies to the West having been cut off as the result of the 1967 defeat of the U.A.R. by Israel) and to pay £135,000,000 to the U.A.R. and Jordan to combat the economic effects of the war with Israel (Libya's share being £30,000,000);

(5) in Cairo on Aug. 30–Sept. 3, 1969, for the discussion of Arab military strategy against Israel;

(6) in Rabat on Dec. 21–23, 1969, when, however, no agreement was reached on President Nasser's demand for specific pledges by all Arab States for the supply of troops, weapons and finance for the struggle against Israel.

The last-named meeting was followed by agreements on increased co-operation between the U.A.R., Libya and the Sudan. After talks between the three countries' leaders in Tripoli (Libya) on Dec. 26–28, 1969, it was announced that regular meetings would be held every four months to co-ordinate military, political and economic action against Israel. At a meeting in Cairo on Jan. 11–13, 1970, it was agreed to set up joint ministerial commissions to ensure co-ordination between the three countries in foreign policy, communications, transport, education, industry, agriculture and land reclamation.

(7) In Cairo on Feb. 7–9, 1970, the U.A.R., Jordan, Syria, Iraq and the Sudan reaffirmed their "determination to liberate violated Arab territories".

(8) In Tripoli, on June 20–22, 1970, at an "informal" meeting of 14 Arab Heads of State, a four-man committee consisting of representatives of Algeria, Libya, the U.A.R. and Syria was formed to mediate between the Government of Jordan and the Palestinian guerrilla organizations then in conflict with each other.

4. ASSOCIATION WITH THE EUROPEAN ECONOMIC COMMUNITY

The Treaty of Rome, which set up the European Economic Community (EEC) and came into force on Jan. 1, 1958, provided *inter alia* that the overseas territories of Belgium, France, Italy and the Netherlands would be associated with the Community. A special convention annexed to the

Treaty laid down the details of this association for the initial five-year period.

The signatories of the Treaty of Rome had also declared their readiness to conclude economic association agreements with independent countries of the French Franc Zone. Morocco and Tunisia accordingly made formal requests for negotiations in October and December 1963 respectively.

Association with the EEC has been negotiated or achieved by the following countries and territories in and around Africa:

(1) Associated French Overseas Territories:

Comoro Islands, French Territory of the Afars and Issas (formerly French Somaliland), Réunion.

(2) Eighteen African States associated under the second Yaoundé Convention [see below]: Burundi, Cameroon, Central African Republic, Chad, Congo (Brazzaville), Congo (Kinshasa), Dahomey, Gabon, Ivory Coast, Madagascar, Mali, Mauritania, Niger, Rwanda, Senegal, Somalia, Togo, Upper Volta.

(3) Nigeria, associated under an agreement signed in Lagos on July 16, 1966.

(4) Morocco and Tunisia, associated under agreements signed in Rabat on March 31, 1969, and in Tunis on March 28, 1969.

(5) Kenya, Tanzania and Uganda, associated as members of the East African Community, under an agreement signed in Arusha (Tanzania) on Sept. 24, 1969.

The Yaoundé Convention

The first Convention on the Association of Overseas Territories with the EEC, annexed to the Treaty of Rome, expired on Dec. 31, 1962. Before this date a number of independent African States which had formerly been French, Belgian, or Italian colonies expressed a wish to continue the association under a new agreement. After protracted negotiations the new Convention of Association between the EEC and associated African states and Madagascar was signed at Yaoundé (Cameroon) on July 20, 1963. This Yaoundé Convention entered into force on June 1, 1964, and expired on May 31, 1969.

After protracted negotiations, an agreement renewing with modifications the first Yaoundé Convention was signed in Yaoundé on July 29, 1969.

The difficulties during the negotiations arose partly through criti-

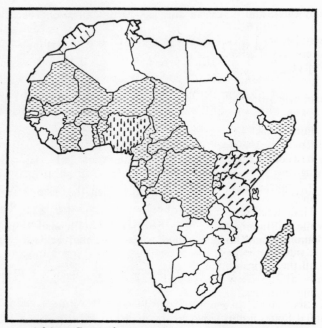

 African Countries
associated with E.E.C.
under the Yaoundé
Convention

 Morocco and Tunisia,
associated with E.E.C.
since March 1969.

 Nigeria – Association
with E.E.C. approved

 East African Community,
associated with E.E.C.
since September 1969.

cisms on the part of the African States of the – from their point of view – unsatisfactory aspects of the working of the first Convention. They pointed out that their exports to the Six had increased by less than 1 per cent in value between 1964 and 1966 – against a rate of 6 per cent for Latin American exports – and that there was a fall of 1 per cent in 1967. The exports of the EEC to the African countries, on the other hand, had risen by some 10 per cent between 1966 and 1967.

The Associated States, in requesting an overall increase in aid to $1,500,000,000 for the new five-year period, were also critical of the way in which European Development Fund aid had been allocated, viz.: (i) only 4 per cent of the investments by the EDF had gone into industrial projects; (ii) aid for agricultural diversification had not been adequately channelled towards import substitution; (iii) there had only been a small increase in "genuine aid" against a high relative increase in loans; (iv) grants for training vital personnel had dropped from 22.50 per cent of the EDF social budget to just over 14.50 per cent; and (v) the delay between EDF approval for specific ventures and their execution often caused an increase of between 10 and 20 per cent in the cost of a project.

The main provisions of the new Convention were as follows:

(1) Both sides affirmed their unanimous wish to continue and strengthen the association, and their readiness to achieve co-operation on the basis of complete equality and mutual confidence with a view to furthering the economic and social development of the Associated States by increasing their trade, financial support and technical co-operation.

(2) Trade Relations. In the sphere of trade relations the new Convention, while continuing to favour the development of commerce between the Community and the Associated States, also conformed to the wish of both sides to help in the development of co-operation and trade among all the African countries, as well as to the principles laid down especially at the New Delhi Conference of UNCTAD on aid to the developing countries.

The Six agreed to grant to agricultural imports originating in the Associated States a more favourable treatment than·had been the case previously, while continuing the complete exemption from customs duty of imports of non-agricultural products originating in the Associated States.

(3) Aid to Associated Countries, etc. A total of $1,000,000,000 would be provided in aid by the Six for the period of the new Convention, viz. $900,000,000 through the European Investment Fund and $100,000,000 through the European Investment Bank.

Of the total to be made available through the European Investment Fund, $748,000,000 would go in grants to the 18 Associated States and $62,000,000 to the French and Netherlands overseas departments, while another $80,000,000 would be provided as loans on specially favourable terms for the Associated States and $10,000,000 for the French and Dutch overseas departments [these special loans are usually made to price-stabilization funds for commodities].

In addition, the European Investment Bank would on its normal terms make loans totalling $90,000,000 to the Associated States and $10,000,000 to the French and Netherlands overseas departments, out of funds obtained from bond issues on the international capital markets. Total aid to the Associated States would thus amount to $918,000,000, and to the French and Dutch overseas departments to $82,000,000. The overall aid total of $1,000,000,000 compared with $800,000,000 under the first Yaoundé Convention and $581,000,000 under the Treaty of Rome.

(4) Schedule of Contributions. After protracted negotiations among the Six, which concerned especially an increase in the Italian contribution, it was finally agreed that France and Western Germany would each contribute 33.14 per cent to the European Development Fund, compared with 33.77 per cent each under the first Yaoundé Convention; Italy 15.61 per cent, against 13.70 per cent hitherto; Belgium and the Netherlands each 8.89 per cent, compared with respectively 9.45 per cent and 9.04 per cent hitherto; and Luxemburg 0.27 per cent (unchanged). In actual figures the German and French contributions would amount to $298,500,000 each (against $246,500,000 to the previous Fund), the Italian contribution to $140,600,000 (against $100,000,000 previously), the Belgian and Netherlands contributions to $80,000,000 each (against $69,000,000 and $66,000,000 respectively), and the Luxemburg contribution to $2,400,000 (against $2,000,000).

(5) Disaster Fund. Of the total grants to the Associated States, $65,000,000 – to be increased to $80,000,000 if circumstances required this – would be set aside in a "Disaster Fund" to be used to make grants to them in the event of (a) exceptionally severe falls in world prices for their exports, or (b) national calamities such as famine, drought or floods.

(6) Other Provisions. In order to help African companies to participate in EEC-financed projects, the new Convention laid down that they would be given a 15 per cent advantage in tendering; this would apply to both smaller building projects costing less than $500,000 and supply contracts which could be fulfilled from home production.

It was also agreed that companies from at least two EEC countries should participate in projects of over $5,000,000. This clause had been insisted on by the Netherlands, which felt that it had received an insufficient share of contracts under the first Convention.

(7) Duration. The new Convention would come into force after ratification by the 18 Associated States and the Six. It would be for five years but, although ratification might not be completed until mid-1970, would expire at the latest on Jan. 31, 1975, with the whole amount of aid becoming payable before that date, irrespective of when it formally entered into force.

Nigeria

An association agreement concluded between the EEC and Nigeria on July 16, 1966, and valid until May 31, 1969 (the expiry date of the first Yaoundé Convention), never came into force, the Nigerian instrument of ratification being handed to the EEC Secretariat in Brussels only on Jan. 19, 1968, and ratification by the parliaments of the six EEC member-countries remaining uncompleted.

Morocco and Tunisia

The Association agreements between the EEC and Morocco and Tunisia were, after lengthy negotiations, confined to strictly commercial relations and excluded financial aid, technical assistance and free movement for Moroccan and Tunisian labour in the EEC member-countries — all sought by both countries.

The main provisions of the two agreements were as follows:

(1) Advantages granted by the EEC. In the industrial sector Morocco and Tunisia would benefit from tariff-free and quantitatively unrestricted entry for most of their exports to the EEC. [In 1967 Morocco sent 52 per cent of her exports to the Common Market, including 28 per cent to France, and Tunisia sent 61 per cent, including 41 per cent to France. Of total Moroccan exports to the Community, non-agricultural products represented 40 per cent, and of total Tunisian exports they represented 55 per cent.] The EEC reserved the right, however, to reintroduce tariffs on certain refined oil products if the exports by Morocco or Tunisia to the EEC rose above 100,000 tons.

In the agricultural sector the EEC would reduce levies on olive oil; offer certain concessions on fish products and fishmeal; and grant a duty abatement for hard wheat and various processed agricultural products. Morocco and Tunisia would benefit from an 80 per cent duty preference in the EEC for citrus fruits provided certain price requirements were fulfilled, compared with a 40 per cent preference to be granted for these products to Israel, Spain and Turkey.

(2) Advantages granted by Morocco. Morocco would make tariff reductions of 25 per cent on certain EEC products, would consolidate existing quotas and tariff quotas, and for other products would open new quotas with the Common Market. Morocco retained the right to reimpose protective quotas for the EEC imports at present liberalized on condition that an equivalent volume of trade was liberated in other sectors.

(3) Benefits granted by Tunisia. Tunisia would grant for 40 per cent of its imports from the EEC tariff reductions equivalent to 70 per cent of the preference given to French exports. New quotas would be opened for EEC exports and existing ones would be consolidated. Tunisia would be able to reintroduce quotas for liberalized products under the same conditions that applied to Morocco.

(4) General Provisions. Products not covered by the agreements would still come under the Protocol annexed to the Treaty of Rome, by virtue of which France might grant preferential arrangements to products from Tunisia and Morocco. Similarly, for products not included in the agreements the Six as well as Tunisia and Morocco undertook to maintain the benefit which they had granted each other on a bilateral basis within existing trade agreements.

The Community was given most-favoured-nation benefits except for (*a*) customs union or free trade area agreements, particularly with regard to the economic integration of the Maghreb; (*b*) various preferential agreements already concluded by Tunisia and Morocco with certain other African countries. The Community also expressed support for any steps on which agreement would be reached in UNCTAD.

For the requirements of their industrialization, Morocco and Tunisia might withdraw concessions previously granted provided these were replaced by other concessions "which maintain the balance of the agreement". Both the associated States and the Community could take traditional safeguards necessary for dealing with difficulties in particular regions or sectors, or with balance-of-payments problems.

(5) Association Councils. These Councils – one for EEC-Moroccan and the other for EEC-Tunisian relations – would have powers to recommend any steps needed to ensure proper implementation of the agreement, but could not take any initiative to widen the agreements, even at a purely commercial level, any widening being only possible through fresh negotiations.

Each Council would consist of all the members of the Community Council of Ministers and some members of the European Commission on one side, and members of the Governments of Morocco and Tunisia respectively on the other.

(6) Duration of Agreements. The agreements would be valid for five years from the date they came into force, i.e. when formally adopted by the EEC Council of Ministers. Negotiations with a view to concluding further agreements on a wider basis could be started at the latest by the end of the third year.

The East African Community

The first Association Agreement between the EEC and Kenya, Tanzania and Uganda had been drawn up in Brussels on June 13, 1968, after three years of protracted negotiations, and signed at Arusha (Tanzania) on July 26.

Apart from the abolition of customs duties on many East African exports to EEC countries, it also provided for East African non-discrimination and most-favoured-nations treatment of EEC countries in respect of the right to settle, freedom of services and payments.

This agreement, however, had not been ratified by all the EEC member-countries before the expiry, on May 31, 1969, of the first Yaoundé Convention, to which it was linked, and had therefore never come into effect. Negotiations for the renewal of the agreement with certain modifications took place in Brussels from June 30 to July 10, 1969.

In its final form the new Arusha Convention, which followed the same pattern as the one signed in July 1968, provided that the EEC would suspend customs duties and quantitative restrictions on imports of all East African products except for cloves, coffee and canned pineapples, which compete with exports of the 18 Associated States and for which tariff quotas were fixed of 56,000 tons p.a. for coffee, 860 tons for tinned pineapple and 100 tons for cloves. In return Kenya, Tanzania and Uganda granted the EEC member-countries tariff preferences varying between 2 and 8 per cent on 58 products, affecting 6.5 per cent of the total imports of the three East African countries, and 10 per cent of their imports from the EEC countries.

The new agreement was for five years, will run parallel to the second Yaoundé Convention, and will therefore also expire on Jan. 31, 1975.

5. THE "NON-ALIGNED NATIONS"

On the initiative of Presidents Tito of Yugoslavia and Nasser of the United Arab Republic, an international conference of "non-aligned countries" was first held in Belgrade on Sept. 1, 1961, and a second conference of such nations took place in Cairo on Oct. 5–10, 1964.

A third conference of "non-aligned nations", held in Lusaka on Sept. 8–10, 1970, was attended by representatives of 32 African countries, among whom the Emperor Haile Selassie of Ethiopia and Presidents Kaunda of Zambia and Nyerere of Tanzania played a prominent part.

The African countries represented at the Lusaka conference were Algeria, Botswana, Burundi, Cameroon, the Central African Republic, Chad, both Congos, Equatorial Guinea, Ethiopia, Gabon, Ghana, Guinea, Kenya, Lesotho, Libya, Mali, Mauritania, Morocco, Nigeria, Rwanda, Senegal, Sierra Leone, Somalia, the Sudan, Swaziland, Tanzania, Togo, Tunisia, Uganda, the United Arab Republic and Zambia.

The essential criterion for admission to the group of non-aligned nations was that they should not be military allies of either of the two super-Powers (the United States or the Soviet Union), and its principal aim was "the quest for peace", i.e. peaceful coexistence among nations and non-interference in each other's internal affairs.

The Lusaka conference was dominated by the problem of "the definitive decolonization of Africa" (in the words of President Tito), and the final conference documents dealt mainly with this problem.

(1) The "Lusaka Declaration on Peace, Independence, Co-operation and the Democratization of International Relations" – designed to

constitute the "Charter of Non-Alignment" — no longer defined non-alignment as "an irreplaceable instrument for the solution of the dangerous contradictions of the contemporary world and the establishment of international relations based upon the principle of active and peaceful coexistence" but rather as "an integral part of the changes in the present structure of the international community in its entirety" and "the product of the anti-colonialist revolution". Instead of "rich" and "poor" countries, it distinguished between "oppressors" and "the oppressed", "aggressors" and "victims of agression". It stated in particular that the immediate danger of a conflict between the super-Powers had diminished as the result of their tendency to negotiate, but that this did not contribute to the security of small, medium-sized or developing nations, nor did it prevent the danger of local wars. At the same time the participants in the conference undertook "to continue their efforts to bring about the dissolution of the great military alliances".

(2) A resolution on *apartheid* and racial discrimination condemned the U.S.A., France, the United Kingdom, Western Germany, Italy and Japan, which "by their political, economic and military co-operation encourage and incite the Government of South Africa to persist in its racist policies".

(3) A resolution on the Portuguese colonies appealed to the member-States of NATO to cease giving assistance to Portugal by selling her arms and equipment.

(4) A resolution on Zimbabwe (Rhodesia) condemned in particular Britain's approval of the presence of South Africa in that territory and called for the application of the Geneva Convention on the protection of prisoners of war and civilians.

(5) A general resolution on "decolonization" appealed urgently to France and Spain to allow the peoples of their dependencies as soon as possible to exercise their right of self-determination under the auspices of the U.N. and OAU. It further proposed that economic and diplomatic relations with Portugal and South Africa should be broken off and that the special fund of the OAU liberation committee should be increased. In particular, it requested the President of the conference to take up contact with NATO member-States (especially the U.S.A., Britain, France, Western Germany and Italy), and also with Switzerland and Japan, and to ask them to end immediately their direct or indirect support for "the regimes of colonial and racial oppression".

(6) A "Declaration on Non-Alignment and Economic Progress" dealt with a working programme and preliminary negotiations among non-aligned countries.

III. POLITICAL DEVELOPMENTS IN AFRICAN STATES
SINCE ACHIEVEMENT OF INDEPENDENCE

1. THE OLDEST INDEPENDENT STATES

ETHIOPIA
[Called Abyssinia until 1941.]

Area: 457,265 sq. miles.
Population 1969 (estimate): 24,769,000.
Capital: Addis Ababa (644,000).
Official language: Amharic.
Chief products: Livestock, cereals, coffee.

Early History

Ethiopia is claimed to have been an independent country since the 11th century B.C. According to tradition the Queen of Sheba, who visited King Solomon of Israel, was Queen of Ethiopia, and it is from their son Menelek that the Kings and Emperors of Ethiopia claim descent and the title "Lion of Judah". After centuries of internecine warfare between the inhabitants of the country's various provinces, the Amharan chief Lij Kassa gained supremacy as "King of Kings" or Emperor Theodore III, defeating his last opponent in 1855. After his death in 1868, however, the country was again torn by conflict until in 1889 Menelek, the ruler of Shoa, proclaimed himself King of Kings.

Meanwhile the Italians had, in 1888, established themselves in that part of the country known as Eritrea, with the port of Massawa as its principal town. The Treaty of Uccialli concluded between Italy and the Emperor Menelek in 1889, and enabling the Italians to occupy Asmara, was denounced by the Emperor in 1893 who feared an alliance between his internal enemies and the Italians. War subsequently broke out and the Italians suffered reverses at Amba Alagai and Makelle (1895—96) and decisive defeat at Adua in March 1896. In a subsequent peace treaty signed in Addis Ababa, the Treaty of Uccialli was annulled and the absolute independence of Abyssinia recognized.

After Menelek had consolidated his regime, the Sudanese-Abyssinian frontier was delimited in a treaty between Britain and Abyssinia in 1902, the frontiers with British East Africa and Uganda were defined in 1908.

An Anglo-French-Italian agreement of Dec. 13, 1906, provided for the completion of the country's only railway line from Djibuti to Addis Ababa and co-operation in maintaining "the political and territorial status quo in Ethiopia". After Menelek's death in 1913, there followed several years of confusion from which Ras Tafari Makonnen emerged as the country's ruler. Ethiopia was admitted to the League of Nations in 1923 and an Italo-Ethiopian treaty of "perpetual friendship" was signed in Addis Ababa on Aug. 2, 1928. Ras Tafari was proclaimed Emperor Haile Selassie I in 1930.

Open conflict with Italy, however, arose late in 1934 out of incidents on the border with Italian Somaliland; despite mediation efforts by Britain and France and an Ethiopian appeal to the League of Nations, forces of the Fascist Italian Government invaded Ethiopia in October 1935 and by the end of May 1936 Italy had annexed Ethiopia and the Emperor had fled to Palestine, subsequently settling in England.

After the outbreak of World War II British and Commonwealth troops, supported by Abyssinian forces, liberated Ethiopia, and the Emperor Haile Selassie returned to Addis Ababa in May 1941.

Constitutional and Political Developments, 1950—70

The British Foreign Office announced on Jan. 4, 1955, that an Anglo-Ethiopian agreement had been signed on Nov. 29, 1954, providing for the return to Ethiopian administration of tribal areas on the border with British Somaliland which had been under temporary British administration since 1944. The agreement preserved the right of tribes in British Somaliland to graze their flocks in the area concerned. [For Somali claims to Ethiopian territory see SOMALIA, page 287.]

On Nov. 4, 1955, a new Constitution was promulgated by the Emperor, superseding that of 1931 which was adopted after his accession to the throne. The reforms introduced included the principle of Ministerial responsibility to Parliament; the broadening of the Chamber of Deputies; the introduction of free, secret and universal suffrage; the independence of the judiciary; the recognition of full civic rights for all Ethiopians without distinction of race or creed; the recognition of fundamental human rights and freedoms and the suppression of all feudal practices. The Ethiopian Orthodox Church remained the established State Church, though full religious freedom was guaranteed to all citizens. The Emperor retained the prerogative of supreme direction of foreign affairs and the rights to conclude and ratify treaties with foreign powers, to dissolve Parliament and to appoint Cabinet Ministers and judges.

The first general elections in the history of Ethiopia were held on Sept. 11—Oct. 10, 1957, to elect a Chamber of Deputies of 210 members. All native-born Ethiopian citizens over the age of 21 were eligible to vote; as there were no political parties in the country, candidates campaigned on their personal records.

A Senate of 35 members was nominated by the Emperor on Nov. 1, 1957; most of the members were officials experienced in government and administration.

On Dec. 14, 1960, a section of the Ethiopian Imperial Guard and the police carried out a *coup d'état* in Addis Ababa in the absence of the Emperor, who was on a visit to Brazil. However, the rebels were not supported by the population nor by the remainder of the armed forces, and the revolt was crushed by the time the Emperor returned on Dec. 17. Nevertheless, 15 members of the Government were massacred during the revolt, the complete casualty list comprising 29 killed and 43 wounded in the armed forces; 174 killed and 300 wounded in the Imperial Guard; 121 killed and 442 wounded amongst the civilian population.

The former commander of the Imperial Guard, General Mengistu Newaye, was found guilty on March 28, 1961, of being the ringleader of the revolt, of attempting to overthrow the Government by armed rebellion and of being concerned in the shooting of 15 people. His sentence of death by hanging was carried out on March 30.

A new Cabinet was announced on April 17, 1961; Mr. Aklilou Habtewold, formerly Deputy Premier, had been appointed Prime Minister on March 29, 1961. On March 23, 1966, the Emperor promulgated a decree under which the Prime Minister would henceforth have power to appoint the members of the Cabinet; the decree laid down that the Cabinet would be collectively responsible to the Emperor and Parliament.

The Eritrean Issue, 1950–70

On Dec. 2, 1950, the U.N. General Assembly adopted a plan providing for a federation of Eritrea with Ethiopia under the Ethiopian Crown and conferring on Eritrea, within the framework of the Federation, a large measure of autonomy in domestic affairs.

A draft Constitution was submitted on May 3, 1952, to the first Representative Assembly in Eritrea, consisting of 33 Coptic Christians and 33 Moslems – the former elected by adult franchise and the latter by electoral colleges; this Constitution would establish Eritrea as an autonomous unit federated with Ethiopia under the terms of the U.N. General Assembly resolution. The new draft Constitution was unanimously adopted by the Eritrean Assembly on July 10, 1952, and ratified by the Emperor of Ethiopia on Aug. 11. On Aug. 28, the Eritrean Assembly elected its chairman, Ato Tedla Bairu, as Chief Executive of Eritrea.

Eritrea became federated with Ethiopia on Sept. 11, 1952, on which date the Emperor formally ratified the Act of Federation; under the federal constitution Ethiopia was responsible for the defence, foreign representation and finances of Eritrea. Great Britain, which had assumed responsibility for Eritrea in 1941, formally transferred sovereignty over Eritrea to Ethiopia at midnight on Sept. 15–16. The Emperor Haile Selassie, while on a visit to Eritrea which began on Oct. 4, announced that Eritreans would take a full part in the administration of the Federation through a joint Federal Council to be established with its Headquarters in Addis Ababa.

It was officially announced on May 20, 1960, that the Eritrean Government would be known as the Eritrean Administration; Ethiopian insignia would be used for all administrative purposes in the territory, and the Eritrean seal would bear the words "Eritrean Administration under Haile Selassie I, Emperor of Ethiopia". It was stated at the same time that the changes had been unanimously approved by the Eritrean Assembly in Asmara.

The final step in the integration of Eritrea with Ethiopia was taken on Nov. 14, 1962, when the Ethiopian Parliament and the Eritrean Legislative Assembly unanimously voted to abolish the federal status possessed by Eritrea and to make the territory a province of the Ethiopian Empire.

The activities of Moslem Eritrean Nationalists and the alleged aid given to them by the U.A.R. in their fight against Ethiopia were two factors affecting relations between Ethiopia and Arab countries during the sixties, Ethiopian recognition of Israel in October 1961 being a further factor. On May 13, 1967, the Ethiopian Government asked the Arab League's representative in Addis Ababa to leave Ethiopia because of his "unauthorized activities". The Arab Liberation Front for Eritrea announced its responsibility for a series of sabotage incidents involving guerrilla warfare from March 1969 onwards.

LIBERIA

Area: 43,000 sq. miles.
Population 1969 (estimate): 1,150,000
Capital: Monrovia (110,000).
Official language: English.
Chief products: Iron ore, diamonds, rubber.

Liberia as an independent country has its origins in the settlement, under the auspices of the American Colonization Society, of freed slaves from the U.S.A., the first contingent of 88 arriving at Sherbo Island in 1820. By 1838 the settlers had obtained political rights to an area stretching some 40 miles inland between Cape Mount and Bassa Point on the so-called Grain Coast, and in 1847 they achieved independence under a Constitution similar to that of the U.S.A., with an executive headed by the President and a bicameral parliament consisting of a Senate of 10 members and a House of Representatives of 39.

Liberia's economic development began with a lease agreement of 1926 whereby the Firestone rubber company obtained the right to lease up to a million acres for rubber production for 99 years, and a $5,000,000 loan was granted to the Government by a subsidiary of Firestone. In 1930 a League of Nations commission issued a report alleging that forced labour was a common practice in Liberia and this eventually led to a revised agreement with Firestone. In 1942 the U.S.A. and Liberia signed a defence agreement, which was followed by other agreements. A 1959 agreement also provided for economic aid and limited military assistance for the development of frontier forces. The U.S.A. built a military base at what is now the capital's airport, and the port of Monrovia was built under Lend-Lease aid.

President Tubman, elected in 1943, followed an "open-door" policy for foreign investment and ended the Firestone monopoly, introduced universal suffrage and emancipated the women of Liberia.

President Tubman was re-elected for President in 1951, 1955, 1959, 1963 and 1967, each time for a four-year term of office. He stood, each time, as the candidate of the True Whig Party, the only party in Liberia, which has been continuously in power since 1878. President Tubman was last opposed in the presidential elections in 1959 when he received 168,000 votes against 24 votes for Mr. William Bright. In the 1967 elections on May 2, Mr. William Tobert was elected as Vice-President, being the only candidate.

The Constitution now provides for an executive President assisted by a Vice-President and Cabinet, whilst the Legislature consists of the 18-member Senate and the House of Representatives with 52 members.

Three attempts have been made on the life of the President: In 1955 President Tubman escaped without injury when fired at, whilst in September 1961 the discovery of a Communist plot to kill the President was announced by security officials; on Feb. 5, 1963, it was again announced that a plot had been discovered to kill President Tubman and overthrow the Government, and that five people, including Colonel David Y. Thompson, Commander of the Liberian National Guard (the Liberian Army), had been arrested.

On Feb. 12, 1958, legislation was passed by the National Assembly making racial discrimination a crime punishable by fines up to $30,000, and in some cases by imprisonment.

SOUTH AFRICA

Area: 472,359 sq. miles.
Population 1970 census – provisional figures: 21,314,000.
Capitals: Pretoria – administrative (493,000), Bloemfontein – judicial (146,000), Cape Town – legislative (626,000).
Other important towns: Johannesburg (1,365,000), Durban (683,000), Port Elizabeth (381,000), Germiston (197,000).

Constitutional Developments

The Union of South Africa
The Union of South Africa came into being on May 31, 1910, after the

United Kingdom Parliament had passed the South Africa Act of 1909. This Act, which was the Union's Constitution, was framed in South Africa by a National Convention consisting of the representatives of the Parliaments of the four self-governing British colonies in South Africa, viz., the Cape of Good Hope, Natal, the Transvaal and the Orange River Colony. After Union the latter reverted to the former name of Orange Free State. The South Africa Act was approved by the four colonial Parliaments and, in addition, by a referendum in Natal.

The Cape of Good Hope was colonized by the Dutch in 1652. The British took possession in 1795 and again in 1806, after an absence of three years; the territory was formally ceded to Great Britain in 1814. Natal was annexed to the Cape Colony in 1844, placed under separate government in the following year and established as a separate colony in 1856. The Transvaal, on the other hand, was colonized by Boers who left the Cape Colony during the Great Trek in 1836 and the following years. [The Boers — now known as Afrikaners — were the descendants of the original Dutch settlers in the Cape.] In 1852 Britain recognized the independence of the Transvaal which, in the following year, took the name of the South African Republic. Following the annexation of the Republic by Britain in 1877, war broke out between the British and the Boers in 1880; although peace was concluded in 1881, and self-government restored to the Boers, a second Boer War broke out in 1899.
The Orange Free State, which was a British possession from 1848 until its independence in 1854, was again annexed (by the British) as the Orange River Colony in May 1900. In the peace treaty of Vereeniging of May 31, 1902, both the Transvaal and the Orange River Colony lost their independence, but responsible government was restored to the two colonies in 1906.

Under the 1910 Constitution executive power was vested in the Sovereign acting on the advice of His Ministers of State for the Union, and might be administered by the Sovereign in person or by the Governor-General as his representative. Legislative power was vested in the Union Parliament which consisted of the Sovereign, the Senate and the House of Assembly. Although each of the provinces had its own Provincial Council, the Union was not a federal State and the Union Parliament was supreme. The Prime Minister was always the leader of the majority party in the House of Assembly and the other Cabinet Ministers were appointed by the Governor-General on the Prime Minister's recommendations.
Two clauses of the 1910 Constitution were given special protection; these "entrenched clauses" might not be repealed or altered unless approv-

al of a Bill embodying any such change had been given by a two-thirds majority of the members of both Houses of Parliament in joint session. The first related to the Cape franchise rights whereby, in addition to whites holding the vote, suitably qualified Coloured men and Natives in the Cape could vote for members of the Union Parliament. The other "entrenched clause" established English and Dutch as the official languages of the Union; this was amended in 1925 when Afrikaans was substituted for Dutch.

The reason behind the constitutional "safe-guarding" of franchise was to be found in the nominal equality between whites and educated blacks in the Cape Province and Natal, both groups having had the vote prior to the formation of the Union.

The Union's status within the Commonwealth was changed by the Statute of Westminster of 1931, which gave effect to a resolution adopted by an Imperial Conference in 1926 [see pages 22-4]. In 1934, when the Union Parliament passed the Status Act giving statutory effect to the constitutional changes brought about by the Statute of Westminster, the Speaker gave a considered ruling that ". . . the Statute of Westminster does not in any way derogate from the entrenched clauses of the South Africa Act, and the position will not be changed by the passing of the Status Bill . . .".

The Republic of South Africa

A referendum on whether South Africa should become a Republic, held on Oct. 5, 1960, in the Union and South West Africa, resulted in 52.05 per cent of the 1,633,772 votes cast by the all-white electorate being in favour, and 47.49 per cent against. The individual returns from the four provinces and South West Africa varied considerably; the Orange Free State (76.7 per cent), South West Africa (62.3 per cent), the Transvaal (55 per cent) and the Cape (50.1 per cent) all had a republican majority, whereas only 23.7 per cent voted in favour in Natal. The cities of Cape Town, Johannesburg and Durban all had anti-republican majorities, while Pretoria had a republican majority.

The Republic of South Africa Constitution Bill, first published on Dec. 9, 1960, received its third reading in the Senate on April 23, 1961. It was based almost completely on the South Africa Act of 1909, but the words "the Crown" or "King or Queen" wherever they occurred were replaced by "the State". The powers of the President corresponded to those of the

Governor-General; the President, who had to be a white registered voter at least 30 years of age, was to be elected by secret ballot by a majority of an electoral college consisting of the members of both Houses of Parliament, presided over by the Chief Justice or Judge of Appeal.

Previously, on March 15, 1961, during a Commonwealth Prime Ministers' Conference, it was officially announced that Dr. Verwoerd, the South African Prime Minister, had decided "in the light of the views expressed on behalf of other member-Governments [of the Commonwealth] and the indications of their future intentions regarding the racial policy of the Union Government . . . to withdraw his application for South Africa's continuing membership of the Commonwealth as a Republic". The withdrawal was to be effective from May 31, 1961, the date on which South Africa would become a Republic.

As a result of South Africa's departure from the Commonwealth, legislation was passed in both the South African and British Parliaments governing the future relationship between the two countries. The South Africa Act, designed to regulate finally the operation of United Kingdom law in relation to South Africa, was enacted in the British Parliament on May 24, 1962; this stated, *inter alia*, that as from the enactment of the Bill any person who was a British subject by virtue only of being a South African citizen would cease to be a British subject, with certain provisos. The Commonwealth Relations Act, enacted on June 15, 1962, in the South African Parliament, provided that (*a*) with effect from May 31, 1962, British subjects who were not South African citizens would be classed as aliens in South Africa; (*b*) as from Jan. 1, 1963, Commonwealth citizens being temporary visitors (for six months or more) to South Africa would have to register as aliens; and (*c*) as from Jan. 1, 1963, British subjects already in South Africa, not having applied for permanent residence by Dec. 31, 1962, would have to register as aliens.

The Apartheid Issue

Its Origins

Segregation of the races was practised in the four colonies before Union in 1910. In the Cape Colony, the Glen Grey Act of 1895 first established the principle of entrusting the Africans in the Transkeian territories with some measure of responsibility for their own affairs and with the right to individual land tenure. Africans were compelled, in the Transvaal and Orange Free State, to carry identification passes, to pay hut taxes, to live in ill-defined reserves or to squat on farmers' lands — without the right to own land. Employment of Africans in these two provinces was subject to stringent control and pass provisions.

Legislation which effectively segregated the races was passed following the Act of Union: (a) The Native Labour Regulations Act of 1911 provided uniform legislation for the whole Union, divided into labour districts similar to the Transvaal mining areas; (b) the Natives Land Act of 1913 provided that blacks and whites should not encroach on one another's lands; (c) the Native (Urban Areas) Act of 1923 established uniformity in the housing of Africans in "locations" within urban limits, an amendment of 1925 enacted a consistent system for the taxation of Africans, and the Native (Urban Areas) Consolidation Act of 1945 incorporated the various amendments made, since 1923, with the original act [see also under "Residential Apartheid"]; (d) the Industrial Conciliation Act of 1924 regulating collective bargaining between employers and employees but excluding Africans and Indians from the category "employee"; (e) a Native Affairs Commission, established in 1920, provided *inter alia* for regular conferences with representative bodies of Africans. [The term 'Native' (= black African) was later officially replaced by the term 'Bantu'.]

The Hertzog Government — based on a coalition between Afrikaner Nationalist and the (white) South African Labour Party — in 1926 introduced a legalized "Colour Bar" whereby non-whites were, in specified districts, excluded from engaging in skilled or semi-skilled employment, where they might compete with Europeans.

The Indians in South Africa, descendants of immigrants who had arrived during the latter half of the 19th century, were restricted by: (a) the Immigrants' Act of 1913 which in effect stopped further Indian immigration to South Africa: (b) a diminution of their rights to hold property in the Transvaal in 1919; (c) the Class Areas Act of 1924 whereby Indians in Natal lost their provincial franchise and the Government was empowered to segregate them in reserved areas; (d) the Trading and Occupation of Land (Transvaal and Natal) Restriction Act of 1943, which "pegged" the existing occupation of land or premises in Durban for three years; (e) the Asiatic Land Tenure and Indian Representation Act of 1946, the first chapter of which defined areas in Durban and other parts of Natal where Indians might acquire and/or occupy property. [See also The Franchise Question, page 57.]

The Implementation of Apartheid after 1948

The policy of *apartheid* was first clearly defined as the policy of the Nationalist Party under the leadership of Dr. Malan in 1948, during the campaign preceding the general election of that year.

Dr. Malan, in a speech at Paarl on April 20, declared that the election would be dominated by the question of whether the European race would be able to "maintain its rule, its purity and its civilization or float along until it vanishes for ever in the black sea of South Africa's non-European population". The party's policy, based on the two "fundamental principles" of *apartheid* and trusteeship, should be applied to the three non-European racial groups in the Union – the Natives, the Coloureds and the Indians.

A statement on the Nationalist policy on the coloured question, published on March 29, 1948, had declared that the *apartheid* policy must be applicable to the "social, residential, industrial and political spheres". Following the victory of the Nationalist Party on May 26, 1948, considerable legislation to implement this resolution was passed through the Union Parliament over the period 1949–61, and continued to do so after the declaration of a Republic on May 31, 1961. [See also The Franchise Question, page 57.]

Residential Apartheid

The Native (Urban Areas) Consolidation Act of 1945 [see above] was amended over the period 1950–70 in such a way that the authorities were given wide-ranging powers to control the entry of non-Europeans into urban areas, the principal amendments being: (*a*) The Native Laws Amendment Act – which received its third reading in Parliament on June 19, 1952; (*b*) the Native (Urban Areas) Amendment Act (1955) – which received its third reading in the Senate on March 31, 1955; (*c*) the Native Laws Amendment Act (1957) – approved by the Senate on May 17, 1957; (*d*) the Bantu Laws Amendment Act (1963) which, according to a Government spokesman, was designed to "establish more firmly the migratory labour system" – approved at its third reading on June 21, 1963; (*e*) the Bantu Laws Amendment Act (1964), which came into force on Jan. 1, 1965; and (*f*) the Bantu Laws Amendment Act (1970) – which empowered the Minister of Bantu Administration and Development to prohibit the employment of Africans in any area or any trade – passed at its third reading in the House of Assembly on Feb. 23, 1970.

The Group Areas Act, which became law on May 31, 1950, placed the whole of the Union (except certain areas already set aside for particular racial groups) on a "controlled area" basis in relation to ownership and occupation of land by racial groups, and empowered the Governor-General with Parliament's approval to set aside any part of a controlled area as a group area, in which only members of a particular racial group would be allowed to live, to own property or to conduct a business. For the purpose of this Act the population was divided into three main racial groups – whites, Natives and Coloureds – the last two of which might be subdivided. The Act came into operation in the Cape, Natal and the

Transvaal on March 30, 1951; on Oct. 18, a proclamation was issued applying occupation control to the whole of the Cape Province.

Subsequent amendments to the Group Areas Act included: (1) the Group Areas Amendment Act (1955), given its third reading in the House of Assembly on Feb. 7, 1955; (2) the Group Areas Further Amendment Act, which passed its third reading in the Senate on June 21, 1955; (3) the Group Areas Development Act, which passed its third reading in both Houses of Parliament on June 21, 1955, and set up a Group Areas Development Board which would take control of all affected property on the proclamation of a group area; (4) the Group Areas Amendment Act (1956), which received a third reading in the Senate on May 3, 1956; (5) a proclamation issued on Feb. 12, 1965, applying a section of the Group Areas Act to all public places of recreation so that such places in white areas could not be frequented by non-white and *vice versa*.

The report of a Government Commission on the Socio-Economic Development of the Bantu Areas, under the chairmanship of Professor F. R. Tomlinson, was published on March 27, 1956; this put forward detailed proposals for the consolidation of the Bantu Areas into seven main divisions or blocks, involving the construction of 100 new Bantu townships. The Union Government accepted the factual material of the report "as a basis for the further development of ideas and the determination of policy by the Government" but rejected many of the Commission's detailed recommendations.

Following on this, the Promotion of Bantu Self-Government Bill, which provided for the abolition of Native representation in the South African Parliament, the establishment of eight Bantu "national units" or Bantustans and the conferment of legislative powers on Bantu territorial authorities, received its third reading on June 3, 1959, in the House of Assembly.

The first territorial authority to be constituted under the Bantu Authorities Act [see page 58] was that for the Transkei reserve, which was opened by Dr. Verwoerd on May 7, 1957, but did not function until May 26, 1959. The Transkei Self-Government Bill was enacted on May 24, 1963, its principal provisions being as follows: (*a*) the Transkei, while remaining an integral part of the Republic, would be governed by a Legislative Assembly consisting of the four Transkei Paramount Chiefs, 60 other chiefs and 45 elected members; (*b*) this Assembly would have power to legislate on internal matters, but any such laws would be passed to the Republican President for his assent or reference back to the Assembly; (*c*) executive power would be in the hands of a Chief Minister and five other Ministers who would be elected by secret ballot by members of the Legislative Assembly; (d) the right to vote would be held by all Africans over 21 (or, if taxpayers, over 18) who were either (i) born in the Transkei, (ii) lawfully living in the Transkei, (iii) Xhosa-speaking persons in the Republic, or (iv) Sotho-speaking persons linked with Sotho-speaking tribes of the Transkei. The newly elected Assembly met for the first time on Dec. 6, 1963.

During 1968 a measure of internal self-government was given to the Ciskei and Tswana homelands. The Ciskei Territorial Authority, first established in November 1961, was formally reconstituted on Nov. 14, 1968, as a Legislative Assembly with an Executive Council of six members, having authority over local affairs. The Tswana Territorial Authority which had been established in December 1961 was made a Legislative Assembly on Dec. 12, 1968.

Social and Economic Apartheid

The Population Registration Act, which received its third reading in the Senate on June 9, 1950, provided for the compilation of a register of the population, their classificaton as European, Coloured or Native, and the issue of identity cards to persons over 16, or in the case of Natives, over 18.

After 1952 the various passes which Africans had been required to carry under previous legislation were consolidated into a single reference book, which all African males over 16 were required to carry; the primary purpose of the pass laws, which were introduced in the early 19th century, was to control the influx of African labour into the towns from the reserves, the then Protectorates and other neighbouring territories. As from Dec. 1, 1960, all African women over the age of 16 were also required to carry pass books.

The Prohibition of Mixed Marriages Act, passed by the Senate on June 30, 1949, laid down penalties up to a maximum of a £50 fine for officials who knowingly solemnized inter-racial marriages, and made these marriages void. An amendment, adopted at its second reading in the House of Assembly on Feb. 22, 1968, laid down that a marriage contracted abroad between a male South African citizen and a woman of a different race would not be recognized in South Africa.

Under the Native Labour (Settlement of Disputes) Act, passed in the Senate on Sept. 30, 1953, strikes by Native workers were prohibited under pain of heavy penalties; in addition the Act provided for the settlement of Native labour disputes by means of compulsory arbitration.

The Industrial Conciliation Bill, forbidding the formation of racially mixed trade unions and providing for the division of existing mixed unions into separate racial bodies, received its third reading in the Senate on May 1, 1956. A further provision empowered the Minister of Labour to "safeguard the economic welfare of employees of any race" by reserving specified kinds of work for members of particular races. The scope of this Act was extended by an amendment passed by the House of Assembly on May 1, 1959; under this, commercial as well as industrial workers were included, while the provision that in recommending "job reservation" the Industrial Tribunal must take into account the economic welfare of racial groups affected was removed. The Amendment Bill also stated that the Tribunal's powers should not be affected by the availability of labour.

The Reservation of Separate Amenities Act received its third reading in the Senate on Oct. 1, 1953; this empowered railway and other authorities to provide separate facilities for different races in all public places and vehicles, and made discrimination valid whether these facilities were equal or not. This had been foreshadowed in 1948 when segregation on Cape suburban trains was introduced, firstly on an experimental basis and then permanently on Sept. 12. *Apartheid* was introduced on the buses in Cape Town from April 16, 1956, while a proposal for the introduction of *apartheid* in amenities and offices under Municipal control had been adopted on March 29. Segregation of amenities had long been practised throughout the country except in parts of the Cape Province.

Educational Apartheid

The Bantu Education Act, given its third reading in the House of Assembly on June 25, 1952, transferred the control of the education of Africans from the Provincial Administrations to the Department of Native Affairs. This meant that non-whites would henceforth be educated on the basis of syllabuses specially drawn up for them and widely different from those for whites. The Act also empowered the Minister to withdraw grants in aid of mission schools in order to further community or Government schools, and to cancel the registration of any school. An amendment to this Act, giving greater powers to the Minister and laying down conditions for the registration of private schools, was approved in the Senate on May 9, 1956.

Provision for the progressive exclusion of non-European students from the "open" Universities of Cape Town and the Witwatersrand, and the establishment of five separate University colleges for non-white races (three for African tribal groups and one each for Coloureds and Indians) was made in the Extension of University Education Bill, which received its third reading in the Senate on June 8, 1959.

Under the University College of Fort Hare Transfer Bill, which received its third reading in the Senate on June 27, 1959, control of Fort Hare College for Africans passed from Rhodes University to the Department of Native Affairs; the College, which had hitherto admitted Coloured, Indian and African students, was reserved for the exclusive use of the Xhosa tribal group.

Two new University Colleges, as provided for above, for the Sotho tribes at Turfloop in the Northern Transvaal, and for the Zulus at Ngoya in Natal, were officially established on July 31, 1959, as was a University College at Bellville, Cape Town, for Coloureds, Malays and Griquas, to be known as the University College, West Cape, on Nov. 1, 1959. A University College for Indians was later instituted at Durban.

Bills were adopted in the Senate on April 30, 1969, releasing the three University Colleges for Africans – Fort Hare, Zululand and the North – and the University Colleges of the Western Cape (for Coloureds) and of Durban-Westville (for Indians) from their association with the University of South Africa, and establishing them as Universities.

Measures transferring the control of the education of Coloureds and Indians from the Provinces to the central Government were passed during 1963–65 – the Coloured Persons Education Bill on May 1, 1963, and the Indians' Education Bill on April 30, 1965.

The Franchise Question

Between 1936 and 1970, both the Native and Coloured populations of the Cape lost their place on the general electoral roll; the removal of the Cape Coloured population involved considerable legal and parliamentary debate over the so-called "entrenched clauses" [see page 49].

The Native Representation Bill, which provided for the abolition of the Native franchise in the Cape Province and the creation of a Native Representative Council elected from the four provinces in the Union, was passed on April 6, 1936, in its third reading at a joint session of both Houses of Parliament, in accordance with constitutional procedure on the amendment of "entrenched clauses". Native voters on the existing roll were transferred to a special register for all Natives who subsequently obtained the necessary qualifications. The Bill laid down that the Natives so registered would be entitled to elect three European members to the House of Assembly and two to the Cape Provincial Council. The first meeting of the Native Representative Council was held at Pretoria on Dec.

6, 1937; a purely advisory body, which consisted of 12 elected and four nominated Native members and six Europeans, it could make recommendations on all laws and estimates of expenditure affecting Natives before they were submitted to Parliament.

Important changes in the Union's Native policy after the success of the Nationalist Party in the general elections of 1948 included increased legislative and executive functions for the Native Representative Council, whose membership, it was proposed, should be increased and become exclusively Native. However, on Jan. 4, 1949, it was announced that the Native Representative Council was to be abolished; the Secretary of Native Affairs stated that no Government could concede the demands for the abolition of discriminatory legislation which the Council had made during its previous session in 1946.

The Bantu Authorities Bill, which provided for the replacement of the Native Representative Council by Bantu tribal, regional and territorial authorities with administrative, executive and judicial functions, was passed in the Senate on June 11, 1951, and in the House of Assembly on June 21.

Between 1951 and 1955 several attempts were made in Parliament to introduce legislation providing for the separate representation of the Coloured voters in Cape Province and Natal. The Separate Representation of Voters Act of 1951 was declared illegal by the Supreme Court in 1952 because it had not been passed by the two-thirds majority required for proposed changes in the "entrenched clauses" of the Constitution. Similarly an attempt to repeal the franchise "entrenched clause" failed to obtain the required majority for constitutional amendments.

The problem was solved when Parliament passed, in June 1955, a Bill increasing the membership of the Senate from 48 to 89, which in due course gave the ruling Nationalist Party a two-thirds majority in a joint session of both Houses. By this means a South Africa Act Amendment Bill was passed on Feb. 27, 1956; the Act *inter alia* removed the franchise "entrenched clause" while retaining the "entrenched clause" referring to the official status of the Afrikaans and English languages.

A Separate Representation of Voters Act was given a third reading in the House of Assembly on April 27, 1956, and approved by the Senate during the first week of May. *Inter alia* this laid down that Coloured voters in the Cape Province (who would be on a separate electoral roll) would elect four white members to the House of Assembly and two white members to the Cape Provincial Council.

Subsequently the number of members in the Senate was reduced from

90 to 54 in the Senate Act of 1960; this re-established the system of election of Senators by proportional representation. Native representation in the Senate was also abolished.

On Oct. 2, 1964, the Coloured Representative Council Bill was enacted; the provisions of this Act, foreshadowed in an official statement on Dec. 12, 1961, included the establishment of a Coloured Representative Council of 30 elected and 16 nominated members with an executive council of five. Elections for this Council were to be held every five years, all Coloured people over 21 having the right to vote. The Council would have powers to advise the Government, when requested, on all matters affecting the economic, social, educational and political affairs of Coloured people.

The purpose of legislation introduced on March 26, 1968, was described by a Government spokesman on May 1 as "rounding off the Government's policy of bringing separate or parallel development to the Coloured population group". The Prohibition of Improper Interference Bill, which passed its final stages in Parliament on May 21, 1968, prohibited multiracial membership of, or participation in, political parties. The Separate Representation of Voters Amendment Bill, passed by the Senate on May 20, extended the term of office of the existing white representatives of the Coloured people in Parliament until 1971 — the end of the existing Parliament — and provided that such representation would then end, as would representation on the Cape Provincial Council.

The Coloured Person's Representative Council Amendment Bill provided for the enlargement of the existing Council to one of 40 elected and 20 nominated members — the chairman being nominated by the State President — and for giving it a limited measure of jurisdiction over Coloured affairs. Under the Bill, which received its final reading in the Senate on May 21, 1968, about 700,000 Coloured men and women over 21 would be able to vote for members of the Council.

Elections to this Council were first held on Sept. 24, 1969, and resulted in the anti-*apartheid* Labour Party gaining a majority of the 40 elective seats. They did not command a majority, however, in the 60-member council following the nomination of pro-Government members to fill the 20 remaining seats.

It was further announced on Feb. 6, 1970, that: (*a*) all Coloured people would be removed from the common voters' rolls of municipalities and divisional councils in the Cape Province by September 1972; and (*b*) Coloured people would in future elect their own representatives to councils in separate municipalities still to be created for them.

59

The Indian community in South Africa never received the franchise.

On Feb. 26, 1968, a South African Indian Council Bill received its second reading; this Bill established the Council as a statutory body with 25 nominated members to serve a three-year term of office.

Legislation against Opponents of *Apartheid*

Of the organizations opposing the policy of *apartheid*, the most influential among Africans was the African National Congress, which had a tradition of pursuing its objects by peaceful means. After it was declared illegal in 1960, however [see below], a minority of its former members began to resort to violence.

The Pan-Africanist Congress, founded on April 6, 1959, by former ANC members who objected to the ANC's alliance with white and Indian left-wing organizations, immediately began to organize a militant arm known as Poqo, which was not committed to non-violence.

From 1960 onwards some members of both the ANC and the PAC received military training outside South Africa (especially in Tanzania and in Communist countries) with the object of waging guerrilla warfare against the South African Government's forces.

From its accession to power in 1948, the Nationalist Party had made it clear that it would introduce legislation as deemed necessary to suppress organizations which might resort to violent means in their fight against *apartheid.*

The Suppression of Communism Act, which was designed to restrict the activities of Communist and near-Communist organizations and agitators, came into force on July 17, 1950. During the Bill's passage through the South African Parliament, the then Minister of Justice, Mr. C. R. Swart, had stated that the doctrine of Communism in South Africa was not confined to the teachings of Marx, Trotsky and Lenin but also had "a special aim of its own, viz., the creation of hostilities between Europeans and non-Europeans". The South African Communist Party, which was declared under the Bill to be an illegal organization, went into voluntary liquidation with effect from June 20, 1950, almost a month before the Bill became law.

On March 21, 1960, the date selected by the PAC for a non-violent campaign against the pass laws, the police fired on a large crowd of Africans at Sharpeville (an African township near Johannesburg), killing 67 people, while three more Africans were killed when the police fired on a demonstration at Langa location near Cape Town. In protest against the shootings African workers launched a strike which continued until April 7 in Cape Town and Durban.

As a result an Unlawful Organizations Bill, whose provisions were modelled on those of the Suppression of Communism Act and which declared the PAC and the ANC to be unlawful organizations, was rushed through Parliament between March 28 and April 5, 1960.

Powers of detention without trial for a maximum period of 90 days, given temporarily to the police under the General Law Amendment Act of 1963, were extended permanently to 180 days under the Criminal Procedure Amendment Act, enacted on June 25, 1965.

Among other legislation, the General Law Amendment Act ("Terrorism Act"), which came into force on June 21, 1967, made terrorism an offence to be equated with treason and provided for the arrest of suspects without warrant and for indefinite detention, including solitary confinement, penalties ranging from a minimum of five years' imprisonment to the death sentence.

On Jan. 1, 1970, according to an official statement, there were 801 persons serving prison sentences imposed under security laws — 14 whites, 11 Coloureds, 15 Asians and 761 Africans.

THE UNITED ARAB REPUBLIC (EGYPT)

Area: 386,000 sq. miles.
Population 1969 (estimate): 32,501,000.
Capital: Cairo (800,000).
Other important town: Alexandria (1,900,000).
Official language: Arabic.
Chief products: Crude oil, cotton, rice.

The Monarchy, 1922–53

Egypt, formerly a British Protectorate, became independent in 1922, Sultan Ahmed Fuad being proclaimed King of Egypt. [The Egyptian Royal House had been founded by Mehemet Ali who was appointed Pasha of Egypt by the Sultan of Turkey in 1805, Egypt then forming part of the Ottoman Empire. The position of Pasha became hereditary among his descendants, who held the title of Khedive from 1867 and Sultan from 1914.]

Under the Constitution of 1923 Egypt was governed by a hereditary monarch and a Parliament of two Houses, the Senate and the Chamber of

Deputies. The King acted through a Council of Ministers who were appointed and dismissed by him but were responsible to Parliament.

The accession of King Farouk (King Fuad's son) in 1936 was closely followed by the signing on Aug. 26, 1936, of the Anglo-Egyptian Treaty, terminating the military occupation of Egypt by British troops which had started in 1882, following an Egyptian military revolt. The treaty, however, also provided for British troops to be stationed in the vicinity of the Suez Canal to ensure, with Egyptian co-operation, the defence of the Canal.

During the years 1937–52 the Government of the country was in the hands of the nationalist parties – the Wafdist Party led by Nahas Pasha, and the Saadist Party which had been formed by a group of dissident Wafdists in 1932. General elections held in 1942 were boycotted by all parties except the Wafdist Party, which itself boycotted elections held in 1945; however, all parties contested those held in 1950 which resulted in an overwhelming majority for the Wafdist Party.

On Oct. 15, 1951, the Egyptian Parliament approved a decree abrogating the Anglo-Egyptian Treaty of 1936; this unilateral action was not recognized by the British Government and strong British naval and military reinforcements were moved into the Suez Canal zone. Terrorist activities against the British troops ensued, which culminated in serious riots in Cairo on Jan. 26, 1952; Nahas Pasha was dismissed as Prime Minister on the night of Jan. 26–27 by King Farouk, and Aly Maher Pasha was appointed in his stead.

After six months of changes in the leadership of the Government, the crisis reached its climax on July 23, when a bloodless military coup was carried out in Cairo by General Mohammed Neguib.

The General declared in a broadcast proclamation that the object of the coup was to end governmental instability and corruption in high places, and emphasized that the Army had no political aims and desired to work for the interests of Egypt within the Constitution. The Premier, Hilaly Pasha, who had been in office for less than 24 hours, resigned following the coup and was replaced by Aly Maher Pasha, who formed his new Government on July 24. On July 26, in response to a demand by General Neguib and the Army, King Farouk abdicated in favour of his infant son, the seven-month old Prince Ahmed Fuad, and left Egypt the same day. The Egyptian Cabinet assumed the royal prerogatives pending the appointment of a Regency Council which would hold these prerogatives until the infant King came of age.

Statements praising General Neguib's action, and denouncing the former regime of King Farouk, were issued by the leaders of the principal political parties, including the Wafdists, Saadists, Liberals and Nationalists, as well as by the extremist Moslem Brotherhood organization [see below].

Despite repeated warnings by General Neguib to rid themselves of corrupt elements, none of the political parties carried out any drastic reorganization; in consequence the Army took action by arresting some 50 leading members of political parties as well as former associates of ex-King Farouk. Aly Maher resigned the premiership and a new Government was formed with General Neguib as Prime Minister; in explanation of his resignation Aly Maher stated that it was "in the best interests of the nation that power should be transferred to a single hand". During the last week of September the Government carried out an extensive purge of the Diplomatic Corps, the Officer Corps and senior ranks of the Civil Service, whilst at the same time strengthening its control of the administration by placing Army officers in every department.

Supreme powers were conferred on General Neguib for a six-month period on Nov. 14, 1952, with retrospective effect from the time of the July coup to Jan. 23, 1953.

On Dec. 10, 1952, the General announced the abolition of the 1923 Constitution and the Government's intention of drafting a new Constitution "to realize the aspirations of the Egyptian people". However, on Jan. 16, 1953, General Neguib announced that there would be a "transitional period" of three years before constitutional Government was restored.

All political parties in Egypt were dissolved and their funds confiscated under a decree issued on Jan. 16; General Neguib announced, on Jan. 23, the formation of the "Liberation Rally" as the sole political party.

On Feb. 10, 1953, General Neguib announced his assumption of sovereign powers and the formation of a "Congress", composed of the Council of the Revolution (the Army committee of 13 officers which, under General Neguib's chairmanship, had been the effective instrument of government since the abdication of King Farouk) and the Council of Ministers and charged with the discussion of general policy; in addition he emphasized that the monarchy still existed and that the Regent would sign future decree-laws.

The Republic of Egypt, 1953–58

Egypt was proclaimed a Republic on June 18, 1953, by the Council of the Revolution, with General Neguib assuming presidential powers as well as the post of Prime Minister under a provisional Constitution. In his Cabinet Lieut.-Colonel Gamal Abdel Nasser was appointed Vice-Premier and Minister of the Interior.

By February 1954 disagreements had arisen between General Neguib and other members of the Council of the Revolution, but when General Neguib offered to resign popular demonstrations in his favour caused him to withdraw his resignation. On April 17, 1954, however, he resigned as Prime Minister but remained President both of the Republic and of the Council of the Revolution. The latter thereupon nominated Colonel Nasser as Prime Minister and Military Governor.

The Council of the Revolution announced on Sept. 15, 1953, that it had established a Revolutionary Tribunal, composed of members of the Council, to try all persons accused of "conspiring against the interests of the country and attempting to undermine the revolution". The tribunal, on June 22, sentenced 13 cavalry officers to imprisonment or dismissal from the Army for conspiring to overthrow the Government. The tribunal was, however, dissolved on June 30, 1954.

The Council of the Revolution had meanwhile taken measures to remove its opponents among former political leaders from public life; the latter included 38 persons, among them three former Prime Ministers, deprived of their political rights for 10 years on April 15. [This measure was subsequently annulled on Jan. 31, 1960, by presidential decree.]

The principal opponent of the Government was the Moslem Brotherhood – an organization founded in 1928 by Sheikh Hassan el Banna with the aim of establishing a theocratic society in Egypt and ultimately world-wide domination by Islam. The Brotherhood was eventually dissolved by the Government on Oct. 29, 1954, following an alleged attempt on the life of Colonel Nasser three days earlier.

It was subsequently claimed that President Neguib had been involved in a conspiracy by the Moslem Brotherhood, and on Nov. 14, 1954, the Cabinet and the Council of the Revolution jointly decided to relieve him of his post. After further allegations that he had conspired with left-wing officers to remove Colonel Nasser and to return to power himself, it was officially decided that in order "to deprive enemies of the regime of any opportunity to sow discord" General Neguib would not be tried. Seven leading members of the Brotherhood, however – including its "Supreme Guide" (Dr. Hassan el-Hodeiby) – were sentenced to death by a special court on Dec. 4, 1954.

Colonel Nasser proclaimed a new Constitution on Jan. 16, 1956, thus bringing to an end the three-year transitional period [see page 63].

It was officially stated that the new Constitution was of a "socialistic nature and would abolish social distinctions and prohibit the creation of civil titles". It laid down that sovereignty would be vested in the people and that the regime of the State would be "republican and democratic"; the presidential system would be the basis of government, with legislative powers vested in a National Assembly and executive power in a President.

At the same time it was stated that political parties would remain suspended until the Government introduced a law regulating them; pending such a measure "a National Union would be established by the people to work for the realization of the aims of the revolution". Colonel Nasser described the National Union as "a kind of Popular Front organization with no political orientation".

A referendum on the Constitution, held on June 23, 1956, resulted in an overwhelming majority of 99.8 per cent or 5,488,225 votes in favour. The presidential election, which took place at the same time, resulted in 99.9 per cent or 5,496,965 votes being cast for Colonel Nasser, the sole candidate for the presidency. The Council of the Revolution had been dissolved on June 24, and the new Cabinet, which had a civilian majority, was sworn in by President Nasser on June 30.

The first general elections since the 1952 revolution were held on July 3, 1957, all Egyptian citizens over 18 being eligible to vote; as all political parties had previously been dissolved, there was no organized opposition. All candidates had to be approved by the executive committee of the newly-established "National Union"; as nearly half the candidates were rejected by this committee, 62 deputies were returned unopposed to the National Assembly. About 100 candidates were returned with the required absolute majority but a second ballot had to be held on July 14 in the remaining constituencies; the new Assembly, with a total of 350 seats, met for the first time on July 22.

The United Arab Republic, 1958–61

Under a proclamation signed by President Nasser and President Kuwatly of Syria on Feb. 1, 1958, the two Republics of Egypt and Syria were merged into a single country, the United Arab Republic.

This was preceded on Sept. 4, 1957, by the signing of an agreement establishing an economic union between the two countries, while unanimous approval for a Federal Union between the two States was given on Nov. 18 in Damascus, at a joint session of 35 members of the Egyptian Parliament and the whole of the Syrian Chamber of Deputies, and in Cairo by the Egyptian National Assembly.

The proclamation stated that the United Arab Republic (U.A.R.) would have a "presidential democratic system of government" in which executive power would be vested in the Head of State. Legislative powers would be held by a Council of the Nation, whose members would be chosen by the President of the U.A.R.; at least half the members would be selected from the existing Parliaments of Egypt and Syria. The U.A.R. would consist of two regions (*aqlim*) – Egypt and Syria – and each of these would have an Executive Council. Any other Arab country could accede to or federate with the U.A.R., which had been described as "a preliminary step toward the realization of Arab unity".

It had previously been stated in Damascus on Jan. 31 that Cairo would be the capital of the U.A.R. and that existing diplomatic missions in Damascus would be replaced by consulates-general. Cairo radio announced on Feb. 4 that President Nasser had decided to dissolve the Syrian political parties and to form a "National Union" in Syria on the Egyptian model.

The official result of a referendum held on Feb. 21 showed an overwhelming majority in favour of union between the two countries, the detailed figures being: 6,102,128 votes "for" and 247 "against" in Egypt; 1,312,759 "for" and 39 "against" in Syria. At the same time the electorate voted for the election of Colonel Nasser as first President of the U.A.R.; this resulted in 6,102,116 votes in Egypt and 1,312,809 in Syria being cast in favour, and 265 votes in Egypt and 186 in Syria being cast against such action.

On Dec. 23, 1958, President Nasser admitted that difficulties had arisen in integrating Syria's economy with that of Egypt.

A decree issued by him on Oct. 21, 1959, appointed Field-Marshal Abdel Hakim Amer (the third Vice-President of the U.A.R.) as supervisor of general policy in the Syrian region. President Nasser thus demonstrated that he was determined to press ahead with the welding of the two regions into a single administrative unit and to overcome the delays which the execution of his industrial programme and land reform measures had encountered in Syria.

Measures to further the integration of the two regions of the U.A.R. continued to be taken during the next two years. The first joint Parliament was opened by President Nasser on July 21, 1960; this comprised 400 Egyptian and 200 Syrian deputies who had been appointed by the President from among candidates nominated by the National Union, and superseded the system of regional parliaments.

Mr. Nureddin Kuhala, President of the Syrian Executive Council, was nominated Vice-President of the U.A.R. by a presidential decree of July 19, thus filling the vacancy which had existed since the resignation on Dec. 30, 1959, of Mr. Akram Hourani, the last Syrian to hold the office of Vice-President.

Cabinet changes announced by President Nasser on Sept. 20, 1960, resulted in an increase in the number of Syrian members in the Cabinet from three to seven; these changes meant a strengthening of Syrian participation in the Central Government, which had been considerably reduced since the resignation of Mr. Hourani and three other members of the Syrian *Baath* party in December 1959. [Although the Syrian political parties had nominally been dissolved, many former party members adhered to their policies; the *Baath,* or Arab Socialist Party, was primarily responsible for union with Egypt and largely dominated the Syrian central administration.]

The abolition of the Regional Executive Councils and the reorganization of the Central Government were decreed by President Nasser on Aug. 16, 1961; there would now be five Egyptian Vice-Presidents, 22 Egyptian Ministers, two Syrian Vice-Presidents and 14 Syrian Ministers. According to a Government spokesman the purpose of this action was (*a*) to further the unity of the two regions of the U.A.R.; (*b*) to raise the standard of living throughout the country; and (*c*) to enable the nationalized enterprises [see page 74] to play an important part in the Government's economic plans.

Despite these attempts to bring the two regions together, a successful army coup aimed at the secession of Syria from the U.A.R. and the restoration of Syrian independence took place in Damascus on Sept. 28, 1961. The coup followed secret talks between its leaders and Field-Marshal Amer, during which strong dissatisfaction was reported to have been expressed by the Syrian officers at the alleged preferment of Egyptian officers and the increasing introduction of the latter in Syrian units.

The leaders of the coup declared that Syria, while a champion of Arab unity, had always been strongly opposed to any dictatorship, and denounced those who "under the cloak of union and socialism" had spread in Syria an "atmosphere of terror and injustice". Subsequent broadcasts accused the "Egyptian junta" of having "betrayed the confidence of the Syrians" and Arab unity, and of having been responsible for a "regime of terror".

President Nasser immediately ordered the armed forces of the U.A.R. to suppress the rebellion; this order was, however, withdrawn later in the day.

Although Cairo had continuously denounced the new civilian regime in Syria, and President Nasser had on Oct. 1 broken off diplomatic relations with Jordan and Turkey because of their recognition of the regime, the President indicated on Oct. 5 that he accepted the situation when he announced that his Government would not oppose the application of the new regime to renew her U.N. membership nor stand in the way of Syria's admission to the Arab League.

As a result of Syria's secession from the U.A.R., the dissolution of the Union of Arab States – a loose association between the U.A.R. and Yemen established on March 8, 1958 – was announced on Dec. 26, 1961. The reason given for the ending of the Union was that the two Governments had been "unable to shape this union into an effective political instrument capable of positive participation in the promotion of the Arab cause". The Egyptian decision to dissolve the Union followed a broadcast by President Nasser on Dec. 23 in which he strongly attacked the Imam of Yemen as a "reactionary".

The United Arab Republic, 1962–70

The name "United Arab Republic" was retained by Egypt even after the secession of Syria.

A "Charter for National Action" published by the President on May 21, 1962, was designed to form the basis for the U.A.R.'s future political, economic and social development; it proposed that the future Constitution should be based on principles of "scientific socialism". In addition it stated that the "objectives of the Arab struggle" were "freedom, socialism, unity" and emphasized the necessity for collective leadership.

In implementation of this last principle President Nasser announced the forthcoming creation of a Presidency Council as the highest authority in the country, headed by himself, and of an Executive Council to act as a Cabinet; the latter would be presided over by Wing-Commander Ali Sabry, who would carry out the duties of Prime Minister, an office abolished under the 1956 Constitution.

Elections for a new National Assembly of 350 members were held on March 10 and 19, 1964, immediately before the publication of a new Constitution. It had been laid down that at least half the members of this would have to be workers or small farmers owning not more than 25 acres of land and that all candidates would have to be members of the Arab Socialist Union [see below]. Only 110 deputies, including 48 workers and small farmers, were elected on March 10 and therefore a second ballot was held on March 19; this resulted in 108 small farmers, 71 workers and 61 professional and business men and members of the armed forces being returned. A further 10 members were subsequently nominated by President Nasser under the new Constitution.

This new Provisional Constitution was proclaimed by President Nasser on March 23, 1964, to come into effect on March 25 and to remain in force until a Permanent Constitution had been drafted by the new National Assembly and approved by the electorate in a referendum.

This Constitution stated that the U.A.R. was "a democratic, socialist State based on the alliance of the working powers of the people" and that Islam would be the State religion. It laid down that "social solidarity is the basis of Egyptian society" and that "the economic foundation of the State is the socialist system", and provided for equality before the law and for equal public rights and duties. The National Assembly would exercise legislative power and control the work of the executive authority and would be elected by secret public ballot. The President would be chosen by a two-thirds majority in the National Assembly, this choice to be approved by an absolute majority of the votes cast in a popular referendum; he would have executive power and could appoint or dismiss one or more Vice-Presidents. The Government, consisting of the Prime Minister, Deputy Prime Ministers and Ministers would be "the supreme executive and administrative organ of the State". Amendments to the Constitution might be proposed by the President or at least one-third of the members of the National Assembly; a two-thirds majority in the Assembly would be required for the approval of any proposed changes.

Field-Marshal Abdel Hakim Amer was appointed First Vice-President on March 25 by President Nasser, who also named three other Vice-Presidents — Mr. Zakaria Mohieddin, Mr. Hussein el Shafei and Mr. Hassan Ibrahim. A new Council of Ministers was sworn in on the same day under the leadership of Wing-Commander Ali Sabry.

The Arab Socialist Union, the sole legal political organization in the country, was created by an Act of Dec. 7, 1962, and replaced the National

Union; the general objective of the new Union was the "realization of the socialist revolution". The party organization was pyramidal in structure, ranging from about 6,000 basic units through district and provincial councils to a General National Congress; every six years this Congress would elect a general committee from which the supreme party organ – the "Supreme Executive Committee" – was appointed.

President Nasser, whose term of office expired on March 26, 1965, under the new Constitution, was re-elected for a further six-year term in a referendum held on March 15; on a 98.5 per cent poll (voting being compulsory for males over 18 and optional for females) 99.99 per cent of the votes were cast in favour of the President.

A U.A.R.-Iraqi Unified Political Command met for the first time on May 19–25, 1965, under the joint chairmanship of President Nasser and President Aref of Iraq, comprising 25 members – the Presidents and Prime Ministers of the two countries, the four Vice-Presidents of the U.A.R. and a number of Ministers of both countries. This joint body was to constitute the highest political authority of the two States and would take "all practical steps to achieve constitutional unity between the two countries within a maximum of two years".

> During the next eighteen months, the leadership of the Government changed twice: on Oct. 2, 1965, Mr. Zakaria Mohieddin succeeded Wing-Commander Ali Sabry, who was appointed a Vice-President of the Republic on the same day; while on Sept. 10, 1966, it was announced that the Mohieddin Government had resigned and that Mr. Mohammed Sidki Soliman had been appointed Prime Minister. Although Mr. Mohieddin had carried out a far-reaching purge and re-organization of the Egyptian police and had uncovered and broken up a plot by the Moslem Brotherhood (which continued to be active in other Arab countries) to overthrow the Government and assassinate its leaders, his economic policies had led to a sharp rise in the cost of living and he encountered opposition from those quarters which advocated expansionist rather than restrictive methods.

Following the defeat of the Egyptian forces in the Arab-Israeli War of June 1967 [see page 73] President Nasser announced on June 9, less than 24 hours after the cease-fire had come into force between the U.A.R. and Israel, that he had asked Mr. Mohieddin to take over the post of President of the Republic and that it was his [i.e. President Nasser's] intention to give up all official and political functions and to become a private citizen. However, after popular demonstrations in favour of President Nasser, calling on him to remain Head of State, the President withdrew his resignation on the following day (June 10). A new Government was formed on June 19, in which President Nasser assumed the premiership; in addition he took over the post of Secretary-General of the Arab Socialist Union.

A far-reaching re-organization of the Cabinet was announced on March 20, 1968; this continued the move towards a more civilian and "technocratic" Government begun in 1966 under Mr. Soliman's leadership.

A referendum on a fundamental programme of reform of the Arab Socialist Union, to be followed in due course by the drawing up of a new Constitution, was held on May 2, 1968; the official result was 99.989 per cent in favour. President Nasser, in announcing this referendum on March 30, had stated that the single-party system would remain but stressed that this "must be rebuilt through elections from the bottom to the top". The principal reforms were (a) that elections would be organized to elect the basic units of the Arab Socialist Union; (b) that the National Congress should undertake the responsibility of drawing up a new Constitution [a task normally within the competence of the National Assembly] ; and (c) the Central Committee of the Union would *inter alia* "fix the objectives of national action and participate in framing the main lines of the Constitution".

On Sept. 28, 1970, President Nasser died of a heart attack in Cairo; Mr. Anwar Sadat, Vice-President of the U.A.R. since Dec. 20, 1969, was unanimously nominated for the Presidency on Oct. 5 by the eight-member Supreme Executive Committee of the Arab Socialist Union. This choice was unanimously approved by the National Assembly on Oct. 7 and in a national referendum on Oct. 15, when Mr. Sadat received 90.4 per cent of the total votes cast on an 85 per cent poll.

On Oct. 21 Dr. Mahmoud Fawzi was appointed Prime Minister and Mr. Abdel Mohsen Abu el Nur Secretary-General of the Arab Socialist Union, both of these posts having previously been held by President Nasser; while on Nov. 1 Mr. Ali Sabry and Mr. Hussein el Shafei were nominated Vice-Presidents by President Sadat.

Following the resignation of Dr. Mahmoud Fawzi as Prime Minister and his acceptance of a request by President Sadat to form a new Cabinet, the new administration was sworn in on Nov. 18, 1970. On the same day the creation of a Council of National Defence, to be responsible for ensuring the security and defence of the Republic, was announced; its members would comprise the President, the Prime Minister, four Cabinet Ministers (including those of Foreign Affairs and War), the Chief of Intelligence and the Chief of the General Staff.

President Sadat, President Nemery of the Sudan and the Libyan leader, Colonel Kadhafi, had previously agreed on Nov. 8, at the end of a five-day summit meeting in Cairo, to take steps for the eventual federation of the three countries – the first such measure being the formation of a joint triumvirate leadership comprising the three Heads of State.

Foreign Relations

The Conflict with Israel

Egypt's relationships with foreign countries were strongly coloured by President Nasser's policy of "Arab Unity", which implied conflict with Israel, owing to the fact that the Arab States considered that the creation of the State of Israel was a violation of Arab territory, and Israel was not recognized by any Arab country. This conflict erupted on Oct. 29, 1956, when the Israeli Army launched an attack on Egyptian positions in the Sinai Peninsula with the avowed aim of eliminating Egyptian commando bases, from which frequent attacks had been launched into Israeli territory. As the result of the rejection by Egypt of a cease-fire ultimatum delivered by the British and French Governments, the air forces of the latter countries began an offensive against Egyptian airfields and other military installations on Oct. 31, followed a few days later, on Nov. 5, by paratroop landings in the Canal Zone. Operations ceased at midnight on Nov. 6–7 after Egypt and Israel had accepted an unconditional cease-fire and subject to the despatch of a U.N. police force to the Middle East to keep the peace between Israel and the Arab countries, pending a final settlement of the political problems of the area. The withdrawal of Allied forces from the Suez Canal Zone and Israeli forces from the Sinai Peninsula was "phased" with the progressive take-over of these areas by the United Nations Emergency Force (UNEF) in the Middle East – the British and French withdrawal being completed on Dec. 22, 1956, and the Israeli on March 6–7, 1957.

Officially, however, the U.A.R. and Israel continued to be at war. After a period of comparatively peaceful armed confrontation, open warfare broke out on June 5, 1967, between Israel and the Arab States. During the month immediately preceding the outbreak of hostilities the UNEF had withdrawn from the Egyptian-Israeli frontier on May 19 at the demand of the U.A.R. Government, while on May 23 an Egyptian blockade of the

Straits of Tiran, at the entrance to the Gulf of Aqaba, had begun, thus denying passage to shipping proceeding to the Israeli port of Eilat.

Within 80 hours of the outbreak of war Israel achieved a complete military victory over her Arab opponents – the U.A.R., Syria and Jordan – before all hostilities ceased on June 10 in response to repeated cease-fire calls by the U.N. Security Council. After virtually destroying the air forces of Egypt, Jordan and Syria on June 5, the Israeli armed forces had, by the end of the war, apart from their gains on other fronts, overrun the entire Sinai Peninsula, captured the Gaza strip and advanced to the Suez Canal.

The Suez Canal was closed by the U.A.R. authorities on June 6 as a result of the war; the official explanation was that Anglo-American air intervention on the side of Israel had been "categorically established". [President Nasser later, in an interview published on May 15, 1968, admitted that he had been mistaken in making this allegation.] On July 17, United Nations observers took up their positions on the cease-fire line [i.e. the Suez Canal] with the aim of preventing violations of the cease-fire, while on Aug. 26, 1967, both Egypt and Israel agreed to abstain indefinitely from navigation on the Suez Canal; frequent incidents continued to occur, however, across the Canal, usually ending after the agreement of local cease-fires.

The Soviet leaders publicly supported the Arab cause in their confrontation with Israel, e.g. in a statement made by Mr. Kosygin (the Soviet Prime Minister) on Dec. 10, 1969. Although official silence was maintained both in Egypt and in the Soviet Union, reports from press correspondents in the Middle East, both Communist and Western, stated that large quantities of Soviet arms and military equipment were being sent to Egypt to replace the heavy losses suffered by the Egyptian Army and Air force in the war.

The Israeli Government issued a statement on April 29, 1970, declaring that Soviet pilots were flying operational missions in Egypt; this was described by President Nasser, on May 1, as "Israeli propaganda". The President did not deny the reports, however, saying that "Russian assistance to Egypt is no secret and nothing new; it is the assistance of a friend to a friend". On May 4, Mr. Kosygin said that Soviet military advisers were "attached to the armed forces of the U.A.R." under an agreement between the two countries.

Following the acceptance of a peace initiative launched by the U.S. Secretary of State, a cease-fire agreement between Egypt and Israel came into force on the Suez Canal front on Aug. 7, 1970, for a period of 90 days. Despite mutual accusations of infringement of the agreement, it was extended for another 90 days on Nov. 3, 1970, and for a further 30 days on Feb. 4, 1971.

Involvement in Yemen

Egypt was also involved in the prolonged Yemeni Civil War of 1962–70, which was caused by the overthrow of the hereditary ruler of Yemen, the Imam Mohammed, by the Army and the proclamation of a Republic on Sept. 27, 1962. Almost immediately after the setting-up of a royalist Government-in-exile in Saudi Arabia, civil war broke out and forces were sent from Egypt to aid the Republican Government and from Saudi Arabia to assist the royalist cause. Relations between the U.A.R. and Saudi Arabia deteriorated as a result of this participation, and in July 1965 the civil war threatened to lead to war between the two countries. However, under an agreement concluded in Khartoum between President Nasser and King Faisal of Saudi Arabia on Aug. 31, 1967, Egyptian forces, which had numbered some 60,000 during the five-year period, were withdrawn from the Yemen by Dec. 9, 1967.

The Economy

The principle of "Arab socialism" on which the Egyptian economy was based after the coming-to-power of President Nasser resulted in the almost complete nationalization of industry and commerce.

As a result of the Suez affair of 1956 [see page 72] various measures to bring British and French interests in Egypt under Egyptian control were taken. Three decree-laws ordering the Egyptianization of foreign banks and insurance companies and the sales agencies in Egypt of foreign manufacturers or exporters were signed by President Nasser on Jan. 31, 1957. A further decree issued on April 8 empowered the Administrator of "enemy property" to sell or liquidate British and French banks and insurance companies under sequestration since November 1956; this was completed on April 17, and on the following day it was announced that banks of "friendly" countries had been given a five-year time-limit for their "Egyptianization". The sequestration of Anglo-Egyptian Oilfields Ltd., the largest British interest in Egypt, had previously been announced on Nov. 3, 1956, while on June 5, 1957, it was announced that six British and French pharmaceutical companies, sequestrated in the previous November, had been "Egyptianized".

During 1960 the nationalization of the Bank of Egypt and the *Banque Misr* – the largest industrial enterprise in the U.A.R. – was announced on Feb. 11, and that of all newspapers, periodicals and publishing houses on May 24. The nationalization of over 400 private firms including banks, insurance companies and manufacturing and trading concerns was ordered by President Nasser on July 20, 1961; this was followed by a decree on July 26 which limited the maximum individual land holding to about 100 acres.

After the secession of Syria from the U.A.R., President Nasser intensified his policy of "Arab socialism". Between Oct. 21, 1961, and Jan. 10, 1962, the property of "capitalist reactionaries" was sequestrated, while President Nasser announced on Dec. 23, 1961, that the Government had decided to nationalize all foreign-owned agricultural land for distribution among the peasants. It was reported on Jan. 7, 1962, that all foreign schools would be taken over by the Government if not sold to U.A.R. nationals by September 1962.

By November 1963 practically all industrial enterprises and large and medium-sized trading concerns had been nationalized, following a series of measures announced over the previous year. On Sept. 25, 1962, a presidential decree was promulgated empowering the U.A.R. Government to take over a share of not less than 50 per cent in the capital of all shipping and ship-repairing firms operating in Alexandria and the Suez Canal Zone. Foreigners were no longer allowed to own land under a law approved by the Presidential Council on Jan. 2, 1963; any land under foreign ownership was officially taken over by the Office for Land Reform on Nov. 1. The nationalization of all cotton-exporting and cotton-ginning companies in the U.A.R. became effective under a decree issued during the weekend of April 13–14, 1963; this completed the nationalization of the Egyptian cotton industry which had begun on June 22, 1961, with the passing of an Act creating a State organization to buy and export the Egyptian cotton crop. All flour-mills and rice-mills were nationalized on May 18, 1963; all pharmaceutical factories and distributing firms on June 16; and 16 road transport and eight maritime and river transport concerns on June 19. The nationalization of some 240 companies in a wide field of light industry and the cancellation of all contracts and licences for private firms carrying out mining and quarrying operations (but not oil-drilling) were announced on Aug. 12; another 177 companies were nationalized by a decree issued on Nov. 11, 1963. Only small retail traders remained unaffected; the Government stated that it wanted to reorganize the retail trade and that it would encourage small shopkeepers to become part of a "grouping system" in the interests of greater efficiency and the prevention of excessive profits.

Despite the programme of nationalization which was carried out, the Egyptian economy relied to a certain extent on foreign aid. The most important single project in receipt of foreign support was the Aswan High Dam [see below]; the Soviet Government, in addition to financing this scheme, also gave considerable aid in various other projects. It was announced on Dec. 22, 1958, that three projects — the construction of five new airfields, the creation of new industrial schemes and the building of several factories and a thermal power station at Suez — were to be carried out with Soviet co-operation. Further Soviet assistance in the building of more than 100 industrial projects was announced on Feb. 19, 1960; while two agreements on economic aid were signed on Jan. 27, 1962, and Sept. 22, 1964. Plans to build an $800,000,000 iron and steel complex at Helwan, 15 miles south of Cairo, with Soviet aid were announced by the U.A.R. Government on May 15, 1968.

The U.A.R. also received aid from Western countries; this was interrupted following the Suez affair of 1956 and again after the Arab-Israeli War of June 1967. The United States took measures between 1957 and 1960 aimed at resuming economic relations with, and economic aid to, the U.A.R., while British and Dutch credits for industrial development in the U.A.R. were announced on May 4, 1961, and similar aid from West Germany on July 5, 1961, and France on March 6, 1965.

An agreement was signed on July 13, 1969, for the construction of an oil pipeline from Suez on the Red Sea to Alexandria on the Mediterranean by the U.A.R. with the SOCEA Consortium; this group consists of five French companies, three Italian and one each from Britain, Spain and the Netherlands. The projected pipeline, which would bypass the Suez Canal (which had been blocked and out of action since the 1967 Arab-Israeli war), was expected to be in service towards the end of 1971.

The Aswan High Dam

The most important economic scheme undertaken during President Nasser's term of office was the building of the Aswan High Dam in the middle reaches of the Nile; the object of the scheme was (a) to control the waters of the Nile, which had previously caused annual flooding of the river valley in Egypt, and (b) to provide Egypt with a source of hydro-electric power.

> The High Dam, which was 370 feet high and three miles long, formed a reservoir with an area of some 750 square miles and a capacity of about 28,600,000 million gallons of water. Irrigation projects based on this reservoir, named Lake Nasser, were intended to convert 700,000 acres of intermittently irrigated land to dependable irrigation and to open an additional 1,300,000 acres to irrigation for the first time.
>
> A hydro-electric power station, built on the dam itself, was expected to reach an annual capacity of up to 10,000,000,000 kwh by 1972, thus making Egypt virtually self-sufficient for the medium-term future.

The cost of the High Dam was estimated at about £400,000,000, of which about one-third had been supplied as loans "on especially generous terms" by the Soviet Union; about 5,000 Soviet workers and technicians had helped in the completion of the building of the dam and the power station.

Work on the High Dam was officially started on Jan. 9, 1960; the first phase of the construction work was completed in May 1964 with the diversion of Nile waters through a specially built canal, and the second phase early in 1968 with the completion of the dam. The turning on of the twelfth and last power-generating turbine on July 21, 1970, marked the essential completion of the scheme.

2. FORMER BRITISH TERRITORIES AND PROTECTORATES

THE SUDAN

Area: 977,000 sq. miles.
Population 1969 (estimate): 15,186,000.
Capital: Khartoum (194,000).
Other important town: Omdurman (206,000).
Official language: Arabic.
Chief product: Cotton.

The "Independent and Democratic Republic of the Sudan" was officially proclaimed on Jan. 1, 1956, bringing to an end the Anglo-Egyptian condominium established in 1898.

Parliamentary Regime, 1956–58

The Sudanese House of Representatives had adopted unanimously four resolutions on Dec. 19, 1955, which *inter alia* declared the Sudan a sovereign independent republic and provided for the election of a Constituent Assembly and of a five-man committee to exercise the powers of the Head of State. The latter committee was formally established on the achievement of independence and represented all the main political groupings. Mr. Ismail al Azhari, leader of the National Unionist Party and Prime Minister before independence, formed an all-party National Government in Khartoum on Feb. 2, 1956; his Government was defeated, however, on

July 4, 1956, in the House of Representatives on a no-confidence motion. On the following day (July 5) Mr. Abdullah Khalil, leader of the Umma Party, was elected Prime Minister by 60 votes to 30 for Mr. Azhari.

The first general elections since independence were held between Feb. 27 and March 8, 1958, when 173 members of the House of Representatives and 30 out of the 50 members of the Senate were elected. The ruling alliance of the Umma and the People's Democratic parties under Mr. Khalil was victorious, the results for the House of Representatives being as follows: —

Umma Party	63
National Unionist Party (NUP)	45
People's Democratic Party (PDP)	27
Southern Liberals	20
Anti-Imperialist Front	1
Southern Federalist	1
Uncommitted Southern members	16

and those for the Senate:

Umma Party	14
National Unionist Party (NUP)	5
People's Democratic Party (PDP)	5
Southern representatives	6

Members for the remaining 20 seats in the Senate, distributed in proportion to the party strengths in the House of Representatives, were nominated by the Supreme Commission which exercised the functions of the Head of State. Thus the Umma Party received seven, the NUP five, the PDP four and Southern representatives four seats.

Sudanese males over 21 had the vote in the House of Representatives elections whilst the lower age limit for the Senate elections was 30.

On March 20 Mr. Khalil was re-elected Prime Minister by 103 votes against 44 for Mr. Azhari and 25 for Mr. Stanislaus Paysama, who had formed a new parliamentary group, the Southern Sudanese Federal Bloc, from Liberals and independents the day before (March 19). Mr. Khalil announced the membership of his Cabinet on March 27, consisting of nine Umma members and four PDP members.

General Abboud's Military Regime, 1958—64

On Nov. 17, 1958, the Sudanese Army under the command of General

Ibrahim Abboud overthrew Mr. Khalil's Government in a bloodless coup, dissolved Parliament and all political parties and suspended the Constitution.

The coup followed a period of political tension; the Government was strongly attacked by the National Unionist Party during October for its alleged failure to cope with the economic crisis arising from difficulties in disposing of the Sudan's cotton crop, and its acceptance of British and U.S. aid which, it was held, was tying the Sudan too closely to the Western powers. In addition, the two parties in the Government were known to disagree on the Sudan's policy towards Egypt and on the acceptance of Western aid, and these differences were expected to lead to the fall of the Government.

Under the new regime power was to be divided between the "Supreme Council of the Armed Forces" and the Cabinet; a group of seven officers under General Abboud, who became both President and Prime Minister, formed a majority in both bodies. President Abboud announced on March 4, 1959, that all the members of the Supreme Council of the Armed Forces had resigned, as a result of pressure exerted by Brigadier Abdel Rahim Shenan, who had sent troops to Khartoum to present his demands on March 2 and 4. A new Council was appointed on the following day, five members of the previous Council being replaced by Brigadier Shenan, Brigadier Mohieddin Ahmed Abdullah and Brigadier Makboul El-Amin, both of whom had also sent troops to Khartoum.

Following unauthorized troop movements on May 22, it was announced on June 1 that Brigadier Shenan, Brigadier Abdullah and a number of other officers had been arrested. Their trial before a court martial began on June 21, the accused being charged with inciting and conspiring with others to cause a mutiny by launching an armed attack on Khartoum on May 22 with the aim of overthrowing the regime. Brigadiers Shenan and Abdullah and four other senior officers were found guilty and sentenced to death on Sept. 22; the sentences were subsequently commuted to life imprisonment by President Abboud.

The Supreme Council announced on July 11, 1961, the arrest of 15 politicians, including Mr. Ismail al Azhari, Mr. Abdullah Khalil, two former Ministers in Mr. Khalil's Government and Mr. Abdel Khaliq Mahgoub, secretary-general of the banned Sudan Communist Party. President Abboud stated that a group of Sudanese had opposed the regime and had "unscrupulously invented and spread rumours to mislead their countrymen". Most of those arrested were sent to Juba in the southern Sudan.

Legislative elections were held between April and October 1963 for the elective seats on the local and provincial councils (April 26 and the beginning of August respectively) and the Central Council. The latter, to which provincial councils elected their representatives on Oct. 12, 1963, had complete legislative powers, unlimited financial control and the right to direct and supervise the Administration. The Council was formally inaugurated by President Abboud on Nov. 14.

Parliamentary Regime, 1964—69

The military regime was, however, overthrown by a popular uprising at the end of October 1964, the immediate cause of the revolt being an incident at Khartoum University, one of the main centres of opposition to the regime.

An unauthorized meeting of students was held there on Oct. 22 by the Anti-Imperialist Front, an opposition movement in which Communists played an important role, to protest against the alleged brutality of the Government's repression of the autonomist movement in the southern provinces [see below]. The police, who were attacked when attempting to break up this meeting, opened fire, killing one student and wounding eight others. In the demonstrations which followed, the students were joined by other sections of the population and the banned political parties, who called for a general strike. This began on Oct. 26 and met with widespread support among manual and office workers. On the same day the situation developed further when open support was given to the anti-Government forces by a section of the Army.

Discussions held on Oct. 28—29 between the Army faction opposed to the military regime and the United National Front, an alliance of political parties and professional organizations, resulted in the following agreements. President Abboud was to remain Chief of State and C.-in-C. of the Armed Forces; the Central Council was to be dissolved and a civilian Cabinet was to be formed which would exercise legislative powers pending general elections and would have power to override the President's veto by a two-thirds majority; free elections to a Constituent Assembly were to be held not later than March 1965, and the state of emergency in force since the 1958 coup was to end.

A civilian government was formed by Mr. Serr al Khatim Khalifa on Oct. 30 and included one member from each of the five principal political parties — Umma Party, NUP, PDP, Communist Party and Moslem Brotherhood – as well as representatives of professional organizations and universities and a number of civil servants.

However, on Nov. 8, President Abboud, without consulting the Prime Minister, ordered the arrest of seven senior Army officers who, during the recent crisis, had submitted a note to the Army High Command calling for the Sudan to co-operate with the policies of the United Arab Republic. Mr. Khalifa and other Ministers protested on Nov. 9 against these arrests which, they alleged, were the first step towards the dismissal of all officers who had supported the "people's revolution" of Oct. 22–26. On the following day (Nov. 10) the United National Front demanded the removal of President Abboud; the President on Nov. 15 announced his decision to resign in accordance with "the people's desire to liquidate the military regime in all its forms". Mr. Khalifa stated that the prerogative of Chief of State would be transferred to a five-member Council of Sovereignty, as laid down in the 1956 Provisional Constitution, and that a National Defence Council, consisting of the Premier, four other Ministers and the C.-in-C. of the Armed Forces, would be responsible for the affairs of the armed forces.

One of the main reasons for the fall of the military regime was its failure to solve the long-standing problem of the southern provinces of Equatoria, Bahr-el-Ghazal and Upper Nile.

The three main reasons for the antagonism of the southerners, mainly pagan and negroid, towards the Moslem and Arab north, were: firstly, traditional hostility caused by Arab slave-raiding in the south during the nineteenth century; secondly, the policy of separate administration of the south pursued by the British Government in 1930–46, under which northerners were excluded and Arab dress, customs and religion were forbidden whilst Christian missions were encouraged; finally, the facts that after attainment of self-government in 1954 many northerners had to be sent to the south to replace the former British administrators because of the almost complete absence of higher education in the south, and that Arabic was introduced as the official language in schools, the administration and the Army, giving rise to a fear that Islam would be forcibly imposed on the south.

A mutiny in the Sudan Defence Force in Equatoria in 1955 developed into a popular revolt; after its suppression many southerners fled into neighbouring countries. A further exodus occurred in 1958 with the abolition of political parties, which made peaceful agitation in support of southern claims impossible.

Southern refugees were organized in two main bodies – the Sudan African National Union, SANU, whose secretary was Mr. William Deng, and the Sudanese Christian Association. In September 1963 a terrorist organization, *Anya Nya*, acting as the military arm of the secessionists, launched a guerrilla campaign in the Ethiopian frontier area of the Upper Nile province, which rapidly spread into Equatoria and Bahr-el-Ghazal. On Feb. 27, 1964, the expulsion of all the 300 foreign missionaries in the southern Sudan was announced; the Government stated that it had "proof and documents" that "some foreign priests had and still have close responsibility for the unrest in the south and that they are working for the disunity of the Sudanese nation by misleading the citizens and inciting them against their northern brothers". Allegations of brutal treatment of priests and nuns by the Sudanese authorities were made by many of the deported missionaries on their arrival in Rome.

Mr. Khalifa's Government attempted to enter into negotiations with the southern rebels. On taking office the Prime Minister, at the end of a two-day tour of the southern provinces, announced an unconditional amnesty for all southern Sudanese who had fled since 1955 and appealed to the exiles to return home and to work for freedom and equality in the Sudan. This offer was rejected by exiled SANU leaders who demanded complete independence for the south; the Government on the other hand refused an offer of negotiations on neutral territory.

A short-term agreement on the status of the southern provinces was announced on March 29, 1965, after a round-table conference in Khartoum attended by all political parties, including two conflicting factions of SANU, and by observers at ministerial level from Algeria, Ghana, Kenya, Tanzania, Uganda and the United Arab Republic, all of whom had been invited. During the conference the southern leaders issued a demand for self-determination on a federal basis, while the northern leaders aspired to a solution within a framework of national unity. The final agreement covered *inter alia* the formation of an economic development council with a subsidiary agency for the south; the establishment of a southern university; the appointment of more southerners to administrative posts, in particular in prison administration, police and information; and greater autonomy for the south in education, employment and the exercise of religion.

The efforts of the Government to reach a peaceful settlement with the southern Sudanese were nullified by renewed outbreaks of violence and by determined military action against the rebels by Government forces during the period July 1965 to February 1966.

Meanwhile a serious Cabinet crisis had developed during the first week of February 1965 owing to the differences between the right-wing Umma Party, the NUP and the Moslem Brotherhood on the one hand, and the

Communists, pro-Nasserites and their supporters on the other. The right-wing parties had accused several of the representatives of professional organizations in the Government of being Communists or "fellow-travellers" enabling the Left to dominate the Cabinet. The immediate cause of the crisis was a dispute over the date of general elections preparatory to the restoration of parliamentary government.

On Feb. 18 Mr. Khalifa submitted his resignation to the Council of Sovereignty, this having been demanded on the previous day by the Umma Party, the NUP and the Moslem Brotherhood. However, he accepted an invitation from the Council to form a new coalition Government on condition that it was confined to representatives of political parties (implying the exclusion of the professionals' National Front). The new Government formed on Feb. 23 was denounced by the People's Democratic and the Communist parties, both of which had refused an invitation to join it, and by the professionals' National Front and the Khatmiyya Moslem sect.

The general elections – in which women had the vote for the first time – took place in the five northern provinces from April 21 to May 8, 1965; supplementary elections were to be held in the three southern provinces after agreement had been reached at the round-table conference [see above]. Voting took place for 173 seats out of the total of 233, the remaining 60 being reserved for the south. The Umma Party and the NUP, with 75 and 54 seats respectively, were victorious; the remaining seats were split between the Communists (11), the Beja Tribal Association (a pro-Umma group) (10), the Moslem Brotherhood (5), the PDP (3) and Independents (15). The Constituent Assembly on June 10 elected Mr. Mohammed Ahmed Mahgoub, the Umma Party leader, as Prime Minister, and Mr. Azhari as permanent President of the Council of Sovereignty; a Government consisting of six Ministers each from the Umma Party and the NUP was announced on June 14. Following further consultations with the secretary-general of SANU, Mr. William Deng, the appointment of three Ministers representing the southern bloc – one SANU member and two independents – was announced on June 17.

On July 25, 1966, the Constituent Assembly, on the initiative of the parliamentary Umma Party, passed a motion of censure on the Prime Minister by 126 votes to 30 with 15 abstentions. Mr. Mahgoub thereupon tendered his resignation, which was accepted by the Council of Sovereignty. Dr. Sadiq el Mahdi, president of the Umma Party, was elected Premier by 138 votes to 29 on July 27. The formation of a coalition Government composed of members of the Umma Party and the NUP was announced on July 31, while Mr. Mahgoub became leader of the Opposition. The change in leadership of the Government led to a split in the ruling Umma party; 22 members of its conservative right wing, followers of the Imam el Hadi el Mahdi (leader of the Ansar Moslem sect) and Mr. Mahgoub, refused to be represented in the new Cabinet.

In an attempt to assist the Prime Minister to reunify the party, all Cabinet Ministers offered their resignation on Sept. 29, 1966. A Cabinet re-organization did not occur, however, until early in December when *inter alia* two supporters of the Imam joined the Cabinet. Shortly afterwards the National Unionist Party decided to end its co-operation with the Prime Minister and its six Cabinet Ministers ceased to attend to their ministerial duties from Dec. 22.

On the same day (Dec. 22) a constitutional crisis arose when the High Court decided to uphold an appeal by the former Communist members of the Constituent Assembly against the banning of their party. A Bill to this effect had been passed on Dec. 9, 1965, following a demand for the dissolution of the Party by the Umma Party and the NUP. The Constituent Assembly refused, on Dec. 23, to reinstate the Communist deputies and the Government instructed the Attorney General to appeal against the High Court's decision. The Council of Sovereignty decreed on April 17, 1967, that the ban was lawful; as a result Chief Justice Babiker Awadalla resigned because of his disapproval of the Government's "interference with the Judiciary".

The Council's decision was in sharp contrast to a statement made by President Azhari in mid-March at the opening of a Sino-Sudanese Friendship Centre in Khartoum, in which he hoped that the Sudanese people would follow the example of the Chinese "Cultural Revolution" against "reaction, superstition and imperialism" and draw inspiration from its "great leader" Mao Tse-tung.

On April 28, 1967, the NUP decided to withdraw completely from the coalition Government and to call for a National Government, including the PDP, under a neutral Premier, which would hold power until new elections to take place not later than January 1968. The Imam announced on May 9 that he had directed his supporters in the Umma Party to co-operate with NUP members in order to overthrow the Government; this followed a decision taken at a meeting of the Ansar Moslem sect in February 1967 that the Umma Party should be re-organized so as to strengthen its conservative and religious character, in contrast to the modernizing tendencies of the Prime Minister. Following the rejection of a confidence motion in the Assembly by 86 votes to 112 with five abstentions on May 15, Dr. Mahdi resigned; the Assembly decided on May 18 by 111 votes to 93 to request the former Premier, Mr. Mahgoub, to form a new Government; he thereupon formed a Cabinet which included three Umma, six NUP and four PDP Ministers and one Minister from each of the three southern parties — Southern Front, Southern Liberals and SANU.

Elections had previously been held in the southern provinces from March 8 to mid-April; these had been postponed repeatedly since 1965 because of the opposition of the majority of southern political parties and of secessionist activities in many areas. The elections, boycotted by the Southern Front, the left wing of SANU, the PDP and the Communists, resulted in the Umma Party winning 15, SANU 10, the NUP five and Independents three seats, and the Liberals one seat. Agreement was reached during the election period on the political future of the south. This provided for regional assemblies in each of the country's nine provinces, to be reconstituted as regions, to deal with specified regional questions, members being elected for five years, and regional governors to be selected by each regional assembly from a list of three candidates to be presented by the Central Government. At the same time, however, the Government continued in its campaign against the secessionist rebels.

At the beginning of 1968, talks were held between the Government and the Opposition, led by Dr. Mahdi, to consider the possibility of forming a new Government supported by both sides, extending the validity of the provisional Constitution and prolonging the mandate of the existing constituent Assembly; these were broken off, however, by the Government Democratic Unionist Party, DUP (formed in December 1967 by the amalgamation of the NUP and the PDP).

The reason for this action lay in the fact that the Government's majority in the Assembly had been lost after a number of defections from the Imam's faction in the Umma Party, which supported the Government, to the Opposition, which consisted of Dr. Mahdi's progressive faction of the Umma Party. Although the Opposition could not muster the two-thirds majority in the Assembly required to extend the validity of the Provisional Constitution, the Government feared that it might, by a simple majority, force a vote of no-confidence. To prevent this happening, the Government asked its followers, early in February to resign their seats in the Assembly; 80 did so while 119 deputies, who belonged to Dr. Mahdi's faction or were allied with it, refused. President Azhari thereupon announced on Feb. 7 that, as more than one-third of the Assembly's membership had resigned, the Assembly was unable to continue its work on the proposed new Constitution; he accordingly dissolved it and ordered general elections to be held on April 26 – May 2. A complaint made by Dr. Mahdi on Feb. 8 and 9 accusing the Government of having violated the provisional Constitution was dismissed outright by the Constitutional Court on Feb. 13 for procedural reasons.

The elections resulted in the defeat of the Opposition groups; the DUP gained 101 seats, while the remainder were shared amongst Dr. Mahdi's faction (36), the Imam's faction (30), SANU (15), the Southern Front (10), Independents (9), Umma Party adherents of the original party before its split (6), and six other groups who each gained six or less seats. Dr. Mahdi was himself defeated by a follower of the Imam. The new Constituent Assembly on May 27 re-elected Mr. Mahgoub as Premier and Mr. Ismail al Azhari as President of the Council of Sovereignty.

Establishment of Military Regime, 1969

A crisis arose in Mr. Mahgoub's coalition Government after the two factions of the Umma Party had officially announced their reunification in one party in April 1969 and had demanded a greater share in the Government than represented by the Ministries held by the Imam's faction. Before the crisis was resolved, the Government was overthrown by a Revolutionary Council led by Colonel Jaafar Mohammed al Nemery in a bloodless coup on May 25, 1969. Mr. Babiker Awadalla, the only civilian member of the Council, headed a new Government announced on May 25. The first decree issued by Mr. Awadalla's Government announced the suspension of the Constitution and of all parliamentary bodies and declared: "The Sudan is a Democratic Republic. Sovereignty lies with the people who are represented by the Revolutionary Council."

Mr. Awadalla disclosed in a statement on May 26 that all but four of the Ministers in the previous Government had been placed under "protective arrest"; ex-President Azhari and Mr. Mahgoub were transferred to prison on May 29, while eight Ministers were released on June 1. He also stated that the Sudan would follow a neutral policy in international affairs, but that its relations with foreign countries would depend on those countries' attitude to the Arab-Israeli conflict. He said: "We are Arabs and fanatical on the question of Palestine. We shall not allow the surrender to Israel of one inch of Palestine territory." The Government would work for "a modern Sudan" and Sudanese socialism. He added on May 27 that the country's principal industries would be nationalized and the State's role in the economy strengthened. On

May 31 General al Nemery declared that the Sudan would never be allowed to return to multi-party democracy, but added that there was "no opening for the creation of a Communist regime".

On Oct. 28, General al Nemery announced that Mr. Awadalla, who had resigned as Prime Minister on the previous day, would become deputy chairman of the Revolutionary Council and Minister of Foreign Affairs in a re-organized 25-member Cabinet to be headed by the General himself.

A number of attempts to overthrow the new military regime were made from July 1969 onwards. What, according to *Le Monde*, was the tenth such plot led to a violent confrontation between Government forces and followers of the Ansar sect under their leader, the Imam, in March 1970; this insurrection was suppressed and the Imam killed while trying to escape.

The situation in the south had been relatively calm in the twelve months preceding the military coup. On June 10, 1969, General al Nemery announced that his Government would grant the three southern provinces local autonomy; he reiterated, however, that there would always be a "unified Democratic Republic of the Sudan" and that any attempt at secession would be regarded as high treason and severely repressed. Two-thirds of the Sudan's troops continued to be stationed in the south, and were engaged in sporadic clashes with the *Anya Nya*, the military arm of the secessionist movement.

GHANA

Area: 92,000 sq. miles.
Population 1969 (estimate): 8,600,000.
Capital: Accra (634,000).
Other important towns: Kumasi (282,000), Sekondi-Takoradi (128,000).
Official language: English.
Chief product: Cocoa.

Ghana, the former British Colony of the Gold Coast, achieved independence as a sovereign State within the Commonwealth at midnight on March 5–6, 1957, under the premiership of Dr. Kwame Nkrumah, who subsequently took office as President when Ghana became a Republic on July 1, 1960.

The four administrative areas into which the country had been divided before independence had come under British control at different times during the 19th and 20th centuries, the original Gold Coast Colony in 1874, Ashanti in 1901 and the Northern Territories in 1902, whilst Transvolta-Togoland (part of the former German Colony of Togo) was administered by Britain under a League of Nations Mandate from 1918 and under U.N. trusteeship from 1946.

Constitutional Developments before Independence

The Gold Coast was the first British colonial territory to enjoy an increasing measure of internal self-government, and also the first to attain independence within the Commonwealth. This development was largely due to the early formation of political parties, in which ex-servicemen from World War II played an important part. The first political mass organization was the United Gold Coast Convention led by Dr. Joseph Danquah, but in June 1949 Dr. Kwame Nkrumah, breaking away from Dr. Danquah's movement, founded the Convention People's Party (CPP). Agitating from the outset for Dominion status for the Gold Coast, the CPP soon emerged as the most tightly organized of the country's political movements.

The constitutional developments which led to the granting of independence to the Gold Coast are summarized below.

1. The first Africans were appointed to the Administrative Service in the Gold Coast in July 1942, and they included Dr. (then Mr.) K. A. Busia (the later Prime Minister), who became an Assistant District Commissioner.

2. The first "unofficial" (i.e. African) members of the Gold Coast Executive Council (which had until then consisted of European officials only), appointed in September 1942, were Sir Ofori Atta and Mr. K. A. Korsah (who became the first African Chief Justice on April 18, 1956).

3. After consultations between the British Governor of the Gold Coast and representatives of African political opinion, the British Government approved in October 1944 the formation of a Legislative Council with an "unofficial" majority partly elected by provincial councils and municipalities and partly nominated by the Governor. The latter, however, retained powers to override decisions by the Council. These constitutional measures, by which the Gold Coast became the first British colony in Africa to have a majority of Africans in the Legislature, came into operation on March 29, 1946.

4. Following serious riots which had occurred in Accra and other towns in the Gold Coast in February – March 1948, when 21 Africans were killed and over 200 other persons wounded, and the Watson

report on the riots issued by a Commission of Inquiry, the British Government issued a statement on Aug. 4, 1948, containing new political, economic and social proposals.

The Watson report described the 1946 Constitution as "outmoded at birth"; referred to African suspicions that the Government was using the chiefs as "an instrument for the suppression or delay of the political aspirations of the people"; and recommended the creation of an Assembly with legislative functions and parliamentary status, with a Board of Ministers acting as an Executive Council. The British Government, however, in its statement disagreed with the Commission's criticism of the 1946 Constitution and stressed that any agreement to further proposals "already largely envisaged" were "not the fruits of an outbreak of disorder".

5. A committee under Mr. Justice Coussey, having examined the proposals of the Watson report, suggested further constitutional changes in its report of Oct. 26, 1949. Apart from reforms in local and regional government, the Coussey Committee decided, by 20 votes to 19, to recommend a bicameral Legislature, i.e. a Senate of 38 members and a House of Assembly of 78, the latter to consist mainly of members elected regionally by universal suffrage, which would be direct in certain municipalities and indirect elsewhere. The new Executive Council was to have 12 members who would be responsible to the House of Assembly and include five Ministers appointed from the House (administering Internal Affairs and Justice, Health, Education, Agriculture, Public Works, Commerce and Industry). The Governor was to retain, *inter alia*, a power of veto on legislation.

The British Government accepted the proposals on Oct. 26, 1949, with certain provisos, especially that of ultimate retention of responsibility by the Governor, and the establishment of a single-chamber Legislature instead of the proposed bicameral one.

Shortly afterwards a civil disobedience campaign by the CPP led to the declaration of a state of emergency on Jan. 13, 1950, and the arrest of party leaders, including Dr. Nkrumah who, with nine others, was sentenced to 12 months' imprisonment on Feb. 22, 1950, for incitement to strike and publication of seditious material.

The new Constitution of the Gold Coast, based on the Coussey Report, published on Dec. 30, 1950, provided for (a) a Legislative Assembly of 84 members, of whom 75 would be Africans, and (b) an Executive Council headed by the Governor and consisting of eight African Ministers and three European ex-officio members who would retain responsibility for Defence, External Affairs, Justice and the Civil Service. The Governor retained the right to veto Bills passed by the Assembly and to enact legislation on his own initiative.

Although the franchise was extended to all men and women over 21, the majority of the members of the Legislative Assembly would be chosen in indirect elections and only the five members representing the principal towns would be returned by direct election.

In the first elections held on Oct. 5–10, 1951, the CPP led by Dr.

Nkrumah won an overwhelming victory, gaining 34 seats, against three won by the United Gold Coast Convention led by Dr. Joseph Danquah, and one Independent. The other members of the Assembly were 37 Territorial Council representatives elected by the paramount chiefs, six European representatives of the Chambers of Commerce and of Mines, and the three ex-officio members.

In the Executive Council formed on Feb. 26, 1951, Dr. Nkrumah – who had meanwhile been released from prison "as an act of grace" – became Leader for Government Business and Minister without Portfolio. On March 21, 1952, however – under an Order in Council amending the Constitution – Dr. Nkrumah was appointed Prime Minister.

6. A White Paper published by the Gold Coast Government on June 19, 1953, contained proposals for 'the limited transitional period' before independence, by which the ex-officio Ministers would be replaced by representative Ministers; the Governor would retain responsibility only for External Affairs, Defence and Internal Security; and the position of the Prime Minister and his Ministers should be brought into line with that prevailing in other Commonwealth countries. These and other proposals contained in the White Paper were approved by the Legislative Assembly on July 15, 1953.

After the British Government had approved the proposed constitutional changes in April 1954, and the Legislative Assembly had, on Nov. 18, 1953, unanimously increased the number of seats from 84 to 104 – all to be elected by direct universal suffrage – new elections held on June 10–15, 1954, resulted in the CPP gaining 71 seats and thus an absolute majority. Dr. Nkrumah's new Cabinet of 11 members, announced on June 21, 1954, was accordingly composed of CPP members only and was the first all-African Cabinet to be appointed in British Africa.

7. Proposals for the independence of the Gold Coast as a full member of the Commonwealth, published by the Gold Coast Government on April 19, 1956, included the provision that the Gold Coast should have full responsibility for Defence and External Affairs. In general elections held on July 12–17, 1956, the CPP retained 71 seats, while the National Liberation Movement, led by Professor K. A. Busia, gaining 12 seats and the Northern People's Party, with 15 seats, were the principal Opposition parties.

The British Government's Bill approving the proposed independence of the Gold Coast under the name of Ghana was enacted on Feb. 7, 1957 – after the U.N. Trusteeship Council, and subsequently the U.N. General Assembly, had agreed that, following a plebiscite held in British Togoland in 1956 which resulted in an overwhelming vote for union with an independent Gold Coast, the Togoland territory should be included in Ghana.

On Aug. 3, 1956, the National Assembly passed by 72 votes to nil, with the Opposition abstaining, a motion calling for independence within the Commonwealth.

The proposed independence Constitution provided for a Cabinet and a Parliamentary system of government, the legislature to be the National Assembly consisting of a Speaker and 104 members. The country would be divided into five regions — the Eastern and Western Regions, Transvolta-Togoland, Ashanti and the Northern Territories (including the northern section of Togoland) — each of which would have a Regional Assembly and a House of Chiefs which would have power to consider any matter referred to it by a Minister or the Regional Assembly. These proposals were accepted by the Government and Opposition leaders, by the former because the draft Constitution retained the unitary form of Government on which the ruling CPP had insisted, and by the Opposition because sufficient powers had been given to the Regions and the traditional authorities to counter-balance any undue concentration of power at the centre.

Consolidation of Dr. Nkrumah's Regime

The dominant feature of the three years 1957–60 was the Government's action, in varied guises, against opponents of the regime.

A Deportation Bill was passed on Aug. 23, 1957, empowering the Minister of the Interior to deport anyone without "appeal to or review in any court" whose presence was "not conducive to the public good" (i.e. for political reasons). This Bill was presented as a result of the violence which accompanied legal proceedings concerning deportation orders issued against two leading members of the Moslem Association Party, one of the Opposition parties. By Dec. 3, 1958, the number of persons expelled under this Act totalled 61.

The Emergency Powers Bill, to replace the Emergency Powers Orders in Council which were due to expire in March 1958, having been in force since independence, was given its third reading on Dec. 12, 1957. The main provisions of the new Act were: (a) If the Governor-General was satisfied that a state of emergency existed he might, by proclamation, issue such regulations as he deemed necessary or expedient for the maintenance of law and order; (b) the Government was given powers of detention, exclusion and deportation, orders for the latter having to bear the Governor-General's signature; and (c) any emergency regulations would lose their effect if not approved by Parliament within 28 days. [The Act was invoked for the first time on Dec. 30, 1957, when the Government proclaimed a local state of emergency in Kumasi.]

Further legislation to aid the Government in taking action against opposition movements was presented on July 5, 1958, with the publication of the Preventive Detention Bill; under this the Ghanaian Government sought powers to detain Ghanaians for actions considered "prejudicial to the security of the country and its relations with other countries". The Minister of Information and Broadcasting explained that the Bill aimed at forestalling subversive activities and preventing their taking effect.

New security legislation was announced by the Government on June 4, 1959, following the publication on May 22, 1959, of the report of a Commission of Inquiry into the activities of two former Opposition M.P.s, who had been detained in December 1958 and unseated on April 6, 1959. This report stated that the Commission believed that the two men, Mr. R. R. Amponsah and Mr. M. K. Apaloo, had been engaged since June 1958 in "a conspiracy to carry out at some future date in Ghana an act for unlawful purpose, revolutionary in character". The new legislation included the amendment of the law of treason to ensure that persons engaged in such activities could be tried on a charge of treason, which carried the death penalty; other provisions included imprisonment of not less than five years for sedition, legislation to make it an offence, punishable by up to 15 years' imprisonment, to make false statements which were "likely to injure the credit or reputation of Ghana or the Government of Ghana", and powers to enable the House of Assembly to expel members in certain cases of abuse of privileges.

Conflict between the Government and the regional chiefs, who were by tradition the religious, political and military leaders of their peoples, arose very soon after the achievement of independence.

A Statute Law Amendment Bill, introduced in the National Assembly on Aug. 26, 1957, provided for the abolition of European chief regional and regional officers and the appointment of regional commissioners, who would be resident Ministers. The Minister of the Interior, in support of the Bill, stated that relations between the Government and the people would benefit from these appointments. Opposition to the Bill had previously been expressed by the paramount chiefs of the Coastal Province, the Asanteman Council in Ashanti and the Northern House of Chiefs, whilst Dr. Busia declared that the Bill had "objectionable implications" because it would lead to the introduction of party control over regional administration.

In October 1957, the two most powerful chiefs in Ghana, the Asantehene and the Okyenhene (paramount chiefs of Ashanti and Akim Abuakwa) made public declarations of neutrality in reply to a letter from Dr. Nkrumah inviting them to define their attitude towards party politics. As a result the Government appointed a Commission of

Inquiry into the administration of the Akim Abuakwa region and suspended the Okyenhene from the exercise of his statutory functions pending the Commission's report.

In reply to an appeal by the Joint Provincial Council (the council of chiefs from southern Ghana) to the Government to reconsider this decision, Dr. Nkrumah stated on Nov. 22, 1957, that it would be prepared to do so if the Okyenhene undertook not to take part in or encourage activities likely to cause unrest in his State. On Nov. 27, the Joint Provincial Council unanimously recommended that Chiefs should not take part in party politics.

Relations between the two sides deteriorated further after the Government on Feb. 2, 1958, announced its decision to create eight new States in Ashanti and to recognize the chiefs of these areas as paramount chiefs whilst withdrawing recognition from two of the existing States. At an emergency meeting of the Asanteman Council in Ashanti on Feb. 17, the Asantehene accused the Government of seeking to usurp his powers to reduce or elevate chiefs; a resolution was adopted by the meeting denouncing the Government's action as unconstitutional.

After 1957 political opposition to the Government centred on the United Party, whose parliamentary leader was Professor Busia, and which was an amalgamation of six political organizations, formed at a conference in Kumasi on Oct. 6, 1957. The six were the three main opposition parties – the National Liberation Movement (NLM), the Northern People's Party (NPP) and the Moslem Association – and three regional groups – the Ga People's Association, the Wasaw Youth Association and the Ashanti Youth Association. At its inauguration, the United Party had 24 representatives in the National Assembly – 12 NLM members, 11 NPP members and one member representing the Federation of Youth Organizations.

Legal action was taken during the period 1957–60 against Opposition M.P.s, mostly on charges of subversive activity, which were denied vigorously by the accused.

On Nov. 30, 1957, two Opposition M.P.s, Mr. S. G. Antor and Mr. Kojo Ayeke, were arrested on charges of conspiring to attack certain people with armed force; both men were leaders of the then defunct Togoland Congress, which had agitated against the integration of British Togoland with Ghana. At their trial, the prosecution alleged that the aim of the conspiracy had been to show that this integration was a failure and to persuade the United Nations to intervene. The two M.P.s were found guilty and sentenced to six years' hard labour.

Arrests under the Preventive Detention Act [see above] were ordered on Nov. 10, 1958, of 43 Ghanaians, many of them members of the United Party, said to be involved in an alleged conspiracy "to assassinate the Prime Minister and two of his Ministers and to overthrow the Government"; 38 of those wanted were eventually arrested. The two Opposition M.P.s who were the subject of an inquiry in 1959 [see page 92] were arrested on Dec. 20, 1958, on similar charges.

The Speaker of the National Assembly notified the Governor-General on July 27, 1959, that Dr. Busia had been disqualified from membership of Parliament under the National Assembly (Disqualification) Act, which *inter alia* laid down that a member forfeited his seat in the Assembly if he absented himself from 20 consecutive sittings of the House without the Speaker's permission. Dr. Busia with his family had meanwhile arrived in England on June 29, prior to undertaking a pre-arranged lecturing tour in Europe. As a result of the Speaker's statement, Mr. S. D. Dombo became leader of the United Party in succession to Dr. Busia.

The Republic under Dr. Nkrumah

The two main features of the Government's proposals for a Republican Constitution for Ghana published on March 6, 1960, were, firstly, provision for the eventual surrender of Ghana's sovereignty, in whole or part, to a union of African States, and, secondly, the extensive powers given to the President, who would combine the functions of Head of State and Head of Government and have power to veto legislation, to dissolve the National Assembly and to appoint the judiciary. The Constitution was designed so that as far as possible the man chosen to be President would be the leader of the majority party in the National Assembly, which with the President would form Parliament. Other provisions included a House of Chiefs for each region.

The draft Constitution was strongly criticized by the Oppositon United Party who described it as "worse than the crudest colonial Constitution of the 19th century"; the Constitution was nevertheless approved by 1,008,740 votes to 131,425 in a referendum held on April 19, 23 and 27, 1960. In the Presidential elections held at the same time Dr. Nkrumah received 1,016,076 votes against 124,623 votes for the United Party candidate, Dr. Danquah, on a 54 per cent poll.

Dr. Nkrumah's Assumption of Personal Powers

President Nkrumah assumed progressively greater powers during the years following the proclamation of a Republic, confirming in his opponents' view the comment made by Dr. Busia on Aug. 30, 1957, on a policy statement made by Dr. Nkrumah, that "the trend towards dictatorship has become more evident".

The Criminal Code (Amendment) Bill enacted on Aug. 23, 1960, gave powers to the President to impose press censorship in certain cases and to restrict the importation of publications which might be "contrary to public interest". On May 1, 1961, President Nkrumah took over full executive direction of the CPP, assuming the posts of General Secretary of the party and chairman of its central committee. In explanation of his action he stated that the country, led by the party, was entering a "new political revolution regarding the struggle for the total liberation of the African continent" and that, internally, Ghana had entered "a new phase of the industrial and technical revolution". A further announcement was made on June 4, to the effect that the President had taken over direct responsibility for the main aspects of Ghana's development programme. The country's broadcasting system came under the President's direct supervision, following an announcement to this effect on July 22, 1961, whilst on Sept. 22 it was announced that the President had become Supreme Commander of Ghana's armed forces and that British Army Officers in the Ghanaian forces would be replaced by Ghanaians. On Aug. 31, 1965, the Armed forces came under the direct command of the President.

Measures to consolidate President Nkrumah's regime and to silence his opponents continued, orders under the Preventive Detention Act being issued against many leaders and supporters of the Opposition Party. [The Government was empowered to extend this Act for a further five years in a Bill passed on Nov. 4, 1963.]

Mr. Justice Bossman on Jan. 9, 1961, in a judgment given in a case in which 13 detainees had sought writs of *habeas corpus*, ruled (1) that the English *Habeas Corpus* Act of 1816 was not in force in Ghana, and (2) that only common law rights of *habeas corpus* were in force locally. The Ghana Supreme Court ruled on Aug. 28, 1961, that the Preventive Detention Act was neither unconstitutional nor in conflict with the declaration of fundamental human rights made by the President on assuming office. On May 5, 1962, the President stated that he had decided not to proceed with an earlier intention of extending the maximum period of detention to 20 years for second offenders under this Act; instead a further five years' detention and the possible loss of rights as a citizen would be the penalty for such offenders.

Other legislation aimed at opponents of the regime, which became effective during this period, included a Bill extending the jurisdiction of Ghanaian courts to offences committed outside the country, passed on

Nov. 3, 1961, and a Bill which came into force on Feb. 22, 1964, giving President Nkrumah power to remove any judge of the Supreme Court or the High Court at any time "for reasons which seem to him sufficient".

Restriction of Political Opposition, 1960–64

Dr. J. B. Danquah declared on Dec. 11, 1960: "President Nkrumah has dealt the last fatal blow at our experiment with parliamentary democracy."

This comment followed a ruling by the Speaker that he could no longer allow "members of the former Opposition to occupy the front benches" on his left, since Standing Orders recently adopted by the Assembly made no provision "for an Opposition or for majority or minority groups". This decision appeared to abrogate the earlier arrangement, decided after the declaration of the Republic, that the terms "majority and minority" would replace those of "Government and Opposition" in the Assembly, following the adoption of a horse-shoe seating pattern in the House.

A number of prominent Opposition personalities were arrested under the Preventive Detention Act on Oct. 3, 1961, after the discovery of an alleged plot to murder Dr. Nkrumah and other Ministers; those arrested included Dr. Danquah and Mr. Joe Appiah (deputy leader of the Opposition). Also arrested were leaders of a recent strike which had broken out in the twin towns of Sekondi and Takoradi, involving thousands of railway, dock and other workers, and which subsequently spread to Accra and Kumasi. The strikes were in protest against rises in the cost of living following the introduction of an austerity budget on July 4 and 7.

After being released on June 20, 1962, as part of a general amnesty for detainees, Dr. Danquah was re-arrested under the Preventive Detention Act on Jan. 8, 1964; according to a Government statement on Jan. 14, this detention order was made "in connexion with the recent attempt [on Jan. 2] on the life of the President". Dr. Danquah died in prison on Feb. 4, 1965, the official cause of death being "heart failure"; allegations of ill-treatment and torture of political prisoners were made by Dr. Busia and a prominent political prisoner, whose identity was not disclosed, during February and March 1965.

Establishment of One-Party State

Following a referendum held on Jan. 24–31, 1964, and resulting in a practically unanimous vote in favour on a 96.5 per cent poll, Ghana became a one-party State at midnight on Feb. 21, after the President had given his assent to a Bill amending the Constitution. A further amendment provided for a standing three-man presidential commission to be appointed by the President to perform his functions in the event of his death, resignation or absence from Ghana, or of his being declared incapable of acting by Parliament. The National Assembly was formally dissolved on May 25, 1965; at the same time the holding of elections on June 9 was announced. Candidates were to be selected and allocated to their constituencies by the CPP Central Committee, the CPP being the sole permitted political party. When nominations closed on June 1 only CPP candidates had been announced and were thus returned unopposed. The new Parliament met for the first time on June 10 and unanimously elected President Nkrumah for a second five-year term.

Dissension among Dr. Nkrumah's Supporters

Even within the ranks of Dr. Nkrumah's supporters, there appeared to exist "subversive elements".

On Sept. 28, 1961, President Nkrumah announced that he had asked six members of his Government, including two Cabinet Ministers, Mr. K. A. Gbedemah and Mr. Kojo Botsio, to resign in view of their "varied business connexions", and that six other Ministers and members of the Government had accepted his request that they should surrender parts of their assets to the State; the Central Committee of the CPP informed the two former Cabinet Ministers on Jan. 16, 1962, that they had been deprived of their "rights and privileges" as party members and requested them "to resign as a party member of the Assembly", but added that they would be permitted to retain their ordinary party membership. Mr. Gbedemah was expelled from the party on Jan. 24 and from the Assembly on Feb. 11 (on the ground of having been absent from 20 consecutive sessions without the Speaker's permission). Mr. Botsio, who resigned his seat in the Assembly on Feb. 11, 1962, was nevertheless appointed Foreign Minister in March 1963.

The Foreign Minister, Mr. Ako Adjei, the Information Minister, Mr. Tawiah Adamafio, and the executive Secretary of CPP, Mr. H. H. Cofie-Crabbe, were detained on Aug. 29, 1962, under the Preventive Detention Act "in the interests of the security of the State" and dismissed from their posts. No further official announcement was made as to the reasons for this action but the Ghanaian Press and Government leaders denounced the men as "traitors" who had plotted against Dr. Nkrumah and the regime. On Dec. 9, 1963, the three men were acquitted, by the Special Court, of treason charges arising out of the alleged assassination attempt on President Nkrumah. After an emergency Cabinet meeting the President announced, without giving a reason, that he had dismissed Sir Arku Korsah, who had conducted this trial, as Chief Justice of Ghana; on Dec. 23, a Bill giving the President power to annul decisions of the Special Court was passed with retroactive effect from Nov. 22, 1961, and on the following day (Dec. 24)

President Nkrumah announced that "the judgment of the Special Court [see above] is declared null and void by virtue of this new legislation".

On Sept. 6, 1962, President Nkrumah ordered the dissolution of the propaganda unit of the CPP pending its reorganization; this action followed rumours of the arrest of the head and deputy head of the unit.

Economic Measures

President Nkrumah, on Oct. 9, 1960, strongly denied reports to the effect that Ghana intended to adopt a collectivist economy and to nationalize all foreign and Ghanaian firms, beginning in 1961. In his statement he emphasized that his Government's economic policy was based on four sectors — State-owned; joint State-Private enterprise; co-operatives; and the private sector. However, on Dec. 19, 1960, proposals for a planned socialist-type economy for Ghana, including a bigger role for co-operatives in farming and the retail trade, were published following a conference of the CPP and its affiliated organizations, the Ghana Trade Union Council, the United Farmers' Council and the National Co-operative Council.

This tendency towards nationalization became more apparent during the next two years. Firstly, the Government published on Jan. 24, 1961, a Mines (Abandonment) Bill, under which a gold-mining company which closed mines or allowed mines to be flooded without governmental permission would become liable to up to 10 years' imprisonment. On Feb. 13, however, the Government stated that it would not proceed with the Bill if the shareholders of five of the seven U.K.-controlled gold-mining companies operating in Ghana accepted the Ghana Government's offer for their entire share capital. The directors of these companies subsequently recommended acceptance, and on March 4 an official announcement was made in Accra to the effect that the Government had set up the Ghana State Mining Corporation as a holding company for the shares taken over, the Corporation to determine the overall policy of the mines subject to directions from the Government. Three further Government take-overs were the nationalization of Ghana Airways on Feb. 16, 1961, the establishment on Jan. 1, 1963, of a State Diamond Marketing Board and the announcement on June 1, 1962, of the impending formation of a Ghana State Farms Corporation to establish State farms, which scheme would receive Soviet aid.

The Volta River Scheme

The Volta River hydro-electric scheme, which was expected ultimately to revolutionize the Ghanaian economy by providing cheap power for the country's industrialization, was inaugurated by President Nkrumah on Jan. 22, 1966, four years to the day since work on the hydro-electric station began.

The project had three main components: (a) the £58,000,000 concrete dam, 2,200 ft. long and 440 ft. high, spanning the Akosombo Gorge, on the Volta River, and impounding a lake 250 miles long; (b) the £35,000,000 new seaport of Tema, 17 miles east of Accra, which was built to serve the project and was opened in 1962; and (c) a £46,000,000 aluminium smelter, which was to be the main customer for the power produced and which came into full production in November 1967.

The cost of building the dam (originally estimated at $168,000,000) was met initially by international loans, the largest being $47,000,000 by the World Bank, with the U.S. Export-Import Bank, the Agency for International Development and the British Government providing a total of $84,000,000, while Ghana found the remainder from her own resources. Ghana, in order to repay these loans, signed an agreement with the company owning the aluminium smelter – the Volta Aluminium Company (VALCO) – in which VALCO guaranteed to buy £2,500,000 of electric power a year for a period of 30 years from the Volta River Authority. Under the same agreement, VALCO was free to import its own raw product – alumina – and to export aluminium. [VALCO is owned by the Kaiser Aluminium and Chemical Corporation (90 per cent) and Reynolds Metals Company (10 per cent) both of the U.S.A.]

The total maximum capacity of the hydro-electric station was 833 MW, which was far in excess of Ghana's estimated domestic requirements and the power required for the aluminium smelter at Tema. An agreement was signed in August 1970 on the construction of a transmission line linking Ghana, Togo and Dahomey, thus bringing to fruition the idea that Ghana should export the surplus power generated under the Volta River scheme.

Disputes with other Countries

Ghana's relations with other countries during this period were dominated by the repeated accusations made by Ghana against her neighbours, European States and the United States of involvement in attempts to overthrow or undermine President Nkrumah's regime.

On March 15, 1960, the Ghanaian Government published details of an alleged plot for the invasion of Ghana from bases in Togo; it also announced that it possessed a copy of a document "purporting to be a draft Constitution" for independent Togoland, which laid claim to the former British Togoland territory incorporated in Ghana. The accusation — which came after a period of worsening relations between the two countries resulting from suggestions by Dr. Nkrumah that Togo should unite with Ghana after becoming independent — was immediately denied by the French and Togolese Governments.

Further accusations against the Government of Togo were made on Dec. 11, 1961, when the Ghanaian Government published a White Paper on events leading up to the arrest of some 50 opponents of the Government on Oct. 3, 1961. The White Paper gave details of an alleged plot by the Opposition to overthrow the regime; others accused included the British Press and unnamed foreign companies in Ghana, whilst the attitude of British officers formerly serving with the Ghanaian forces was criticized. Again all the accusations were denied by the parties concerned.

Following a series of bomb outrages in Accra during September 1962 in which 10 people were killed, the Ghanaian Press alleged that Britain and the United States were implicated in these outrages and that Western Germany was involved in plots aimed against Dr. Nkrumah. The U.K. High Commissioner in Accra (on Sept. 12), the U.S. Ambassador (on Sept. 18) and the West German Ambassador (on Sept. 19) protested strongly against these allegations from which the President, however, dissociated his Government on Sept. 20 and 22. The committee of the "United Party in Exile", an organization of Ghanaian political refugees, also denied, on Sept. 14, that it was involved in these outrages.

Ghana's foreign policy resulted in "a diplomatic offensive" by President Houphouët-Boigny of the Ivory Coast and Heads of State of other member-countries of the *Conseil de l'Entente* [see page 18] against alleged Ghanaian and Chinese Communist support for subversive activities in a number of independent African countries. This campaign preceded a conference of the Heads of State of French-speaking Africa held at Nouakchott, Mauritania, which opened on Feb. 10, 1965. Persistent antagonism had arisen between certain of these States and Ghana, due partly to the presence in Ghana of exiled Opposition groups from these countries and to border incidents and in part to their different attitudes over the Congo (Kinshasa). The Council of Ministers of the Organization of African Unity (OAU) appointed a five-member committee to examine charges of alleged subversive activities made against Ghana who had denied the charges. On June 13 the committee reported that agreement had been reached after Mr. Botsio (the Ghanaian Foreign Minister) had conceded that (*a*) the Ghanaian Government would remove from Ghana all refugees considered undesirable by any other country and (*b*) Ghana would "forbid the formation of any political group" whose aims were to oppose any member-States of the OAU.

The overthrow of Nkrumah's Regime –
Return to Democratic Government

President Nkrumah was deposed on Feb. 24, 1966, while on a visit to Communist China, as the result of swift action in an Army coup which established in power a National Liberation Council (NLC) led by Major-General Joseph A. Ankrah (former Chief of Defence Staff of the Army). The leader of the military action, Colonel Emmanuel Kwashie Kotoka, declared in a broadcast on the same day that the CPP had been declared illegal, that Parliament had been dissolved and that all political detainees had been released. Mr. K. A. Gbedemah and Dr. Kofia Busia returned from exile whilst Mr. S. D. Dombo, the former parliamentary leader of the United Party, was amongst those released from detention. All political parties were banned by the NLC on March 1, and the Young Pioneer movement (the CPP's youth movement) dissolved. The overthrow of President Nkrumah's rule was greeted with enthusiastic popular demonstrations in favour of the new regime.

The NLC announced on Feb. 26 that it had no political ambitions but would appoint as soon as was practicable a committee to draft a new Constitution for approval by the NLC and by the people of Ghana in a referendum. This Constitution was to provide for a division of power between the executive, the legislature and the judiciary, so that there should never again be a concentration of power in the hands of one individual. It would also provide for "free and fair general elections" after which the NLC would hand power over to any Government duly elected under the Constitution.

On March 2, President Touré of Guinea announced that Dr. Nkrumah had been appointed joint Head of State of Guinea and Secretary-General of Guinea's sole party. At the same time, Dr. Nkrumah declared: "I have come here purposely to use Guinea as a platform to tell the world that very soon I shall be in Accra, in Ghana"; the ex-President continued to appeal over Radio Conakry to the people of Ghana on March 24 and April 10 and 24 to rise against the military regime and to prepare for his return to Ghana. On Dec. 28, 1966, the Ghanaian police charged Dr. Nkrumah and three of his security men with murder and conspiracy and offered a reward of £10,000 to anyone bringing him to Ghana "alive or dead".

Measures were taken by the NLC to set the Ghanaian economy on its feet again and to oust supporters of the Nkrumah regime from public life. On March 2, 1966, General Ankrah, giving an outline of the

CARL A. RUDISILL LIBRARY
LENOIR RHYNE COLLEGE

Council's economic policy, forecast a liberal economy in which "active State participation" would be limited to "certain key and basic projects" and the private sector would remain "the largest sector in terms of numbers of persons engaged and gross output". By December 1966 the NLC had taken a number of administrative and economic measures designed to reduce Government spending and at the same time to remove those officials appointed merely for political reasons by ex-President Nkrumah; these included the replacement, announced on Sept. 11, of unqualified local court magistrates, whose only claim to their position was "their loyal support of Kwame Nkrumah", by qualified lawyers, and the appointment, on June 30, of an advisory political committee with Mr. Justice Akufo-Addo as chairman and Dr. Busia as vice-chairman. A decree was published on Sept. 16, 1967, establishing the Ghana Industrial Holding Corporation to manage, on a purely commercial basis, 19 out of the 55 companies wholly owned by the Government; this was the beginning of the reorganization of Ghana's State-run enterprises.

Several attempts to overthrow the new regime were made without success. On Jan. 15, 1967, a Government statement was issued declaring that a small minority of the CPP had been committing sabotage, encouraging strikes and smuggling messages to and from Dr. Nkrumah in Guinea whilst on Jan. 23 the NLC announced that it had uncovered a plot for its overthrow and the assassination of its members. Three of the leaders of this conspiracy were sentenced to death on May 29, the sentence being commuted to 40 years' imprisonment on June 4. As the result of an abortive attempt to overthrow the NLC by a small section of the Ghanaian army, Lieut.-General Emmanuel Kwashie Kotoka, deputy chairman of the NLC, was fatally wounded. Two of the three officers described as leaders of the coup were sentenced to death by a military tribunal on May 5, whilst the third defendant received 30 years' imprisonment. Three Communist journalists and one Communist diplomat were expelled on June 6 for the official reason of carrying out "activities aimed at bringing ex-President Nkrumah back to power". Certain legislation enacted during the Nkrumah regime was abolished by the NLC; on April 5, 1966, the Preventive Detention Act was repealed while on Sept. 1, 1966, the lifting of censorship on outgoing news, imposed in September 1962, was announced.

The main proposals of the draft Constitution published on Jan. 26, 1968, were for a President with no executive powers, an elected National Assembly of 140 members and an independent judiciary. Late in October 1968 General Ankrah announced that, because of difficulties in registering voters, the Constituent Assembly, which would discuss the above draft, would not be directly elected but would have a majority of members elected by specified groups, professions and bodies.

During the period between the publication of the draft Constitution and its promulgation on Aug. 22, 1969, a considerable reorganization of the country's leadership occurred.

In March 1968 General Ankrah surrendered his responsibilities as C.-in-C. of the Armed forces to General A. Otu, who was, however, arrested on Nov. 20, 1968, on suspicion of complicity in subversive activities. On Sept. 30, 1969, it was officially announced that General Otu had been re-instated in Ghana's armed forces, the Government having accepted the conclusions of a Commission of Inquiry which had absolved the General of complicity in any subversive acts. The General was reappointed C.-in-C. early in November 1969.

General Ankrah resigned as Head of State and Chairman of the NLC on April 2, 1969, being succeeded by Brigadier Akwasi Amankwa Afrifa. This action was taken, according to an NLC statement, because the result of investigations into allegations that "certain persons had been collecting moneys from various companies, particularly expatriate firms, for building up political funds" had established that General Ankrah was involved in these transactions. At a meeting of the NLC in April, the General "accepted full responsibility for the unfortunate incident and offered to resign honourably". Brigadier Afrifa announced on April 8 that by decree it would be made a serious offence for officials or politicians to accept money or other contributions from individuals or companies.

In the first general elections since ex-President Nkrumah's overthrow, held on Aug. 29, 1969, and regarded as the first free elections since the pre-independence elections in 1956, the Progress Party led by Dr. Busia won an unexpected overwhelming victory.

One of the first events leading up to the elections was the publication of a decree on April 28, 1969, on the formation of political parties, after the announcement on April 8 that the ban on political activities would be lifted on May 1, 1969. This decree laid down *inter alia* (1) that no such party was allowed to be formed on a tribal or religious basis or have a name intended to arouse tribal or religious feelings; (2) that former M.P.s and certain office-holders in ex-President Nkrumah's Government, also certain CPP officials, were disqualified from being founder-members or office-bearers of new parties. The principal parties to emerge, as a result, were Dr. Busia's Progress Party (PP), the National Alliance of Liberals (NAL) led by Mr. K. A. Gbede-mah (who had been officially exempted from the above disqualification provisions), the United Nationalist Party (UNP) led by Mr. J. Appiah and the People's Popular Party (PPP) led by Dr. Willie Lutterodt. The last-named party was, however, banned on June 4 because it was considered to constitute an attempt to resurrect the CPP. The Constituent Assembly had previously on April 16 unanimously adopted a Bill, prohibiting any future civilian Government from setting up a one-party regime.

The new Constitution under which the elections were held (promulgated on Aug. 22) provided for democratic government in strong terms designed to prevent a return to a dictatorial regime. It had been decided by the Constitutional Assembly, however, that as an interim measure the functions of the President would be carried out by a Presidential Commission consisting of the NLC chairman and deputy chairman and the Chief of the Defence Staff; this arrangement would be for three years or until the National Assembly decided otherwise.

The final election results gave the Progress Party 105 seats, the NAL 29 and the UNP two seats, the remaining four seats going to three smaller groupings. Dr. Busia was sworn in as Premier on Sept. 3 and the membership of the civilian Cabinet was announced on Sept. 7.

On July 30, 1970, the National Assembly, upon a motion by Dr. Busia supported by the Opposition, decided unanimously to dissolve the Presidential Commission. Brigadier Akwasi Afrifa, the Commission's chairman, who was too young to qualify as a candidate for the office of President, retired from the Army on Aug. 7 after being promoted "in recognition of his services to Ghana".

Mr. Edward Akufo-Addo, a former Chief Justice and the nominee of the Progress Party, was elected President of Ghana for a four-year term on Aug. 28, 1970; in a secret ballot by the members of the National Assembly and 24 Chiefs, he obtained 123 votes against 35 for Dr. Isaac Asafu-Adjaye, a former member of the Council of State.

NIGERIA

Area: 356,669 sq. miles.
Population 1969 (estimate): 63,870,000.
Capital: Lagos (700,000).
Other important towns: Ibadan (1,000,000), Ogbomosho (320,000), Kano (295,000), Oshogbo (209,000), Abeokuta (187,000), Port Harcourt (180,000), Ilesha (166,000), Zaria (166,000), Onitsha (163,000), Iwo (158,000).
Official language: English.
Chief products: Tin, oil, groundnuts, palm produce, cocoa, timber.

Nigeria, a British colony since 1900, attained independence as a sovereign federal State within the Commonwealth on Oct. 1, 1960; two of the country's three regions – the Eastern and the Western – had been self-governing since 1957, while the Northern Region achieved this status in 1959.

Nigeria became a Republic within the Commonwealth on Oct. 1, 1963, Dr. Nnamdi Azikiwe, the Governor-General, being appointed President with executive powers and acting in accordance with the advice of the Premier of the Council of Ministers.

Elections for a new Federal Legislature (Nigeria having been a federation since 1954) had been held on Dec. 11, 1959, all male Nigerians over 21 being eligible to vote. The three main parties contesting the elections, each of which controlled one of the three regions of Nigeria, were the Northern People's Congress (NPC) led by the Sardauna of Sokoto, Premier of the Northern Region; the National Council of Nigeria and the Cameroons (NCNC) led by Dr. Nnamdi Azikiwe, Premier of the Eastern Region; and the Action Group led by Chief Obafemi Awolowo, Premier of the Western Region. It was announced on Dec. 21 that the NPC had won 142 seats, the NCNC 89 and the Action Group 72 seats, while the remaining nine seats went to smaller groups and independent candidates. Accordingly the outgoing Federal Premier, Alhaji Abubakar Tafawa Balewa, who was a leading member of the NPC, formed a new Federal Cabinet on Dec. 20, with 10 NPC and seven NCNC Ministers.

During 1961 elections to the Regional Houses of Assembly were held in the Northern Region on May 4, and in the Eastern Region on Nov. 16, the ruling parties being returned to power (the NPC in the Northern and the NCNC in the Eastern Region). Dr. Michael Okpara, who had succeeded Dr. Nnamdi Azikiwe on his appointment as Governor-General of Nigeria, remained Premier of the Eastern Region, while in the Northern Region the Sardauna of Sokoto was re-appointed Premier. [The Northern Region was enlarged on June 1, 1961, by the addition of the Northern Cameroons – see CAMEROON, page 211.]

Central Government versus the Regions

Political developments during the period 1962–67 were dominated by the conflicts which arose between the Federal Government and the various Regions, culminating in the secession of the Eastern Region as "Biafra" in 1967. The underlying cause of these dissensions was the fact that the population consisted of a number of different ethnic groups, predominant among them being the Hausa and Fulani in the Northern, the Yoruba in the Western and the Ibo in the Eastern Region. While the people of the Northern and Western Regions were predominantly Moslems, Christianity was widely adhered to among Ibo and other ethnic groups. The Ibo were generally more advanced, and many of them lived as traders among non-Ibo peoples.

The Western Region Crisis of 1962–63

In May 1962, a political crisis occurred in Western Nigeria, culminating in the declaration of a state of emergency and the suspension of parliamentary government in the region by the Federal Parliament, as a result of a split inside the Action Group, the main Opposition party in the Federal Parliament. The dispute was caused largely by differences in tactics between Chief Samuel Akintola, then Premier of the Western Region and deputy leader of the party, who advocated that the Action Group should enter a Federal coalition Government, and Chief Obafemi Awolowo, Leader of the Opposition in the Federal Parliament, who strongly opposed this view. On May 20, the party's Federal executive asked Chief Akintola to resign the regional Premiership and the party's deputy leadership, while on the following day a majority of Action Group members of the Regional Legislature addressed a memorandum to the Governor of the Region, Sir Adesoji Aderemi, requesting the dismissal of Chief Akintola from the Premiership. The Governor complied with this request ánd asked Alhaji Dawodu Adegbenro to form a Cabinet.

When the House of Assembly met on May 25 to debate a motion of confidence in the new Government, fighting broke out between the two factions of the Action Group, leading to the proclamation of a state of emergency. Restriction orders were served on 15 leading political figures in Western Nigeria on May 30, including Chief Akintola and Chief Awolowo.

Chief Akintolo had, meanwhile, filed a High Court action challenging the Governor's right to dismiss him without a vote of no-confidence from the House of Assembly, and on July 7 the Supreme Court ruled the Chief's dismissal to be invalid. With the ending of the state of emergency on Dec. 31, 1962, and the return to parliamentary government, Chief Akintola returned to Ibadan to head a Coalition Government of the United People's Party, founded by the Chief's supporters following the split in the Action Group, and the NCNC. An innovation to emphasize the close co-operation of the two coalition parties was the appointment of an NCNC member, Mr. R. A. Fanikayode, as Deputy Premier.

Following the reversal of the Supreme Court's ruling by the Judicial Committee of the Privy Council on May 27, 1963, on appeal from Alhaji Adegbenro, the Western Regional House of Assembly immediately approved a Government-sponsored amendment to the Regional Constitution expressly laying down, with retrospective effect to Oct. 2, 1960, that the Governor could remove a Premier only in consequence of a majority decision of the Regional Legislature. This amendment, which invalidated the appointment of Mr. Adegbenro as Premier in May 1962, was adopted by 83 votes to none after the 38 members of the Action Group had walked out; it was passed by the Upper House on the same day and enacted by the Governor on May 28. An emergency session on June 3 of the Federal House of Representatives approved a Government motion ratifying this amendment by 242 votes to 18.

Chief Awolowo was sentenced to 10 years' imprisonment on charges of conspiring to overthrow the Federal Government by force on Sept. 11, 1963; at the same time 18 other members of the Action Group were sentenced to varying lengths of imprisonment on the same charges. Chief Anthony Enahoro (deputy leader of Action Group), who had escaped to Britain, was deported on May 16, 1963, in response to an extradition demand by the Nigerian authorities, and was sentenced to 15 years' imprisonment, on the same charge as Chief Awolowo, on Sept. 7.

Creation of Mid-West Region

A referendum on the creation of a Mid-West Region was held in the areas concerned – the Benin and Delta provinces of Western Nigeria – on July 13, 1963, resulting in 579,077 votes or 89 per cent of the electorate in favour and 7,218 votes against. The Federal House of Representatives accordingly approved the Mid-West Region (Transitional Provisions) Bill on Aug. 8; this laid down that the new region would have an Administrator, three Deputy Administrators and 12 commissioners to govern for an interim period of six months. Chief Dennis Osadebay, President of the Nigerian Senate, was appointed Administrator on Aug. 12.

A previous unsuccessful attempt had been made in 1962 to introduce a Bill creating such a Region; this had in fact been approved by the Federal Parliament on March 23, 1962, and subsequently by the Northern House of Assembly and the Eastern Houses of Assembly and of Chiefs, but rejected by the Western House of Assembly. The Regional Premier introducing a motion of rejection maintained that the proposals were intended to destroy Western Nigeria by progressive "fragmentation".

General Elections, 1964

The first national elections since independence were held on Dec. 30, 1964, the date having been postponed because of discrepancies between the voters' rolls and the 1963 census. A new delimitation distributed the 312 constituencies amongst the Regions thus – Northern 167; Eastern 70; Western 57; Mid-West 14; and Lagos, the Federal capital, four. The two main alliances contesting the elections were (a) the Nigerian National Alliance (NNA) led by Sir Ahmadu Bello, Sardauna of Sokoto and Premier of Northern Nigeria, comprising the NPC – the Northern Region's ruling party led by Sir Ahmadu, the Nigerian National Democratic Party (NNDP) – the Western Region's ruling party, formed by former members of the NCNC and Action Group, and led by Chief Akintola, and five other regional groupings; and (b) the United Progressive Grand Alliance (UPGA) led by Dr. Michael Okpara, Premier of Eastern Nigeria, comprising the NCNC – the ruling party in the Eastern and Mid-Western regions led by Dr. Okpara, the Action Group and two parties opposed to the Northern Government. The various parties within each alliance contested differing Regions or parts of Regions; the main issues in the election arose from tribal and regional differences and antagonisms.

Widespread unconstitutional practices were reported from many parts of the country long before the start of the election campaign; President Azikiwe appealed to political leaders in a broadcast on Dec. 10 (a) to "uphold with strict impartiality the Constitutions of Nigeria" and (b) to preserve national unity. Dr. Okpara on Dec. 24 asked for a postponement of the elections and threatened that Eastern Nigeria would secede from the Federation unless its demands for the removal of irregularities and the postponement of elections were met. On Dec. 28 the UPGA stated that it had decided to call on its supporters to boycott the election.

The final results announced on Jan. 6, 1965, made it clear that only about four million of the total electorate of about 15 million had voted, the NNA gaining an overwhelming majority with 198 seats, 162 in Northern Nigeria and 36 in Western Nigeria. President Azikiwe had announced on Jan. 4, after the NCNC members returned resigned their seats on Jan. 2, that the Constitution left him no alternative but to call on the outgoing Premier, Sir Abubakar, to form a new Government which would be of "a broadly-based national" character. The President declared that he was in agreement with Sir Abubakar that in those constituencies where elections had not been held arrangements should be made to hold them as soon as possible. Dr. Okpara stated on Jan. 6 that new elections would be held in the Eastern Region as soon as possible and that, if the UPGA received an invitation to join the Federal Government, it would give it "careful consideration"; in effect this meant the abandonment of his previous demand for renewed elections throughout the country.

These supplementary elections were held on March 18, 1965, the UPGA gaining all 51 seats in Eastern Nigeria and the remaining three in Lagos; the final state of the parties in the Federal Parliament was therefore – NNA 198 seats, UPGA 108 seats and Independents five seats, with one seat vacant.

The First Military Coup

A number of young, mostly Ibo, officers of the Nigerian Army, carried out a *coup d'état* on Jan. 15, 1966, by striking simultaneously at widely different centres, killing two Regional Premiers – Alhaji Sir Ahmadu Bello, Northern Region, and Chief Samuel Akintola, Western Region – and abducting the Federal Prime Minister, Sir Abubakar, and the Federal Minister of Finance.

This followed a period of post-election violence in Western Nigeria, where the elections held on Oct. 11, 1965, had resulted in the return to power of Chief Akintola's Government. The UPGA, represented in this region by the Opposition Action Group, alleged irregular conduct by electoral officers; new impetus was given to the riots and demonstrations directed against the Regional Government when the Chairman of the Federal Electoral Commission announced in November that grave irregularities had occurred during the elections.

Immediately after the coup, the remaining Federal Ministers decided as a temporary measure on Jan. 16 to hand the country's administration over to the Army and the police under the control of General Johnson Thomas Umunakwe Aguiyi-Ironsi, Army C.-in-C., who assumed the post of Supreme Commander of the Armed forces. On the same day General Ironsi announced the suspension of the offices of Federal Premier and President and Regional Governors and Premiers, as well as of the Regional Legislatures, and the appointment of Military Governors. Expressions of support reached the General from every Region and major political party, while tribal and regional disturbances ceased as a result of the wide powers given to the four Regional Military Governors. General Ironsi announced on Jan. 21 that his Government would consist of a Supreme Military Council and a Federal Executive Council, which would perform the functions of the Federal Cabinet.

The death of Sir Abubakar was officially announced on Jan. 22, his remains having been found on the previous day. Three days' official mourning was ordered by General Ironsi who referred to Sir Abubakar as "this great son of Nigeria". The discovery of the body of the former Federal Minister of Finance had previously been announced on Jan. 18. The former Federal President, Dr. Azikiwe, was in Britain on a private visit at the time of the coup and did not return to Nigeria until Feb. 25.

On May 24 two decrees were signed by General Ironsi: one dissolving all existing political parties and banning tribal unions propagating political ideas and tribalism, and the other announcing the change of the country's name from Federal Republic of Nigeria to Republic of Nigeria, the former Regions being abolished and replaced by four groups of provinces. This second decree, which was a transitional measure taken without prejudice to the pending report of a study group set up by the military Government on March 1 with the object of making recommendations of a unitary system of government for Nigeria, led to an immediate protest by the Emirs in the Northern Provinces and disturbances between May 28 and June 1, again in the North.

Second Military Coup

General Ironsi's Government was overthrown after units of the Nigerian Army seized the General and the Governor of the Western Region on July 29, 1966, at Ibadan. On Aug. 1, Lieut.-Colonel Yakubu Gowon, Army Chief of Staff, announced that he had taken over control of Nigeria while the Military Government published a decree on Aug. 31 formally restoring the federal system of Government as from Sept. 1. It was reported from Cotonou, Dahomey, that General Ironsi and the Western Region Governor had been murdered shortly after their arrest; but their death was not officially confirmed in Nigeria until Jan. 14, 1967.

The Secession of "Biafra"

Relations between the Federal Government and the Eastern Region deteriorated over the next year until finally on May 30, 1967, Lieut.-Colonel Odumegwu-Ojukwu, Governor of the Region, announced the establishment of the independent Republic of Biafra.

Serious and widespread violence directed against the Ibo minority in the Northern Region took place at the end of September 1966 and continued into October in many areas of Nigeria. The number of persons killed in these riots was never established with certainty but was believed to run into many thousands. As a result of the persecution of the Ibo tribes in the North, retaliation against the Hausa, of Northern origin, occurred in the Eastern Region. Consequently a large-scale exodus of Ibo from the North to the Eastern Region and of Northerners from the Eastern Region to their areas of origin took place. Most of the Ibo population from the other Regions and Lagos also returned to the Eastern Region, which was faced with the problem of resettling over 300,000 persons. Many of the Ibo were skilled technicians and their flight disrupted transport, communications and business in general in many areas of Nigeria.

The Eastern Region refused to take part in discussions on the constitutional future of Nigeria and in consequence the *ad hoc* committee on this subject abandoned its meetings in mid-November 1966. On Nov. 20, Lieut.-Colonel Ojukwu described proposals made by Colonel Gowon for discussion on possible constitutional reform as "anti-democratic, unilateral and dictatorial" and reiterated that the Eastern Region would resist any attempt to impose a Constitution. Colonel Gowon declared his determination, on Nov. 30, to maintain the unity of the Federation of Nigeria as, in his view, a Confederation of sovereign States as proposed by Chief Awolowo (released along with Chief Enahoro on Colonel Gowon coming to power) was unworkable, adding: "If circumstances compel me to preserve the integrity of Nigeria by force, I shall do my duty to my country."

In order to overcome the continued opposition of the Eastern Region, the Military Government of Ghana secretly took steps during December 1966 to bring about a meeting between Colonel Gowon and the four Military Governors of Nigeria. The most important outcome of this meeting, held on Jan. 4–5, 1967, in Aburi (Ghana), was that it gave an effective power of veto to the Regional Governors within the Supreme Military Council. However, the crisis between the Eastern Region and the Federal Government intensified during February and March 1967 when Lieut.-Colonel Ojukwu repeatedly declared that the Aburi agreement had not been implemented and that, unless it were, he would be forced to take unilateral action; on March 2, Colonel Ojukwu stated that his government no longer recognized Colonel Gowon as Head of the Federal Military Government.

The decree implementing the Aburi decisions was issued on March 17, becoming law with immediate effect; it made secession illegal and empowered the Supreme Military Council to assume executive and legislative functions of any Regional Government during any period of emergency which might be declared in the Region by the Council. Strong opposition to the new law, in particular to this clause, was expressed on the same day by Colonel Ojukwu's Government.

On March 31, after the Federal Government had published a Budget Statement making no provision for the Eastern Region's demands for control of its resources, Colonel Ojukwu's Government issued a Revenue Collection Edict, the effect of which was to deprive the Federal Government of all customs revenues and export duties col-

111

lected at Eastern ports as well as of company taxes and oil rents and royalties in the Region as from April 1, 1967. A further move was made on April 18, when the Regional Government in a "Statutory Bodies Edict, 1967" took over 10 Federal installations in the Region.

On May 27 a Consultative Assembly of 300 delegates from all parts of Eastern Nigeria overwhelmingly decided to authorize Colonel Ojukwu to proclaim the Region an independent State – the Republic of Biafra – "at the earliest possible date". Colonel Gowon in a countermove on the following day declared a state of emergency and announced the promulgation of a decree creating 12 States in the Federation of Nigeria replacing the existing four Regions [see map below].

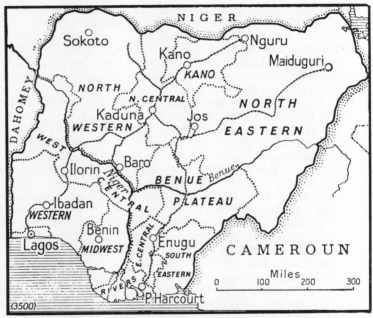

Boundaries of 12 New States as proposed by Federal Military Government of Nigeria.

(Reproduced by permission from *The Times*)

The Eastern Region reacted to this by declaring on May 29 that the proposed division could not be enforced in the East and issued a warning of a possible "bloody conflict", the creation of the Republic of Biafra occurring on the next day.

The Biafran War, 1967—70

The secession of the Eastern Region was immediately denounced by Colonel Gowon as "an act of rebellion" which would be "crushed"; he imposed economic sanctions against the East and ordered a general mobilization of all able-bodied servicemen. On June 14, the Permanent Secretary of the Federal Ministry of Industry stated at a press conference in London that a total and complete blockade of the secessionist Region was in operation.

Colonel Ojukwu had meanwhile established his own Administration in Biafra and it was officially announced in Enugu, the capital of the breakaway State, on June 4 that Biafra had been declared a disturbed area and that full mobilization had been ordered.

During June 1967 there were only sporadic border clashes between the Federal troops and the forces of Colonel Ojukwu; early in July, however, full-scale warfare began, involving thrusts by small forces, guerrilla attacks and the breakdown of law and order in many areas of Nigeria. At the same time unrest arose in the Mid-West State, because of increasing agitation by the resident Ibo for a merger with Biafra; on Aug. 10 the Federal Government admitted that Biafran forces were in control of the whole of this State. Colonel Ojukwu announced on Aug. 16 that he had appointed Major-General Okonkwo as military administrator in Benin, Mid-West State, which had been seized on Aug. 9 by mutinous troops including the Major. Two days later (Aug. 18) Major Okonkwo declared the Mid-West State to be independent both of Nigeria and of Biafra.

The situation was largely reversed during September and October 1967 when the Biafran troops were driven from the Mid-West State and from many urban areas in the former Eastern Region, including Enugu (the capital) and Calabar. By the second half of October, however, the Federal offensive appeared to have been halted by successful Biafran resistance at Onitsha, a key town on the Niger, and the failure of the Federal forces to cross the Niger River led to a period of virtual military stalemate which lasted until the beginning of February 1968. On March 22, 1968, the Federal forces announced the capture of Onitsha — yet the fate of this town, control of which was claimed by both sides, remained obscure for several weeks.

By the beginning of April 1968 the Federal forces were reported to be closing in on the administrative and commercial centre of Aba, but later in the month three successive attempts to ford the Cross River were reported to have been repulsed by Biafran troops. Meanwhile other Biafran units were reported to have crossed the Niger into the Mid-West State in an attempt to cut off the Federal troops in Onitsha

113

from their only remaining supply line; on April 25, however, the Federal Government denied that its hold on Onitsha was precarious.

The war swung decisively in favour of Federal Nigeria in May when its forces occupied Port Harcourt, Biafra's last remaining supply link with the outside world. The capture of this important industrial and strategic centre virtually confined the Biafran forces to a small area in the Ibo heartland, where sporadic fighting was reported during June and July 1968.

August and September 1968 saw the Civil War appearing to draw to a close, with the Federal forces advancing in strength into the Ibo heartland, capturing the strategic towns of Aba and Owerri and surrounding the last important Biafran stronghold of Umuahia. Nevertheless, from the beginning of October onwards increasing Biafran resistance virtually halted the Federal offensive and at the end of 1968 heavy fighting was reported on almost all fronts.

The military situation remained static during 1969, only being broken by the almost simultaneous capture by the Federal forces of Umuahia and the Biafran reoccupation of Owerri in April.

Over the weekend of Jan. 10–11, 1970, Biafran resistance suddenly collapsed with the capture by Federal troops of Owerri and the decision of General Ojukwu to leave the country. Major-General Phillip Effiong, Biafran Chief of Staff, who had been left in charge of the secessionist regime by General Ojukwu, ordered his troops on Jan. 12 to cease fighting and at a ceremony in Lagos on Jan. 15 formally proclaimed the end of secession and accepted the authority of the Federal Government. The Government of the Ivory Coast announced on Jan. 23 that it had granted General Ojukwu political asylum, but this was revoked in October 1970.

Foreign Involvement

Foreign involvement in the Nigerian Civil War centred around the thorny problems of military aid, relief for civilians and attempts at a negotiated peace settlement on both sides.

Military Aid

During the first few months of the war the Federal Government succeeded in building a military superiority by obtaining arms from abroad, both from Britain and Communist countries, to which the Biafran authorities repeatedly made strong objections. On Aug. 27 and Dec. 12, 1968, the British Government's policy of continued arms supplies to the Federal Government was strongly criticized by members of all parties during debates in the British House of Commons. Both sides in the Civil

War had previously, during the early months of 1968, accused each other of soliciting foreign aid and contradictory statements were also made by the Federal and Secessionist Governments on the employment of mercenaries.

Relief Efforts

Despite the grave plight of refugees and other civilians on both sides of the fighting line, international efforts to organize relief, during 1968, were frustrated by the failure of both Biafra and the Federal Government to reach agreement on the methods of transportation and distribution. The attempts of the International Red Cross to fly supplies in from Fernando Poo were temporarily halted in January 1969 because of a ban imposed by the newly independent Government of Equatorial Guinea and again at the beginning of March 1969 during the crisis between Equatorial Guinea and Spain. On Jan. 28, 1969, however, the International Red Cross announced that it had concluded negotiations with Dahomey for the use of the airport at Cotonou (Dahomey) as a base for the airlift of relief supplies into Biafra, the first such flight taking place during the night of Feb. 1–2. Airlifts from Cotonou continued without interruption as had the flights under the auspices of Inter-Church Aid, from the Portuguese island of São Tomé, since April 1968.

A serious dispute over the conduct of relief operations arose between the Federal Government and the International Committee of the Red Cross in June 1969. On June 10 the ICRC suspended the airlift from Fernando Poo and Cotonou following the shooting down of a DC-7 aircraft provided by the Swedish Red Cross, while on June 19 Dr. August Lindt resigned as ICRC Relief Co-ordinator for Nigeria and Biafra after being declared *persona non grata* by the Federal Government.

On June 30, 1969, Chief Enahoro (Federal Commissioner for Information) informed representatives of relief organizations in Lagos that the Federal Government's National Rehabilitation Commission would "take over immediately" from the ICRC responsibility for co-ordinating all relief operations on both sides of the fighting line. The President of the ICRC in reply on July 1, described the Federal Government's decision as a "conscious insult to every humanitarian act". After discussions between the Federal Government and the ICRC an agreement was signed on Sept. 13 governing daytime flights; this agreement was, however, rejected by the Biafran Government on the following day, on the ground that it contained "no adequate guarantee against Nigerian military exploitation of the flights". The formal agreement terminating the role of the ICRC as a relief co-ordinating authority in Federal territory was signed in Lagos on Oct. 2.

Peace Efforts

Numerous attempts to obtain a peace settlement were made, without success, from November 1967 onwards by various international organizations, foreign governments and individuals.

The Organization of African Unity (OAU), after attempts to achieve a cease-fire made during November 1967, held a meeting of its Consultative Committee on Nigeria at Niamey (Niger) on July 15–19, 1968; this was followed by formal negotiations in Addis Ababa which opened on Aug. 5 but which were indefinitely suspended on Sept. 9. Further peace moves by the OAU Consultative Committee later in 1968, in April 1969 and at the Seventh Assembly of Heads of State and Government in Addis Ababa on Sept. 6–9, 1969 [see page 6], all proved unsuccessful.

The British Government similarly made repeated moves to bring peace to Nigeria. The Commonwealth Secretariat, in December 1967 and again in May 1968, attempted to bring about peace; following the second initiative, negotiations between the Federal Government and Biafra took place from May 23–31, but broke down over conditions for a cease-fire. Towards the end of 1968, further peace initiatives were made, which included two visits to Lagos by Lord Shepherd, U.K. Minister of State for Foreign and Commonwealth Affairs, again meeting with no success, as did an attempt made during the Commonwealth Conference in London in January 1969.

Other unsuccessful peace initiatives included an attempt by the Vatican in December 1967, discussions between representatives of both sides in the war and Pope Paul VI during his visit to Uganda on July 31 – Aug. 2, 1969, and appeals for peace on Feb. 16 and Aug. 28, 1969, by the former President of Nigeria, Dr. Nnamdi Azikiwe, who was also a leading Ibo.

Post-War Relief

On the surrender of the Biafran forces, a major relief effort was mounted in many countries to help avert the feared disaster of mass starvation and death in the areas affected by the Civil War and to assist in the rehabilitation of the population. The Federal Government insisted, however, that it alone would control and co-ordinate the relief programmes for the former enclave of Biafra through its own administrative agencies and, while communicating the immediate requirements for relief to a number of "friendly Governments", it rejected outright any relief from certain countries and organizations which it accused of "hostility" towards the Federal cause.

116

The reports of fact-finding missions to Nigeria led by Lord Hunt, the British Prime Minister's personal emissary, by the United Nations Military Observer Team, which had been operating in the country since October 1968, and by M. Said-Uddin Khan, U Thant's representative for relief activities, showed that conditions throughout the territory were better than had been expected. This was in direct contradiction to the far more pessimistic accounts of eye-witnesses, international journalists, relief workers and missionaries.

On Feb. 6, 1970, the ICRC announced its impending withdrawal from Nigeria because of difficulties with the Federal Government and on the ground that, with the cessation of hostilities, its presence would no longer be required. This was followed on June 30 by the end of the Nigerian Red Cross's relief operations in the former secessionist areas and the handing over of responsibility to the National Rehabilitation Commission.

The Twelve-State Federation

The main internal political development, apart from the Civil War, during the period 1967–70 was the creation of the twelve States, the decree announcing this having precipitated the secession of Biafra. The formal division of the Federation took place on April 1, 1968, as follows. Six of the new States were in the Northern Region, viz.: North Western (consisting of the provinces of Sokoto and Niger); North Central (Katsina and Zaria); Kano (Kano Province); North Eastern (Bornu, Adamawa and Bauchi); Benue-Plateau (Benue and Plateau); and West Central (Ilorin and Kabba). The Mid-West remained as it was, while the Western State consisted of the former Western Region except for the Colony Province, which, with the Federal Territory of Lagos, made up the new State of Lagos. The former Eastern Region was divided into East Central (the whole Region except Calabar, Ogoja and Rivers Provinces); South Eastern (Calabar and Ogoja Provinces); and Rivers (Rivers Province).

SIERRA LEONE

Area: 28,000 sq. miles.

Population 1969 (estimate): 2,512,000.

Capital: Freetown (128,000).

Other important towns: Bo (210,000), Kour (170,000).

Official language: English.

Chief products: Diamonds, iron ore, palm kernels, piassava, cocoa.

The former British Protectorate of Sierra Leone achieved independence within the Commonwealth as a sovereign State owing allegiance to H. M. Queen Elizabeth II on April 27, 1961. Prior to the whole of Sierra Leone becoming a Protectorate in 1896, the area around Freetown had been a settlement for freed African slaves, acquired by the British in 1788.

In the country's first general elections since independence held on May 25, 1962, Sir Milton Margai, Prime Minister since before independence, led his party, the Sierra Leone People's Party (SLPP), to victory, gaining 28 out of the 62 directly-elected seats in the Legislative Assembly; subsequently 12 Independents announced their support for the SLPP. Of the remaining 22 seats, 20 were won by the All-People's Congress (APC), led by Mr. Siaka Probyn Stevens, and the Sierra Leone Progressive Independence Movement (SLPIM) which was allied to the APC, and two by independent candidates.

In March 1966, Sir Albert Margai, who had become Prime Minister on the death of his brother, Sir Milton, on April 28, 1964, introduced a Bill providing for the creation of a one-party State. This was opposed, however, by the All-People's Congress, and on Feb. 8, 1967, the Prime Minister announced that his Government had decided to adhere to the multi-party system.

General elections were held on March 17, 1967, but their final results were never officially announced. Immediately after the swearing-in of Mr. Stevens as Prime Minister on March 21, he and the Governor-General, Sir Henry J. Lightfoot-Boston, were detained on the orders of the Army Chief, Brigadier David Lansana, who declared martial law and stated that the Governor-General had no right to appoint Mr. Stevens while the election results were incomplete.

Within 48 hours of this event, on March 23, a group of young officers seized power, declaring that the Governor-General and all political leaders had been taken into custody, that all political parties were dissolved and all political activity was prohibited, and that the Constitution was suspended. The creation of the "National Reformation Council" was announced with Lieut.-Colonel Andrew J. Juxon-Smith named as chairman and the Commissioner of Police, Mr. William Leigh, as deputy chairman.

The country remained under military rule until a further coup, subsequently referred to as "the sergeants' coup", occurred on April 18, 1968, when a group of Army n.c.o.s took over the administration of the country before handing it over to Mr. Stevens and a civilian government on April 26, 1968. According to the Dove-Edwin Commission, appointed by the

National Reformation Council, Mr. Stevens's party, the All-People's Congress, had in fact won the 1967 elections.

After widespread disturbances, which Mr. Stevens attributed partly to followers of Sir Albert Margai, a state of emergency was imposed throughout the country on Nov. 29, 1968, and two days later Parliament approved far-reaching emergency powers for the Government.

Brigadier Lansana and nine other persons were condemned to death on April 18, 1970, for their part in the action against Mr. Stevens and the Governor-General in March 1967 [see above], and Brigadier Juxon-Smith was sentenced to death on July 30, 1970, for having conspired with others to overthrow the Government and to suspend the Constitution, also in March 1967.

After the Government had proposed the introduction of a republican Constitution under which the Prime Minister was likely to become executive President for a five-year term, and the ensuing unrest in various parts of the country, Mr. Stevens again declared a state of emergency on Sept. 14, 1970; he subsequently banned a newly-formed party, which had been joined by two dissident Cabinet Ministers, and had its leaders arrested.

TANZANIA

Area: 342,221 sq. miles (excl. water).
Population 1969 (estimate): 12,926,000.
Capital: Dar-es-Salaam (273,000).
Official languages: Swahili and English.
Chief products: Diamonds, coffee, cotton, sisal.

The two independent Republics of Tanganyika and Zanzibar were united to form one State on April 27, 1964, on which date the formal exchange of the instruments of ratification of the Act of Union occurred. It had been announced on April 23 that the Presidents of the two Republics, Dr. Julius Nyerere of Tanganyika and Sheikh Abeid Amani Karume of Zanzibar, had signed this Act, which had been ratified by the Zanzibar Revolutionary Council on April 21 and which was subsequently ratified by the Tanganyika National Assembly on April 25. The United Republic of Tanganyika and Zanzibar was renamed the United Republic of Tanzania on Oct. 30, 1964.

119

Tanganyika

Tanganyika, until 1918 part of German East Africa, was administered by Britain until 1946 under a League of Nations Mandate and subsequently under U.N. trusteeship. It achieved independence as a sovereign State within the Commonwealth on Dec. 8–9, 1961, under Dr. Nyerere as Prime Minister. On the first anniversary of independence, the country became a Republic within the Commonwealth. The new Constitution, approved unanimously by the National Assembly on June 28, 1962, provided for an executive President who would appoint a Vice-President from amongst the elected members of the National Assembly as his principal assistant and as the leader of Government business in the Assembly. The President would preside over the Cabinet composed of the Vice-President and Ministers, all of whom would be elected members of the Assembly. Presidential elections by universal suffrage were held on Nov. 1–5; Dr. Nyerere, standing as the candidate of the Tanganyika African National Union (TANU), polled 1,123,553 or 97 per cent of the votes cast against 21,279 for his sole opponent, Mr. Zuberi Mtemvu, leader of the African National Congress. Mr. Rashidi Kawawa, who had succeeded Dr. Nyerere as Prime Minister on Jan. 22, 1962, following the latter's decision to resign, became Vice-President while retaining the functions of Premier.

On Jan. 20, 1964, soldiers of the 1st Battalion Tanganyika Rifles revolted against their British and Tanganyikan officers, arresting 30 British officers and n.c.o.s and flying them to Nairobi. In the ensuing riots in Dar-es-Salaam 14 persons – all non-Europeans – were killed and 120 injured. According to a spokesman for the mutineers, the revolt was "purely an Army affair" resulting from dissatisfaction with having British officers and with the conditions of pay. Later on Jan. 20, the Minister of Defence and Foreign Affairs announced that the mutinous troops had returned to barracks. However, on Jan. 24, in the light of similar events in Uganda and Kenya [see pages 126, 130], President Nyerere asked for and received British troops to help regain control of the Tanganyikan Army; the British troops overcame whatever resistance there still was, killing three African soldiers and wounding nine others.

Zanzibar

Zanzibar achieved independence on Dec. 9, 1963 – after being a British Protectorate for 73 years – under a coalition Government based on an alliance of the Zanzibar Nationalist Party (ZNP) and the Zanzibar-Pemba

People's Alliance (ZPPA), both representing the Arab minority which ruled the country. On Jan. 12, 1964, this Government was overthrown by a "Revolutionary Party" led by the self-styled "Field-Marshal" John Okello, which proclaimed the establishment of a Republic on the same day. In a broadcast it was announced that Sheikh Abeid A. Karume, leader of the Afro-Shirazi Party, representing the African majority, had been installed as President and that a new Government had been formed, with Sheikh Abdulla Kassim Hanga as Premier and Vice-President. It was confirmed later that the Afro-Shirazi leaders did not know of Okello's plan. The Sultan of Zanzibar, Seyyed Jamshid bin-Abdullah, fled to Britain, arriving there on Jan. 19.

The new Government rounded up and "screened" supporters of the former regime suspected of possessing weapons; declared the ZPPA and the ZNP illegal; and banned the Sultan from the island for life. The revolution was accompanied by violence and looting of shops belonging to Arabs and Asians.

On Jan. 23 it was officially announced that the Cabinet and all Government departments would be placed under the control of a Revolutionary Council of 30 members, consisting of the Cabinet, officials such as the Commissioner of Police and the "Revolutionary Committee of Four" headed by Okello; the latter's position was described by President Karume as that of a member of the Council who must abide by its decisions and execute those falling within his province. [Okello admitted in Dar-es-Salaam on March 11 that the Zanzibar Government refused to allow him to return to the island, after a visit to Nairobi and Dar-es-Salaam, because "there were difficulties".]

The President announced on Jan. 30 that the country, which had been proclaimed the People's Republic of Zanzibar, was to be a one-party State under the Afro-Shirazi party. The interim Constitution stated that the Government would consist of the President, Vice-President and Cabinet, all members of which would be members of the Revolutionary Council. The Council would have legislative powers and the President was given detention powers.

In the two months immediately preceding the union of Zanzibar and Tanganyika, various developments took place which were widely interpreted as indicating the gradual establishment of a communist-type regime on the two islands, Zanzibar and Pemba, forming the Republic of Zanzibar. These included Cabinet changes involving the replacement of two Ministers considered as moderates; the issue of a decree allowing the confiscation of property by the Government without compensation; the issue of immigration control decrees; the dismissal of British officials; the removal of a United States tracking-station from the island; and the expropriation of Indians and Arabs in Zanzibar.

The United Republic of Tanzania

On April 24, 1964, a Bill was published in Dar-es-Salaam with the following provisions:

(1) The United Republic of Tanganyika and Zanzibar would have Dr. Nyerere as its first president, Sheikh Abeid A. Karume as First Vice-President and a Tanganyikan as Second Vice-President.

(2) Until a new Constitution had been approved the new Republic would be governed in accordance with the Tanganyikan Constitution, modified to provide for a local legislature and executive for Zanzibar with limited powers and dealing with internal affairs.

(3) The Union Parliament, in which Zanzibar would be represented, and the Union's executive would have reserved powers over foreign affairs, defence, police, citizenship, immigration and external trade.

Thus Tanganyika no longer had a separate Government whilst Zanzibar retained its Revolutionary Council and its own Government.

The extensive nationalization programme continued to be implemented in Zanzibar, which also maintained the close relationships with Communist countries established before union. On June 5, 1964, the Zanzibar Electricity Board was nationalized and renamed the State Fuel and Power Co-operative; a similar fate befell the Zanzibar Clove Grower's Association on Oct. 5, 1964, being renamed the Zanzibar State Trading Co-operative; and a further 25 firms were nationalized in April 1965. The confiscation of 24 properties of Arabs and Indians was announced on Dec. 19, 1964, following 25 previous confiscation orders made since April 1964.

On May 11, 1965, it was announced that the Zanzibar Revolutionary Council had approved a new Constitution making the Afro-Shirazi party the supreme authority in the island, from whom the Government would take its orders; all other parties would become illegal under the new Constitution.

A Presidential Commission on the future constitutional status of Tanzania was established on Jan. 28, 1964; President Nyerere stated that the decision that the country should be a one-party State had already been taken, and that the Commission's task was merely to state what kind of one-party State it should be. The two basic facts of the Commission's report (published on April 7, 1965), according to President Nyerere, were: (a) that it rejected an "élite" party for Tanzania and urged that TANU should remain a mass movement of the people; and (b) that it urged that the mass party must have a political creed. The Commission's recommendations included proposals that (a) all candidates for parliamentary seats should be TANU members; and (b) for the Presidency there should be only one candidate, nominated jointly by TANU and the Afro-Shirazi party in Zanzibar and elected on a plebiscite basis.

After lengthy debate on the Commissions's report and a Government White Paper incorporating amendments to the proposals – including the reduction of the voters' choice from three to two TANU candidates, and the establishment of a Permanent Commission on the Abuse of Power instead of "mobile Ombudsmen" – the National Assembly on July 5 approved the Government's proposals as part of a new interim Constitution, and thus formally established Tanzania as a one-party State.

The United Republic received foreign economic and military aid from both Western and Communist countries during its first year of existence; Zanzibar also signed, independently, aid agreements with the German Democratic Republic. Between November 1964 and February 1965 relations with several Western countries deteriorated; following an allegation by the Government in November 1964 of a U.S. plot against Tanzania, diplomats from both countries were expelled, and in February 1965 West German aid was ended as a result of the opening of a Consulate-General by Eastern Germany in the United Republic. President Nyerere signed a 10-year Treaty of Friendship with Communist China on Feb. 20, 1965, during a visit to that country.

General elections were held on the mainland of Tanzania on Sept. 21 and 26, 1965 – no elections occurring on the islands of Zanzibar and Pemba, which had been allotted 52 seats out of the maximum number of 204 seats in the Assembly. 101 out of the 107 constituencies were contested, voters in each constituency choosing between two TANU members. All candidates were Africans with the exception of one European and three Asians.

At the same time a plebiscite was held throughout the whole of Tanzania to approve or reject the appointment of Dr. Nyerere as President for another five-year term; in this Dr. Nyerere received more than 96 per cent of the votes cast.

The new Cabinet announced on Sept. 30 by the President included Sheikh Abeid A. Karume as First Vice-President and Mr. Rashidi M. Kawawa as Second Vice-President, both men having held these posts in the previous Cabinet. President Nyerere himself took the portfolio for External Affairs.

On Feb. 5, 1967, President Nyerere announced that his Government intended to place "the major means of production" under "the control of the farmers and workers" of the country. The assets and industries to be taken over by the State would include any big industry upon which a large section of the population depended for its living, or which provided essential components for other industries and large plantations, especially those producing essential raw materials. This programme had been outlined in a document drawn up by President Nyerere and approved by the TANU executive at Arusha during the last week of January 1967 — so that it became known as the "Arusha Declaration".

In the following week measures implementing this policy were carried out. On Feb. 6, the immediate nationalization of all commercial banks in Tanzania was announced; on Feb. 10 the Government took control of the eight biggest flour-milling companies, acquired a 60 per cent interest in two breweries, the Metal Box Company of Tanzania, the British-American Tobacco Company, the Bata shoe factory and the Tanganyika Extract Company, and a 50 per cent interest in a new cement plant. The President announced on Feb. 11 that eight leading import-export houses and the country's insurance business were to be nationalized; he stressed that after these moves there would be no further nationalization measures taken. Partial settlement of compensation claims arising out of these nationalization measures was reached by August 1967.

The Revolutionary Council continued to maintain its rule over the two islands of Zanzibar and Pemba. On April 25, 1968, Sheikh Abeid A. Karume (Vice-President of Tanzania, but generally described by Zanzibar authorities as President of Zanzibar) stated that he wanted no further integration with Tanzania, that the current interim Constitution providing for internal self-government on Zanzibar and Pemba was to continue indefinitely; and that no free elections would be permitted on the islands for "at least 50 years". President Nyerere did not interfere in the island's internal affairs except that a decree published in Zanzibar on Oct. 28, 1966, setting up secret courts to try political offenders, was suspended on Dec. 3, 1966, at his insistence.

On Sept. 1, 1969, it was reported from Dar-es-Salaam that Mr. Abdullah Kassim Hanga (Prime Minister of the Revolutionary Government formed after the overthrow of the Sultan of Zanzibar in January 1964), Mr. Othman Shariff and Mr. Ali Mwange Tambwe, both former Ministers in Zanzibar, had been arrested and flown to Zanzibar. Vice-President Karume announced on Oct. 26 that 14 persons including the above three had attempted to overthrow the Revolutionary Government and that four of them had been sentenced to death and executed by firing squad, nine sentenced to 10 years' imprisonment and one to three years' imprisonment. It later became known that those executed included Messrs. Hanga, Shariff and Tambwe.

Presidential elections throughout the Republic and parliamentary elections on the mainland were held on Oct. 30, 1970. President Nyerere, the sole candidate for the presidency, was re-elected by 3,465,573 votes to 109,828, on a poll of 72.3 per cent. The national executive committee of TANU had previously selected two candidates for each constituency, except for those constituencies where only one candidate had been nominated; four members of the previous Parliament were returned unopposed (including three Ministers) while all the remaining Cabinet Ministers except two were returned in the parliamentary elections.

UGANDA

Area: 91,076 sq. miles.
Population 1969: 9,526,000.
Capital: Kampala (332,000).
Official language: English.
Chief products: Copper, cotton, coffee, sugar.

Uganda, a British Protectorate since 1890, achieved independence as a sovereign State within the Commonwealth on Oct. 9, 1962, under the premiership of Mr. Apollo Milton Obote. On Oct. 4, 1963, the Kabaka (King) of Buganda, Sir Edward Frederick Mutesa II, was elected President, and Sir William Wilberforce Nadiope, the Kyabazinga (traditional ruler) of Busoga, Vice-President; this followed the passing of a Constitutional Amendment Bill by the National Assembly for the purpose of declaring Uganda "an independent sovereign State which shall cease to form part of Her Majesty's dominions". This Bill provided that the President would have no executive powers. Mr. Obote announced on the first anniversary of independence that Uganda would remain within the Commonwealth.

President Obote's Regime, 1962–70

The original Independence Constitution provided for a federal relationship between the Kingdom of Buganda and the Ugandan Central Government; relations between Buganda and the remainder of the Ugandan Protectorate had been strained since the Kabaka's request in 1953 for Bugandan independence and separation from Uganda. The three other kingdoms in Uganda — Ankole, Toro and Bunyoro — were also to have a federal relationship with the Central Government.

A commission headed by Lord Molson was appointed in 1962 to investigate the territorial dispute between Buganda and Bunyoro known as the "Lost Counties" problem; this involved six *sazas* (counties) which had formed part of Bunyoro until, in 1894, they were handed over by the then British Commissioner to Buganda in return for the latter's help in a war against Bunyoro. The report of the commission recommended that two of the six countries should be restored to Bunyoro.

In 1967, however, Uganda became a Republic under a new Constitution which provided for an executive President who would be concurrently Head of State and of Government, and for the abolition of the four hereditary kingdoms of Uganda — Buganda, Ankole, Bunyoro and Toro. The Central Government also received wider powers than those laid down in the 1962 Constitution.

Between 1962 and 1969, Uganda progressively moved towards becoming a one-party State. Dr. Obote, Prime Minister at the time of independence, had previously led his party, the Uganda People's Congress (UPC), to victory in the general elections on April 25, 1962, when it gained 43 seats against 24 gained by the ruling Democratic Party, while the remaining 24 seats went to the Kabaka's party, the *Kabaka Yekka*, which was in coalition with the UPC.

Between August 1962 and April 1963, the Ugandan Central Government was successful in suppressing the separatist Rwenzururu movement in several counties of the Kingdom of Toro in the Western Province. On Jan. 23–25, 1964, mutiny broke out in the Army; order was restored, however, by British troops at the request of the Ugandan Government.

On Jan. 7, 1964, Dr. Obote stated that Uganda would restrict the growth of political parties and develop as a one-party socialist State. On Aug. 24, 1964, the *Kabaka Yekka* joined the official Opposition Democratic Party and called for new elections. The UPC received some new support, however, when the Leader of the Opposition in the National Assembly and five other members of the Democratic Party went over to the Government, giving it a two-thirds majority in the Assembly, on Dec. 31, 1964.

On Feb. 22, 1966, Dr. Obote announced that he had assumed full powers of government and imprisoned five Cabinet Ministers "pending an investigation into their activities". Two days later (Feb. 24) he announced that he had suspended the Constitution, and on March 2 he proclaimed that he was assuming the powers of President and Prime Minister. This move was opposed in a statement by Sir Edward Mutesa the next day (March 3).

The Republican Constitution was first introduced in 1966, when on April 15 Dr. Obote was declared President under the Constitution. On the following day the Parliament of Buganda approved a resolution rejecting the new Constitution and re-affirming that the 1962 Constitution was still in force.

A centralized Government under President Obote, however, became firmly established in May 1966, when the new Constitution limited the rights of the constitutional kingdoms – as laid down in the 1962 Constitution – particularly those of Buganda, where President Obote subdued all opposition by force, the Kabaka of Buganda being compelled to flee the country. [The Kabaka subsequently arrived in London on June 23, 1966, via Burundi. He died, in exile, in London on Nov. 21, 1969.]

The new Constitution was ruled lawful on Feb. 2, 1967, by the Uganda High Court which declared that it was the result of events which were "a revolution in law". Proposals for the declaration of a Republic and the abolition of the four hereditary kingdoms were made on June 9, 1967, and adopted on Sept. 8, 1967 – the date on which Uganda officially became a Republic.

By August 1968 the parliamentary Opposition had decreased to six seats out of 89 in the National Assembly; however, the state of emergency in Buganda, which had been announced on Oct. 9, 1966, was extended for six months at a time on Nov. 3, 1967, April 25, 1968, and again in November 1968. Under the emergency regulations a number of persons continued to be detained, including 21 men and one woman who were formally discharged in the High Court at Kampala in July 1967 after being accused of treason and of plotting to kill President Obote and his Ministers and install the Kabaka as Emperor of Uganda.

A document known as the "Common Man's Charter", published on Oct. 8, 1969, was unanimously adopted in December 1969 by a UPC conference; the Charter aimed at "creating a new political culture and a new way of life in which the people as a whole are paramount" and involved a "move to the left". The conference also adopted a resolution calling upon the Government to amend the Constitution so that Uganda would become a one-party State; President Obote declared that this would be implemented without delay.

At the close of the above conference, on Dec. 19, an attempt was made on the life of the President, who was injured but discharged from hospital on Dec. 24. The Vice-President, Mr. John K. Babiiha, temporarily assumed control of the Government and declared a national state of emergency, the Opposition Democratic Party and all other parties with the exception of the UPC being banned. Six defendants were sentenced to life imprisonment (the maximum penalty) on May 6, 1970, for their part in this attempt on the life of the President. The judge stated that the attempt had been organized by Paul Juko, a member of the Bugandan royal family and a relative of the late Kabaka.

President Obote announced on July 17, 1970, that in order to overcome tribal voting in a general election a candidate in a given constituency would have to stand simultaneously in a constituency in each of the country's other three regions outside his own. Voters would have to cast votes for their own "basic" candidate and also for one more candidate from each of three other regions. The votes obtained by each candidate would be totalled on a percentage basis, so that the candidates with the highest percentage would win the seats.

Nationalization

President Obote, describing the "Common Man's Charter" [see above] said: "The guiding economic principle will be that the means of production and distribution must be in the hands of the people as a whole. The fulfilment of this principle may involve nationalization of enterprises privately owned."

From Jan. 1, 1970, non-Ugandan traders were restricted to specified areas and barred from trading in goods specified as reserved for Ugandans.

On May 1, 1970, President Obote announced that the country's export and import trade (except for the import of oil and petroleum products) would be nationalized and that the Government would acquire a 60 per cent share-holding in all manufacturing and plantation industries, banks, oil companies, public transport companies and the Kilembe copper mine. The Trade Union Act would be amended so as to outlaw strikes.

The 1971 Military Coup

The Government of President Obote was overthrown on Jan. 25, 1971, by units of the Ugandan Army led by Major-General Idi Amin, the Army's commander, while Dr. Obote was about to return to his country from a Commonwealth Conference in Singapore.

Despite some resistance by troops and police loyal to Dr. Obote, General Amin had little difficulty in gaining control of the whole country and, suspending the Constitution and dissolving Parliament, he proclaimed himself Head of State and was able to appoint an advisory Council of Minsters, consisting mainly of former permanent secretaries in various Ministries and of other civilian experts, on Feb. 2.

Dr. Obote had meanwhile settled in Dar-es-Salaam, where he was assured of continued support by the Governments of Tanzania, Zambia, Somalia and Guinea.

General Amin's regime, however, was officially recognized by Britain (on Feb. 5) and the great majority of countries (both of the West and of the Communist world) with diplomatic representatives in Uganda.

KENYA

Area: 220,000 sq. miles.
Population 1969: 10,890,000.
Capital: Nairobi (480,000).
Other important town: Mombasa (246,000).
Official language: English.
Chief products: Coffee, tea, pyrethrum, meat.

Kenya achieved independence as a sovereign State within the Commonwealth on Dec. 12, 1963, under the premiership of Mr. Jomo Kenyatta, leader of the Kenya African National Union, which had been successful in the general elections held from May 18–26, 1963, prior to the attainment of full internal self-government on May 31. Formerly the British East Africa Protectorate from 1895 to 1920, the country was given Crown colony status, in the latter year, under the name Kenya.

On the first anniversary of independence the country became a Republic within the Commonwealth. The new Constitution provided for a President who would be Head of State and the leader of the majority party in Parliament and would appoint his Cabinet from among Members of Parliament; the President's term of office would be related to the life of Parliament, and the Cabinet would be responsible to Parliament. In a statement on Aug. 14, 1964, announcing the forthcoming establishment of a Republic, Mr. Kenyatta gave an assurance that the regional character of the existing Constitution would be maintained but added that the powers of the regions would be substantially diminished. [Kenya is divided territorially into seven regions – Central, Coast, North-Eastern, Eastern, Rift Valley, Western and Nyanza – and the District of Nairobi.]

On Dec. 12, 1963, *The Times* pointed out that perhaps "the most serious problem for Kenya today springs from the uneven development of its tribes. Some – and notably the Kikuyu – have adopted change but others – and here the Masai are outstanding – have sought to maintain traditional ways." There are two main streams ethnographically:– the Bantu which comprises 70 per cent of the population and includes the Kikuyu (largest of Kenya's tribes), Kamba, Emba and Meru tribes; and the Nilo-Hamitic, the principal tribes being the Masai and the Kalenjin. The second largest tribe in Kenya, the Luo, is of Nilotic origin, while the coastal tribes – the Digo, Durama, Giriama and Pokomo – have cultural, racial and linguistic affinities with the Bantu. Politically, there were two main parties: the Kenya African National Union (KANU) mainly supported by the Kikuyu, Kamba, Kisii, Embu and Meru tribes, all of which are Bantu, and the Luo tribe: and the Kenya African Democratic Union (KADU), mainly supported by the two Nilo-Hamitic tribes. The Kikuyu are regarded as the most politically advanced of the Kenyan African peoples.

On Jan. 23–24, 1964, British troops requested by Mr. Jomo Kenyatta suppressed a mutiny among about 250 members of the 11th Battalion of the Kenya African Rifles at their camp at Lanet, Rift Valley. The Prime Minister announced on Jan. 24 that a committee was to be set up to examine the soldiers' suggestions on pay, allowances and conditions of service; action was also taken against the mutineers.

A Defence Agreement was subsequently signed in Nairobi on March 6, 1964, granting Britain training facilities for her Army, overflying and staging rights for the Royal Air Force and port facilities for the Royal Navy. British troops were, however, withdrawn from Kenya at the end of March 1964.

The British Secretary of State for Commonwealth Relations on June

3, 1964, announced British aid to Kenya totalling over £50,000,000 for civil and defence purposes, partly in the form of gifts of money, equipment and buildings and partly as long-term loans. This aid included a grant of £11,000,000 towards the completion of Kenya's land settlement scheme.

The Constitution Amendment Bill, providing for the establishment of a Republic, obtained the required 75 per cent majority by 101 votes to 17 – these being cast by KADU led by Mr. Ronald Ngala – on Nov. 3, 1964. During the first week of November, six Senators defected from KADU; on Nov. 10, Mr. Ngala announced the voluntary dissolution of the Opposition, he and his followers in the House of Representatives and the Senate crossing the floor to the Government benches and thus making Kenya in effect a one-party State. Immediately afterwards the Constitution Amendment Bill was given a unanimous first reading in the Senate and subsequently passed through its remaining stages.

President Kenyatta, whose appointment along with that of the Vice-President, Mr. Oginga Odinga, had been announced on Dec. 10, 1964, emphasized on May 31, 1965, that Kenya wanted to remain "truly non-aligned". The President's decision to reject a Soviet arms consignment on April 29 was, however, strongly opposed by Mr. Odinga, who on May 30 accused Britain and the U.S.A. of "creating tension" in Kenya.

Mr. Odinga's left-wing views became more apparent over the next twelve months; action against him was taken by the KANU, now the sole political party in Parliament. In the election for the vice-presidency of KANU in July 1965, Mr. Ronald Ngala, the former KADU leader, was elected by 75 votes to six for Mr. Odinga; the latter had been criticizing Kenya's policy as being too pro-Western and advocating much closer ties with the Soviet Union and China. Left-wing propaganda in favour of Mr. Odinga, partly originating outside the country, was spread in Kenya from 1965 onwards. On the first day of the conference of the Parliamentary group of KANU, held on March 11–13, 1966, a decision was taken by the conference to abolish the office of deputy president of the party, then held by Mr. Odinga. Just over a month later, on April 14, Mr. Odinga resigned as Vice-President from the Kenyan Government, announcing his intention of leading an Opposition to KANU; on April 19, a parliamentary Opposition formed by 19 members of the House of Representatives and nine Senators, all of whom had resigned from KANU, elected Mr. Odinga as leader, Mr. Bildad Kaggia as deputy leader and Mr. J. D. Kali as Opposition Chief Whip.

On April 25, Mr. Ramogi Achieng Oneko, Minister of Information and Broadcasting, announced his resignation from the Cabinet and from

KANU in order to join the Opposition group led by Mr. Odinga – the Kenya People's Union (KPU – formerly the Kenya African Union or African People's Union). On the following day President Kenyatta announced that Parliament would be recalled to pass a Bill forcing the dissident parliamentarians to resign their seats and seek re-election; the House of Representatives approved this Bill by 95 votes to eight on April 28 and the Senate by 33 votes to two on the next day. The President ended the current session of Parliament on May 2, six months before its normal end, terminating the mandates of the 30 Odinga supporters.

In the 30 by-elections which followed, held on June 10–26, KANU won 21 seats (13 in the House of Representatives and eight in the Senate) while the KPU, which received its principal support from the Luo tribe, won nine seats (seven in the House and two in the Senate).

Several measures were taken during 1965 and 1966 to ensure public security. In July 1965 and again in March 1966 the Government expelled a number of non-Kenyans, mostly from Communist countries, for reasons of internal security. On Sept. 2, 1965, President Kenyatta announced a complete reorganization of the trade unions which would place the final choice of trade union officials in the hands of the President; this followed repeated clashes between rival factions in the trade union movement. New security legislation giving the President wider powers, including those of preventive detention, was approved by the House of Representatives on June 2, 1966; the first application of the new law was made on Aug. 4 when six officials of the KPU were arrested and detained without trial. On Aug. 14, the Government ordered that six Hindus should leave the country immediately "for reasons of national security".

A further incident relating to national security occurred in June 1967. During a debate in the Kenya National Assembly [formed by the amalgamation of the Senate with the House of Representatives, provided for in a Constitution Amendment Bill approved by the Senate on Dec. 20, 1966, and by the House of Representatives on Dec. 22] on the activities of the United States Central Intelligence Agency in Kenya, Mr. Tom Mboya declared that developing countries were constantly exposed to danger and intrigue from the great Powers and that not only the Americans, but also the Russians, British, French and Chinese must be watched. As a result of this statement the Chinese Embassy in Kenya made a violent attack on Mr. Mboya. Following this the Kenya Government, on June 29, ordered the Chinese Chargé d'Affaires to leave the country; the Chinese retaliated on July 14 by ordering the Kenyan Chargé d'Affaires to leave China.

Legislation on immigration and trade licensing to implement the Government's policy of Kenyanization came into force towards the end of 1967 and early in 1968. An Immigration Act, which came into force on Dec. 1, 1967, limited immigrants to 12 permissible categories and required all residents of European and Asian origin who had not become Kenyan citizens, but who wished to continue working in

Kenya, to apply to the immigration authorities for entry-work permits. These would only be granted where, in the opinion of the Kenyanization Bureau of the Minister of Labour, no suitably qualified Kenyan citizen was available for the employment in question; each permit would be renewable annually for a maximum period of five years. Legislation requiring all traders to be licensed and restricting areas where non-citizens could carry on business in Nairobi and other main towns was passed in the summer of 1967 to take effect from April 1, 1968.

A further Trade Licensing Act came into force on Jan. 1, 1969; this forbade non-citizens to trade in areas predominantly inhabited by Africans, only Kenyan citizens and more particularly Africans being allowed to do so. Non-Kenyan traders affected by this legislation, mostly Asians holding British passports, were given between one and six months to leave their shops and business premises. The estimated number of persons expected to leave Kenya as a result was 15,000, most of whom were Asians. The two leading Asian organizations in Kenya, the Association of British Citizens and the United Kingdom Citizens' Committee, were warned by the Kenyan Government on Jan. 13 that, if they did not dissolve themselves immediately, they would be banned. Kenya, Tanzania and Uganda took joint action on Jan. 22 through their central banks to prevent a large-scale flight of capital from these countries in the event of another exodus of British citizens of Asian origin similar to that which had occurred in 1967 and early 1968 as a result of the legislation on immigration and trade.

On June 25, 1968, a constitutional amendment was approved by Parliament by 113 votes to nil with eight abstentions (including KPU members). This provided for a popular vote in presidential elections to replace the existing electoral college method, and laid down that, in the event of the President's death or incapacity, the Vice-President would take his place, with restricted powers, for a maximum period of 90 days, within which time new elections would have to be held. A further amendment was adopted in November 1968; this laid down that no candidate could stand for Parliament without endorsement by a registered political party. [The only two registered groups with parliamentary representation were KANU and the KPU.]

In local government elections held on Aug. 22, 1968, in over 2,000 wards into which the country was divided, more than 1,800 KPU candidates were disqualified on President Kenyatta's orders; thus KANU candidates were overwhelmingly returned unopposed in nearly every ward. Mr. Odinga, the leader of KPU, had on Aug. 8, withdrawn his party from the elections, which he later described as fraudulent, and accused President Kenyatta of hypocrisy. Further action was taken against alleged opponents of the regime between November 1968 and February 1969, while Soviet diplomats and journalists were expelled in February 1968 and April 1969. Finally, on Oct. 30, 1969, the KPU was banned as a result of a Luo demonstration against President Kenyatta in Kisumu (a stronghold of the KPU) in which 11 people were killed. The Government statement announcing the ban claimed *inter alia* that the Kisumu riots had been "calculated to become a critical milestone in the unfolding programme of disorder and chaos, from which the KPU and their external promoters would have hoped to benefit". Mr. Odinga, who had been placed under house arrest on Oct. 27, was placed in a secret detention centre on Nov. 1; Vice-President Daniel arap Moi, who had been appointed on Jan. 5, 1967, in succession to Mr. Joseph Murumbi, announced a few days later that Mr. Odinga would be detained until no longer considered a danger to the country's security.

Mr. Tom Mboya, Minister of Economic Planning, was assassinated in Nairobi on July 5, 1969; this was followed by large-scale rioting mainly by members of the Luo tribe, of which Mr. Mboya was a member, who suspected that the murder had been committed by a Kikuyu. Nahashon Isaac Njenga Njoroge, a Kikuyu, was charged with the murder of Mr. Mboya on July 21 and sentenced to death in Nairobi High Court on Sept. 10. President Kenyatta appointed two Luo tribesmen to his Cabinet on July 24; this was seen as an attempt to ensure a fair measure of inter-tribal balance in the Cabinet and Civil Service.

Reports began to circulate after Mr. Mboya's assassination that widespread secret meetings were taking place at which oath-taking ceremonies were held for the purpose of enjoining the Kikuyu to take up arms, if necessary, to keep their tribe in power. Such ceremonies were condemned by Christian clergymen, M.P.s belonging to KANU and the vice-president of KANU, which gained much of its support from the Kikuyu.

Following the dissolution of the National Assembly by President Kenyatta on Nov. 7, 1969, primary elections for the 158 elective seats in the Assembly, held on Dec. 6, resulted in the defeat of 77 former M.P.s, the re-election of 50 members of the previous Assembly including 14 Cabinet Ministers, and the election of 108 new members, on a 55 per cent poll. All candidates had to be approved by KANU, the only political party legally allowed, and to comply with strict conditions. 10 out of the 158 seats were uncontested – those of President Kenyatta, Vice-President Moi, the Minister of Lands and Settlement, five other former M.P.s and two new members.

The newly elected Luo members issued a joint declaration on Dec. 9 affirming their support and appreciation of "the President's sagacity and political acumen" and appealing for a review of the cases of all persons detained under the Public Security Act, including Mr. Odinga and other KPU leaders.

On Dec. 12 President Kenyatta declared that his Government would not turn Kenya into a one-party State and would maintain the freedom of the judiciary and of the Press; he gave a warning, however, that those who sought to "spread communal hatred" or "subversive opposition" would not be tolerated.

[For Somali claims to Kenyan territory see SOMALIA, page 286.]

THE CENTRAL AFRICAN FEDERATION OF RHODESIA AND NYASALAND

The Federation of Rhodesia and Nyasaland, which embraced the self-governing British Colony of Southern Rhodesia and the then British Protectorates of Northern Rhodesia (now Zambia) and Nyasaland (now Malawi), came into existence on Oct. 23, 1953, but was destined to have a life span of only 10 years, characterized by conflicts between Europeans in the Federation and the British Government, and by the gradual enfranchisement of the African population, often against the will of the ruling European Governments both at Federal and at territorial level. Eventually the granting of independence to the two Protectorates on the attainment of majority rule led to the dissolution of the Federation on Dec. 31, 1963, and indirectly to the unilateral declaration of independence of Southern Rhodesia by Mr. Ian D. Smith's Government [see RHODESIA, page 174].

The idea of a Federation of the three territories was first conceived at a conference of senior officials of the Governments of Southern and Northern Rhodesia and Nyasaland, the Central African Council and the U.K. Commonwealth Relations and Colonial Offices, held in London on March 5–31, 1951. The conference's report recommended the formation of a Federation and stated *inter alia*: "Closer associaton between the three territories, by the economic and political strength which it would bring with it, would, in our view, provide a surer foundation than exists at present for developing and extending the policy of racial co-operation and partnership, on which all three territories are agreed, without the fear of influences from outside the borders of British Central Africa."

The Federation's Constitution provided for a Federal and three Territorial Legislatures, which, within their exclusive spheres, would be in no way subordinate to one another. In particular, the Territorial Legislatures would retain control of those matters which most closely concerned the daily life of the African population; the protection of African interests would, however, be entrusted to an African Affairs Board, drawn from members of the Federal Assembly having special responsibility for African interests. A further provision in the Constitution was that, for 10 years after the latter became effective, no change was to be made in the division of powers between the Federation and the Territories without the consent of all three Territorial Legislatures.

In the first general elections held on Dec. 15, 1953, the Federal Party, founded on April 30, 1953, by Sir Godfrey Huggins, Premier of Southern Rhodesia, Mr. Roy Welensky and Mr. Malcolm Barrow, respective leaders of the elected members in the Northern Rhodesia and Nyasaland Legislatures, won all but two of the 26 elected seats with the franchise almost completely limited to Europeans. Sir Godfrey, who had been Prime Minister in Southern Rhodesia since 1933, became Federal Premier.

On April 12–17, 1957, Sir Roy Welensky, who had succeeded Sir Godfrey Huggins on Nov. 1, 1956, visited London for discussions with the British Government on aspects of the Constitution. A joint statement was issued on April 26, announcing *inter alia* (*a*) that the Federation would be entrusted with greater responsibility for its external affairs; (*b*) that the U.K. Government would not in future initiate any legislation to amend or repeal any Federal law or deal with any matter on which the Federal Government was competent to legislate except at the Federal Government's request; (*c*) that both Governments were opposed to any proposal either for the amalgamation of the Federation's component territories into a unitary State or for the secession of any territories from it; and (*d*) that a review of the Federal Constitution would take place at a conference to be convened in 1960.

> This agreement followed a period of discontent on the part of the Federal authorities with the British Government's attitude on independence for the Federation; after the rejection by the U.K. Government of a request for semi-Dominion status for the Federation, Sir Roy Welensky, then Deputy Premier, had stated on Oct. 6, 1956, that despite Southern Rhodesia's proven record of self-government, "we are going to be told that the African people are against the granting of independence and therefore we cannot have it."

A Constitution Amendment Bill – enlarging the membership of the Federal Legislature by increasing *(a)* from nine to 15 the members "specifically concerned with African interests", and *(b)* the number of elected members from 26 to 44 (thus reducing the comparative representation of African interests) – passed its third reading in the Federal Legislature on July 31, 1957.

A further clause in the Bill provided, however, for the ultimate elimination of members elected on a racial basis, laying down that if and when an African was elected as an "ordinary elected member" by all races, then from the next general election the number of "ordinary elected members" for the territory concerned would be increased by one, whilst the number of "specially elected members" for African interests would be reduced accordingly. Following a request by the African Affairs Board (whose chairman, Sir John Moffat, the specially appointed European member for Northern Rhodesia representing African interests, had been an opponent of the Bill) that the Bill be reserved for the Royal assent on the grounds that it was a differentiating measure, U.K. parliamentary approval for the Queen's assent was given on Nov. 25.

A greater potential number of Africans were enfranchised with the passing of the Federal Electoral Bill, which received the Royal assent on Feb. 20, 1958. The proposals which this embodied had first been published on Sept. 19, 1957, the main provisions being as follows:– (a) There would be two voters' rolls – the "A" or general roll and the "B" or special roll – both open to persons over 21 of all races, being Federal Citizens or British-protected persons and having been resident in the Federation for at least two years; (b) the qualifications for the two rolls would be on an income and education basis, those for the "A" roll being higher than for the "B" roll; and (c) general voters would elect 44 ordinary members (24 from Southern Rhodesia, 14 from Northern Rhodesia and six from Nyasaland) whilst both general and special voters would elect eight African members (four from Southern Rhodesia and two each from Northern Rhodesia and Nyasaland) and one European representative of African interests in Southern Rhodesia. An estimate of the electorate at that time was about 119,000 of whom 85,000 were general voters, including 3,000 Africans, and 34,000 special voters, including 23,000 Africans.

In the first general elections under the extended franchise on Nov. 12, 1958, Sir Roy Welensky's United Federal Party (UFP), formed on Nov. 21, 1957, by the merger of the Federal Party and the United Rhodesia Party [see page 142], was returned to power with 44 seats; the Dominion Party, created on Feb. 18, 1956, from the majority of political groups in opposition to the Government, and led by Mr. Winston Field, gained eight seats, and one seat went to an Independent. The principal issue on which

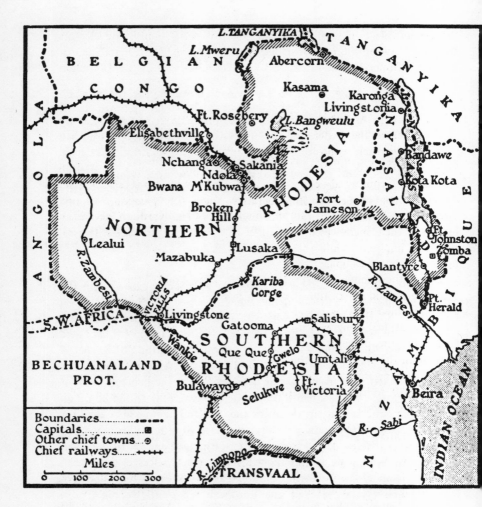

Territories in the Central African Federation, 1953-63, with the names then in use.

the general election was fought was that of racial amity, the electors choosing between the racial partnership principle of the UFP and that of taking a "firmer line" with the Africans, as advocated by the Dominion Party.

Opposition to Federation, 1953–60

Even before the Federation was established African nationalists had made known their opposition to it; members of the African National Congress, founded in 1944 as a convention of a number of African associations concerned with African welfare and advancement, had declared their opposition to Federation when the question was first discussed in 1949. Again, in 1953, members of the Northern Rhodesian branch of the Congress pledged themselves to passive opposition if Federation was imposed, while the African leaders in Nyasaland called for a non-co-operation campaign.

During the summer of 1958, Dr. Hastings Banda, one of the founders of the Congress and one of the chief organizers of the opposition expressed in 1949, returned to Nyasaland to resume active leadership of the Nyasaland African National Congress (NANC), after living in the U.S.A., Britain and Ghana for the previous 30 years. His return was followed by a sharp increase in the activities of the NANC; Dr. Banda himself made a number of speeches regarded by the authorities as inflammatory and leading on Jan. 5, 1959, to his being declared a prohibited immigrant in Southern and Northern Rhodesia.

Serious disturbances occurred in Nyasaland during February – March 1959, causing the proclamation of a state of emergency in the territory, the arrest and deportation of Dr. Banda and many of his supporters and the outlawing of the NANC. The Governor (Sir Robert Armitage) said on March 6 that the prompt action taken against the NANC had disrupted a plot to seize power in Nyasaland by violence which would have involved a massacre of the European population and of Africans friendly to the Government. Similar action was taken by the Governor of Northern Rhodesia (Sir Arthur Benson), who announced on March 12 that he had outlawed the Zambia African National Congress (ZANC) and its affiliated organizations who, he stated, had been waging a campaign of intimidation designed to prevent African electors from exercising their vote freely in the forthcoming territorial elections. [The ZANC was set up in October 1958 by Mr. Kenneth Kaunda as a breakaway group from the Northern Rhodesia African National Congress.]

Sir Edgar Whitehead, Premier of Southern Rhodesia, also took action in view of the "grave situation" which had arisen in Nyasaland; he announced a state of emergency in the territory on Feb. 26 and, at the same time, declared that the four African Congresses in the Federation – Southern Rhodesia African National Congress, NANC, ZANC and NRANC – had all been banned in Southern Rhodesia as illegal organizations and their leading members taken into custody.

A Committee of Inquiry under the chairmanship of Mr. Justice Devlin, set up on March 24, 1958, "to inquire into the recent disturbances in Nyasaland and the events leading up to them", in its report on July 16 concluded that the Nyasaland Government were justified in resorting to a state of emergency since, in the situation then existing, they "had either to act or abdicate" but that there was no evidence of any "murder plot" by the NANC, although that organization had adopted a policy of violence. The report also commented on African opposition to Federation:– "Federation means the domination of Southern Rhodesia; the domination of Southern Rhodesia means the domination of the settler; the domination of the settler means the perpetuation of racial inferiority and of the threat to the African's land; that is the argument. . . ."

[The state of emergency ended in Southern Rhodesia on May 20, 1959, and in Nyasaland on June 15, 1960, while the emergency regulations in Northern Rhodesia expired on Jan. 8, 1960.]

Territorial Constitutional Developments, 1953–60

Northern Rhodesia

The British Government announced on Sept. 22, 1953, that, as a conference on the revision of the Northern Rhodesian Constitution had ended without agreement, it was making known its own proposals for change in the Constitution. These were that the number of European elected members in the Legislative Assembly was being increased from 10 to 12 and of African members (elected by the African Representative Council) from two to four, while the number of official members would be reduced from nine to eight when the Federal Government took up its economic responsibilities. The Executive Council would also be affected by federation, the number of official members being reduced from seven to five, while all four elected members would receive portfolios instead of just two European members. These proposals were criticized by Africans as giving too little, and by Europeans as giving too great a say, to the African. However, they were brought into force and in the first elections under the new rulings on Feb. 18, 1954, the Federal Party won 10 of the 12 seats, the two remaining seats going to Independents.

Further constitutional changes were proposed on March 28, 1958, by the Northern Rhodesian Government, affecting franchise qualifications, representation in the Legislative Council and the composition of the

Executive Council. Two voters' rolls – a "general" and a "special" – were proposed, based on income and education qualifications. The initially lower qualifications for the special roll would be raised over a period of 10 years, in accordance with the anticipated African advance educationally and economically, until they achieved parity with the "general" qualifications, thereby permitting the substitution of a single category of "ordinary" voters. The number of elected members in the Legislative Council would be increased from twelve to eighteen – twelve elected from "ordinary" constituencies covering the principal European residential districts and six from "special" constituencies including the predominantly African areas; four additional seats would be created – two reserved for Africans in the area of the "ordinary" constituencies and two for Europeans in the area of the "special" constituencies; while the number of official members would remain at eight and the six nominated seats responsible for African interests would be abolished. The proportion of unofficial to official ministers in the Executive Council would be reversed, resulting in five "unofficials" and four "officials"; in addition two Assistant Ministers would be appointed, one of whom would be an African.

As no agreement had been reached in the Legislative Council or elsewhere on the original proposals, the U.K. Colonial Secretary (Mr. Alan Lennox-Boyd) published his own modified version of the proposals in September 1958, the principal amendments being (a) that the raising of the "special" roll qualifications should be determined by the rate at which the African population actually became enfranchised; (b) that, although (in accordance with the original proposal) "the total of special votes cast should not count for more than one-third of the ordinary votes cast" in "ordinary" constituencies, the value of ordinary votes should not be similarly limited in other constituencies; and (c) that there should be 10 Ministers including six unofficial ones, four of whom should be Europeans and two Africans.

Although neither set of proposals met with any approval from the NRANC or the Dominion Party, and only some of them were accepted by the UFP, the amended proposals were effective by March 1959. In the first general elections held under the new Constitution on March 20 and April 9, the UFP gained 11 ordinary seats and both African reserved seats, while the Dominion Party gained the remaining ordinary seat, the Central African Party two special seats and both European reserved seats, the NRANC one special seat and Independents the three remaining special seats. [The Central African Party was formed on Feb. 9, 1959, following negotiations between its leader, Sir John Moffat, Mr. Garfield Todd and other "realist-liberals", and followed a policy of the varied races in the Federation working together.]

On Jan. 15, 1960, the Northern Rhodesian Government announced the abolition of the African Representative Council, which had been established in 1946 to advise the Governor on matters directly affecting the African population. In explanation it was stated that the need for special representation had disappeared with the introduction of the new Constitution, which provided for a wider franchise and a system of representation designed to break away from racial representation.

Southern Rhodesia

The first general elections since federation were held on Jan. 27, 1954, and resulted in a sweeping victory for the United Rhodesia Party (URP) which won 26 out of the 30 seats in Parliament. [The URP was formed on Nov. 5, 1953, by the ruling United Party and a substantial section of the (Opposition) Rhodesia Party.] The outgoing Premier, Mr. Garfield Todd, formed a new Cabinet on Jan. 28.

The Tredgold Commission, appointed on April 19, 1956, by the Southern Rhodesian Government to make recommendations on the qualifications required for franchise and for candidates for the Legislative Assembly, in its report (published on March 14, 1957) recommended a common electoral roll divided into "ordinary" voters with higher income and educational qualifications and "special" voters with lower qualifications whose votes would be reduced in value if they exceeded one-third of the total votes cast in any constituency. This report met with strong criticism from the Opposition Dominion Party and a section of the ruling URP, which maintained that it would lead to a "swamping" of the European voter, and from all sections of the African community. However, the Southern Rhodesia Electoral Amendment Act, the details of which were published on June 23, accepted the Tredgold report with certain qualifications; provision was made for the inclusion, in the "special" voters category, of persons with certain educational standards, irrespective of income, whilst the "fractionalization" of special votes' plan (i.e. reduction in the value of these if comprising more than one-third of the total votes cast) was replaced by a provision that the number of special voters must not exceed 20 per cent of the number of ordinary voters.

A political crisis was precipitated on Jan. 11, 1958, by the resignation of all four members of Mr. Garfield Todd's Cabinet following a clash between them and the Premier over racial policy; Mr. Todd, who had been criticized by many Europeans as an "extreme liberal" for advocating

142

excessively rapid social and political advancement for Africans, formed a new Cabinet on Jan. 14. Following the election of Sir Edgar Whitehead as leader of the territorial division of the UFP on Feb. 8, Mr. Todd and his Cabinet resigned, and on Feb. 17 a new Cabinet was formed by Sir Edgar, who became Prime Minister.

As a result of Sir Edgar Whitehead's defeat at a by-election on April 16, 1958, a general election was held on June 5, in which the UFP gained 17 seats and the Dominion Party 13 seats while the United Rhodesia Party failed to win a seat. [It had previously been announced on April 23 that Mr. Garfield Todd had left the UFP and would resuscitate the United Rhodesia Party which had been merged with the UFP in 1957.] Sir Edgar Whitehead formed a new Cabinet on June 11, 1958.

Nyasaland

On Feb. 9, 1955, the Governor of Nyasaland announced proposals for constitutional changes, which were strongly criticized by all three racial groups in the Protectorate. When, after further discussion, no agreement had been reached, the U.K. Colonial Secretary, Mr. Lennox-Boyd, announced on June 15 that the proposals would nevertheless be implemented.

These changes provided for an increase in the membership of the Legislative Council from 21 to 23, 12 of whom would be officials, five "unofficial" Africans and six "unofficial" non-Africans. This compared with the existing system of three African, five European and one Asian unofficial members. The existing system of nominating European and Asian members would be replaced by an electoral system; the selection of African members – through Protectorate and provincial African councils – would remain as before.

The Bill providing for the implementation of the above proposals was passed on Sept. 6, 1955; in the first general elections to be held on March 15, 1956, Europeans gained all six non-African seats while members of the Nyasaland African National Congress, which advocated withdrawal from the Federation, were returned for three of the African seats.

Sir Robert Armitage, Governor of Nyasaland, announced further constitutional changes on Aug. 24, 1959, which took effect immediately. The main proposals were (a) that the membership of the Legislative Council would be increased by the nomination of two African members by the Governor and the appointment of two more official members; and (b) that two African members of the Legislative Council would be appointed to the

Executive Council, on which Africans had not previously been represented.

At a conference on constitutional reform in Nyasaland, held in London from July 25 to Aug. 4, 1960, agreement was reached on a new Constitution with the following principal points: (*a*) The Executive Council, composed of 13 members presided over by the Governor, would include three ex-officio and five unofficial members of whom three would be chosen from among the members of the Legislative Council elected on the lower of the two proposed electoral rolls [see below], and two from among those elected on the higher roll; (*b*) the Legislative Council would consist of 28 unofficial members plus the three ex-officio and two nominated official members of the Executive Council; of the elected members, 20 would be elected in one set of constituencies by voters who satisfied lower qualifications, and eight in another set of constituencies by voters satisfying higher qualifications; (*c*) there would be two electoral rolls based on monetary and educational qualifications, one having higher standards than the other.

The Monckton Commission, 1960

An advisory Commission, under the chairmanship of Viscount Monckton of Brenchley, was established during 1959, to prepare for the proposed 1960 review of the Federal Constitution, and consisted of 11 U.K. members (including six Privy Councillors) as well as two members from other Commonwealth countries and 13 from the Federation, including five Africans.

The Commission was accepted by Sir Roy Welensky and by the Southern Rhodesia Parliament and Northern Rhodesia Legislative Council, although in the latter all seven African members walked out in protest against the composition of the Commission.

African reaction to the Commission was divided; three African leaders in voluntary exile from Southern Rhodesia and Nyasaland – Mr. Kanyama Chiume, publicity secretary of the NANC, Mr. Joshua Nkomo, president of the SRANC, and Mr. Orton Chirwa, president of the Malawi Congress Party [a nationalist party founded on Oct. 1, 1959] – issued a statement in London on Dec. 10 "completely deploring" the composition and terms of reference of the Commission, while on Dec. 21 Mr. Harry Nkumbula, president of the NRANC, announced that his party would boycott the Commission because its terms of reference excluded secession and because the Africans lacked confidence in its members. On the other hand two prominent Nyasa leaders appealed to Africans to give evidence to the Commission – Mr. T. D. T.

Banda, president of the Nyasaland Congress Liberation Party (the rival organization to the NANC) and Mr. J. R. N. Chinyama, the senior African member of the Nyasaland Legislative Council.

In their report published on Oct. 11, 1960, the members of the Monckton Commission expressed the opinion that the break-up of the Federation at that crucial point in the history of Africa would be an admission that there was no hope of survival for any multi-racial society on the African continent and would, economically, lead to hardship, poverty and distress. Nevertheless they found that the existing form of Federal association was too much disliked by Africans, whose opposition had "hardened to a pitch of distrust and hatred that would be impossible to dispel without fundamental changes". The Commission recommended various changes to remove African objections, including the abandonment of the word "Federation" in favour of a new name and a recommendation to the British Government that any territory should be permitted to secede from the Federation if its inhabitants so desired, after a stated period (five, seven, or more years), or on the attainment of self-government.

The report met with varied response from the Federation and from the British Government.

Sir Roy Welensky declared on Oct. 11 that the recommendations for secession were in direct conflict with previous assurances on the Commission's terms of reference given to the Federal Government and himself; in addition he stated that the right of a Territory to secede from the Federation would "sound the death-knell of the Federation" and that he was therefore "compelled utterly to reject this recommendation". Dr. Hastings Banda declared on the same day, "we want secession and nothing but secession. So far as we are concerned, the Federation is dead. All that remains now is to bury it . . .". Mr. Macmillan stated, on the other hand, in the House of Commons on Oct. 25: "It is not a question of accepting [the report] or declining it; it is a question of discussing it with all those concerned. . . ."

Break-up of the Federation, 1960—63

During the three years between the publication of the Monckton Commission report and the dissolution of the Federation on Dec. 31, 1963, the two Protectorates moved along the road to internal self-government under majority rule whilst Southern Rhodesia, still ruled by Europeans, fought unsuccessfully for her independence. The Federal Premier, Sir Roy Welensky, was one of the most vocal opponents of secession and engaged in continuous conflict with the British Government on this subject.

One of the detailed recommendations which the Monckton Commission made was that a new Constitution for Northern Rhodesia should be negotiated and implemented "without awaiting the full revision of the Federal structure". A conference with this aim in view was held in London from Dec. 19, 1960, to Feb. 17, 1961, but failed to reach any agreement. In view of this result the British Government's plans for constitutional reform were published on Feb. 21, 1961. These provided for a Legislative Council composed of members elected from three types of constituencies containing voters on an Upper Roll, voters on a Lower Roll, and voters on both rolls combined. Members elected in the third type of constituency – the "national" constituencies – would have to receive the same prescribed minimum percentage of the votes cast on each roll. The franchise proposals, by extending the qualifications for both the Upper and Lower Rolls, would result in approximately 2,000 additional Africans being eligible for registration on the Upper Roll, while the adjustments of the Lower Roll franchise would give the vote to some 70,000 Africans.

These proposals, however, were rejected by Europeans and Africans alike in Northern Rhodesia. Sir Roy Welensky issued a statement immediately before the proposals were published, when it was apparent that no agreement had been reached in the Constitutional Conference, accusing the British Government, by implication, of capitulating to the "vicious" forces of African nationalism and declaring that the UFP was determined "that the reins of Government should remain in the hands of responsible people".

As agreed in talks between Mr. Macmillan and Sir Roy Welensky during the latter's visit in March 1961 to the London Conference of Commonwealth Prime Ministers, the Governor of Northern Rhodesia (Sir Evelyn Hone) had meetings during April-June with leaders of the three European parties and representatives of the Asian community. On the basis of these discussions Sir Evelyn presented his detailed recommendations on constitutional reform to Mr. Iain Macleod (U.K. Colonial Secretary), who issued these on June 26, 1961, as a White Paper, the British Government having accepted them.

The new proposals were based on the original plan published in February and accepted the idea of three types of constituencies and the suggested numbers – 15 – of members from each type; in addition it was recommended that there should be seven double-member and one-single member national constituencies. Sir Evelyn also suggested that "the minimum support required by a candidate in order to qualify for election [in a "national" constituency] should be expressed as 12½ per cent or 400 votes (whichever is the less) of the European votes cast in the election and [the same proportion] of the African votes cast in the election. . . . This recommendation gives practical effect to the concept that national members should be obliged to seek support from voters of both races [first mentioned in the February plan] ." There would still be two electoral rolls, both being open to voters of all races; Sir Evelyn made a further recommendation that a voter qualified to register on the Upper Roll would not be at liberty to register on the Lower Roll.

Reaction to these proposals was mixed; Sir Roy Welensky described them as "a reasonably workable instrument", while the African parties in the Protectorate, in particular the United National Independence Party (UNIP), rejected the plans. [UNIP was formed towards the end of 1959 by members of the banned Zambian African National Congress and dissident members of the Northern Rhodesian African National Congress. Mr. Kenneth Kaunda, formerly leader of ZANC, was elected president of UNIP on Jan. 30, 1960.] Mr. Kaunda announced on July 9 his intention of waging a passive resistance campaign against the Constitution but, despite this call for non-violent action, widespread disorders fomented by UNIP members occurred from mid-July to the end of October 1961, this campaign being strongly condemned by the ANC.

On Feb. 28, 1962, Mr. Reginald Maudling (U.K. Colonial Secretary) announced, in the House of Commons, revised and "final" constitutional proposals for Northern Rhodesia with two technical changes being made in the White Paper electoral proposals of June 1961: in qualifying for a national seat the figure of 12½ per cent was reduced to 10 per cent and the numerical alternative of 400 votes abolished. Despite renewed opposition by Sir Roy Welensky and leaders of the ANC and UNIP the new Constitution was made effective from Sept. 11, 1962.

In the first general elections under the new Constitution on Oct. 30, 1962, the UFP led by Mr. H. J. Roberts gained 13 of the 15 Upper Roll seats and two National seats, UNIP led by Mr. Kenneth Kaunda gained 12 Lower Roll seats, one Upper Roll seat and one National seat (won by a pro-UNIP Independent), and the ANC led by Mr. Nkumbula gained three Lower Roll seats and two National seats. The Liberal Party, formed by the merger of the Northern Rhodesian division of the Central African Party with other liberal groups and led by Sir John Moffat, failed to win any seats and announced its disbandment on Nov. 5, recommending its followers to support UNIP. By-elections for the remaining 10 national seats, where no candidates qualified, and one Upper Roll seat, where the UNIP candidate had died before polling day, were held on Dec. 10; the UFP gained the Upper Roll seat while the ANC won two national seats, the other eight national seats remaining unfilled. On Dec. 12, the ANC confirmed that they would enter into a coalition with UNIP to form the first African-dominated Government in the territory, the final strength being 16 UFP, 14 UNIP and seven ANC members.

Meanwhile developments in Nyasaland were moving towards the achievement of internal self-government. Under the new Constitution [see page 144] which had become effective on July 4, 1961, elections were held on Aug. 15, resulting in an overwhelming victory for the Malawi Congress Party led by Dr. Hastings Banda, which won 22 of the 28 elected seats and received 94 per cent of the total vote.

The remaining six seats, all on the Upper Roll, were divided between the UFP (five) and Independents (one). Dr. Banda described the result as a direct mandate to secede from the Federation as soon as possible.

Sir Roy Welensky announced his intention on March 8, 1962, to call a general election and "ask for a mandate to prevent the break-up of the Federation". These elections, held on April 27, were boycotted by all the African parties in the Federation and also by all the European Opposition Parties with the exception of the extreme right-wing Rhodesian Republican Party. 40 UFP candidates were returned unopposed, while 14 UFP candidates and one Independent were elected; as the remaining four members were specially elected or nominated, there was no official Opposition. [On April 19, 1963, the UFP announced its reorganization in four separate political organizations – the Federal Party in the Federation, the Rhodesia National Party in Southern Rhodesia, the National Progress Party in Northern Rhodesia and the Nyasaland Constitutional Party in Nyasaland.]

The final stages of the dissolution of the Federation began on Feb. 1, 1963, when Nyasaland achieved internal self-government with the coming into effect of the first stage of further constitutional reforms, on which complete agreement had been reached at a conference in London from Nov. 12–23, 1962. Mr. Richard A. Butler, U.K. Minister of Central African Affairs [see below], had announced on Dec. 19 in the House of Commons that the British Government accepted in principle that Nyasaland should be allowed to withdraw from the Federation; this action was immediately denounced as "an act of treachery" by Sir Roy Welensky. In doing this Sir Roy quoted extracts from the minutes of the 1953 Conference on the establishment of the Federation including *inter alia:* "The general view expressed by delegates was that . . . any proposal to terminate the Constitution could only be put into effect with the concurrence of the Federal Government and of the three Territorial Governments, and of H.M. Government in the United Kingdom . . .": he then said: "By its action today, the British Government . . . have gone back on the most solemn understandings and intentions." [On March 15, 1962, it was announced in London that the U.K. Home Secretary, Mr. Butler, was to assume responsibility for Central African affairs as head of a new Central African Office taking over the responsibilities of the Secretaries of State for the Colonies and for Commonwealth Relations insofar as they related to the Rhodesias and Nyasaland.]

The second part of the new Nyasaland Constitution came into force on May 9, 1963; on Sept. 27, after talks between Dr. Banda (Prime Minister), Mr. Butler and Sir Glyn Jones (Governor of Nyasaland), it was announced that Nyasaland would be granted independence by July 6, 1964. [For a summary of events after independence see MALAWI, page 151.]

Meanwhile discussions on the future relationship of the three territories after Nyasaland's secession became effective were held in the early months of 1963. Mr. Butler, after a visit to the Federation for informal talks with political leaders from Jan. 19 to Feb. 3, issued a statement on Feb. 3 to the effect that he had found "a general view" in Central Africa that a new form of association would be preferable to the existing one, as there was wider agreement on the basis of an economic association than any other.

On Feb. 13, 1963, a White Paper was published in London dealing with the question of whether any pledges had been given not to consider secession of any Territory from the Federation without the consent of the Federal as well as of the three Territorial Governments; this followed Sir Roy Welensky's accusations in December [see above] and declared: "The statements made [in 1953] cannot be construed as constituting a pledge by the British Ministers to the effect that no change would be made by the United Kingdom without consent of the four [Central African] Governments." In reply to the White Paper, Sir Roy repeated, on Feb. 16, that the Federal Government adhered to its view that "valid pledges against secession were made and these pledges have been broken by the British Government".

Further discussions on the future of Central Africa were held in London on March 21–29 between Mr. Butler and the three Territorial Governments. On March 29 Mr. Butler issued a statement that H. M. Government "accept that none of the territories can be kept in the

Federation against its will and . . . therefore accept the principle that any territory which so wishes must be allowed to secede".

This announcement immediately aroused comment from the Federal and Territorial authorities. In a statement the same evening Sir Roy Welensky declared *inter alia:* "Under threat from the Northern Rhodesian elected Ministers the United Kingdom has, before any discussion has taken place about future relationships, decided one of the massive questions which are for consideration. . . .

"I have always said that the U.K. Government had the legal right to dissolve the Federation by Act of Parliament, although this contravened solemn pledges and conventions entered into in the past. If the Parliament at Westminster are prepared to endorse the decision to break up the Federation, then I . . . [shall] declare to H.M. Government that I will not co-operate in the dissolution of the Federation unless the vital interests of the people of Northern Rhodesia and Southern Rhodesia and the Federal citizens in Nyasaland are taken care of. These are the vital interests, and I do not state them in any special order of priority: (1) that Southern Rhodesia be granted its independence; (2) that the new Constitution for Northern Rhodesia protects the interests of the European community, the various regional interests of the African communities . . . and in particular the special status of Barotseland.

"When I have had assurances on these matters my Government will work to bring about the new order that must now take the place of the present Federal agreement."

Mr. Winston Field, the Premier of Southern Rhodesia, stated: "Southern Rhodesia will have been seceded from. The Federation is at an end. We consider that this means we are entitled to the independence we would have had by 1955 had federation not come about." [For details of events in Southern Rhodesia after 1960 see RHODESIA, page 167.]

A statement issued jointly by Mr. Kaunda and Mr. Nkumbula, the Northern Rhodesian leaders, claimed that the 3,000,000 African people of Northern Rhodesia were on the way to "freedom and independence".

Mr. Butler announced in the U.K. House of Commons on June 18 that the Federal Government and the Governments of Northern and Southern Rhodesia had agreed to attend a conference, to begin on June 28 at the Victoria Falls, to discuss "the orderly dissolution of the Federation and the consequential problems therein". In his opening speech at this conference on June 28 Mr. Butler stressed the full agreement existing among all delegates that arrangements should be made for the orderly and speedy transfer of Federal responsibilities to the Territories. Agreement was reached *inter alia* on the timetable for the dissolution of the Federation, the target date being set at Dec. 31, 1963, conditional on the settlement of important general issues.

The Rhodesia and Nyasaland Bill, an enabling measure to start the process of dissolution, was given an unopposed third reading in the British House of Commons on July 16, and in the House of Lords on July 25.

The Federation was officially dissolved as planned on Dec. 31, 1963; this immediately preceded the achievement of internal self-government on Jan. 3, 1964, by Northern Rhodesia and the success of UNIP in the elections for the Northern Rhodesian Legislative Assembly. [For subsequent events in Northern Rhodesia see ZAMBIA, page 154.]

MALAWI

Area: 36,145 sq. miles.
Population 1969 (estimate): 4,398,000.
Capital: Zomba (20,000).
Official languages: English and Chichewa.
Chief products: Tea, tobacco, maize, groundnuts.

Malawi, the former British Protectorate of Nyasaland, achieved independence on July 6, 1964, as a sovereign State within the Commonwealth, owing allegiance to Queen Elizabeth II, after 73 years of British rule. From 1953–63 Malawi was a member of the Federation of Rhodesia and Nyasaland.

Elections to the National Assembly had been held in May 1964; candidates for 50 seats were elected by voters on a general roll while the remaining three members were chosen by the European community on a special roll with the object of ensuring European minority representation. Apart from the racial qualification of the latter, the franchise was extended to all persons over 21 with continuous residence in the country for two years. All 53 members were returned unopposed, the 50 general-roll candidates being nominated by the Malawi Congress Party [see page 144] and the three special-roll candidates by the Nyasaland Constitutional Party [see page 148].

On the second anniversary of independence the country became a Republic within the Commonwealth, Dr. Hastings Banda, Prime Minister since before independence, being elected the first President in terms of the Republican Constitution.

This Constitution stated that Malawi would be a one-party State, with the Malawi Congress Party as the sole political party, and that the Head of State and of the Government would be an executive President, with no Vice-President or Prime Minister. The President would appoint the members of the Cabinet, including up to three Ministers who were not elected M.P.s, and would be C.-in-C. of the Armed Forces. Two provisions in the existing Constitution which were not retained in the Republican Constitution were the Bill of Rights and the special electoral roll for Europeans. The President would, however, nominate at least three, but not more than five, European members of Parliament at his discretion.

The "Chipembere Rebellion"

In 1964 a Cabinet crisis occurred when five Ministers were dismissed on Sept. 7. On the following day Dr. Banda described them as men "of avarice and ambition", who would have murdered him "in cold blood", and accused them of having tried to stir up the people against him under the guidance of "the steering hand of the Chinese Ambassador in Dar-es-Salaam". The National Assembly, with the five dissident Ministers participating, gave Dr. Banda a vote of confidence on Sept. 9.

However, following the crisis, Dr. Banda was faced with resistance by rebel groups in various parts of the country supporting the former Ministers, notably Mr. Henry B. Masauko Chipembere. The Prime Minister took far-reaching measures against his opponents and introduced increasingly stringent security legislation which gave wider powers to the security forces. In addition the Assembly approved on Oct. 30, 1964, a Constitution Amendment Bill which gave new powers to the Premier to detain anyone "when such detention is reasonably required in the interests of defence, public safety or public order"; to dismiss any member of Parliament who ceased to represent the party for which he was elected; to veto any application for Malawian citizenship; to appoint as Ministers persons who were not Members of Parliament and to place the Director of Public Prosecutions directly under the authority of the Attorney General. A Bill establishing a Malawi Army was announced on Dec. 29, 1964, and a Bill subjecting the Malawi Young Pioneers to the orders and control of police officers while engaged on security operations on March 22, 1965. Military operations against the followers of Mr. Chipembere and another dissident Minister, Mr. M. W. K. Chiume, continued throughout 1965; on Feb. 1, 1966, Medson Silombela, a rebel leader condemned to death in November 1965, was hanged publicly in Zomba.

Measures against opponents of Dr. Banda's regime continued until by the end of 1969 there appeared to be no articulate opposition; the

Pan-African Democratic Party led by Mr. Chipembere in exile was in complete disarray. Eight men were sentenced to death on conviction of treason on June 14, 1968, while the Jehovah's Witnesses' sect had been outlawed as a subversive organization in October 1967.

Increase in President's Powers — Trade and Diplomatic Relations with South Africa

In November 1969 a Local Courts (Amendment) Bill and Constitution (Amendment) Bill were passed, under which President Banda was empowered, firstly, to authorize traditional African courts to try all types of criminal cases and to impose the death penalty and, secondly, to deny the right of appeal to the High Court against sentences passed by such traditional courts — a right formerly guaranteed by the Constitution. As a result of this legislation the Chief Justice, Sir Peter Watkin-Williams, and three High Court Judges announced their resignation on Nov. 22, declaring: "We cannot believe that justice will be adequately safe-guarded." It was officially announced on Oct. 5, 1970, that Mr. James Skinner, former Chief Justice of Zambia, had been appointed Chief Justice of Malawi. [See ZAMBIA, page 155.]

Malawi became the first Black African country to conclude a trade agreement with South Africa; this was announced by the South African Minister of Economic Affairs on March 13, 1967.

> President Banda, commenting on the agreement, declared in the Malawi Parliament on March 29 that he was unmoved by threats of isolation or expulsion from the OAU. He also said: "South Africa is militarily the strongest power on our continent. No single or combination of African States can ever hope to expel or obliterate South Africa from the face of Africa. It would be wrong for the United Nations to do so for political reasons. Other African leaders are pinning their hopes on Eastern Powers as allies against South Africa. I have no such delusion."

Formal diplomatic relations, to be established by Jan. 1, 1968, were announced on Sept. 10, 1967. These two decisions on relations with South Africa were followed by an increasingly greater number of South African economic activities in Malawi, including the granting of two major loans to the Republic in 1968, notably for the building of a new capital at Lilongwe, and by a visit to Malawi by Mr. B. J. Vorster, the South African Prime Minister, in May 1970.

ZAMBIA

Area: 288,130 sq. miles.
Population 1968: 4,144,000.
Capital: Lusaka (238,000).
Other important towns: Kitwe (179,000), Ndola (151,000).
Official language: English.
Chief product: Copper.

Constitutional Developments, 1964–70

Zambia, formerly a British Protectorate and a member of the Federation of Rhodesia and Nyasaland until its dissolution on Dec. 31, 1963, achieved independence as a Republic within the Commonwealth on Oct. 24, 1964. Formerly known as Northern Rhodesia, the country had achieved internal self-government on Jan. 3, 1964. Mr. Kenneth Kaunda, Prime Minister since Jan. 23, became the Republic's first President.

The achievement of independence was complicated by the question of the status of the British Protectorate of Barotseland; agreement was reached following discussions in London from May 15–18, 1964, between the Litunga (Ruler) of Barotseland and the British and Northern Rhodesian Governments, to the effect that Barotseland would form an integral part of Zambia. A further complication was the fact that the country's mineral rights – one of its chief assets – were vested, not in the British Crown, but in the private British South Africa Company; after considerable discussion it was agreed that Zambia should take over these rights and that Zambia and Britain should each pay the company £2 million by way of compensation.

The Republican Constitution included the following provisions:– The President would be Head of State and would be elected by the registered electorate at the same time as the members of the National Assembly; the Cabinet, presided over by the President, would consist of a Vice-President, who would also be the Leader of the House in Parliament, and not more than 14 Ministers, appointed by the President; Parliament would consist of the President and the National Assembly of 75 elected members plus up to five members nominated by the President.

Presidential and parliamentary elections were held on Dec. 19, 1968; under a constitutional change approved by Parliament on Dec. 19, 1967, the voting age had been lowered from 21 to 18 and the National Assembly enlarged from 75 to 105 elected members, the President retaining the right to add five nominated members. President Kaunda was re-elected by more than half the maximum possible number of votes, whilst his party, the United National Independence Party (UNIP — see page 147), won 81 seats in Parliament, the African National Congress (ANC), 23 seats and Independents one seat. The National Progress Party [see page 148], which in the previous Parliament had held 10 seats, based on a special electoral roll for whites, did not retain any of these as the roll became defunct at the end of Zambia's first Parliament.

In a referendum held on June 17, 1969, the Government sought the electorate's approval of a change in the Constitution, whereby Parliament would be empowered to amend by a two-thirds majority any of the entrenched clauses in the Constitution without holding a referendum in each case. The clauses concerned provided safeguards for fundamental human rights; the right to own property without fear of confiscation by the Government without due compensation; and the independence of the judiciary. The Government was successful, receiving a "yes" vote of over 53 per cent.

A conflict arose between President Kaunda and the judiciary, after sentences on two Portuguese soldiers, accused of illegally entering Zambia, were quashed on appeal by Mr. Justice Evans on July 3, 1969, in the Lusaka High Court. Giving this decision, Mr. Justice Evans commented that the incident was "trivial, and a mere technical breach", the two soldiers having been "enticed" or requested by a Zambian immigration official to cross into Zambian territory. President Kaunda stated on July 14 that he found that these comments had been politically motivated to discredit the Government. Questioning whether the judiciary was "working in the interests of a foreign Power" he called for an explanation from the Chief Justice, Mr. James J. Skinner, who totally rejected President Kaunda's complaint. As a result of demonstrations demanding the dismissal of the Chief Justice and Mr. Justice Evans, and of threats on their lives, both men left the country on July 17 and 25, respectively. President Kaunda called for an end to the demonstrations while promising the swift Zambianization of the courts. [Mr. Skinner subsequently resigned and was succeeded by Mr. Brian Doyle, according to an official statement issued in Lusaka on Sept. 23, 1969.]

Internal Security

The United National Independence Party (UNIP), led by President Kaunda, has commanded an absolute majority in Parliament ever since independence, yet the President has repeatedly declared (e.g. on Jan. 17, 1965) that, although he favoured a one-party system, it would not and could not be forced on the people.

Difficulties arose for President Kaunda's regime from time to time partly as the result of activities of the African National Congress (ANC) — the official Oppositon — and of certain religious sects, as well as of dissension within UNIP, and partly arising from the fact that the 50,000 whites in Zambia, largely employed in the copper mines, included many Rhodesians and South Africans unable or unwilling to adapt themselves to the policies of a UNIP Government.

A report by a Commission of Inquiry into disturbances involving followers of the Lumpa Church published on Sept. 21, 1965, blamed the Lumpa Church and provincial officials of UNIP for having caused the unrest; it absolved the party's national leadership and President Kaunda from any responsibility. The Lumpa Church, an exclusive African sect founded in 1955 by Mrs. Alice Lenshina, was characterized by an attitude of intolerance and intimidation, in particular in preventing its followers from being recruited by UNIP, and serious disturbances had occurred towards the end of July and early in August 1964. Immediately before the report's publication, on Sept. 17, the National Assembly had extended for a further six months, in a modified form, emergency regulations enforced in the northern areas where the Church had been active.

President Kaunda had stated on April 11, 1965, that the security of the country was his "first responsibility", and in this context his Government subsequently took a number of administrative measures.

Early in 1966 a member of the British High Commission was declared *persona non grata* and several journalists were expelled. On June 16 it was disclosed that the Leader of the Opposition in the Rhodesian Legislative Assembly, Mr. Chad Chipunza, had been declared a prohibited immigrant in Zambia. President Kaunda dismissed seventeen European police officers on July 14, having decided, according to an official statement, that the "police security forces are not in a sufficient state of preparedness to deal with the present situation, caused by Rhodesia's unilateral declaration of independence"; finally, on Oct. 27, the Government served orders on 25 non-Zambians to leave the country within 24 hours, all of them being accused of racialism or of causing industrial unrest. In the same year on Feb. 22, the President had warned that the Government would not tolerate any situation which would bring about "industrial chaos" nor would it meet any unreasonable demands; this followed a series of unofficial strikes by white miners over terms of employment and pension funds. On Sept. 22, 1966, President Kaunda's powers to enforce special security regulations and to introduce new measures were extended for a further six months by Parliament.

President Kaunda alleged on April 30, 1967, that Zambia had for some time been exposed to efforts by the Smith regime to obtain information on political and economic matters from Zambia and "to create a climate of doubt and despondency among the people of Zambia".

Earlier, on April 13, a number of British citizens, allegedly Rhodesian agents, were detained under the Preservation of Public Security Regulations; others were served with deportation orders, whilst a few left the country secretly for Rhodesia.

During 1968 President Kaunda was faced with dissension within UNIP and with further incidents endangering internal security. Disagreement among the leaders of UNIP came to a head at a meeting of the party's national council in Lusaka early in February 1968, when President Kaunda, after castigating party officials for allowing tribalism to split the organization, announced his resignation on Feb. 4; however, after "anguished" discussions, he agreed to resume the presidency.

Dissatisfaction amongst UNIP members had contributed to the formation in 1967 of the United Party by Mr. Nalumino Mundia. Following many months of inter-party strife between UNIP and the United Party, an open clash occurred on Aug. 13, 1968, near the Congo border, in Chililabombwe, resulting in six deaths. The next day (Aug. 14) President Kaunda stated that the United Party had been declared unlawful because his security intelligence had revealed that its members were engaged in acts threatening public security and peace.

Economic measures against the eight Opposition M.P.s elected in Barotse Province in the elections of Dec. 19, 1968 [see above], were taken by the Government; President Kaunda, announcing this on Dec. 23, 1968, added that he would ensure that nothing these eight would say would become effective and that he would not allow Barotse Province "to have enemies within it". Measures of a similar nature were taken by local authorities against ANC supporters, apparently without the approval of the Government. At the opening of the new National Assembly on Jan. 22, the Speaker announced that he could not accord recognition to the ANC as the official Opposition on the grounds that it could form "neither a quorum to execute the business of the House nor a Government".

Widespread unrest and acts of violence largely caused by local organizers and followers of UNIP, and directed against ANC followers and other political dissidents, especially the sect of Jehovah's Witnesses, continued after the elections into the early months of 1969.

Further clashes between UNIP and ANC followers took place in the Mumbwa and Livingstone districts between December 1969 and February 1970.

State Participation in Industry and Trade

Far-reaching political and economical measures were announced by President Kaunda on Aug. 11, 1969. They involved the assumption of majority control in mining companies by the Government through its Industrial Development Corporation (Indeco), a new taxation formula for the mines based on profitability and new industrial projects to be carried out by Italian firms.

The economic plan was a continuation of the process set in motion on April 19, 1968, when the President had announced the proposed acquisition of majority control by the Government, through Indeco, in 26 large companies. Dr. Kaunda had stated, however, on April 23, 1968, that he did not visualize total State control or nationalization of private enterprise; expressed the hope that there would be no necessity to nationalize the copper-mining industry; and added that the object of these reforms was to put "Zambian business firmly in Zambian hands".

Following the Zambian Government's acquisition of a 51 per cent interest in the country's copper mining industry with effect from Jan. 1, 1970, President Kaunda announced on Nov. 10, 1970, that (a) the State would acquire a 51 per cent interest in all private banks and in certain industrial companies and (b) building societies and insurance companies would be nationalized. Such State participation would be controlled by the Mining and Industrial Development Corporation (established on April 1, 1970) which would have two wholly-owned subsidiaries: (a) Indeco [see above], and (b) the Mining Development Corporation (Mindeco).

In addition the President stated that by the beginning of January 1972 the retail trade would have to be in the hands of Zambians or State-owned companies, and he gave all expatriates engaged in wholesale trade in Zambia 14 months in which to close their businesses or sell them to Zambians.

The Effect of UDI in Rhodesia on Zambia

On the unilateral declaration of independence by Rhodesia on Nov. 11, 1965 [see page 174], a state of emergency in Zambia was declared by

President Kaunda who, on Nov. 14, denounced Mr. Ian Smith as a "rebel and traitor".

The President disclosed on Nov. 17 that he had asked for British troops to be sent to Zambia to defend the Kariba Dam, situated on the Rhodesian border and supplying power for the copperbelt; although the British Prime Minister (Mr. Harold Wilson) announced on Dec. 1 that military aid – in the form of a squadron of jet fighters to be stationed at Ndola – to Zambia would be under "unequivocal British command" and "purely for defensive purposes", no agreement was reached on the despatch of British ground forces to Zambia, as Dr. Kaunda insisted that they should be stationed on the Rhodesian side of the frontier, to protect the Kariba power installations, as well as on Zambian territory, and the British Government did not agree to do so.

In regard to help for the Zambian economy, it was announced in Lusaka on Dec. 19, 1965, that President Kaunda and Mr. Cledwyn Hughes (then U.K. Minister of State for Commonwealth Relations) had reached full agreement on measures to aid Zambia to overcome the effects of sanctions against Rhodesia, and especially the ban on exports of oil from Rhodesia to Zambia imposed by the Smith regime. Britain agreed to bear the cost of an airlift of oil supplies and would also spend £3½ million to aid surface routes other than those through Rhodesia to bring oil to Zambia.

The Canadian Government agreed to contribute transport facilities, whilst the United States Government, in a joint communiqué with Zambia on Dec. 27, announced that it would make a "significant contribution" to the airlift of oil supplies. After petrol rationing had been introduced in Zambia on Dec. 22, 1965, the oil airlift continued until May 28, 1966; the total lifted exceeded 8,300 tons and had enabled Zambia to build up stocks, whilst for future supplies she would rely on surface transport.

Zambia's fuel crisis was ended on July 22, 1968, when an oil pipeline from Dar-es-Salaam to Ndola in the Zambian copperbelt (built by a subsidiary of the Italian State-owned ENI) went into operation.

Relations between Britain and Zambia over the next three years were dominated by the Zambian Government's continued demand for the use of force against the Smith regime in Rhodesia and for increased financial aid to Zambia in compensation for losses suffered as a result of Rhodesian UDI – British contingency aid for the latter purpose amounting to £7,000,000.

On Nov. 15, 1966, in the U.N. General Assembly, President Kaunda accused the British Government of "seeking to disengage from the Rhodesian problem" and to leave the fate of Rhodesia's Africans "at the mercy of a ruthless minority". An agreement was signed, nevertheless, in Lusaka on Feb. 1, 1967, making provision for British aid.

After talks between President Kaunda and the British Government in London on July 16–20, 1968, President Kaunda claimed on July 21 that the British Government had agreed to give more aid to Zambia.

The effect of UDI on the Zambian economy varied over the years immediately following the Rhodesian declaration. In April 1966 the Zambian economy was strengthened by an increase in the price of copper (April 24), the announcement of a new export tax (April 26) and the discovery of large coal deposits. However, between July and November 1966, the economy, in particular the copper mines, became increasingly affected by difficulties arising out of the sanctions imposed against the Smith regime; copper production fell to three-quarters of the normal figure, largely because of the shortage of coal imports needed for refining.

On July 22, 1966, the Zambian Government authorized resumption of copper exports via Rhodesia until alternative routes were sufficiently developed; active steps were taken in 1966 to open up new trade routes to the north and east.

As a first step, the road from the copperbelt to the port of Dar-es-Salaam (Tanzania) was speedily developed early in 1966. A National Transport Corporation set up in March 1966 reached agreement with the Italian Fiat Motor Company for an initial supply of about 800 trucks for use on this road.

It was announced in Lusaka on Aug. 21, 1968, that a Tanzania-Zambia Railway authority had been formed to handle the affairs of a proposed railway line from Zambia to Dar-es-Salaam, to be built by Communist China. The line, which would start from Kapiri Mposhi (135 miles north of Lusaka), was expected to take five years to build, while its estimated cost was about £120,000,000 (excluding rolling stock). According to an official announcement in Dar-es-Salaam on July 12, 1970, China was to grant Tanzania an interest-free loan of about £169,000,000 (at the prevailing exchange rates) in connection with the proposed line.

Details of a four-year development plan were published on Oct. 31, 1966; the object of this plan was to lay "the foundations for Zambia's future prosperity by increasing rural productivity, by creating 100,000 new jobs and by diversifying the present copper-bound economy".

In order to make Zambia independent of the electric power supply from the power station on the southern shore of Lake Kariba (in Rhodesia), the construction of a new hydro-electric scheme was begun by a Yugoslav enterprise at Kafue in 1968, and a World Bank loan of

$40,000,000 was obtained in July 1970 for the construction of a power station on the north bank of Lake Kariba (i.e. on Zambian territory).

GAMBIA

Area: 4,000 sq. miles.
Population 1968 (estimate): 360,000.
Capital: Bathurst (30,000).
Official language: English.
Chief product: Groundnuts.

After an association with Britain lasting over 350 years, the Crown Colony of Gambia became an independent sovereign State within the Commonwealth on Feb. 17, 1965.

In the first general elections since independence held on May 17–26, 1966, the ruling People's Progressive Party (PPP), led by Sir Dauda Jawara, the Gambia's Prime Minister since the country had obtained internal self-government in June 1962, obtained 24 out of the 32 seats in the House of Representatives. The remaining eight seats were won by the opposition United Party led by Mr. Pierre N'Jie. In addition to the 32 directly elected members there were four members elected by the Chiefs, two non-voting members appointed by the Governor-General, and the Attorney General, who was also a non-voting member. In April 1968 the House approved a Bill increasing the members to be nominated by the Government from two to four and making the office of Attorney General a ministerial position.

In September 1968 four former Ministers (expelled from the PPP) formed a new party, the People's Progressive Alliance (PPA), and as a result of changes in allegiance the distribution of seats in the House in December 1969 was PPP 21, United Party seven and PPA four.

A resolution that Gambia should become a Republic within the Commonwealth, although approved by the House of Representatives on June 2, 1965, had not been given the required two-thirds' majority vote in a national referendum in November 1965. However, following a second referendum, in which 84,968 votes were cast for republican status and 35,683 against, Gambia was proclaimed a Republic within the Commonwealth on April 24, 1970, and Sir Dauda Jawara became its first President, replacing the Queen as Head of State.

BOTSWANA

Area: 220,000 sq. miles.
Population 1969 (estimate): 629,000.
Capital: Gaborone (30,000).
Official language: English.
Chief products: Diamonds, manganese, cattle.

The former British Protectorate of Bechuanaland achieved independent status as the Republic of Botswana within the Commonwealth on Sept. 29–30, 1966, thus ending eighty-one years of British rule. Sir Seretse Khama, the former Prime Minister, was sworn in as the first President of Botswana during the independence ceremony, under one of the provisions of the proposed Constitution outlined by him on Dec. 13, 1965. This was that the existing Prime Minister and Deputy Prime Minister would automatically become President and Vice-President but that at the end of his first term of office the President would be elected by the members of the Legislative Assembly.

Other provisions of the Constitution were that the President would be empowered to force any expatriate administrative officers to retire in favour of local men, and that the franchise would be held by adults of all races, but dual citizenship would not be allowed.

The country had been given self-government under an "advanced type of Constitution" published on June 2, 1964, and the first general elections for the Legislative Assembly of 32 members (elected in single-member constituencies on a common roll) were held on March 1, 1965. They gave 28 seats to the Bechuanaland Democratic Party led by Seretse Khama, the advocate of a multi-racial society which, however, would have to maintain good-neighbourly relations with the Republic of South Africa despite the latter's *apartheid* policies. The Bechuanaland People's Party, favouring Pan-Africanism, gained three seats.

The second general elections (the first in the Republic of Botswana) held on Oct. 18, 1969, resulted in a victory for the ruling Botswana Democratic Party, which won 24 out of 31 seats in the Assembly against three each for the Botswana National Front and the Botswana People's Party (formerly the Bechuanaland People's Party) and one for the Botswana Independence Party. Sir Seretse was sworn in as President for a second term of office on Oct. 22, 1969.

LESOTHO

Area: 11,716 sq. miles.

Population 1969 (estimate): 890,000 (excl. Lesotho citizens in South Africa).

Capital: Maseru (14,000).

Official language: English.

Chief products: Diamonds, cattle.

Basutoland, which had been under British rule for 97 years, was granted internal self-government on April 30, 1965, when its Paramount Chief Moshoeshoe II became the Queen's representative.

The country's first general elections held on April 29, 1965, gave the Basutoland National Party 31, the Basutoland Congress Party 25, and the Marematlou Freedom Party four seats in the House of Assembly. The Basutoland National Party formed a Government of which Chief Leabua Jonathan (the party's leader) became Prime Minister on July 7, 1965.

The Basutoland National Party is conservative and in favour of maintaining the traditional powers of the chiefs. The Basutoland Congress Party is a left-wing nationalist party which is ready to accept support from Communist countries. The Marematlou Freedom Party was originally monarchist but later gave support to the Congress Party.

During a conference on the granting of full independence held in London on June 8–17, 1966, the Paramount Chief expressed his concern lest independence should be given against the wishes of the two Opposition Parties, which had obtained 56 per cent of the votes in the general elections and which objected to independence being given to Chief Jonathan's "minority Government" which would be unable, he claimed, to defend the country's interests "against foreign interference" (i.e., by implication, from South Africa).

Basutoland became the independent Kingdom of Lesotho on Oct. 4, 1966, with Moshoeshoe II as King. Previously, on July 12, 1966, he had announced that he would hold a referendum on the acceptance of the Independence Constitution, but the College of Chiefs, which had powers to depose him as Paramount Chief, decided on July 14 that he should abandon his involvement in politics under pain of being deposed. He nevertheless continued to express his determination not to accept the Independence Constitution.

Meanwhile Chief Jonathan had, as the first Prime Minister of a Black

African country, together with two of his Ministers, visited Dr. Verwoerd, the South African Prime Minister, on Sept. 2, 1966, in order to establish "good-neighbourly relations and co-operation".

As the King continued his political activities in an endeavour to obtain greater political powers than afforded to him under the Constitution, the Prime Minister took drastic action against him on Dec. 28, 1966, when the King was placed under house-arrest and thus prevented from addressing further political meetings.

On Jan. 5, 1967, the King finally agreed to accept the demands of the Council of Chiefs to abstain from further political activity and to act strictly as a constitutional monarch, failing which he undertook to abdicate.

A new crisis arose in January 1970 when it became apparent that general elections held on Jan. 27 would result in the defeat of Chief Jonathan's party, unofficial returns showing that the Congress Party had won 33 out of the 60 seats in the National Assembly.

Chief Jonathan declared a state of emergency, suspended the Constitution and ordered the arrest of Opposition leaders. Restrictions were also imposed on the King, who subsequently left the country on April 2, 1970, for the Netherlands, the Government of which had granted him permission to reside in that country for six months.

After a period of unrest and clashes between police and Congress Party followers, Chief Jonathan declared on March 31 that Lesotho would remain an independent sovereign Kingdom in which the King would be bound to act in accordance with the advice of his Ministers.

In view of the continued state of emergency, however, the British Government did not renew its aid programme which had amounted to over £4,000,000 a year and expired on March 31, 1970. The resumption of normal relations between the two countries was announced subsequently on June 11, 1970, by the British Government, while U.K. economic aid was resumed at the end of July.

King Moshoeshoe II returned from exile on Dec. 4; on the following day he took a new oath undertaking to "abstain from involving the monarchy in any way in politics or with any political party or group" under pain of being declared deposed by a simple announcement in the Government Gazette.

MAURITIUS

Area: 805 sq. miles.
Population 1969 (estimate): 795,000 (excluding Rodrigues and other small islands).
Capital: Port Louis (138,000).
Official language: English.
Chief product: Sugar.

Mauritius became an independent Monarchy within the Commonwealth, owing allegiance to H. M. Queen Elizabeth II, on March 12, 1968, after 158 years of British rule.

The political parties in Mauritius had not arrived at unanimous agreement on the country's future status. The Mauritius Labour Party led by the Prime Minister, Sir Seewoosagur Ramgoolam, and the Independent Labour Bloc advocated full independence, whilst the Moslem Committee of Action supported independence subject to electoral safeguards for the Moslem community. The *Parti mauricien social démocrate,* founded by Mr. Jules Koenig and later led by Mr. Gaëtan Duval, however, opposed independence and advocated some form of continued association with Britain.

The multi-racial population of Mauritius and its island dependency of Rodrigues posed a particular problem concerning the form of electoral system to be adopted. A Commission under the chairmanship of Sir Harold Banwell was appointed by the British Government after the London Constitutional Conference of Sept. 7–24, 1965, to visit Mauritius and make recommendations for an electoral system after consultations with the local political parties and leading personalities. Certain of the proposals made by the Commission and published on June 3, 1966, were accepted wholly by the Mauritians. These were that the Legislative Assembly should have sixty-two members elected by block voting in multi-member constituencies, including two members for Rodrigues; that the three candidates receiving the largest number of votes in a constituency would be declared elected; and that each voter would have one vote for each seat in the constituency.

A further proposal, subsequently adopted in an amended form, was that there would be eight specially elected members to be returned from amongst unsuccessful candidates who had made the best showing in the election. The first four would go, irrespective of party, to the "best losers" of whichever communities in the island were under-represented in the Assembly after the constituency elections, and the remaining four seats would be allocated on the basis of both party and community. It was hoped that these proposals would result in a fair representation of all parties and races in the Legislative Assembly.

Shortly before the declaration of independence, violent clashes between Moslems and Creoles, leading to murder and looting, caused the death of at least 27 persons and injury to several hundred. Order was restored with the help of British troops.

On the attainment of independence a six-year defence agreement with Britain was signed, providing for the continuation of existing British facilities for the Royal Air Force and the Royal Navy. A Mauritian agreement with the Soviet Union, concluded in July 1970 for granting facilities to Soviet trawlers and aircraft, was considered by the British Government to have "implications for the overall defence of the area". A Government spokesman subsequently stated, on Nov. 2, 1970, that this agreement did not imply a re-orientation of Mauritian foreign policy, which was to remain firmly linked to the West.

On Dec. 1, 1969, a coalition Government of National Unity was formed by Sir Seewoosagur Ramgoolam in order to overcome the latent antagonism between the predominantly Hindu community and the Moslem, Chinese, Creole and European minorities. Mr. Gaëtan Duval, Leader of the Opposition, became Minister of Foreign Affairs, Tourism and Emigration.

SWAZILAND

Area: 6,705 sq. miles.
Population 1969 (estimate): 410,000.
Capital: Mbabane (14,000).
Official language: English.
Chief products: Iron ore, asbestos, timber, sugar.

The last British territory in Africa (apart from Rhodesia) to achieve independence, Swaziland became a constitutional Monarchy within the Commonwealth on Sept. 6, 1968, after sixteen months of internal self-government from April 25, 1967.

General elections held on April 19–20, 1967, resulted in all seats in the new Parliament being won by the ruling *Imbokodvo* National Movement, a royalist party founded and directly controlled by the Ngwenyama (Ruler),

King Sobhuza II. Prince Makhosini Dlamini, leader of the *Imbokodvo* and a great-grandson of Sobhuza I, was appointed as the country's first Prime Minister.

The Independence Constitution laid down that executive authority would be vested in the King, who would appoint the Prime Minister and, on the latter's advice, a Deputy Prime Minister and up to eight other Ministers. The Swaziland Parliament would consist of (i) a House of Assembly with a Speaker, 24 members elected by adult suffrage in eight three-member constituencies, six members appointed by the King, and a non-voting Attorney-General, and (ii) a Senate of six members elected by the House of Assembly and six appointed by the King. The Swazi National Council, consisting of the King, the Queen Mother and all adult male Swazis, would continue to advise the King on all matters regulated by Swazi law and custom through the traditional councils of advisers. The King was empowered to dispose, at his discretion, of the mineral rights held by him in trust for the Swazi nation.

RHODESIA

Area: 150,820 sq. miles.
Population 1969: 5,090,000.
Capital: Salisbury (400,000).
Other important town: Bulawayo (250,000).
Official language: English.
Chief products: Asbestos, gold, copper, coal, chrome, tobacco.

Rhodesia, which had been, under the name of Southern Rhodesia, a self-governing British Colony from 1923 to 1953 and a member of the Federation of Rhodesia and Nyasaland [see page 135] from 1953 until its dissolution in 1963, was unilaterally declared independent by the Prime Minister, Mr. Ian D. Smith, on Nov. 11, 1965. After almost five years of attempts to reach a negotiated settlement between Rhodesia and the United Kingdom, the Smith regime assumed republican status on March 2, 1970.

The unilateral declaration of independence (UDI) came after drawn-out negotiations between the Rhodesian authorities and the British Government, on the question of independence, had foundered on the crucial issue of "no independence before majority rule" [NIBMAR] – the principle on which successive British Governments stood firm.

167

From the 1961 Constitution to UDI

[For a summary of events prior to 1961 see THE CENTRAL AFRICAN FEDERATION OF RHODESIA AND NYASALAND.]

The 1961 Constitution

The main provisions of a new Constitution for Southern Rhodesia, published in London on June 13, 1961, and replacing the 1923 Constitution, were as follows: (*a*) The Governor would represent the Sovereign in the Territory; (*b*) there would be two electoral rolls – the "A" Roll having higher property ownership and educational qualifications than the "B" roll; (*c*) the Legislative Assembly would consist of 50 members elected in "A" roll constituencies and 15 in "B" roll electoral districts – both rolls voting together in all 65 constituencies but the votes cast being adjusted in value if necessary so that the total number of "B" roll votes would be equivalent to no more than 25 per cent of "A" roll votes in an "A" roll constituency, and *vice versa* in "B" roll electoral districts [a system known as "cross-voting"] ; (*d*) the Constitution included a Declaration of Rights [see below] , and provided for the establishment of a Constitutional Council, whose main function would be to advise the Legislative Assembly as to whether its Bills were in conformity with this Declaration; (*e*) the existing Native Reserves and the Special Native Area would together be placed in one category to be described as "Tribal Trust Land" for occupation by tribesmen on a basis of communal tenure, provision being made for converting Tribal Trust Land to individual freehold ownership. The Declaration of Rights contained elaborate guarantees ensuring to every person in Southern Rhodesia "the fundamental rights and freedoms of the individual ... whatever his race, tribe, place of origin, political opinions, colour or creed, subject to respect for the rights and freedoms of others."

The British House of Commons approved these proposals on June 22 by 313 to 219 votes; the Southern Rhodesia Parliament also gave its approval on June 21, the only opposition coming from the nine Dominion Party members. [For origins of the Dominion Party see page 137.] A referendum in Southern Rhodesia held on July 26 resulted in 41,949 votes in favour of, and 21,846 against, the constitutional proposals on a 77 per cent poll; eligible voters included 78,000 Europeans, 4,000 Africans, 1,000 Coloureds and 1,000 Asians. Sir Edgar Whitehead, the Prime Minister, described the result as "the birth of the Rhodesian nation" and declared that "the stage is set for African people to play their part fully in the political life of the country".

168

Opposition to the new Constitution was voiced, however, by both African political organizations. On June 17–18, a congress of the National Democratic Party (NDP) condemned the proposals as "an evil attempt by both the Southern Rhodesian and British Governments to entrench settler minority rule" in Southern Rhodesia. [The policy of the NDP, formed on Dec. 29, 1959, was defined as the establishment of democratic government elected on the principle of "one man, one vote", the total emancipation of all peoples and the abolition of all forms of racial or national oppression.] The party leader, Mr. Joshua Nkomo, after pointing out that "the majority of the African people will be excluded from expressing an opinion" in the referendum, announced that the NDP would hold its own secret referendum among the African population "to give the African a chance to say 'No' to the proposals". The results of this ballot, in which all Africans over 21 were eligible to vote, were announced by Mr. Nkomo on Aug. 9 as 467,189 votes against the Constitution and only 584 in favour. The NDP's rival organization – the Zimbabwe National Party – denounced both the new Constitution and the NDP's secret ballot, which it described as a "phoney referendum" designed "to hoodwink the African people".

The Southern Rhodesia (Constitution) Bill was enacted on Nov. 22, 1961, after its passage through both Houses of the British Parliament; the new Constitution was promulgated as an Order in Council on Dec. 6, thereby coming legally into force.

Under the new Constitution, in operation as from Nov. 1, 1961, general elections to the new Legislative Assembly were held on Dec. 14, when all voters were expected to cast two votes each – one for the constituency candidate and the other for the electoral district candidate of their choice.

As a result of a boycott by African nationalists the elections were contested almost entirely by Sir Edgar Whitehead's United Federal Party (UFP – see page 137) and Mr. Winston Field's Rhodesian Front (RF) with the following result:

	Constituency Votes	Electoral District Votes	Seats
RF	38,282	35,224	35
UFP	30,943	29,308	29

The remaining seat was won by an independent candidate.

Mr. Winston Field accordingly, on Dec. 15, formed a new Cabinet including Mr. Ian D. Smith (Treasury) and Mr. Clifford W. Dupont (Justice and Law and Order).

169

The Rhodesian Front was formed on March 13, 1962, by the merger of the four main right-wing European parties in the Federation of Rhodesia and Nyasaland – the Federal Dominion Party, the Southern Rhodesian Dominion Party, the Southern Rhodesia Association and the Rhodesia Reform Party (led by Mr. Ian D. Smith).

Internal Security Measures

As a result of the militant action of the African nationalists, in particular members of the Zimbabwe African People's Union (ZAPU – formed on Dec. 17, 1961, by leaders of the banned NDP including Mr. Joshua Nkomo), involving acts of violence and intimidation, the Government of Southern Rhodesia introduced during 1962–64, a number of Bills dealing with internal security.

These Bills included: (*a*) amendments to the Unlawful Organizations Act and the Law and Order (Maintenance) Act, enacted on Sept. 7, 1962: (*b*) a Law and Order (Maintenance) Amendment Bill, introducing the mandatory death sentence for crimes involving the use of petrol bombs or inflammable liquids or explosives against persons; and amendments to the Unlawful Organizations Act and the Preservation of Constitutional Government Bill – all adopted on March 20, 1963; (*c*) the Foreign Subversive Organizations Bill, approved at its second reading on July 23, 1963; (*d*) a renewal of the Preventive Detention Act of 1959, approved on March 4, 1964; (*e*) an extension of the Unlawful Organizations Act for another five years on March 10, 1964; (*f*) a Law and Order Maintenance (Amendment) Bill, 1964, providing for increased mandatory sentences.

ZAPU had been declared unlawful on Sept. 20, 1962; Mr. Nkomo was first placed under restriction at that time. In July 1963 a split took place, as a result of which a ZAPU faction led by the Rev. Ndabaningi Sithole formed the Zimbabwe African National Union (ZANU) on Aug. 8, 1963.

In April 1964 Mr. Nkomo and other African nationalists were sent to a restriction area at Gonakudzingwa (in south-eastern Rhodesia). The People's Caretaker Council (a successor to ZAPU) and ZANU were banned on Aug. 26, 1964.

The Independence Issue, 1963–65

On March 23, 1963, Mr. Field formally applied to the British Government for full independence for Rhodesia at the moment of secession from the Federation by either Northern Rhodesia or Nyasaland, but Mr. Butler (U.K. Minister for Central African Affairs) replied on April 11: "H.M. Government accept in principle that Southern Rhodesia, like the other

Territories, will proceed through the normal processes to independence. . . . Our legal advice is that it would not in any event be possible to make Southern Rhodesia an independent country in the full sense of the word while remaining a member of the non-independent Federation. . . . The secession of one member of the Federation would not in itself end your membership of the Federation."

Mr. Field, on May 9, again asked for independence to be granted not later than the date when the dissolution of the Federation occurred; following discussions between Mr. Field and Mr. Butler, the latter made it clear, on June 18, that "the position had not yet been reached which would enable H.M. Government to arrive at a decision on the question of Southern Rhodesia's independence".

Following further requests for independence by the Prime Minister, on Sept. 20 and Oct. 25, Mr. Duncan Sandys (U.K. Secretary of State for Commonwealth Relations and the Colonies) defined the British Government's attitude on Nov. 15 as follows: "We are prepared to grant independence to Southern Rhodesia in the same circumstances as we have granted it to other British territories. In particular, we look for a widening of the franchise so as to cover representation of Africans. . . . If we were to give independence to Southern Rhodesia on terms which were unacceptable to our fellow members [in the Commonwealth], we would be likely to cause grievous injury to the unity of the Commonwealth. . . . It is clear, therefore, that the whole Commonwealth will have to be consulted." This proposal was rejected by Mr. Field on Nov. 20.

Following the dissolution of the Federation of Rhodesia and Nyasaland on Dec. 31, 1963 [see page 151], further talks on independence were held from Jan. 24—Feb. 2, 1964, between Mr. Field and the British Government. Shortly afterwards, the Governor of Southern Rhodesia, Sir Humphrey Gibbs, opening Parliament on Feb. 24, declared: "It is now plain that the British Government is not prepared to be brought to any conclusions except on most extravagant terms. My Ministers consider that they have done their utmost and there is no obligation upon them to initiate further discussions."

Following disagreements between the Rhodesian Front and Mr. Field, the latter resigned as Prime Minister on April 13, 1964, and was succeeded by Mr. Ian D. Smith, who declared that he would try to negotiate independence for Rhodesia. After further exchanges with the British Government, however, he stated on June 25 that, if the negotiations failed, his Government would "consider and place before the people of Southern Rhodesia all the pros and cons of a unilateral declaration of independence".

As a result of talks between Mr. Ian Smith and the British Government on Sept. 7–10, it was announced that the Southern Rhodesian Government would seek the consent of the majority of the territory's population to a declaration of independence on the basis of the existing Constitution and franchise. The method of consulting African opinion in this referendum would be via an *indaba*, a traditional meeting of chiefs and headmen convened in order to obtain the views held on a particular subject in the tribal areas. The British High Commissioner in Salisbury announced on Oct. 21, however, that both the outgoing Conservative and the incoming Labour Governments in Britain had advised Mr. Smith that this method was not acceptable; Mr. Smith said the same day that this was "a fantastic decision" which prejudged the outcome of the consultation. The *indaba* was held as planned on Oct. 21–26 at Domboshawa near Salisbury and resulted in a unanimous vote in favour of independence under the existing Constitution.

Mr. Harold Wilson, the new British Prime Minister, on Oct. 27 issued this warning: "In [the British Government's] view, the inevitable consequences of UDI would be very serious indeed. . . . In short, an illegal declaration of independence in Southern Rhodesia would bring to an end relationships between her and Britain, would cut her off from the rest of the Commonwealth, from most foreign Governments and from international organizations, would inflict disastrous economic damage upon her and would leave her isolated and virtually friendless in a largely hostile continent."

The attitude of the British Government was strongly supported by Commonwealth leaders and the U.S. Government, while in Rhodesia the Association of Rhodesian Industries came out strongly against UDI on Oct. 27. The Rhodesian Government, on the other hand, denied that it was about to take unilateral action or that it would do so if it obtained a massive "yes" vote in the forthcoming referendum on Nov. 5. Voters in this referendum were asked the question "Are you in favour of independence based on the 1961 Constitution?" The official results showed that 58,091 voters had said "Yes" and 6,096 voters "No", with 944 spoilt papers. 61 per cent of the total number of registered voters – 89,886 whites and 12,729 Africans – had voted, but it was apparent that almost all African and other non-European voters had abstained.

Unsuccessful Negotiations: January–September 1965

In general elections held on May 7, 1965, the ruling Rhodesian Front was overwhelmingly returned to power; Mr. Smith had previously stated, on March 31, that the main reason for calling a general election was that

172

since the previous elections in 1962 the situation had so altered that "a fresh mandate" from the country was necessary.

The Rhodesian Front won all 50 seats on the "A" roll, 22 of these being unopposed; the "B" roll seats, which were not contested by the Rhodesian Front, were distributed between the Rhodesia Party (10) and Independents (5). [The Rhodesia Party was formed on Aug. 12, 1964, by Sir Roy Welensky as a "party of national conciliation", and incorporated the former Rhodesia National Party, the Southern Rhodesian division of the United Federal Party, see page 148.] The vast majority of African voters abstained, following an African nationalist call for a boycott; the poll in the electoral districts, where most Africans were resident, was about 16 per cent.

Following a fact-finding mission to Rhodesia by Mr. Arthur Bottomley (the U.K. Minister of State for Commonwealth Relations) on July 22–27, 1965, Mr. Smith and Mr. D. W. Lardner-Burke (Minister of Law and Order) conferred with the British Government in London on Oct. 4–8 without agreement being reached. The British Government on Oct. 9 gave in detail the principles on which it insisted and which Mr. Smith had found unacceptable, as follows:

"(1) The principle and intention of unimpeded progress to majority rule, already enshrined in the 1961 Constitution, would have to be maintained and guaranteed.

"(2) There would also have to be guarantees against retrogressive amendment of the Constitution.

"(3) There would have to be immediate improvement in the political status of the African population.

"(4) There would have to be progress towards ending racial discrimination.

"(5) The British Government would need to be satisfied that any basis proposed for independence was acceptable to the people of Rhodesia as a whole."

Mr. Smith replied to the British statement on Oct. 9, maintaining that the Rhodesian Government had accepted the first three points in principle but that, under the fourth point, it would be "quite unrealistic" to suggest that the Land Apportionment Act of Rhodesia could be "abolished overnight", and that the fifth point was "quite meaningless or merely a device to ensure that no understanding reached between the Governments can with certainty be implemented".

In spite of the breakdown in talks, Mr. Wilson continued to explore possibilities of preventing UDI by the Rhodesian Government and of resuming negotiations. On Oct. 21, he announced his decision to visit Rhodesia with Mr. Bottomley, in order to "find some means of breaking the deadlock"; this was in reply to a letter from Mr. Smith on the previous day, offering to agree to a "solemn treaty" to guarantee that an independent Rhodesia would stand by the principles of the 1961 Constitution. Mr. Smith described the proposed visit as "an honest and genuine attempt to solve our problem", adding, however, that at their talks in London he and Mr. Wilson "really did get to the end of negotiations".

Mr. Wilson visited Southern Rhodesia on Oct. 25–30 and had discussions with persons representing all shades of opinion. On Oct. 29, when it had emerged that no common ground had been found between the points of view of the British and Rhodesian Governments, Mr. Wilson suggested two alternative courses of action to Mr. Smith; (a) that the Rhodesian Government should consult the Rhodesian people in a referendum as to whether they wanted independence based on the 1961 Constitution; or (b) that the two Prime Ministers should jointly recommend to the Queen the setting-up of a Royal Commission to produce an independence Constitution based on that of 1961, acceptable to the people as a whole. The Rhodesian Government, having rejected these proposals, on Oct. 30 put forward a compromise scheme whereby a joint Royal Commission would be set up with the task of finding out whether the 1961 Constitution, with suitable amendments to be agreed upon by both Governments, was acceptable to the Rhodesian people as a whole; no agreement could be reached, however, on the terms of reference of the Commission. On Nov. 7 Mr. Wilson, in a further attempt to enable the proposed Royal Commission to start its work, suggested that its chairman-designate, Sir Hugh Beadle (the Rhodesian Chief Justice), should come to London for discussions and that the two Prime Ministers might thereafter meet again. In reply, on Nov. 8, Mr. Smith ignored both these proposals and concluded that the stage had again been reached where the two opposing views could not be reconciled; he also announced that Sir Hugh Beadle was flying to London "entirely on his own initiative", talks between Sir Hugh and Mr. Wilson taking place on Nov. 9–10.

The final step was taken when, following an exchange of letters between the Queen and the Rhodesian Government on Nov. 9 and a telephone conversation in the early morning of Nov. 11 between the two Prime Ministers, Mr. Smith announced his Government's unilateral declaration of independence for Rhodesia in a broadcast to the nation at 1.15 p.m. (Local Time) on Nov. 11.

The Immediate Effects of UDI

A new Constitution, published on Nov. 11, in general followed the 1961 Constitution but contained the following major new provisions: (1) The section in the 1961 Constitution on the Governor of Rhodesia was replaced by one providing for the appointment of an "Officer Administering the Government"; (2) the British Parliament's power to legislate for Rhodesia was removed and the Crown's power to issue Orders in Council under U.K. legislation repudiated; (3) the concept of allegiance to the "Constitution of Rhodesia" was introduced; (4) certain constitutional amendments, previously subject to approval by separate referenda of the four races or by the Sovereign on British ministerial advice, could now be implemented by a two-thirds majority of the total membership of the Rhodesian Parliament, viz., the franchise qualifications as well as sections dealing with judicial independence, the Declaration of Rights, the Constitutional Council, safeguards for laws dealing with racial ownership of land and the procedure of constitutional amendment.

Immediately after Mr. Smith's broadcast, Mr. Wilson repudiated the action taken by the Rhodesian Government in a statement in the House of Commons, and outlined the immediate consequences of this action.

Mr. Wilson said: "The British Government condemns the declaration of independence . . . as an illegal act and one ineffective in law. . . . The Governor, in pursuance of the authority vested in him by Her Majesty, has today informed the Prime Minister and the other Ministers of the Rhodesian Government that they cease to hold office . . . [and] can exercise no legal authority in Rhodesia. . . . The British Government wish to make it clear that it is the duty of British subjects – including all subjects of Rhodesia – to remain loyal to the Queen and the law of the land. . . .

"We shall have no dealings with the rebel regime. The British High Commissioner is being withdrawn and the Rhodesian High Commissioner in London has been asked to leave. Exports of arms . . . have . . . been stopped. All British aid will cease. Rhodesia . . . has been . . . removed from the sterling area. . . . The Ottawa Agreement, 1932, which governs our trading agreements with Rhodesia, is suspended. . . . There will be a ban on further purchases of tobacco from . . . Rhodesia. We propose . . . to ban further purchases of Rhodesian sugar.

"We shall not recognize passports issued or renewed by the illegal Southern Rhodesian regime. . . .

"It is the duty of everyone owing allegiance to the Crown, in

Rhodesia or elsewhere, to refrain from all acts which would assist the illegal regime to continue in Rhodesia in their rebellion against the Crown. . . ."

A Southern Rhodesia Bill, whose purposes had been described by the U.K. Attorney General, Sir Elwyn Jones, on Nov. 12 as (*a*) to declare "the legal position, which is that Southern Rhodesia is part of Her Majesty's dominions, and that the Government and Parliament of the United Kingdom have responsibility and jurisdiction in respect of it", and (*b*) "to give power to make Orders in Council in relation to Southern Rhodesia", was enacted, unopposed in either House, on Nov. 16. The continuation of the Act was subsequently approved by the British Parliament at yearly intervals, beginning in 1966.

The Rhodesian Unilateral Declaration of Independence evoked expressions of violent opposition in virtually all countries of Africa, and of explicit support for the application of economic measures against Rhodesia from most countries throughout the world. No Government officially granted recognition to the Smith regime, although several continued to maintain consular missions in Rhodesia.

The South African Prime Minister, Dr. Verwoerd, issued a statement on Nov. 11 making it clear that the Republic would not take part in any sanctions against Rhodesia. The Portuguese Foreign Minister subsequently indicated that his country similarly refused to participate in such sanctions.

The U.N. General Assembly approved on Nov. 11, 1965, by 107 votes to two (Portugal and South Africa) with France abstaining and Britain not taking part in the vote, a resolution condemning UDI and "inviting" Britain to take the necessary steps "to end the rebellion". On Nov. 19 the U.N. Security Council adopted by 10 votes to none (with France abstaining) a resolution confirming previous U.N. resolutions on Rhodesia and, in addition, calling on all States "not to entertain any diplomatic or other relations" with the Smith regime and "to refrain from any action which could assist and encourage" it, in particular to desist from providing it with arms, equipment or military material and to do their utmost to break all economic relations "with Rhodesia, including an embargo on oil and petroleum products".

Export of oil products to Rhodesia was banned by Iran (Nov. 22), Kuwait (Nov. 23) and Libya (Dec. 1). On Nov. 23, Mr. Wilson made a statement in the House of Commons on the British Government's attitude to the proposed oil embargo. He declared: "I have said repeatedly . . . that whatever measures we take must be effective. The quicker they are, the less the lasting damage. What I have said is that we reject the idea of military intervention. We will examine any measures – tobacco is the first – necessary to get a quick solution of the problem in Rhodesia, and that includes an oil embargo."

In Rhodesia the Government had meanwhile assumed wide powers, including censorship of the Press, radio and television; power to impose rationing; the cancellation of import licences; and the introduction of export control. [Prior to UDI, import control had been introduced on Nov. 3, and a state of emergency declared throughout Rhodesia for three months from Nov. 5.]

On Nov. 12, Mr. Smith issued a statement saying that the Governor of Rhodesia, Sir Humphrey Gibbs, had been "advised that in view of the new Constitution which has been given to the people of Rhodesia by the *de facto* Government in control, he no longer has any executive powers in Rhodesia". Sir Humphrey replied to this on Nov. 14 by reiterating that he remained the "lawful Governor"; that he would not recognize the "illegal Government or the new Constitution they have presented to the country" and that he would only resign "if asked by Her Majesty to do so". A Government statement, issued on Nov. 18, announced that Mr. Clifford Dupont had resigned as Minister of External Affairs and Defence, and also as an M.P., and had been appointed by the Executive Council as "Acting Officer Administering the Government in terms of the 1965 Constitution".

British Sanctions, December 1965 – March 1966

On Dec. 1, 1965, further British embargoes on Rhodesian exports were announced by Mr. Wilson, who stated: "The embargoed items now account for over 95 per cent of Rhodesia's exports to us, so that we, who were once Rhodesia's best market, have virtually ceased to buy from her". The same day the U.K. Treasury announced stringent new restrictions which almost entirely cut off the flow of current account funds from Britain to Rhodesia.

The British Government announced the imposition of oil sanctions against Rhodesia on Dec. 17, the effect of this being to prevent British companies and ships from supplying oil to the Mozambique port of Beira and, provided the necessary support was also forthcoming from other countries, thus to prevent the use of the oil pipeline from Beira to Umtali (Rhodesia). American participation in the oil sanctions was announced on

Dec. 28. As a result, the Feruka refinery near Umtali slowed down production to a virtual standstill on Jan. 15, 1966, no oil having been pumped through the pipeline from Beira since Dec. 31, 1965.

Following numerous unconfirmed reports of tankers with oil for Rhodesia being allegedly bound for Beira, the British Government, in March 1966, ordered strict surveillance of the seaward approaches to Beira by British naval and air forces. On April 7, 1966, the U.N. Security Council adopted a British resolution which called *inter alia* "upon the Government of the United Kingdom to prevent, by the use of force if necessary, the arrival at Beira of vessels reasonably believed to be carrying oil destined for Rhodesia".

Various counter-measures where taken in Rhodesia against British sanctions during this period.

On Dec. 7 all banks, commercial concerns and industry in the country were brought under Government control. On the following day Mr. Smith announced plans for national service and direction of labour to counter the effect of British sanctions, which he admitted would prove "injurious" and would inevitably cause unemployment among certain sections of the community. The Smith Government prohibited, on Dec. 22, the publication of news of the measures which were being taken to meet the sanctions imposed by Britain and other countries. Petrol rationing was first introduced on Dec. 27, and by Jan. 25, 1966, the ration was reduced to 40 per cent of previous consumption.

Constitutional Developments, 1966—68

The Smith Government proceeded during 1966—68 to give a legal basis to the country's unilaterally declared independence.

The independence Constitution of 1965 was "legalized" by the Rhodesian Legislature on Feb. 18, 1966, by 49 votes to two in the absence of the African Opposition.

An Emergency Powers Bill consolidating the powers taken by the Government since Nov. 11, 1965, was adopted on March 8, 1966.

A Constitution Amendment Bill, agreed by Mr. Clifford Dupont as "Officer Administering the Government" on Sept. 14, 1966, gave the Government powers to legislate on preventive detention (until then held under emergency regulations).

Meanwhile the Rhodesian judiciary gradually gave recognition to the Smith regime.

A judgement given in the Salisbury High Court on Sept. 9, 1966, recognized the Smith Government as "the only effective" one in the country, and on Aug. 9, 1968, the same court ruled that the Government had achieved "internal *de jure* status", this opinion being confirmed by the Appeal Court on Sept. 13.

Security Measures, 1966—69
Legislation to curb subversive activities against the Smith Government included an amendment to the Law and Order (Maintenance) Act, providing the mandatory death sentence for possessing "arms of war" — brought into operation on Nov. 16, 1967. On Sept. 27, 1968, however, the mandatory death sentence was abolished both under the above amendment and for the throwing of petrol bombs [see page 170].

From 1965 onwards both ZAPU and ZANU [see page 170] organized raids into Rhodesia by armed infiltrators operating from Zambia and Tanzania, which repeatedly led to clashes with the Rhodesian armed forces. On Dec. 26, 1968, the Rhodesian Government gave the number of infiltrators killed by security forces as over 160.

Mr. Sithole, the ZANU leader, was sentenced to six years' imprisonment on Feb. 12, 1969, for incitement to murder Mr. Smith and other Rhodesian Ministers.

Negotiations: From UDI to the *Fearless* Talks
Mr. Wilson defined his Government's immediate aims in Rhodesia on Jan. 25, 1966, as "to bring the Rhodesian rebellion to an end as quickly as possible, without lasting damage to the country", and "to help the people of Rhodesia . . . in making a fresh start towards establishing, in the words of the Lagos communiqué [see below], 'a just society based on equality of opportunity . . .' "; he also defined the British Government's plans for an interim Government under the Governor to be formed after the return to constitutional rule and to replace the Smith regime. At the same time he restated his Government's view on future constitutional changes in Rhodesia, adding a sixth principle to the five already specified [see page 173], viz. "the need to ensure that, regardless of race, there is no oppression of majority by minority or of minority by majority".

Following secret negotiations between May and November 1966, Mr. Wilson and Mr. Smith met on board the British cruiser *Tiger* off Gibraltar on Dec. 2—3, 1966, and produced a working document proposing a return to the 1961 Constitution with certain changes to meet the "six principles", including the extension of the "B" roll franchise to all Africans satisfying citizenship and residence qualifications. The document was approved by the British Cabinet but rejected by the Rhodesian regime on Dec. 5.

The British Government thereupon decided to withdraw all previous offers made to the Smith regime and to ask the U.N. Security Council to adopt a resolution providing for selective mandatory sanctions. [For details of this resolution see page 182.]

Following further negotiations between the two sides between November 1967 and September 1968, Mr. Wilson and Mr. Smith met on Oct. 9–13, 1968, on board H.M.S. *Fearless* in Gibraltar, with the result that a document setting out the basis on which a proposal for settlement of the Rhodesian question would be introduced in the U.K. Parliament met with no acceptance by Mr. Smith.

> The principal points of the *Fearless* document were: (*a*) a reiteration of the six principles; (*b*) the composition of the legislature should be such that it "secured at all times a 'blocking quarter' of directly and popularly elected Africans"; (*c*) "the 'B' roll franchise to be extended to include all Africans over 30 who satisfy the citizenship and residence qualifications"; (*d*) any amendment of the "specially entrenched provisions of the Constitution will require a vote of at least three-quarters of the total membership of both Houses [of Parliament] voting together"; (*e*) the establishment of a Commission "to study recommendations on the problems of racial discrimination" in Rhodesia; (*f*) the establishment of a Royal Commission "for the purpose of testing the acceptability to the people of Rhodesia as a whole of a new Independence Constitution"; (*g*) the provision of "additional facilities for the education and training of Africans in Rhodesia".

Further negotiations during November 1968 failed to end in any agreement.

Outside Pressures against Rhodesia

African Nations' Call for Use of Force

Many African countries pressed continuously for the use of force to overthrow the illegal regime, but Britain and a number of her Western allies held out against this demand and refused to turn to military means of ending the rebellion.

The first demand for the use of force after UDI was made by the Council of Ministers of the Organization of African Unity (OAU). Following the adoption of a resolution (the text of which was not made public) at a special meeting on Dec. 5, the Secretary-General of the OAU announced that the Council had recommended that all the 36 OAU member-countries should break off diplomatic relations with Britain by Dec. 15, 1965, if by that date the British Government had "not crushed the rebellion and restored law and order in Southern Rhodesia". In the event, only nine African countries subsequently broke off relations with Britain – Tanzania, Ghana, Algeria, Congo (Brazzaville), Guinea, Mali, Mauritania, Sudan and the U.A.R.

Following a conference of representatives of 19 Commonwealth countries held in Lagos on Jan. 11–12, 1966, a communiqué was published containing the following principal points: (a) The Governments represented affirmed their determination that "the rebellion must be brought to an end"; having "discussed the question of the use of military force in Rhodesia", they accepted that "its use could not be precluded if this proved necessary to restore law and order"; (b) the conference had decided to set up two committees (i) to keep the effect of sanctions under regular review and (ii) to help accelerate the training of Rhodesian Africans; and (c) it was reaffirmed that authority and responsbility for guiding Rhodesia to independence rested with Britain, but it was acknowledged that the problem was "of wider concern to Africa, the Commonwealth and the world".

A further Conference of Commonwealth Prime Ministers, held in London from Sept. 6 to 15, 1966, was characterized by a basic difference of opinion on the Rhodesian problem. On the one hand, African, Asian and Caribbean members, supported by Canada, were reported to favour mandatory sanctions or, in the case of many African members, the use of force against the Smith regime; and, on the other hand, Britain, Australia, New Zealand, Malta and Malawi took a more moderate attitude. A communiqué issued on Sept. 14 gave expression to both views, the principal sections being: (1) the reaffirmation of the "one man, one vote" principle as the basis of democracy in Rhodesia; (2) agreement that the British Government would not recommend to Parliament any constitutional settlement that did not conform to the six principles [see pages 173, 179] ; (3) an undertaking that the British Government would not consent to independence before majority rule unless the people of Rhodesia as a whole were shown to be in favour of it, by a referendum based on universal adult suffrage; (4) Britain's readiness – if by the end of 1966 no action had been taken on the "initial and indispensable steps" to bring the rebellion to an end – to join in sponsoring, with Commonwealth support, a resolution providing for mandatory sanctions; (5) assistance to be given to Zambia "to produce a more complete cut-off to trade with Rhodesia" and "to withstand any serious [resultant] effect on her economy".

[For the effect of UDI and sanctions on Zambia see page 158.]

The main international action against UDI in Rhodesia took the form of economic sanctions; these had only a limited success largely because of the incomplete support given by various nations and by the refusal of South Africa and Portugal to participate in any economic sanctions against the Smith regime.

As a result of the failure of the *Tiger* talks [see page 179] Mr. Wilson stated on Dec. 5, 1966, that the British Government was accordingly bound to proceed in accordance with the terms agreed upon at the September Commonwealth Conference [see above] and to request the United Nations to impose selective mandatory sanctions.

The U.N. Security Council met at the request of the British representative, Lord Caradon, on Dec. 8, 1966, and adopted by 11 votes to none with four abstentions, on Dec. 16, an amended British resolution on selective mandatory sanctions. These (*a*) operated on 12 key Rhodesian exports – tobacco, sugar, chrome ore, asbestos, iron ore, pig iron, ferro-alloys, meat, meat products, copper, leather, and hides and skins; (*b*) prohibited the supply of aircraft, motor vehicles, their small parts and equipment, and arms to Rhodesia; and (*c*) imposed a ban on the supply of oil and oil products to Rhodesia.

The immediate implementation of this resolution was undertaken by several countries; the resolution was brought into force in Britain by an Order in Council on Dec. 23, 1966, and in the United States by an Executive Order on Jan. 5, 1967. Japan announced on Dec. 23 the suspension of motor vehicle exports to Rhodesia.

The Portuguese Foreign Minister indicated, however, on Dec. 27, that the Portuguese Government was still awaiting replies to letters sent to the U.N. Secretary-General and the President of the Security Council, in particular querying the legality of the resolution which was not adopted unanimously. He claimed further that, over the Rhodesian dispute, Britain had used Portugal "as a scapegoat in a situation for which Britain knows we have no responsibility". South Africa stood by her pledge, made immediately after UDI, not to take part in sanctions.

The U.N. Secretary-General, U Thant, reported to the Security Council on March 9, 1967, on the implementation of the selective mandatory sanctions; a total of 92 member-States had by then supplied information on their policy towards the resolution, most of them being willing to comply with it.

The Malawi Government, however, informed U Thant on Feb. 16 that it could not enforce all the sanctions decreed by the Security Council without imposing hardship on her own people. Neither South Africa nor Portugal replied to U Thant's inquiries on the implementation of the resolution.

Virtual *de facto* recognition was granted to the Smith regime by the Rhodesian judiciary when in January 1968 it refused a Rhodesian African the right of appeal to the Judicial Committee of the Privy Council in London. The Rhodesian authorities subsequently executed a number of Africans condemned to death but granted a reprieve under the Queen's prerogative of mercy. As a result of this action, the British Government introduced a resolution calling for comprehensive mandatory sanctions in the U.N. Security Council, and this resolution was unanimously adopted on May 28, 1968. It imposed mandatory sanctions on Rhodesia in the spheres of trade, financial transactions, communications and travel, involving a complete boycott of Rhodesian goods with certain humanitarian exceptions.

An Order in Council implementing the Security Council resolution was approved by the British House of Commons on July 15 and by the House of Lords on July 18; implementation of comprehensive mandatory sanctions was announced by Japan (June 4), New Zealand (Aug. 29) and the U.S.A. (July 16 and Aug. 12).

The Security Council's sanctions committee, created under the resolution of May 29, in its first report to the Council on Dec. 30, 1968, gave information covering mainly the first half of 1968 and stated that by the middle of that year Rhodesia's trade remained quite substantial, partly because the Security Council's resolution of Dec. 16, 1966, had been confined to selective sanctions and partly because some States had contravened the resolution. All available evidence indicated that South Africa had become Rhodesia's main trading partner and that Portugal had failed to implement both the 1966 and the 1968 resolutions.

Mr. Roy Jenkins, the British Chancellor of the Exchequer, told the House of Commons on July 8, 1969, that the direct cost to the Exchequer of sanctions between UDI and May 31, 1969, amounted to £37,700,000.

III – The Republic

On May 20, 1969, Mr. Smith declared that the "intractable British attitude" had ended hopes of a negotiated settlement of the independence dispute and announced that constitutional proposals due to be published in a White Paper on the next day, together with the question whether Rhodesia should become a Republic, would be the subject of a referendum on June 20. This statement followed the abortive discussions in November 1968 [see page 180] and an inconclusive exchange of messages with the British Residual Mission in Salisbury during the period Jan. 23 to May 14, 1969.

The proposals on the White Paper were based, to some extent, on a set of proposals made on July 17, 1968, by the Rhodesian Front, recommending a Republican Constitution to be implemented in two stages.

The introduction to the White Paper stated: "The Government of Rhodesia believe that the present Constitution is no longer acceptable to the people of Rhodesia because it contains a number of objectionable features, the principal ones being that it provides for eventual African rule and inevitably the domination of one race by another, and that it does not guarantee that government will be retained in responsible hands. Therefore it is proposed that there should be a new Constitution, which, while reproducing some of the provisions of the existing Constitution, will make certain major changes in order to remove these objectionable features. . . ."

The White Paper proposals provided for a Head of State who would be chosen by an Executive Council consisting of the Prime Minister and other Ministers. There would be a bicameral legislature comprising a House of Assembly and a Senate. The former would initially have 66 members including 50 Europeans (non-Africans) elected by European, Asian and Coloured voters; and 16 Africans, eight of whom would be elected by electoral colleges of chiefs, headmen and representatives of African Councils, while the other eight would be elected by African-roll voters. With increasing contributions to the national exchequer from the African community, the number of African seats would gradually be enlarged to a maximum of 50, thus ensuring parliamentary parity. The Senate would comprise 10 Europeans elected by European members of the Lower House, 10 African chiefs elected by all the chiefs of Rhodesia sitting in electoral colleges, and three members of any race to be appointed by the Head of State. Any Bill to amend the Constitution, including entrenched clauses, or the Declaration of Rights, would require an affirmative vote of two-thirds of the total membership of each of the two Houses, voting separately. The "A" and "B" electoral rolls would be replaced by separate

European and African rolls; cross-voting [see page 168] would cease to exist and the nomination of Africans for European seats or *vice versa* would be prohibited. Voting qualifications would be on a basis of income, education and property ownership, and would be higher for Europeans than for Africans.

Amongst the proposed changes to the existing Declaration of Rights were that the preamble would give equal emphasis to the rights and duties of citizens; that exceptions to the right to personal liberty would be increased to cover arrests ordered by quasi-judicial authorities and preventive detention in the interests of public safety; and that protection from search and entry of premises would be limited, and the right of a person to refuse to give evidence at his trial would be omitted. The Declaration would not be enforceable by the courts and the Senate's legal committee would take over the functions of the Constitutional Council.

Mr. Michael Stewart, the U.K. Foreign and Commonwealth Secretary, expressing the British Government's views on the White Paper proposals, stated on May 21, 1969, that the proposals were a "complete and flat denial of at least five of the six principles". He declared that the British Government, although "prepared to be flexible on details, on form and . . . on timing", would not compromise on the principle of "unimpeded progress within reasonable time to majority rule", and he added: "It is inescapable from Mr. Smith's pronouncement that he does not accept that."

The results of the referendum, in which "A" and "B" roll voters voted together, were announced on June 22 as follows:

Republic	"Yes"	61,130
	"No"	14,372
Percentage of majority:		81
New Constitution	"Yes"	54,724
	"No"	20,776
Percentage of majority:		73.

Of the total electorate (over 81,000 Europeans and 6,645 Africans) 75,500 cast their votes.

Mr. Stewart told the House of Commons on June 23 that this result had "pushed the *Fearless* proposals [see page 180] off the table" and declared that it remained the policy of the British Government to work for an honourable settlement "when there are people in power in Rhodesia who share our principles. . . . Meanwhile, sanctions and the international isolation of Rhodesia must continue".

The following day (June 24) Mr. Stewart announced the closure of the British Residual Mission in Salisbury and of Rhodesia House in London, as well as the forthcoming resignation of the Governor, Sir Humphrey Gibbs; Sir Humphrey announced his resignation on the same day that Mr. Stewart's statement was made (June 24).

The Constitution Bill, incorporating the basic White Paper proposals of May 21, was signed by Mr. Clifford Dupont on Nov. 29, 1969. It also laid down that the Head of State and C.-in-C. of the armed forces would be a President appointed by the Cabinet for not more than two five-year terms with limited constitutional powers.

Mr. Smith had previously, on Sept. 3, told the Legislative Assembly that there would be no formal declaration of a Republic and that in any case the new status could not come into effect until the electorate had accepted the proposed Constitution at a general election, probably early in 1970.

Mr. Dupont signed two further Bills on Nov. 29, both of which had also been foreshadowed in the White Paper – a Land Tenure Bill and an Electoral Bill. Under the former, designed to replace the Land Apportionment Act, all land in Rhodesia would be divided into a European area of 44,952,900 acres, an African area of 44,944,500 acres and an area of 6,617,500 acres to be designated "national land"; the Bill also provided for legislation on the ownership and occupation of land in European areas "which makes provision for different classes of Europeans". The Electoral Bill provided for methods of election for members of the new House of Assembly and the Senate.

Following the enactment of this legislation, Mr. Smith declared on Dec. 3 that Rhodesia was now a Republic *de facto*.

On March 2, 1970, Rhodesia officially became a Republic, following the signing by Mr. Dupont on March 1 of a proclamation dissolving the Legislative Assembly and ordering a general election on April 10. Under the Constitution Act [see above] the dissolution of Parliament automatically brought the Republican Constitution into effect, with Mr. Dupont as acting President.

Mr. Stewart, the U.K. Foreign and Commonwealth Secretary, told the House of Commons on March 2 that the "purported assumption of a republican status by the regime in Southern Rhodesia" was illegal and did not in any way affect the British Government's determination to maintain economic sanctions and increase their efficiency whenever possible.

The establishment of a Republic was followed during March by the withdrawal of consular representation of 11 of the 13 countries who, up to March 2, had maintained this form of external contact with the Smith regime, the two exceptions being South Africa and Portugal. During this period, a number of Royal and educational links between Britain and Rhodesia were suspended or broken.

On March 6, the U.N. Security Council met at the urgent request of Britain, who put forward a draft resolution calling on the Council to condemn the Rhodesian action and to decide that "all member-States of the U.N. shall refrain from recognizing this illegal regime or from rendering any assistance to it". As a result of the failure to secure recognition of this resolution and the veto, by the U.S.A. and Britain, against an Afro-Asian resolution calling for the use of force, the Security Council adopted on March 18 a Finnish compromise resolution, which contained, in addition to the substance of the British draft resolution, the following main proposals:

The Council would (1) call upon member-States not to recognize any act performed by officials and institutions of the illegal regime; (2) condemn Portugal and South Africa for continuing to maintain relations with the illegal regime; (3) decide that member-States should "immediately sever all diplomatic, consular, trade, military and other relations that they may have with the illegal regime in Southern Rhodesia; [and] terminate any representation that they may maintain in the territory. . . ."

The U.N. Security Council's Sanctions Committee, however, concluded, in its report of July 13, 1970, that the measures taken against Rhodesia, including sanctions, had not had the desired results, and gave the following figures for Rhodesia's trade with other countries:

	1969	1968
Imports into Rhodesia	£115,000,000	£120,800,000
Exports from Rhodesia	£140,000,000	£106,500,000

The report added that Rhodesia's trade through South Africa and Mozambique had continued virtually unchecked.

In the Rhodesian general elections on April 10 the Rhodesian Front gained all 50 European seats; seven of the eight African-roll seats went to African candidates of the Centre Party and the eighth seat was gained by a candidate of the National People's Union (NPU). [The NPU – the African Opposition – was formed by the merger of the United People's Party (formed in May 1965 by African members of the Rhodesia Party) and the Democratic Party (an African party launched in August 1968 by former ZAPU members) on June 21, 1969, and was dedicated to the principle of majority rule on a non-violent and non-racial basis.] The remaining eight seats in the House of Assembly were reserved for Africans returned by an electoral college of chiefs, headmen and representatives of African Councils. The first Republican Cabinet, with Mr. Ian Smith as Prime Minister, was sworn in by Mr. Dupont on April 13; Mr. Dupont, having been appointed by the Cabinet as the first President of the Republic on April 14, was sworn in on April 16. The 50 European members of the Assembly met on April 30 as an electoral college to elect the 10 European senators.

Continued Opposition to the Regime

The state of emergency in Rhodesia was extended for a further period of three months on Jan. 17, 1969; a Constitutional Amendment Bill to extend the maximum period of states of emergency from three months to one year, introduced the same day, received the required two-thirds majority for final approval on Jan. 24. Under this new legislation the state of emergency was extended for a further twelve months on April 16, 1969, and again on June 11, 1970.

A renewal of infiltration into Rhodesia by African nationalist guerrillas was reported in January 1970; these guerrillas were believed to have crossed the Zambezi river into Rhodesia from Zambia on Jan. 3. On Jan. 29 Mr. Smith warned the Zambian Government of Rhodesian retaliation if it continued actively to support the guerrillas. In reply the Zambian Minister of Home Affairs, Mr. Lewis Changufu, stated on Jan. 30 that any clashes inside Rhodesia were "a direct result of the oppression exercised on the majority of people in Rhodesia" and added: "In the past Zambians along the borders with white minority regimes have suffered constant aggression. . . . Nevertheless, Zambia has avoided measures which would serve to increase tension in the area."

On Aug. 20, 1970, the House extended to two years an Order enabling the Government to restrict the movement of persons without trial or charge. At that time only 56 persons were stated to be under restriction. On Nov. 15 it was announced that death sentences on 20 Africans had been commuted to life imprisonment, and that there were fewer than 20 Africans left under sentence of death.

3. FORMER FRENCH TERRITORIES AND PROTECTORATES

MOROCCO

Area: 171,000 sq. miles.
Population 1969 (estimate): 15,050,000.
Capitals: Rabat — in winter — (261,000), Tangier — in summer — (166,000).
Other important towns: Casablanca (1,177,000), Marrakesh (265,000), Fez (250,000), Meknès (205,000), Oujda (149,000).
Official language: Arabic.
Chief product: Phosphates.

Morocco became an independent sovereign State, under Sultan Mohammed V, after joint declarations recognizing the independence, sovereignty and integrity of the country had been signed with France on March 2, 1956, and with Spain on April 7, 1956.

Under the Treaty of Fez of 1912, Morocco had been a French Protectorate since that date, while a Spanish "sphere of influence" extended over the northern part of the country with the exception of the Tangier Zone. The latter territory, under an International Control Commission, enjoyed a special regime, involving a free monetary system and free trade.

Two parties advocating independence were, in the French sector, the Istiqlal — whose policy called for the abolition of the protectorate system and the conclusion of an agreement with France recognizing Morocco's full independence — and the Democratic Independence Party (PDI), which demanded the opening of negotiations between France and Spain "in order that the whole of Morocco's territory may recover its independence". Demands for the unity and independence of Morocco were put forward, from November 1955 onwards, by two nationalist parties in the Spanish zone — the Reformist Party and the Unity and Independence Party. The amalgamation of the Istiqlal and the Reformist Party was announced in Tangier, on March 17, by Si Allal El Fassi, leader of the Istiqlal.

The French Government announced on April 26, 1956, that agreement had been reached on the formation of a Moroccan Army and that the control of the police would be transferred immediately to the Moroccan Ministry of the Interior.

The ambiguous status of the "Army of Liberation", an organization responsible for a serious revolt in the Rif area prior to independence, led, however, to strained relations between the Moroccan and French authorities and to a number of incidents; the "Army" was not officially recognized by the Moroccan authorities but was allowed to remain in existence side by side with the new Moroccan Army and the French forces retained in Morocco. In the summer of 1956, however, the "Army" decided to incorporate itself in the national Moroccan Army, and by the end of August it was estimated that 10,000 members of the "Army" had arrived in Rabat; 2–3,000 irregulars, however, still remained organized in independent bands.

The Spanish Foreign Minister had announced on June 14, 1965, that it had been agreed to transfer the Spanish zone to the Moroccan authorities within 15 days; this transfer was officially completed on Aug. 1.

On Oct. 29, 1956, a declaration abrogating the international status of Tangier was signed by the Moroccan Foreign Minister and representatives of the International Control Commission. The special status of the city and province of Tangier was finally abolished on April 19, 1960, when Tangier was reintegrated financially and economically with Morocco. However, on Jan. 2, 1962, the King of Morocco signed a decree creating a free zone in the port of Tangier, in accordance with a statement which he had made on July 27, 1961, and which provided for measures designed to revive economic activity in Tangier which had suffered severely since April 1960.

Constitutional Developments

At the achievement of independence the Cabinet of Ministers consisted of members of the Istiqlal and the PDI, while a Consultative National Assembly, consisting of 76 members nominated by the Sultan, reflected not only political groupings but also the various social sectors and regions of Morocco.

Si Bekkai, who had been Prime Minister since November 1955, tendered his resignation on Oct. 26, 1956, but accepted the Sultan's request to form a new Government drawn entirely from the Istiqlal, with the exception of three Independent members, including himself.

Opening the Consultative National Assembly in Rabat on Nov. 12, 1956, the Sultan described the Assembly as "a step towards the final objective which we shall strive to attain – a genuine representative system allowing the people to conduct public affairs within the framework of a constitutional monarchy".

A further step in this direction was made when on July 9, 1957, Prince

Moulay Hassan, the eldest son of the Sultan, was proclaimed heir to the throne. Before nominating the Prince as his heir, the Sultan had obtained not only the consent of the Royal family and *ulema* [doctors of Moslem law] according to tradition, but also that of the Consultative Assembly, the political parties and the trade unions, in order to signify his desire that Morocco should develop into a constitutional monarchy.

It was announced in Rabat on Aug. 14, 1957, that Sultan Mohammed V would be known henceforth as the King of Morocco and that the country would be known as the Kingdom of Morocco instead of the Sherifian Empire.

During 1958 disagreement amongst members of the Government led to the formation of two new Cabinets in succession. M. Ahmed Balafrej, Foreign Minister in Si Bekkai's Cabinet, who formed a new Cabinet on May 8, following the resignation of the Prime Minister on April 16, submitted his own resignation on Nov. 22.

Following the formation of a new Government by M. Abdallah Ibrahim on Dec. 24, 1958, a split occurred in the Istiqlal party; on March 2, 1959, M. Mehdi Ben Barka (President of the Consultative Assembly), M. Mahjoub Ben Seddik (general secretary of the Moroccan Workers' Union – UMT), M. Thami Ammar (Minister of Agriculture) and several other dissident leaders set up their own "national confederation", having been expelled from the Istiqlal party on Jan. 26 by M. El Fassi (the party leader). The dissident faction received the support of the UMT leaders and the student organizations; as a result of the former over 20 constituent unions of the UMT broke away during February 1959 in protest. Under the leadership of M. Ben Barka, the National Union of Popular Forces (UNFP) was formed on Sept. 6, 1959.

This derived its support from (*a*) the dissident Istiqlal faction; (*b*) the UMT; (*c*) dissident sections of the Democratic Independence Party (PDI) led by the former Minister of Labour, M. Abdelhadi Boutaleb; (*d*) a section of the former "Liberation Army" led by M. Mohammed el Basri; (*e*) dissident members of two small political groups – the People's Movement and the Independent Liberals. The main points of the new party's policy were the establishment of a genuine democracy within the framework of a constitutional monarchy, the evacuation of foreign troops and support for Algerian nationalists.

During the last months of 1959 and the early part of 1960 relations were strained between the left-wing members of the Government led by M. Ibrahim and the conservative Ministers, who were generally believed to act under the political direction of the Crown Prince. The left-wing Ministers were supported by the UNFP, the UMT, the Moroccan Students' Union and a section of the "Liberation Army", while the conservative forces controlled the Army and the police. After the formation of the UNFP a number of measures were taken against left-wing organizations, including the banning of the Communist Party on Sept. 14, 1959; 18 members or former members of the "Liberation Army" were arrested during February 1960 and charged in March with conspiracy against the security of the State.

On May 20, 1960, the King dismissed M. Ibrahim's Government and on May 23 he announced that he would himself form a Government, with the Crown Prince as Vice-Premier, and that he would grant Morocco a democratic Constitution before the end of 1962. The new Ministers of the King's Cabinet, formed on May 26 after consultations with former Prime Ministers (MM. Bekkai, Balafrej and Ibrahim), fell into three main groupings: personal friends of the King and the Crown Prince, including M. Bekkai; representatives of political parties; and members of the Ibrahim Government regarded as sympathetic towards the UNFP.

In the first elections ever held in Morocco, the members of 798 municipal and rural district councils were elected on May 29, 1960, all tax-payers of both sexes over the age of 21 (with the exception of members of the armed forces) being eligible to vote. Candidates were put forward by the UNFP, the Istiqlal, the People's Movement, the Constitutional Democratic Party and Independent Liberals; there were also many independent candidates. Between 70 and 75 per cent of the electorate took part in the voting (90 per cent of the eligible population having registered); no official results were announced as the authorities did not regard the elections as a contest between parties. The figures published by the UNFP and Istiqlal were not consistent with each other, both parties claiming a victory in the elections.

King Mohammed V of Morocco died on Feb. 26, 1961, and was succeeded by the Crown Prince as King Hassan II, who took over the Premiership and confirmed in their posts the other Ministers of his father's Cabinet. On June 2, King Hassan formed a new Government under his personal direction; the new Cabinet was representative of all parties except the left-wing UNFP.

In a national referendum held on Dec. 7, 1962, an overwhelming majority voted in favour of a draft Constitution submitted by the King. This Constitution, promulgated on Dec. 14, replaced the interim Basic

Law sealed by King Hassan on June 2, 1961, and provided for the institution of a constitutional monarchy.

The Constitution laid down that (*a*) Morocco was to be a "constitutional, democratic and social monarchy"; (*b*) there would not be a one-party system; (*c*) the franchise and other political rights would be given to all adult men and women; and (*d*) civil freedom would be guaranteed. Parliament would comprise (i) a House of Representatives, elected by universal adult suffrage; and (ii) a House of Councillors, two-thirds of whom would be elected by an electoral college consisting of members of prefectural and provincial assemblies and communal councils, and one third by Chambers of Agriculture, Commerce and Industry and Handicrafts, as well as by trade unions. The Prime Minister and other Cabinet Ministers would be appointed by the King. The revision of the Constitution would rest with the Prime Minister and Parliament; the draft laid down, however, that "neither the monarchical system . . . nor provisions relating to the Moslem religion" might be subject to constitutional reform.

In elections for the first House of Representatives, held on May 17, 1963, the pro-Government Front for the Defence of Constitutional Institutions (FDIC) failed to gain an outright overall majority, obtaining 69 seats against 41 for the conservative Istiqlal party and 28 for the left-wing UNFP; the remaining six seats out of the total membership of 144 went to independent candidates. [The formation of the FDIC had been announced on March 20, 1963, by M. Ahmed Reda Guedira, Minister of the Interior and Agriculture and a leader of the Independent Liberals, with the aim of defending the Constitution against the "dictatorial hopes" of "a certain party" (i.e. the Istiqlal). The Front comprised M. Guedira's Independent Liberal supporters, the People's Movement and a number of independent political personalties.]

The 120 members of the Chamber of Councillors were elected on Oct. 13; the final results gave 107 seats to the FDIC, 11 to the Istiqlal and two to independent candidates. On Nov. 13, the King appointed a new Cabinet headed by Hadj Ahmed Bahnini and composed almost entirely of royalist FDIC members. The first Moroccan Parliament was opened by King Hassan on Nov. 18.

A new political organization, the Democratic Socialist Party (PSD), was formed on April 12, 1964, and on May 10, M. Bahnini was elected its president and M. Guedira its secretary-general. The formation of this party led on June 23 to the division of the 74 FDIC members of Parliament into two groups – 33 following the PSD and the remaining 41 the "People's Movement".

On June 7, 1965, when the Government was defeated in a vote on a new Press law, the King announced that he had proclaimed a state of emergency, that he would himself assume legislative and executive powers and that new elections would not be held until the Constitution had been revised and submitted to a referendum.

The reactions of the different political parties to this announcement were mixed; the PSD declared its full support while the People's Movement was divided and the Istiqlal and UNFP gave it their qualified support.

M. Bahnini tendered his Government's resignation on June 8, and on the same day King Hassan formed his Cabinet; the composition of this reflected the King's desire to concentrate on economic development and increased administrative efficiency. On July 6, 1967, however, Dr. Mohammed Benhima was appointed Prime Minister by the King, Dr. Benhima being succeeded as Premier on Oct. 6, 1969, by Dr. Ahmed Laraki.

A revised Constitution, providing for the ending of the state of emergency and a return to parliamentary democracy under a constitutional monarchy, was approved by 89.7 per cent or 4,443,561 of the valid votes cast in a national referendum on July 24, 1970. The main points of difference between the new Constitution and the 1962 Constitution were that there would be a unicameral legislature made up of members elected in general elections and members elected by an electoral college of representatives of municipal councils, professional bodies and trade unions; and that the initiative for constitutional amendments would lie with the King and no longer with the Prime Minister and Parliament.

This draft constitution was rejected by the Istiqlal, UNFP, UMT and the Moroccan Students' Union (UNEM) when published in mid-July. On July 27, it was announced that the Istiqlal and UNFP had defined the objects of a "National Front" jointly established by them, while retaining their autonomy; these were the achievement of a political, economic and social democracy based on land reform and the nationalization of the economy, the liberation of territories "under foreign domination" and "active support for the people of Palestine". After the date for elections to the Chamber of Representatives had been officially fixed for Aug. 21 and 28, the Istiqlal and the UNFP and its associated trade unions announced early in August that they would boycott these.

In the indirect elections for 150 members, held on Aug. 21, 1970, 95 Independents, known to support the Government, 38 members of the pro-Government People's Movement, 10 members of the *Progrès social*, five Istiqlal members and one candidate each from the *Mouvement populaire démocratique* and the *Parti démocratique constitutionnel* were returned. The direct elections for the remaining 90 members of the Chamber on Aug. 28 resulted in 63 Independents and 22 members of the People's Movement being elected; the successful candidates included all nine members of the Government who had stood for election. M. Abdelhadi Boutaleb was elected President of the new Chamber of Representatives on Oct. 10.

Internal Security

Following the arrest on July 16, 1963, of the leaders of UNFP the Minister of Justice gave further details of an alleged plot on Aug. 15; he stated *inter alia* that a coup was to have been carried out on July 20 and the King himself assassinated.

The trial of the 102 UNFP members and supporters arrested in July opened on Nov. 23, 1963, in Rabat; 67 defendants were found guilty and 35 acquitted by the court on March 14, 1964. M. Mohammed el Basri, M. Moumen Diouri and M. Omar Benjelloun were sentenced to death, as were eight of the sixteen tried *in absentia*, including M. Mehdi Ben Barka and M. Ahmed Akouliz (known as "Sheik el Arab" and said to be one of the leaders of the conspiracy). The remaining convicted defendants were sentenced to varying periods of imprisonment. On Aug. 20, 1964, King Hassan commuted the death sentence on MM. Basri, Diouri and Benjelloun to life imprisonment. Under a general amnesty on April 14, 1965, all those imprisoned following the "July plot" were released; this did not include those tried *in absentia*.

M. Ben Barka, who had been living in exile in Geneva since before the above trial, disappeared during a visit to Paris on Oct. 29, 1965, under suspicious circumstances; no trace of him was subsequently found and it was feared that he had been murdered. Strong feeling was aroused by this incident among the left-wing opposition parties in Morocco.

On March 23, 1965, violent rioting broke out in Casablanca; the immediate cause was a Ministry of Education circular making some form of technical training compulsory for students over 17. Students and schoolboys, fearing that this would exclude them from professional or civil service careers, went on strike on March 22, and organized demonstrations in the city on the following day. Workers who were discontent at growing unemployment and rising prices joined in these demonstrations which soon degenerated into riots. According to an official statement, seven rioters were killed and 69 soldiers and police injured; but unofficially it was estimated that at least six policemen and 103 civilians had been killed and 500–600 injured.

Nationalization

Under a decree of Sept. 26, 1963, the Moroccan State expropriated, between October 1963 and July 1966, some 250,000 hectares of colonized land which had been privately sold to foreign landowners, as opposed to land officially colonized during the period of the French Protectorate.

> This nationalization of agricultural land formed part of a land reform plan envisaging a redistribution of land and limitation of the size of holdings. The redistribution of expropriated land began on July 15, 1966, under a decree published on that day, when 6,000 hectares were distributed amongst 500 peasants grouped in 13 co-operatives. A move towards the decentralization of agrarian organization was made early in 1967 when the *Office de mise en valeur agricole* (the body in charge of land reform) was dissolved and replaced by seven regional offices.

On July 1, 1965, within a few weeks of the declaration of a state of emergency, King Hassan announced a measure which brought over 60 per cent of the country's exports under State control; this was that the export trade in citrus fruits, fresh vegetables, fish products and handicraft goods would be nationalized and transferred to the *Office chérifien de contrôle et d'exportation*, and followed the nationalization of the phosphates trade. By April 1967 nationalization of the export trade had been extended to wines and cotton.

Further nationalization measures were announced by the Government during 1966 and 1967; on Jan. 19, 1966, the Government announced that it was taking over 50 per cent of the shares of the Moroccan Sugar Company, while in April 1967 the Government extended its control over the Spanish iron-mining company, *Minas del Rif*, by taking over two iron-mines near Nador.

"Moroccanization" and "Arabization" measures were taken in the judiciary, health service and education system from early 1965 onwards. Educational reform included a three-year plan over the period 1965 to 1967 at the end of which Arabic would have replaced French as the language of instruction; at the end of 1967, however, French was still the principal language of instruction for senior pupils.

Foreign Relations

The main problems of Morocco's relations with other countries after the achievement of independence were caused by disputes with her neighbours and the existence of foreign bases on Moroccan soil.

Spanish Territories

Relations with Spain centred on the question of the two Spanish "State Territories" of Ceuta and Melilla [on the Moroccan coast facing Spain], and the Spanish enclave of Ifni on the western coast of Morocco. Ceuta had been a Spanish possession since the end of the sixteenth century and Melilla since 1492; Ifni was ceded to Spain by Morocco in 1860 but the Spanish flag was not hoisted there until 1934.

In November-December 1957 Spanish forces repelled an attack on Ifni by Moroccan irregulars. King Mohammed V, however, reaffirmed on Dec. 10, 1957, that his Government intended to "restore Morocco's natural and historic frontiers", and on July 23 and Aug. 20, 1961, Moroccan claims to Ceuta, Melilla, Ifni and the Spanish Sahara (embracing Rio de Oro and Sagura el Hamra) were reiterated.

The Ifni enclave and Spanish Saharan territories. (*Economist*)

In the last-named territory and also in "Southern Morocco" [see map] a "Liberation Army" was active early in 1958. There followed an agreement signed on April 1, 1958, on the transfer of "Southern Morocco" to Moroccan jurisdiction, which came into effect on April 10. Ifni, however, was not transferred to Morocco until June 30, 1969, after an agreement to that effect had been signed in Fez on Jan. 4, 1969.

For the Spanish Sahara the U.N. General Assembly had in December 1968 and again in December 1969 recommended a referendum on its future status, and King Hassan stated in February 1970 that if necessary Morocco would settle this problem in direct negotiations with Spain.

Mauritania

Open support for the concept of a "Greater Morocco" including Mauritania was expressed for the first time by King Mohammed on Feb. 25, 1958; this claim was reiterated in more explicit terms on March 28 by the King when he received four prominent Mauritanian public figures who pledged him their loyalty, this action being condemned by the Mauritanian Government on the following day.

The Moroccan claim to sovereignty over the whole territory of Mauritania was strongly reasserted after the announcement on July 26, 1960, that Mauritania would become independent on Nov. 28, 1960. The Moroccan Government began intense diplomatic activity to gain support for its case, obtaining a favourable response from the Foreign Ministers' Conference of the Arab League in August but failing to secure the passage of a resolution in its favour by the Political Committee of the U.N. General Assembly in November.

On Sept. 26, 1969, however, King Hassan announced at a press conference that he had decided to renounce the Moroccan reservations regarding the recognition of the Islamic Republic of Mauritania; subsequently during a visit by a Moroccan delegation to Nouakchott on Jan. 12–16, 1970, it was decided to establish diplomatic relations between the two countries, while on June 8, 1970, a "treaty of solidarity, good neighbourliness and co-operation" was signed.

Algeria

The border between Morocco and Algeria had never been finally demarcated but this fact did not lead to a serious dispute until July 1963. From then onwards the Moroccans repeatedly alleged that Algerian troops had made incursions into Moroccan territory, while counter-charges were made by the Algerian Government.

From 1964 onwards relations between the two countries gradually improved; a new trade and tariff agreement was signed on Nov. 25, 1964, while a "Treaty of Solidarity and Co-operation" was signed on Jan. 15, 1969, by the two countries' Foreign Ministers.

Finally on May 27, 1970, King Hassan and President Boumedienne agreed to set up a joint commission to demarcate the frontier area from Figuig to Tindouf, it being expected that the definitive line would follow the *de facto* border inherited from French rule.

French and American Bases

The evacuation of French and American military bases in Morocco took place over a period of years.

Between February 1958 and April 1959 French troops in Morocco were gradually reduced, those remaining in Morocco being regrouped, after the Moroccan Government had brought pressure to bear on the French Government. An agreement was signed in Rabat on Sept. 1, 1960, providing for the evacuation of all French military, naval and air forces from Morocco by March 2, 1961, with the exception of Air Force training schools which would be evacuated in stages up to the end of 1963; on March 5, 1961, it was announced by King Hassan that France had agreed to accelerate the evacuation plans so that the last of the air-base schools would be vacated by Oct. 1, 1961, and this date was adhered to.

On Dec. 22, 1959, President Eisenhower of the U.S.A. visited Casablanca for conversations with the King. A joint communiqué announced the same day that the U.S. Air Force would relinquish its base at Ben-Slimane (near Rabat) by March 31, 1960, and that all U.S. Forces would be withdrawn from Morocco by the end of 1963. In the event the Ben-Slimane base was handed over on March 4, 1960.

TUNISIA

Area: 48,319 sq. miles.
Population 1969 (estimate): 5,027,000.
Capital: Tunis (790,000).
Official language: Arabic.
Chief products: Zinc, phosphates, petroleum, olive oil.

Tunisia, formerly a French Protectorate, became independent on March 20, 1956, when France and Tunisia signed a protocol in which France recognized Tunisia's independence and her right to conduct her own foreign policy and to form her own Army.

The five years preceding this agreement had been characterized by nationalist demands for independence and by terrorist activity. Following the rejection by France on Jan. 9, 1952, of a Tunisian demand for autonomy and an all-Tunisian Parliament, serious disturbances broke out in Tunisia and M. Habib Bourguiba, leader of the Néo-Destour (Tunisian Nationalist Party), was arrested. [M. Bourguiba had become one of the leaders of the Tunisian Nationalist Movement in 1930. He was responsible in 1934 for the split in the ranks of the Destour (Constitution) Party, reorganizing the majority as the Néo-Destour Party.] Terrorist activity for which members of the Néo-Destour and Tunisian Communist parties and, on certain occasions, of the French community in Tunisia were held responsible, continued throughout 1952–54.

Finally, on June 2, 1955, an agreement granting autonomy to Tunisia, but protecting French interests in that country, was signed; this received the support of the majority of the Néo-Destour but was opposed by an extremist wing of that party led by M. Salah Ben Youssef, which demanded a strict time-limit on all restrictions of Tunisian sovereignty.

M. Bourguiba, who welcomed the agreement and who had been interned in France since May 1954, following two years' imprisonment on the island of Galite, returned to Tunis on June 1, 1955, while M. Ben Youssef, who had been living in exile since 1952, arrived in Tunis on Sept. 13. On Oct. 12, however, M. Ben Youssef was expelled from the party on the grounds (a) that by his opposition to the autonomy protocol he had pursued a policy contrary to that approved by the political bureau and (b) that he had attempted to create divergencies and sow confusion among the membership. M. Ben Youssef refused to recognize his expulsion and stated on Oct. 30 that he would form branches of the "general secretariat of the Néo-Destour".

During the next three months clashes occurred between Bourguibists and Youssefists; on Jan. 31, 1956, the Government announced the discovery of a Youssefist conspiracy aimed at preventing the application of the agreement granting autonomy to Tunisia. M.Ben Youssef escaped before being arrested and was granted asylum in Libya.

Independent Monarchy

In the first general elections, held on March 25, 1956, on a basis of adult male suffrage, all 98 seats in the Constituent Assembly were won by the National Front, which had been formed before the election out of the Bourguiba wing of the Néo-Destour, the General Union of Tunisian Workers (UGTT), the Union of Tunisian Craftsmen and Traders and a number of independent candidates.

The new Cabinet, under the leadership of M. Bourguiba, was presented to the Bey (the hereditary ruler of Tunisia) on April 15, while M. Djellonli Farès (Néo-Destour) was elected President of the Assembly on April 17.

Tunisia made further progress towards independence with the signing of agreements with France (*a*) on April 18, 1956, in which the Tunisian Government assumed complete responsibility for public order, and (*b*) on June 15, in which France recognized Tunisia's right to possess her own diplomatic representation.

Several political and social reforms were approved by the Tunisian Government in the months following the general elections: the reduction of the Bey's Civil List (June 21); the abolition of the special legal status of the Bey's family (May 31); the reform of the local government system (June 16); the nationalization of religious foundations (May 2); and the improvement of the status of agricultural workers (April 30).

A number of engagements against "Youssefist" rebels took place between April and June 1956, while on Jan. 24, 1957, M.Ben Youssef was sentenced to death *in absentia* on charges of plotting against the internal security of the State.

The Republic

On July 25, 1957, the Constituent Assembly unanimously decided (1) to abolish the Monarchy; (2) to proclaim Tunisia a Republic; and (3) to invest M. Bourguiba with the functions of Head of State and with the title of President of the Republic.

Sentences were passed, on Dec. 23, 1958, on a number of persons who were accused of plotting the assassination of President Bourguiba, of smuggling arms into the country from Libya, and of planning to form an Opposition party, which would act as a cover for "Youssefist" activities. Nine of the defendants, of whom four, including M. Ben Youssef, were tried *in absentia*, were sentenced to death; however, on Dec. 29, President Bourguiba commuted the death sentences on the five defendants who were in Tunisia to hard labour for life.

A further trial of 128 supporters of M. Ben Youssef on charges of plotting to assassinate President Bourguiba and overthrow the Government ended on Oct. 3, 1959, when all but five of the defendants were found guilty, 15 being sentenced to death. [M. Ben Youssef was shot dead on Aug. 12, 1961, at an hotel in Frankfurt (West Germany) by unknown assailants.]

On Nov. 8, 1959, M. Bourguiba was re-elected unopposed as President of the Tunisian Republic in the first elections held under the new Constitution, which had been officially promulgated on June 1, 1959.

This laid down that Tunisia was a Moslem State and guaranteed fundamental human rights. The President, who must be a Moslem, would be elected for a term of five years by universal suffrage and might be re-elected, with a limit of three consecutive terms. He would lay down the policy of the State; choose the members of the Government, who would be responsible solely to himself; and hold the Supreme Command of the armed forces. The National Assembly would be elected for a term of five years at the same time as the President and the Constitution might be amended by a two-thirds majority of the Assembly even without presidential approval.

In the presidential elections over 91 per cent (1,009,127 out of 1,099,577) of the electorate went to the polls and of these 1,005,769 voters (91 per cent) were in favour of the re-election of M. Bourguiba. In the Assembly all 90 seats were won by the ruling Néo-Destour party, which presented lists of "national union". The sole Opposition party, the Communists, supported M. Bourguiba and the only Opposition candidates for the Assembly were two Communists.

A plot to assassinate President Bourguiba was discovered on Dec. 19, 1962; it was alleged that the various elements involved in the conspiracy included members of the Army, supporters of the old Destour Party, followers of the late M. Ben Youssef and former members of the pre-independence resistance movement. 26 conspirators were tried between Jan. 12 and 17, 1963, on charges of plotting against State security and attempting to assassinate the President, to overthrow the Government and to subvert the loyalty of the Army; 13 of the defendants were condemned to death and 13 to varying terms of hard labour or imprisonment.

The Tunisian Communist Party had announced on Jan. 8, 1963, that it had been "officially informed that it must cease its activities" although the party leadership had strongly condemned the assassination attempt. In addition on Jan. 18, President Bourguiba announced that he had recalled the Tunisian Ambassador in Algiers in view of the "encouragement" which the plotters against his life had "received in Algeria"; the Algerian Government announced on Jan. 20 that it had recalled the head of the Algerian diplomatic mission in Tunis and strongly denied M. Bourguiba's "rash accusations". [Diplomatic relations were resumed between the two countries on May 25, 1963.]

At the first party congress to be held since March 1959, on Oct. 19–22,

1964, the Néo-Destour Party adopted the name *Parti socialiste destourien* (PSD), thus emphasizing the party's commitment to "Tunisian socialism". The congress also approved measures designed to ensure closer liaison between the Government, "national organizations", such as trade unions, and local party cells.

In the presidential and general elections on Nov. 8, 1964, President Bourguiba was re-elected for a further five years, receiving 1,255,152 votes out of a registered electorate of 1,301,543, while the ruling PSD won all 90 seats in the Assembly with the support of about 96 per cent of the registered electorate; no Opposition candidates stood in either of the elections. Dr. Sadok Mokkadem was elected President of the new Assembly on Nov. 12.

A decision to set up a Council of the Republic was made on March 15, 1966, at a meeting of members of the political bureau of the PSD and of the Tunisian Cabinet, under the chairmanship of President Bourguiba. The Council would comprise the Ministers and members of the political bureau and would (*a*) examine the general policy of the Government on a consultative basis; and (*b*) in the event of a vacancy in the Presidency through "death, resignation or absolute incapacity" designate an acting President. This second function superseded the existing arrangement under which members of the Government were called upon to elect one of their members as acting President, and was attributed to the President's wish to strengthen the existing regime and its institutions even if he himself could no longer exercise his functions through illness or death.

Following widespread popular opposition to the pace and extent of the implementation of the principle of collectivized farming [which had begun experimentally in 1962 and been authorized on a wider scale by legislation in May 1963], a major reorganization of the Cabinet occurred on Sept. 8, 1969. In particular, this involved the transfer of overall responsibility for economic and planning affairs from M. Ahmed Ben Salah, principal architect of the collectivization policy, to M. Bahi Ladgham, Secretary of State to the Presidency; in a decree issued on the same day, M. Ladgham (who was also Secretary-General of the PSD) received many of the responsibilities of a Prime Minister, although not the title.

The Cabinet reshuffle was accompanied by a decision to "revise" the controversial agrarian reform policy by a Bill which became law on Sept. 20. This laid down that a private sector would remain in agriculture, its text specifying that the categories of farming which would not be obligatorily collectivized would include family farms centred round their owners' residences, family stockbreeding concerns, market gardens, other horticultural enterprises and orchards; thus the co-operative system would essentially involve cereal-producing lands and vineyards.

President Bourguiba, as the only candidate, was re-elected for a third term of office on Nov. 2, 1969, receiving 1,363,731 votes or 99.76 per cent of the total of 1,367,122 votes cast on a 94.71 per cent poll. In the general elections held at the same time PSD candidates were elected unopposed to all 101 seats in the Assembly with 94.69 per cent of the electorate taking part in the vote. On Nov. 7 in a reorganization of the Cabinet, M. Bahi Ladgham was appointed to the newly-created post of Prime Minister.

Further action against M. Ahmed Ben Salah was taken during November 1969. He was dropped from the Cabinet and lost the post of Secretary-General of the PSD on Nov. 7 and expelled from the PSD two days later (Nov. 9) as a result of "a confirmed disagreement between the point of view of the party and that of M. Ben Salah as to the spirit of the party's fundamental opinions and of their methods of application". On Nov. 10 M. Ben Salah was bitterly attacked by the President, who accused him of being "responsible for our misfortunes" and of carrying out an economic policy which had brought the country "to within an ace of catastrophe"; on the following day M. Ben Salah was deprived of his seat in the Assembly. At the beginning of 1970 M. Ben Salah was placed under a form of house arrest while a parliamentary commission of inquiry investigated his management of the economy; he was arrested on March 24 on a charge of having planned since 1956 to achieve ultimate control of the Government. His trial opened on May 19 and he was sentenced to 10 years' hard labour, 10 years' restricted residence and deprivation of his civil rights on charges of treason and mismanagement of the economy on May 24.

On June 8, 1970, M. Ladgham's Cabinet resigned; the President thereupon invited M. Ladgham to form a new Government and also replaced the political bureau of the PSD by a nine-man commission, of his own appointing, with responsibility for drafting amendments to the Constitution and plans for the structural reorganization of the PSD. The appointment of this commission followed the announcement on the same day by the President of plans for reforming the country's political institutions to introduce greater democracy and make the presidential regime more flexible.

M. Hedi Nouira succeeded M. Ladgham as Prime Minister on Nov. 1; this arose out of the latter's continued absence from the country, following his appointment as head of a supervisory committee for the implementation of a cease-fire agreement in the Jordanian Civil War of September 1970.

Relations with France, 1956–70

Tunisia's relations with France remained strained until 1963 when the French Government evacuated the naval base at Bizerta, all French armed forces from other parts of Tunisia having been withdrawn by Oct. 11, 1958.

During the years 1956–61 the deterioration of these relations, resulting from Tunisian support for the Algerian nationalists and insistence on the withdrawal of French troops from Tunisia, led to repeated armed clashes, to mutual discriminatory action against Frenchmen in Tunisia and Tunisians in France, and to the suspension of diplomatic relations for one year from July 20, 1961.

Although Franco-Tunisian relations improved thereafter, an unresolved problem between the two countries arose from their failure to reach agreement on compensation for former French-owned land, which the Tunisian State had taken over under a Land Nationalization Bill unanimously approved by the National Assembly on May 12, 1964.

GUINEA

Area: 96,865 sq. miles.
Population 1969 (estimate): 3,890,000.
Capital: Conakry (172,500).
Other important towns: Kankan (176,000), Kindia (152,000).
Official language: French.
Chief products: Aluminium, iron ore, diamonds, bananas, coffee.

After 68 years of French rule as part of French West Africa, Guinea became an independent Republic on Oct. 2, 1958, following the rejection by the people of Guinea of the new Constitution of the Fifth Republic of France on Sept. 28 by 636,281 votes against 18,012 – Guinea being the only former French colony to vote against the new Constitution.

The French Government informed the Government of Guinea on Sept. 29, 1958, that by its vote Guinea had separated itself from the other territories of French West Africa and that she would "no longer normally receive the aid either of the administration of the French State or of funds for equipment".

On the achievement of independence M. Sekou Touré, until then Prime Minister, assumed office as Head of the first Government of the Republic – which included representatives of the ruling *Parti démocratique de Guinée* (PDG), the Guinea section of the *Rassemblement démocratique africain* (RDA) and the *Parti du regroupement africain* (PRA). The Constituent Assembly, formed on Oct. 2 by the transformation of the Territorial Assembly, adopted a draft Constitution declaring Guinea to be a Republic of the presidential type on Nov. 12.

Technical agreements were signed with France on Jan. 5, 1959, under which French would remain the official language, French assistance in the supply of technicians, civil servants and teachers would be given and Guinea would remain in the Franc Zone. This latter provision was renounced, however, by President Touré on March 1, 1960. France announced the establishment of diplomatic relations with Guinea on Jan. 15, 1959.

M. Sekou Touré was re-elected by direct popular vote as President of the Republic on Jan. 15, 1961; the only candidate, he received over 99 per cent of the votes.

During the following year, a policy of nationalization was implemented; on Jan. 31, the nationalization of two major public utility companies – supplying electric power and water – and the foreign-owned largest private transport company in Guinea was announced, and on March 13 that of the precious minerals industry. On Jan. 8, 1962, all insurance companies were closed by Government order, following the formation of a State insurance company in August 1961.

On Aug. 26, 1961, the Roman Catholic Archbishop of Conakry was expelled from Guinea following his protest against the decision of the PDG that all private schools should be nationalized and against the President's statement that all the Churches in Guinea should become "national". Relations between the Church and the Government improved, however, with the installation of an African prelate as Roman Catholic Archbishop of Conakry on May 31, 1962.

On Dec. 11, 1961, President Touré made a strong public attack against "anti-Guinean" plotters, including Communists, who were alleged to be in contact with "circles in France" and with an unnamed "embassy of an Eastern country" and to have been responsible for an attempt to overthrow the regime in November. Following this attack the Soviet Ambassador in Conakry, Mr. Daniel Solod, left Guinea on Dec. 16, 1961, at the request of the Guinean Government.

In the general elections held on Sept. 28, 1963, a single list of candidates put forward by the PDG for an enlarged Assembly of 75 members was returned.

On Oct. 15, 1963, the denationalization of diamond mines and of certain stores, the closing of State shops and the ending of the control of private retail trade were ordered by presidential decree.

Diplomatic relations between Guinea and France were in effect broken off on Nov. 22, 1965, following official Guinean allegations that two members of the French Government, as well as the French Embassy in Conakry, were implicated in a plot against President Touré. Accusations of involvement in the plot were made against the Governments of the Ivory Coast, Niger and Upper Volta, all of whom, with France, denied the allegations.

Relations between Ghana and Guinea deteriorated following the announcement by President Touré on March 2, 1966, that Dr. Nkrumah – who had been offered political asylum in Guinea after the overthrow of his regime in Ghana [see page 99] – had been appointed joint Head of State of Guinea. Ghana's immediate reactions were to close the Ghanaian Embassy in Conakry, to recall Ghana's diplomatic mission and to send a sharp protest to the Guinean Government.

Two incidents involving the detention of Guinean citizens occurred in October 1966 and June 1967. On Oct. 29, 1966, the Ghanaian authorities detained the four members of the Guinean delegation to the OAU conference to be held on Nov. 5–9; the Ghanaian Government announced that the four would not be released unless the Guinean Government released those Ghanaians who were "illegally detained" in Guinea. The second incident occurred on June 26, 1967, when the Guinean Foreign Minister and Guinea's Permanent Representative at the U.N. were detained by the Ivory Coast authorities, who stated that the Guineans would not be released until a high official of the Ivory Coast and the crew of an Ivory Coast trawler were set free in Guinea. This exchange took place in the last week of September 1967.

Presidential and legislative elections were held on Jan. 1, 1968; M. Touré, nominated by the country's only political party (the PDG) and the only candidate, received 99.9 per cent of the votes in the presidential election, whilst a single list of candidates, also nominated by the PDG, was returned to the Assembly.

In February 1968 President Touré declared that his "Marxist" regime would become more rigid and attack the "remaining vestiges of capitalism, tribalism and religion". Previously a mass expulsion of European mission-aries had been completed by May 31, 1967, and the regime introduced a "cultural revolution", involving educational reforms which would bring school curricula in line with the revolution. The "Guineazation" of commerce was announced by President Touré on Nov. 8, 1968.

Estimates of the number of Guineans who by 1968 had fled the country (mainly to Senegal and the Ivory Coast) because of their opposi-tion to the regime varied widely, the minimum being 250,000. The PDG, on the other hand, was thought to have firm control of its 1,800,000 members organized in some 7,000 local committees of 10 members each.

On May 14, 1969, the National Revolutionary Council sentenced 13 defendants to death and another 27 to terms ranging from hard labour for life to five years' imprisonment on charges of plotting to overthrow the Government of President Touré – all of the accused having confessed, according to Radio Conakry, to taking part in the conspiracy.

Serious incidents occurred in November 1970, when attempts by "mercenaries" and Guinean exiles to invade the country were repulsed by forces loyal to the Government. President Sekou Touré, in announcing the first such attempt on Nov. 22, said that one of the invaders who had been taken prisoner had stated that they had received instructions from a Portuguese general. On Nov. 23, the Guinean Government further stated that the operation was "part of a plan by foreign powers to reconquer African countries with revolutionary regimes".

Although Portugal denied these allegations of having launched the invasion of Guinea, the report of a U.N. special mission sent to investigate the affair concluded from the fact that foreign naval units were involved (as confirmed by eyewitnesses) that another Power was involved. In addition the report declared that the information obtained from other sources appeared to confirm the Guinean Government's conviction that this Power was Portugal.

On Jan. 24, 1971, the National Assembly of Guinea, sitting as a Supreme Revolutionary Tribunal, sentenced 92 Africans (34 *in absentia*) to death and a further 72 persons to hard labour for life; the latter included the Roman Catholic Archbishop of Conakry, Mgr. Raymond-Maria Tchidimbo, and two West Germans, Herr Adolf Marx and Herr Hermann Seibold (who was said by the Conakry authorities to have committed suicide in his cell after arrest). By Feb. 4, according to most informed sources in Conakry, eight of the 92 condemned to death had been executed, four of whom were named by the Government as former senior Guinean officials.

Diplomatic relations were broken with Senegal (by the Senegalese Government on Jan. 24, 1971) and with West Germany (by Guinea on Jan. 29, 1971) following Guinean allegations that both countries were involved with Portugal in the abortive invasion of November 1970.

CAMEROON

Area: 183,000 sq. miles.
Population 1970 (estimate): 5,800,000.
Capital: Yaoundé (120,000).
Other important town: Douala (200,000).
Official languages: French and English.
Chief products: Aluminium, cocoa, coffee, timber.

(economist)

Cameroon is a Federal Republic, constituted on Oct. 1, 1961, out of two former Trust Territories administered respectively by France and Britain: (*a*) East Cameroon, which, as part of the former German colony of Kamerun, had been a League of Nations Mandate and later a U.N. Trust Territory administered by France, and since Jan. 1, 1960, the independent Republic of Cameroon; and (*b*) West Cameroon, which together with Northern Cameroons had formed the other part of the German colony and had been a League of Nations Mandate and U.N. Trust Territory administered by Britain.

The Republic of Cameroon, 1960–61

In the Republic of Cameroon, power was provisionally retained by the Government which was led by M. Ahmadou Ahidjo as Prime Minister and had held office since February 1958 under a statute of 1956 whereby the territory had received internal autonomy whilst remaining under French trusteeship.

A national referendum held on Feb. 21, 1960, produced a favourable majority for the new Constitution, which provided for a President as Head of State, who would appoint the Prime Minister and Cabinet; a National Assembly of 100 members elected by universal suffrage; an Economic and Social Council; and a federal administrative structure to take account of the ethnic and religious diversity of the Cameroon population.

In the first general elections held since independence on April 10, 1960, M. Ahidjo's party, the *Union camerounaise,* received 60 seats in the National Assembly. The remainder were distributed amongst the *Union des populations du Cameroun* (UPC) — a left-wing Nationalist movement — (22), the Democratic Party (11), Moderates (2) and other Opposition parties (11). M. Ahidjo was elected President of the Republic on May 5 by the National Assembly.

Southern Cameroons, 1959–61

The Southern Cameroons, as a U.N. Trust Territory, were administered as an integral part of Nigeria, the Governor-General of Nigeria being also High Commissioner for the Southern Cameroons.

The first elections for the Southern Cameroons House of Assembly based on universal adult suffrage and held on Jan. 24, 1959, were won by the Kamerun National Democratic Party (led by Mr. John N. Foncha and favouring separation from Nigeria) which by gaining 14 out of the Assembly's 26 seats defeated the alliance of the Kamerun National Congress (which gained 12 seats) and the Kamerun People's Party (2 seats) which together had formed the previous Government and advocated joining the Federation of Nigeria.

The U.N. General Assembly's Trusteeship Committee decided on March 12, 1959, that separate plebiscites should be held in the Northern and Southern Cameroons to ascertain the inhabitants' wishes as to their future.

It had previously been announced on Oct. 17, 1960, after meetings between Mr. Foncha, the Premier of the Southern Cameroons Government, and M. Ahidjo, the President of the Cameroon Republic, that it was proposed to set up a federation of the two countries, with a federal Executive and Parliament for the whole of the enlarged Republic but with separate Governments and Legislative Assemblies in each of the two federal States.

The plebiscites, repeatedly postponed, were eventually held on Feb. 11—12, 1961, and resulted in 223,571 voters in the Southern Cameroons favouring union with the Cameroon Republic, against 97,741 for union with Nigeria (out of a registered electorate of 354,163. [In the Northern Cameroons, however, 147,296 votes were cast for union with Nigeria, against 97,659 for union with the Cameroon Republic, out of 292,985 registered voters. The Northern Cameroons accordingly, on June 1, 1961, became part of the Northern region of the Federation of Nigeria — see page 105.]

The Federal Republic

On the entry of the Southern Cameroons, as the Federate State of West Cameroon, into the Cameroon Republic Mr. Foncha became Vice-President of the Republic, and on Jan. 11, 1962, he was reinvested as Premier of West Cameroon. Both President Ahidjo and Vice-President Foncha were re-elected in 1965 and again in 1970.

The country's sole legal party, the *Union nationale camerounaise* (UNC), received the votes of 98 per cent of the registered electorate in general elections held on June 7, 1970, for the 50 seats of the Federal National Assembly and for the 100 seats of the Legislative Assembly of the Federate State of East Cameroon. The UNC came into being on Sept. 1, 1966, through the amalgamation of four political parties: (*a*) the *Union camerounaise*, (*b*) the Kamerun National Democratic Party, (*c*) the Kamerun People's National Convention, led by Dr. E. M. L. Endeley; and *(d)* the Kamerun United Congress, led by Mr. Salomon Tandeng Muna.

The Constitution provided that after May 7, 1965, the Premier of West Cameroon was no longer concurrently Vice-President of Cameroon; Mr. S. T. Muna became Premier of West Cameroon in January 1968. In East Cameroon Dr. Simon Pierre Tchoungi was appointed Premier in November 1965 and reappointed in June 1970.

The illegal UPC, which had formed the largest parliamentary Opposition group in the former Republic of Cameroon [see above], had lost much of its influence since the death of the militant leaders, the latest of these being the party's provisional secretary-general (M. Osende Afana) in March 1966. The movement was held directly responsible for a number of violent incidents which occurred between 1967 and 1970 in the vicinity of the border with the Congo (Brazzaville).

On Jan. 5–6, 1971, the Roman Catholic Bishop of Nkongsamba (Cameroon) and five other defendants accused of subversive activities organized by the UPC were sentenced to death by a military court in Yaoundé. Three of these sentences, including the bishop's, were commuted to life imprisonment on Jan. 14, while on the following day the remaining death sentences were carried out in public.

TOGO

Area: 21,850 sq. miles.
Population 1970: 2,000,000.
Capital: Lome (100,000).
Official language: French.
Chief products: Phosphates, cocoa, coffee.

The French-administered Trust Territory of Togoland achieved independence as the Republic of Togo on April 27, 1960, under the premiership of M. Sylvanus Olympio, who had held office since April 1958. Before 1914 the Territory had formed the eastern part of the German colony of Togo; from 1919 it was administered by France under a League of Nations Mandate and subsequently under U.N. trusteeship from 1946, having the status of an autonomous Republic within the French Community since 1956. [The western part of the former German Togo was administered under similar terms by Britain until 1957, when it joined the independent State of Ghana – see pages 88, 90.]

In the first elections since independence held on April 9, 1961, M. Sylvanus Olympio was elected President of the Republic; at the same time a National Assembly of 51 members was elected and the Constitution of the new Republic approved. M. Olympio was the sole candidate and the list of candidates sponsored by his party, the *Comité de l'unité togolaise* (CUT), the only one submitted. The Opposition candidature of M. Anani Santos and the list submitted by the *Juvento* Movement on behalf of the principal Opposition parties (*Juvento* and the *Union démocratique des populations togolaises* – UDPT) were rejected on the grounds that they had been filed too late. The Opposition parties protested against this decision, alleging that they had been prevented by various governmental measures from submitting their lists within the specified period.

Between May 1961 and January 1962 there were three assassination attempts made against President Olympio.

On May 11, 1961, it was announced that a plot aimed at a rebellion and the assassination of members of the Government had been discovered; it was also alleged that this had been organized by members of the Opposition parties with the support of a "neighbouring country" (i.e. Ghana). A second plot was said to have been discovered on Dec. 1–2, 1961; an official statement declared that the 18 men who had been arrested after this discovery had confessed to having been trained in Ghana under President Nkrumah. Further arrests were subsequently made, including that of the secretary-general and president of the *Juvento* Party, which was dissolved by presidential decree on Jan. 13, 1962. The third attempt was made on Jan. 21, 1962, no political motives being ascribed to the crime.

Following the development of Togo into a virtual one-party State and the emergence of special problems over the future of the Togolese armed forces, President Olympio's Government was overthrown and the President assassinated in a military coup on Jan. 13, 1963. The leaders of the coup established an "insurrectionary committee" which, it was announced, had requested M. Nicolas Grunitzky (the leader of the Opposition UDPT) and M. Antoine Meatchi (head of the affiliated *Union des chefs et des populations du nord*) to return from exile. M. Grunitzky formed a provisional civilian Government on Jan. 16, which was formally presented to the Togolese Assembly on Jan. 17. He then decreed both the abrogation of the existing Constitution and electoral laws and the Assembly's dissolution.

Under the new Constitution approved by a national referendum on May 5, 1963, M. Grunitzky was elected President and M. Meatchi (deputy head of the provisional Government) Vice-President in elections held on the same date (May 5), both being the only candidates. The National Assembly elections held at the same time resulted in the return of a single "National Union" list submitted by the four main political parties – UDPT, *Juvento, Mouvement populaire togolais* and CUT, the party formerly led by the late President Olympio.

On Jan. 13, 1967, a bloodless coup was carried out by the Army, led by Lieut.-Colonel Etienne Eyadema (Army Chief of Staff), and President Grunitzky announced his voluntary withdrawal from office. Colonel Eyadema announced that the Army had taken over full responsibility "in order to stop the political confusion" which was creating "a psychosis of imminent civil war"; that the Constitution was suspended and the National Assembly dissolved; that all political activity would be prohibited; and that a state of emergency had been declared.

On April 14, 1967, Colonel Eyadema announced the dissolution of the Committee of National Reconciliation, which had been formed on Jan. 14 to create within three months conditions necessary to enable free elections to be held, and the formation under his presidency of a new Government consisting of four military men and eight civilians.

A few days later, on April 24, an unsuccessful attempt was made on the life of President Eyadema by Lance-Corporal Norbert Boko Bosso, a distant relative of the former Major Emmanuel Bodjollé (formerly Chief of Staff and directly involved in the assassination of President Olympio in January 1963). Lance-Corporal Bosso confessed to having acted under Major Bodjollé's orders and was sentenced to death on April 27.

On Aug. 31, 1969, President Eyadema declared that Togo would in future have only one political party; the constituent congress of this party, which decided to call itself *Rassemblement du peuple togolais,* elected the President as chairman of the party on Nov. 29.

A plot to overthrow the regime and to "eliminate [the President] physically" was foiled by the Army during the night of Aug. 8–9, 1970. The conspirators who, according to a Government spokesman, were "former military men from Ghana and Dahomey" had named as the instigator of the attempted coup M. Noé Kutuklui, the former leader of CUT; M. Kutuklui was arrested on Aug. 9 by the police in Dahomey, where he had been living as a refugee since 1966.

MALAGASY REPUBLIC

Area: 228,000 sq. miles.
Population 1969 (estimate): 6,643,000.
Capital: Tananarive (343,000).
Other important towns: Finanarantsoa (238,000), Antsirabé (190,000), Tamatave (144,000).
Official languages: French and Malagasy.
Chief products: Coffee, rice, sugar, vanilla, graphite, radioactive minerals.

A French possession since 1896, Madagascar became an independent

Republic within the French Community on June 26, 1960, having been an autonomous Republic within the Community since Oct. 14, 1958. On April 28, 1959, the Constituent Assembly had adopted a new Constitution providing for a strong presidential system of government, and on May 1, 1959, M. Philibert Tsiranana, the head of the former Provisional Government and leader of the *Parti social-démocrate* (PSD), was elected President of the Malagasy Republic, combining the functions of President and Prime Minister. It was announced on June 14, 1960, that the Malagasy Government had approved a constitutional reform whereby the President of the Republic would, after independence, take over the prerogatives formerly exercised by the President of the Community.

On Sept. 4, 1960, the PSD gained 75 seats in the National Assembly; the Opposition *Parti du congrès de l'indépendance* (AKFM) led by Pastor Richard Adriamanjato obtained nine seats, the remaining 23 seats going to Independents.

President Tsiranana was re-elected for a seven-year term on March 30, 1965, receiving 97 per cent of the votes cast, the remainder being shared by his two opponents. On Aug. 8, 1965, the President's party (the PSD), which had previously absorbed the small *Rénovation nationale malgache*, gained 104 out of the 107 seats in the Assembly, the remaining threee seats going to the AKFM in Tananarive, where it obtained 49 per cent of the votes. The President had previously stated on Oct. 1, 1963, that he accepted the existence of an Opposition and was not in favour of a one-party State.

After parliamentary elections held on Sept. 6, 1970, the distribution of seats in the National Assembly remained unchanged.

The Foreign Ministers of South Africa and the Malagasy Republic signed an economic agreement on Nov. 20, 1970, providing for a South African loan to finance the Malagasy tourist industry. President Tsiranana had previously on April 16, 1969, and Jan. 9, 1970, expressed his wish to expand relations with South Africa.

DAHOMEY

Area: 44,913 sq. miles.
Population 1969 (estimate): 2,640,000.
Capital: Porto Novo (85,000).
Other important town: Cotonou (120,000).
Official language: French.
Chief products: Palm produce, groundnuts, cotton.

Dahomey, an autonomous Republic within the French Community since Dec. 4, 1958, and previously part of French West Africa, achieved independence as a Republic outside the Community on Aug. 1, 1960, under the premiership of M. Hubert Maga, who had been elected Prime Minister on May 22, 1959. In the presidential, vice-presidential and National Assembly elections held on Dec. 12, 1960, the *Parti dahoméen de l'unité* (PDU), led by M. Maga and M. Sourou Migan Apithy, received 468,000 votes against 213,000 for the *Union démocratique dahoméenne* (UDD) led by M. Justin Ahomadegbé, president of the outgoing Assembly. M. Maga took office as President of the Republic on Dec. 31, with M. Apithy as Vice-President.

In December 1961 M. Ahomadegbé, whose party had been banned, was sentenced to five years' imprisonment on charges of plotting against State security and planning the assassination of M. Maga. However, M. Ahomadegbé was amnestied together with several other convicted UDD leaders on Nov. 3, 1962.

A new provisional regime was established, after demonstrations and a general strike, under Colonel Christophe Soglo, commander of the Army, on Oct. 28, 1963. In the provisional Cabinet formed the following day, M. Maga, M. Apithy and M. Ahomadegbé all held office. However, on Nov. 27, 1963, Colonel Soglo announced the discovery of a plot to kill him and several of his Ministers and to re-establish the regime of ex-President Maga, who on Dec. 3 resigned all his ministerial posts and was placed in detention.

A draft Constitution was approved in a national referendum on Jan. 5, 1964; this laid down that the President would be the Head of State and that the Vice-President would be Head of Government and "responsible for the maintenance of order and security". The National Assembly would have 42 deputies and all candidates for parliamentary seats would have to be members of the Dahomeyan Democratic Party (PDD) which had been formed on Dec. 13, 1963, by M. Apithy and M. Ahomadegbé. The PDD declared in its manifesto that it would accept a legal and constructive political Opposition.

On Jan. 19, 1965, M. Apithy was elected President and M. Ahomadegbé Vice-President, but on Nov. 29, 1965, M. Apithy and M. Ahomadegbé resigned under pressure from the Army, led by General Soglo. This followed a crisis in which M. Ahomadegbé was appointed in place of M. Apithy as President of Dahomey by the PDD, after President Apithy had refused to sign Government decrees appointing the members of the Supreme Court, on the grounds that they were unconstitutional, and also declined to give his assent to a Bill passed by Parliament, which laid down that the President of the Supreme Court could not be a politician. General Soglo assumed supreme power on Dec. 22, 1965, and issued a proclamation declaring that he had dissolved the National Assembly, all regional and municipal councils and all political parties and had annulled the Constitution.

General Soglo's regime was overthrown in a bloodless coup by the Army, led by Major Maurice Kouandeté, on Dec. 17, 1967; Lieut.-Colonel Alphonse Alley was named as Head of State with Major Kouandeté as Prime Minister on Dec. 21.

In a referendum held on March 31, 1968, a majority vote was registered in favour of a new Constitution, which provided for a one-party State led by an executive President.

Following a virtual boycott of presidential elections held on May 5, 1968, after a call for such action by ex-Presidents Maga and Apithy (in exile in Paris), who claimed that the elections had been rendered null and void by a decree excluding former political leaders from the Presidency, the Army leaders announced on June 28 that Dr. Emile Derlin Zinsou, who had not been authorized to stand for the presidency in May, was to be invested as President and entrusted with the formation of a Government. During his installation as President on July 17, Dr. Zinsou announced that his appointment was to be put to a referendum on July 28; this produced a firm vote of confidence for Dr. Zinsou.

On Dec. 10, 1969, Dr. Zinsou's Government was overthrown by Army officers; a Directorate consisting of Lieut.-Colonel Emile de Souza, Lieut.-Colonel Benoît Sinzogan and Lieut.-Colonel Maurice Kouandeté was formed on Dec. 12. Ex-Presidents Maga, Ahomadegbé and Apithy all stated their support for Colonel Kouandeté and returned to Dahomey shortly afterwards.

The Military Directorate adopted, on Dec. 25, 1969, a Charter authorizing its three members to exercise, pending general elections and the establishment of a constitutional regime, all powers traditionally held by the Head of State.

The presidential elections took place in stages between March 3–31, 1970; three of the candidates – M. Maga, M. Apithy and M. Ahomadegbé – represented different regions, unlike the fourth candidate, ex-President Zinsou, who attempted to overcome regional rivalries. Representatives of M. Apithy, M. Ahomadegbé and Dr. Zinsou protested against alleged atrocities committed against their followers in the north, where M. Maga had overwhelming support.

By March 26 it appeared that M. Maga had won the election; however, on March 28 the Directorate issued an Order to the effect that all election proceedings should cease. On April 3 Lieut.-Colonel Emile de Souza announced the cancellation of the elections and foreshadowed the formation of a Government of National Union within a month.

However, consultations between M. Maga and M. Ahomadegbé led in mid-April to an agreement on the introduction of a presidency by rotation and to the publication of a draft charter establishing the principle of collective leadership of a presidential council, the three members of which would alternately be Head of State. This proposal was subsequently accepted by M. Apithy, while Dr. Zinsou withdrew.

The Military Directorate announced on May 1 that M. Maga had been appointed Head of State for two years, during which he would be chairman of the Presidential Council. He would be succeeded by M. Ahomadegbé in May 1972 and M. Apithy in May 1974. The Council would be assisted by a Cabinet composed of followers of its members.

NIGER

Area: 459,180 sq. miles.
Population 1969 (estimate): 3,909,000.
Capital: Niamey (60,000).
Official language: French.
Chief product: Groundnuts.

Formerly part of French West Africa, Niger became an independent Republic outside the French Community on Aug. 2–3, 1960. M. Hamani Diori, the Prime Minister, was unanimously elected President of the Republic by the National Assembly on Nov. 9, 1960.

In the general elections held on Dec. 14, 1958, 54 out of the 60 seats in the Assembly went to a coalition of the local section of the *Rassemblement démocratique africain* (RDA), dissident members of the *Parti du regroupement africain* (PRA) and tribal chiefs. The Sawaba, the local section of the PRA, led by the former Prime Minister, M. Djibo Bakary, won the remaining six seats; subsequently the elections for these were annulled and at new elections the seats were won by Government supporters. Over 70 per cent of the electorate did not vote in the main elections. Later in December M. Hamani, leader of the local RDA, was elected Prime Minister.

It had been announced on Oct. 18, 1959, that the Sawaba had been dissolved by the Government; by 1964, the party's leader, M. Bakary, was living in exile in Ghana. Incursions by armed Sawaba rebels from Ghana into Niger during October 1964 resulted in the Niger authorities alleging that "two African States" and a "non-African Power" were encouraging terrorist activity, and it became clear that these accusations were directed against Ghana, Dahomey and Communist China. After an attempt on the life of President Hamani Diori, the alleged assassin, who was immediately arrested, was said to have confessed that he was a member of the Sawaba party and that the attempt formed a part of a plan for widespread terrorist action with help from Ghana. This allegation, confirmed on April 17, 1965, by President Hamani, was strongly denied by President Nkrumah and the Ghanaian Government. A reconciliation with Dahomey was effected in December 1965, but the attacks against Ghana and China were intensified.

M. Hamani Diori, the only candidate, was re-elected President of the Republic on Sept. 30, 1965, and again on Oct. 1, 1970. In the legislative elections held in 1965, the ruling *Parti progressiste nigérien* (PPN) – the successor to the RDA – retained complete control of the National Assembly, winning all 50 seats unopposed on a single national list of candidates, this achievement being repeated in 1970. The PPN was the only legally constituted political party.

UPPER VOLTA

Area: 105,879 sq. miles.
Population 1969 (estimate): 5,330,000.
Capital: Ouagadougou (115,000).
Official language: French.
Chief products: Livestock, cotton, groundnuts.

After twenty months as an autonomous Republic within the French Community, dating from Dec. 11, 1958, Upper Volta became a Republic outside the Community on Aug. 5, 1960. The new presidential Constitution was approved in a national referendum on Nov. 27, and on Dec. 8, M. Maurice Yaméogo, Prime Minister since October 1958, was unanimously elected President of the Republic by the National Assembly.

M. Yaméogo's party, the local section of *Rassemblement démocratique africain,* had previously, on April 19, 1959, won 64 of the 75 seats in the National Assembly, the remaining 11 seats going to *Parti du regroupement africain*, led by M. Nazi Boni and M. Joseph Conombo. M. Yaméogo was re-elected Prime Minister on April 27. The two Opposition parties were both dissolved shortly after their formation by the Government prior to independence, the *Parti républicain de la liberté* (the local section of *Parti de la fédération africaine*) in January 1960 and the *Parti national voltaïque* in October 1959. M. Boni, the leader of both parties and the principal Opposition personality, was placed under an order of administrative internment early in 1960, along with other Opposition leaders.

On Oct. 3, 1965, President Yaméogo was re-elected, receiving over 99 per cent of the votes cast, as did the country's sole party, *Union démocratique voltaïque,* in the legislative elections a few weeks later on Nov. 7.

Following a general strike and demonstrations by trade union supporters, President Yaméogo's regime was replaced on Jan. 3, 1966, by a new Administration formed by the Army Chief of Staff, Lieut.-Colonel Sangoule Lamizana, this action being welcomed by President Yaméogo. On Jan. 5, 1966, Lieut.-Colonel Lamizana, now President of the Republic, declared the Constitution suspended and the National Assembly dissolved; he stated that he would exercise legislative and executive powers by ordinance and decree.

On Sept. 8, 1967, President Lamizana announced the arrest of a number of persons who, he said, had plotted "to assassinate the present leaders of the country". Several measures were taken to consolidate President Lamizana's regime; stringent austerity measures had been in operation since February 1966, and it had been announced on Dec. 12, 1966, that all political activities were to be suspended.

Ex-President Yaméogo – who had been under arrest since Jan. 3, 1966, i.e. the day after his overthrow by Lieut.-Colonel Lamizana – was sentenced, on May 8, 1969, to five years' hard labour and a fine on charges of having embezzled nearly $3,000,000, but he was reprieved on Aug. 5, 1970.

During 1970 President Lamizana gradually permitted a return to political activities.

A new Constitution providing for the continuation of his own Presidency for another four years, but also for the direct election of a President thereafter and for the appointment of a Prime Minister and a Cabinet, was approved in a popular referendum on June 14, 1970.

In general elections for a new National Assembly held on Dec. 20, 1970, the conservative *Union démocratique voltaïque* gained 37 out of the total of 57 seats, and on Feb. 13, 1971, this party's leader, M. Gérard Kango Ouedraogo, was appointed the country's first Prime Minister.

CHAD

Area: 495,000 sq. miles.
Population 1969 (estimate): 3,510,000.
Capital: Fort Lamy (132,000).
Official language: French.
Chief products: Cattle, sorghum, millet.

Chad, part of the former territory of French Equatorial Africa, achieved independent status as a Republic within the French Community on Aug. 10–11, 1960, having been an autonomous Republic within the Community since Nov. 28, 1958. The Prime Minister, M. François Tombalbaye, was elected Head of State by the National Assembly by unanimous vote of the 78 deputies present.

Following a series of political crises early in 1959, general elections were held on May 31, 1959, in which the *Parti populaire tchadien* (PPT) won 57 out of the 65 seats. M. Tombalbaye, who had headed a coalition Government since March 24, 1959, was re-elected Prime Minister.

The period following independence was marked by the progressive elimination of opponents or potential opponents of President Tombalbaye. On March 18, 1961, it was announced that the PPT and the opposition *Parti national africain* (PNA) had agreed on a merger, the new party to be known as the *Union pour le progrès du Tchad* (UPT). General elections were held on March 4, 1962, resulting in the return of a single "national union" list of Government supporters in all constituencies; this followed the dissolution of all parties except the UPT by the Government in January 1962.

A constitutional law instituting a presidential type of regime and replacing the existing Constitution, which had provided for a parliamentary system of government, was approved by the National Assembly on April 14, 1962. M. Tombalbaye, the only candidate, was elected the first President of the Republic on April 23 by an electoral college.

During the period 1962–65, the regime of President Tombalbaye was repeatedly threatened, according to both the findings of a Special Criminal Court and the President's own statements, by plots against the President's life and his Government. From 1965 onwards clashes between rebels and Government forces occurred at frequent intervals; in August 1968 President Tombalbaye appealed for, and was granted, French military assistance, in accord with the 1960 defence agreements beween Chad and France, in the Tibesti region of north-eastern Chad where Government forces were again in conflict with rebel forces. [The Tibesti area has a sparse population of Arabic-speaking nomadic herdsmen, strongly opposed to the central Government.]

The principal rebel organization was the *Front de libération nationale du Tchad* (*Frolina*); its leader, Dr. Abba Sidick, explained in January 1970 that the reason why the rebellion had developed in the North was that by "its tactless and extortionate treatment of the Moslem population" the central Government had created conditions favourable to an armed struggle.

A smaller organization known as the *Front national tchadien* (FNT) was operating in east-central Chad under the leadership of Ahmed Moussa.

In April 1969, the French garrison of about 1,000 men at Fort Lamy was reinforced by further French forces numbering about 2,000 men; according to an unofficial French estimate in September 1969, 1,600 officers and men had been sent to Chad in the period since April. This military intervention was subject, however, to increasing criticism in France herself.

By May 1970 the remaining rebel resistance consisted mainly of about 400–500 Toubbous led by Sultan Kédéfemi and concentrated around the village of Zouar in the north.

Presidential elections held on June 15, 1969, resulted in the re-election by universal suffrage of President Tombalbaye, who was the only candidate. In elections for a new and enlarged National Assembly, held on Dec. 14, 1969, a single list of candidates, nominated by the PPT, was officially returned, having obtained 96.69 per cent of the votes cast with a percentage poll of about 95.

IVORY COAST

Area: 124,550 sq. miles.
Population 1969 (estimate): 4,195,000.
Capital: Abidjan (400,000).
Official language: French.
Chief products: Diamonds, manganese, coffee, cocoa, timber.

Formerly part of French West Africa and an autonomous Republic within the French Community since Dec. 4, 1958, the Ivory Coast became an independent Republic outside the Community on Aug. 6–7, 1960. M. Félix Houphouët-Boigny, the outgoing Head of State and Prime Minister, was elected President of the Republic on Nov. 27, 1960; the only candidate, he received over 99 per cent of the votes. M. Houphouët-Boigny's *Parti démocratique de la Côte d'Ivoire* (PDCI) won all 70 seats in the National Assembly in the legislative elections held on the same date.

Two plots to overthrow the President were discovered during 1963; an extreme left-wing plot was averted by Government security measures during January 1963, whilst a plot, regarded as an attempted continuation of the first, was discovered towards the end of August 1963 during the President's absence from the country.

President Houphouët-Boigny, the only candidate, was re-elected in the presidential elections held on Nov. 7, 1965. On the same date, a single list of candidates nominated by the PDCI (the only legal political party) retained all the seats in the National Assembly.

From 1959 onwards, relations between the Ivory Coast and Ghana were adversely affected by the presence in Ghana of Sanwi émigrés who had set up a "provisional Sanwi government-in-exile" with the aim of re-unifying the Sanwi with Ghana. [Sanwi is a territory on the Ivory Coast—Ghana border.] However, after a visit to Abidjan by a mission from the new military Government in Ghana a co-operation agreement was announced in a communiqué issued on March 18, 1966. At the same time, on March 17, the so-called Sanwi king, Amon Ndouffou III, after his repatriation to the Ivory Coast by the Ghanaian authorities, was pardoned by President Houphouët-Boigny.

On May 30, 1969, the Government announced that it had broken off diplomatic relations with the U.S.S.R., after a student strike which the President of the National Assembly alleged had been instigated by "certain foreigners".

A reorganization of the Cabinet on Jan. 5, 1970, followed consultations by President Houphouët-Boigny with representatives from all walks of life, which revealed a widespread desire for swifter Africanization of enterprises and jobs and greater participation of the younger generation in public affairs. The President therefore aimed at rejuvenating his Government (the average age of the new Cabinet being about 40) and also at forestalling further unrest such as had occurred in 1969.

In presidential and legislative elections on Nov. 29, 1970, President

Houphouët-Boigny was re-elected as the sole candidate, while 100 candidates nominated by the PDCI were returned to the National Assembly.

Under President Houphouët-Boigny, considered an "elder statesman" among French-speaking leaders in Africa, the Ivory Coast has enjoyed a stable regime with a declared policy of economic liberalism and the encouragement of foreign investment to speed up economic growth.

CENTRAL AFRICAN REPUBLIC

Area: 238,000 sq. miles.
Population 1969 (estimate): 1,518,000.
Capital: Bangui (302,000).
Official language: French.
Chief products: Diamonds, cotton, groundnuts, coffee.

The territory of Ubangi-Shari, part of French Equatorial Africa, achieved independence as the Central African Republic, within the French Community, on Aug. 12—13, 1960, after having the status of an autonomous Republic within the Community since Dec. 1, 1958.

The country's first Prime Minister, M. Barthélémy Boganda, was the founder of the *Mouvement d'évolution sociale en Afrique noire* (Mesan) and advocated the formation of a single "Latin African" State in the Congo region which might include former French, Belgian and Portuguese territories.

Following the death of M. Boganda, elections held in April 1959 gave the Mesan party an overwhelming majority; its new leader, M. David Dacko, was appointed Prime Minister, and on Nov. 17, 1960, the National Assembly elected him President of the Republic. The Opposition party, the *Mouvement d'évolution démocratique d'Afrique centrale*, was dissolved by the Government in February 1961, and in November 1962 the Central African Republic officially became a one-party State.

M. Dacko was re-elected, being the only candidate, in the first presidential elections to be held by universal suffrage on Jan. 5, 1964. National Assembly elections were held on March 15, 1964, on a single list of candidates nominated by Mesan.

M. Dacko's regime was overthrown on Jan. 1, 1966, when Colonel Jean Bedel Bokassa, C.-in-C. of the armed forces, assumed the presidency in a military *coup d'état*. M. Dacko was first held under house arrest and subsequently in a military camp. The new Cabinet, formed on Jan. 3,

1966, with Colonel Bokassa combining the functions of President and Prime Minister, abrogated the Constitution and dissolved the National Assembly on the following day (Jan. 4).

President Bokassa announced on April 12, 1969, that a plot to overthrow him, organized by Lieut.-Colonel Alexandre Banza, commander of the Republic's paratroops and Minister of Health, had been foiled two days earlier. Lieut.-Colonel Banza was executed on April 12.

PEOPLE'S REPUBLIC OF THE CONGO (Brazzaville)

Area: 132,000 sq. miles.
Population 1969 (estimate): 880,000.
Capital: Brazzaville (160,000).
Official language: French.
Chief products: Diamonds, timber, groundnuts, palm produce.

The Republic of the Congo (Brazzaville) achieved independence on Aug. 14–15, 1960, under President Fulbert Youlou; formerly part of French Equatorial Africa, the Republic had been an autonomous State within the French Community since Nov. 28, 1958, having changed its name then from Middle Congo.

Between the years 1961 and 1969 the Republic developed from a country under a presidential regime to a People's Republic, which was in fact a one-party State, under a military ruler.

Constitutional Developments, 1961–70

The National Assembly approved on March 2, 1961, a Constitution which provided for a presidential system of Government with a clear separation of executive power (held by the President) from legislative power (held by the Assembly). The President was to be elected by direct universal suffrage, and would appoint a Vice-President and a Cabinet whose members could not be members of the Assembly; he also had the right to submit individual policy issues directly to a popular vote by a national referendum.

On Dec. 8, 1963, a new Constitution introducing a partly presidential and partly parliamentary system was approved in a national referendum. Under this Constitution the President was to be elected by an electoral college normally comprising all members of the National Assembly and of the prefectoral, sub-prefectoral and municipal councils; his powers included the appointment of the Prime Minister and other Ministers and the dissolution of the National Assembly if two Cabinet crises occurred within an 18-month period. The National Assembly was to be elected by universal suffrage of all citizens over 18 years old.

In mid-August 1968, this Constitution was replaced by the so-called *Acte fondamental*, under which the *Conseil national de la révolution* (CNR) formed on Aug. 5, 1968, was made the "guarantor of the continuity of the State" and the Prime Minister, who would be responsible to the CNR and not to the President, became the executor of national policies.

However, the *Acte fondamental* was replaced, in its turn, by the 1970 Constitution, promulgated on Jan. 3, 1970, after the establishment of the People's Republic of the Congo [see page 231] on Dec. 31, 1969. This laid down that sovereignty was to be vested in the people's councils in municipalities, districts and regions; that freedom of speech, the Press, association and religion would be recognized but the use of religious activities for political purposes would be prohibited; and that the chairman of the Congolese Workers' Party would also be Head of State and President of the Council of State which would supersede the Cabinet. The President of the Council of State would appoint its Vice-President and could dismiss him, on the Party's central committee's advice; other members of the Council would be appointed or dismissed by the President on the proposal of the Vice-President.

Other Political Developments from 1958 to 1970

The Youlou Regime

The Abbé Fulbert Youlou, a former priest and the leader of the *Union démocratique de défense des interêts africains* (UDDIA, the local section of the *Rassemblement démocratique africain*), was elected Prime Minister on Nov. 28, 1958, by 23 votes to 22 votes for the outgoing Premier, M. Jacques Opangault, the leader of the *Parti populaire congolais* (PPC, affiliated to the *Mouvement socialiste africain*). In February 1959, M. Opangault's party began a boycott of Assembly sessions to enforce his demand that new elections should be held in view of the Congo's accession to independent status, the Government having previously prolonged the life of the National Assembly until 1962. Disorders broke out in Brazzaville on Feb. 16, as a result of political rivalries, reinforced by the long-standing hostility between the M'Bochi tribe, supporters of M. Opangault, and the Balali tribe, followers of the Abbé Youlou. French troops were called in to maintain order but by Feb. 20, when calm had been restored, at least 100 Africans had died. M. Opangault was arrested on

Feb. 19 on charges of incitement to sedition, rebellion and destruction of property. The Abbé Youlou subsequently announced that fresh elections would be held; these took place on June 14 and resulted in the UDDIA gaining 51 seats against 10 for the PPC and its allies.

On Nov. 21, 1959, the Abbé Youlou was unanimously elected President of the Republic by the National Assembly; he continued to act as Prime Minister in terms of a constitutional law which provided that the two posts could be held by the same person.

On the achievement of independence, it was announced that M. Opangault, who had been released from detention under a general amnesty on July 3, 1959, had accepted office as Minister of State in President Youlou's Government.

President Youlou, who had taken over the portfolios for Defence and the Interior on Jan. 11, 1961, was re-elected President by popular vote under the 1961 Constitution; he was the only candidate and was supported by all the main political parties. M. Opangault was appointed by the President as Vice-President on June 5, 1961. He resigned from this post in April 1962 and from the post of Minister of Public Works in November 1962, but was appointed Minister of State on May 25, 1963.

A Bill to establish a one-party State was approved by the National Assembly on April 13, 1963, when 61 deputies (out of a full membership of 64) voted in favour. Such a proposal had been announced by the President in August 1962, and had immediately received the approval of the President's party and the other two principal parties, the PPC and MSA.

During discussions on the final details of the new single-party structure held on Aug. 6–8, 1963, disagreement arose between the President and certain trade union delegates, who demanded that the President should "immediately" form a new and smaller Government, hold fresh elections and carry out urgent reforms. The President, on the other hand, maintained that any changes must await the inauguration of the new party. The situation was worsened by the Government's decision on Aug. 8 to ban all political meetings until the formal establishment of the new party.

The disagreement was brought to a head on Aug. 12 by the arrest of four trade union leaders and the remaining trade union leadership calling a general strike to begin on Aug. 13. Three days of demonstrations followed and French troops were called in to assist in maintaining internal security, under the 1961 defence agreement between France and the Congo. On Aug. 15 President Youlou held a meeting with the trade union leaders, at the end of which his resignation was announced; on the same day he was taken into detention in a military camp.

M. Youlou and his family escaped from detention during the night of March 25–26, 1965, and were granted political asylum first in the Congo (Kinshasa) and then in Spain, having been refused entry into France on Jan. 29, 1966. On June 8, 1965, the "People's Court" sentenced M. Youlou to death *in absentia*; M. Stéphane Tchitchelle, Foreign Minister in M. Youlou's Government, was sentenced to 15 years' hard labour on June 11, while other Ministers in the same Government were sentenced to varying lengths of imprisonment.

The Massemba-Débat Regime

A new Provisional Government was formed on Aug. 16, 1963, under the leadership of M. Alphonse Massemba-Débat, who had been President of the Assembly and subsequently Minister of Planning – a post which he had given up in May 1963, reportedly as a result of his opposition to the increasingly authoritarian nature of the regime.

General elections held on Dec. 8, 1963, resulted in all 55 Assembly seats being won by a single list of candidates nominated by the *Mouvement national de la révolution* (MNR); the valid votes cast were all in favour of the list which included M. Massemba-Débat and four of the Ministers in the Provisional Government. M. Massemba-Débat was elected unopposed as President by the electoral college, as laid down in the 1963 Constitution, on Dec. 19, and appointed M. Pascal Lissouba as Prime Minister on Dec. 24.

On July 2, 1964, the MNR was officially established as the country's sole political party. The policy of nationalization, which had been announced by M. Lissouba on Jan. 21, 1964, had already, by March 1964, been applied to the Air Congo airline, electricity and water distribution, and urban transport in Brazzaville.

The policies of the President and Prime Minister – "moderate socialist" according to *The New York Times* – were subjected to strong pressure from the *Jeunesse* branch of the MNR whose spokesman, M. Albert Martin, gradually took an openly pro-Communist line. The situation came to a head on Aug. 27, 1964, when M. Léon Angor, President of the National Assembly, demanded the dismissal from the Cabinet of the moderate Ministers, some of whom had been associated with ex-President Youlou's Government. An open Cabinet crisis was avoided until the end of October 1964, when certain Ministers resigned.

On Dec. 21, 1964, all existing trade unions were dissolved by a decision of the National Assembly, which at the same time approved the formation of a single trade union, the *Confédération nationale des syndicats congolais*, with M. Diallo Idrissa as secretary-general. This development, according to French press reports, was also brought about by strong pressure from the *Jeunesse* leaders, and directed against the influential Christian trade unions, which had played a prominent part in the overthrow of M. Youlou.

It was officially announced on Feb. 19, 1965, that the Attorney General and the Director of the Government Information Agency had been found murdered and that the President of the Supreme Court had disappeared. [He was later also found to have been murdered.] A *New York Times* special correspondent reported from Brazzaville on March 5 that all three had been killed on Feb. 15 by gangs of *Jeunesse* members during a night of widespread violence.

A major Cabinet re-organization was announced on April 6, 1965, under which six new members, most of them *Jeunesse* leaders, entered the Government.

On April 26, 1966, it was officially announced that M. Pascal Lissouba had resigned from the post of Prime Minister; this action had been approved by the political bureau of the MNR on April 15, which had also given its approval to a Cabinet formed by M. Ambroise Noumazalay, considered the country's leading Marxist theoretician, on April 19. [The political bureau's primacy over the Government had been officially established on Jan. 8, 1966.] M. Georges Mouyabi, a moderate, was elected President of the National Assembly on May 10 in succession to M. Léon Angor, who had advocated closer ties with Communist China.

Following a period of unrest marked by attempted coups and plots against the Government, President Massemba-Débat, in a broadcast on July 22, 1968, offered to hand over power to anyone who felt himself to be "better equipped and more gifted" than the President "to lead the Congo out of a state of under-development". No one, however, took up this offer before the deadline of July 27. The situation remained tense, unrest breaking out in Brazzaville on July 31; on the following day, the President announced the dissolution of the National Assembly and the suspension of the activities of the political bureau of the MNR. On Aug. 2, the President withdrew from the capital; it was generally assumed by foreign correspondents that he did so under Army pressure. The Army assumed power on the following day but was unable to muster sufficient popular support and recalled the President.

On Aug. 5, the day after his return, the President announced the formation of a *Conseil national de la révolution* (CNR) which would "co-ordinate the policies of the Government and the MNR and control and direct the action of the State" and would be led by the Chief of General Staff, Colonel Marien Ngouabi. It would be responsible for drafting all documents concerning the functioning of the State and would nominate the Prime Minister and Government on the recommendation of the President of the Republic who would not, however, play a leading role in the Council. Colonel Ngouabi thus emerged as the most influential personality on the political scene. The powers of the President were further reduced with the adoption of the *Acte fondamental* in mid-August [see Constitutional Developments, page 226].

The situation changed once more with the announcement on Sept. 4 of the resignation of President Massemba-Débat and the decision of the CNR to give power to a Provisional Government under Captain Alfred Raoul, who had been appointed Prime Minister on Aug. 22. [He was the first person to hold this post since the dismissal of M. Ambroise Noumazalay on Jan. 12, 1968, by President Massemba-Débat on the ground that the post of Premier was superfluous.] Captain Raoul announced on Sept. 5 that he was taking over the functions of Head of State; he also took the post of Prime Minister and the Defence portfolio in the Provisional Government, in which M. Pascal Lissouba became Minister of State for Planning. A Government statement was made on Sept. 16, from which it appeared that M. Massemba-Débat was under a form of house arrest.

On Oct. 13, 1968, it was officially announced that the CNR had been reorganized; all members who had collaborated with ex-President Massemba-Débat were dropped, notably two former Prime Ministers, M. Pascal Lissouba and M. Ambroise Noumazalay, and two former prominent members of the MNR, M. Julien Boukambou and M. Léon Angor.

The CNR nominated Major Marien Ngouabi, the Army commander, as Head of State on Jan. 1, 1969; on the same day a new Cabinet was formed replacing the Provisional Government but with Major Raoul remaining as Prime Minister.

On June 21, 1969, the Cabinet was reorganized, M. Pascal Lissouba being left out, and the Directorate of the CNR was reduced to five members – President Ngouabi, Major Raoul and the chairmen of three newly-created commissions (Education, Press and Propaganda; Economic Affairs, Finance and Social Affairs; Organization).

During the period 1968–69 the CNR took action against any potential opposition to the regime; a number of political trials involving supporters of ex-Presidents Youlou and Massemba-Débat occurred between December 1968 and November 1969. An attempt to overthrow the Government was foiled on Nov. 8, 1969; President Ngouabi stated that the conspirators had been led by M. Bernard Kolela, who was arrested, and M. Batsimba, who had escaped. M. Kolela had been a party secretary under the Youlou regime, was sentenced to death *in absentia* on June 22, 1965, but reprieved in July 1968 and made an official in the Foreign Ministry. The alleged plotters were sentenced by a military court, M. Kolela and three others to death, 10 defendants to death *in absentia*, and certain other defendants to varying terms of imprisonment. The President accused the Congo (Kinshasa) of involvement in the plot; this resulted in a subsequent deterioration in relations between the two countries.

Rule of Congolese Workers' Party

A decisive step was taken late in 1969 with the formation of the avowedly Marxist Congolese Workers' Party as the country's sole political party.

This step was foreshadowed by the CNR on Oct. 21, 1969, when it decided to establish a new party and to reorganize the workers and peasants as well as the People's Army. During a congress held in Brazzaville on Dec. 29–31, 1969, the new party, named the Congolese Workers' Party, was formally established as the country's sole political party which would have the decisive voice in all matters affecting the State.

On Jan. 3, 1970, President Ngouabi was sworn in as Head of State under the new 1970 Constitution [see Constitutional Developments, page 226]; he undertook to devote all his strength to "the triumph of the proletarian ideals of the Congolese people in work, democracy and peace". A new Council of State was announced on the following day composed of all except one of the Ministers in the former Cabinet, which had resigned at the President's request on Jan. 3. The one exception was M. Charles Assemekang, who became President of the Supreme Court.

On April 1, the Congolese Workers' Party decided that a people's militia was to be set up to replace the existing gendarmerie, a high proportion of whose members, they claimed, had been involved in an unsuccessful coup on March 23, 1970, led by Lieut. Pierre Kikanga, who was reported as having been killed with 30 of his men.

Foreign Relations

The country's move towards a one-party socialist State was matched by a corresponding move towards closer relationships with Communist countries.

On Feb. 22, 1964, it was announced that the Republic and Communist China had decided to establish diplomatic relations at ambassadorial level. Similar agreements were reached with the Soviet Union (March 10), North Vietnam (July 16) and Bulgaria (January 1965), while on May 11, 1964, it was announced that diplomatic relations (at an unspecified level) were to be established with Cuba. The then Prime Minister, M. Pascal Lissouba, repeatedly affirmed, however, that the country's policy in foreign affairs was one of non-alignment.

On Oct. 2, 1964, President Liu Shao-Chi of Communist China and President Massemba-Débat signed a Treaty of Friendship during the latter's visit to Peking; this Treaty was ratified by the Congolese National Assembly in November 1964.

It was announced on Jan. 9, 1970, that diplomatic relations at legation level were to be established with the German Democratic Republic, the Congo being the first Black African country to do so.

Relations between the two Republics of the Congo were tense during 1964; President Massemba-Débat accused President Tshombe, on Aug. 15, of "interference" in Brazzaville's internal affairs, whilst the latter gave "a last warning" that he would take "extreme measures" unless Brazzaville ceased all aid to the rebel forces [see CONGO (Kinshasa), page 263]. The situation improved, however, to the point where, on Oct. 30, 1965, a joint communiqué published after a meeting in Léopoldville between the Foreign Ministers of the two States expressed regret at the events which had caused the breakdown in relations and announced the establishment of a joint commission to study mutual problems. The two Ministers also decided to restore diplomatic relations at ambassadorial level.

On Oct. 9, 1968, the Brazzaville Government announced that they had broken off diplomatic relations with the Congo (Kinshasa) after the execution of M. Pierre Mulele, the leader of the 1963 rebellion, although the Brazzaville Government had received solemn guarantees of M. Mulele's safety from the Kinshasa Government, prior to their allowing him as a political refugee to contact the Congo (Kinshasa) embassy in Brazzaville with a view to returning home.

Following attempts by the Presidents of the other Central African republics to bring about a reconciliation between Kinshasa and Brazzaville, an agreement — entitled the "Manifesto of June 16" — was signed on June 16, 1970, by Presidents Mobutu and Ngouabi, normalizing relations between their two countries.

Relations with other foreign countries were marked by two incidents during August 1965 and a continuing deterioration in relations with France.

On Aug. 16, 1965, the Congolese Government announced that it had broken off diplomatic relations with Portugal because that country had "failed to observe the U.N. Charter and the Declaration of the Rights of Man" and because the Congo Government wanted "to assist in the total liberation of the African continent from colonial domination".

A few days earlier, on Aug. 13, the U.S. Government withdrew its diplomatic staff from Brazzaville because of alleged mistreatment of U.S. officials by the Brazzaville authorities; the Congolese embassy in Washington was withdrawn to New York under Congolese orders. The Americans stated that their action did not constitute a break in relations but simply a withdrawal of diplomatic personnel.

GABON

Area: 102,317 sq. miles.
Population 1969 (estimate): 485,000.
Capital: Libreville (65,000).
Official language: French.
Chief product: Timber.

Originally part of French Equatorial Africa and since Nov. 29, 1958, an autonomous Republic within the French Community, Gabon achieved independence as a Republic within the Community on Aug. 16, 1960.

M. Léon M'Ba, formerly Prime Minister, became Head of State on the proclamation of independence and was elected President of the Republic on Feb. 12, 1961. Elections for the 67 seats in the National Assembly, held on the same date, resulted in victory for the single list of candidates put forward jointly by M. M'Ba's *Bloc démocratique gabonais* (BDG) and the former Opposition party, *Union démocratique et sociale du Gabon* (UDSG), led by M. Jean-Hilaire Aubame. The National Assembly unanimously approved on Feb. 17 the new Constitution which was of the presidential type.

An attempted coup occurred in February 1964, following developments since the beginning of 1963 tending towards the establishment of a virtual one-party system. President M'Ba was compelled to resign on Feb. 17–18 by a "revolutionary committee" led by four junior Army and gendarmerie officers who, on Feb. 18, announced the creation of a "Provisional Government" under M. Aubame. On the same date, however, French troop reinforcements began to arrive and on Feb. 19 these troops, acting as "Community forces" under Franco-Gabonese defence agreements of 1960–61, put down the rising. President M'Ba resumed power on the following day.

General elections were held on April 12, 1964, resulting in the BDG winning 31 seats and the Opposition the remaining 16 — equally divided between *Défense des institutions démocratiques* lists sponsored by M. Aubame's UDSG, and *Défense de la démocratie* lists organized by M. Fidèle Otandault.

President M'Ba died on Nov. 28, 1967, and was succeeded by M. Bernard-Albert Bongo, the Vice-President. General elections held on Feb. 16, 1969, resulted in the almost unanimous election of candidates of the BDG to Parliament and to municipal and rural councils.

SENEGAL

Area: 77,814 sq. miles.
Population 1970 (estimate): 3,980,000.
Capital: Dakar (600,000).
Official language: French.
Chief products: Phosphates, groundnuts.

Senegal, formerly part of French West Africa and an autonomous Republic within the French Community from Nov. 25, 1958, first became independent as part of the Federation of Mali on June 20, 1960 [see MALI, page 237]. It became an independent Republic in its own right a month later on Aug. 20 after its Government had alleged that the Federal Government had taken measures which constituted an attempted coup directed against Senegalese interests. A new Constitution was adopted on Aug. 25 by the Senegalese National Assembly, and on Sept. 5 M. Léopold Sédar Senghor, formerly President of the Federal Assembly, was elected President. M. Mamadou Dia was invited to continue in the office of Prime Minister and received a vote of confidence from the National Assembly on Sept. 7.

M. Senghor's and M. Dia's party, the *Union progressiste sénégalaise* (UPS), had captured all 80 seats in the Legislative Assembly in the elections held on March 22, 1959. The UPS was the local section of M. Senghor's *Parti du regroupement africain* (PRA) which had a "federalist" policy. Both the dissident *PRA – Sénégal* (advocating immediate independence) and the *Solidarité sénégalaise* (representing the extreme right) failed to win any seats. M. Dia was re-elected Prime Minister on April 5, 1959, whilst the third leader of the UPS, M. Lamine Gueye, was elected President of the Legislative Assembly.

The Prime Minister, M. Dia, attempted to carry out a *coup d'état* in Dakar on Dec. 17, 1962, in order to prevent the adoption by the National Assembly of a vote of censure on his Cabinet. The attempt was frustrated by troops loyal to President Senghor and M. Dia was arrested; M. Senghor took over the duties of Prime Minister at the Assembly's request, also being empowered to prepare a revised draft Constitution based on a presidential type of regime. M. Dia was, on May 13, 1963, sentenced to life detention in a fortress on charges arising out of the attempted coup.

M. Dia's unsuccessful attempt to depose President Senghor was the culmination of a crisis which had been developing for some months between supporters of the two leaders. The President's supporters opposed the continuation of the state of emergency which had been in force since independence, and alleged that the emergency powers were being abused by M. Dia; his supporters, amongst whom were advocates of a socialist-type economy, accused the President (a Christian) of alleged sympathy with the interests of the wealthier classes and the traditional Moslem leaders. The censure motion, specifically attacking M. Dia, stemmed from M. Dia's critics and condemned the use of the state of emergency as "an instrument of blind repression".

On Dec. 19, 1962, President Senghor formed a new Government; the National Assembly on Jan. 2, 1963, approved a Bill extending the state of emergency until July 1, 1963.

The new Senegalese Constitution, which *inter alia* provided for the President assuming the powers previously exercised by the Prime Minister, was overwhelmingly approved in a national referendum held on March 3, 1963.

In the presidential and legislative elections held on Dec. 1, 1963, President Senghor obtained 1,149,935 votes out of 1,156,059 votes cast. During the election campaign a number of clashes occurred between supporters of the UPS and PRA, several people being killed.

Between 1964 and 1966, measures were taken by the Government against opposition movements; on Oct. 3, 1964, the Senegalese National Front, which included supporters of M. Dia, was banned, and on May 22, 1965, the National Assembly passed a Bill on "seditious associations" empowering the Government to dissolve organizations working against the State. The PRA, the legal Opposition, was gradually absorbed in the UPS during this period.

An unsuccessful attempt was made on the life of the President on March 22, 1967, by a certain Moustapha Lo; it was officially announced that the attempt had been organized by followers of M. Dia. Moustapha Lo was executed on June 29, the second time the death sentence had been used since independence; a few months earlier, on April 11, a certain Abdou Faye had been executed for the assassination of M. Demba Diop, chairman of the parliamentary group of the UPS.

President Senghor, the only candidate, was re-elected President on Feb. 25, 1968, receiving 100 per cent of the valid votes cast, as did the sole list of candidates for the National Assembly, sponsored by the UPS. In a Cabinet reorganization on June 6, 1968, the President took over the Defence portfolio.

The period 1968–69 was marked by student demonstrations and strikes, partly in sympathy with student strikes in France, and by illegal strikes organized by the trade unions. The Cabinet adopted various measures to deal with emergencies on April 1, 1969; a state of emergency was declared on May 31, 1968, and again from May 30, 1969, to June 23, 1969.

In 1969 the country's deteriorating economic situation caused particular hardship amongst the peasants who were, as a group, loyal to the Government. The groundnut crop, accounting for about three-quarters of Senegal's exports, had been severely reduced by three successive drought years. President Senghor stated on June 13, 1969, that it was the Government's duty to look first of all after the needs of the countryside; measures already taken included the agrarian reform of July 1964 and a 1965 Act on the modernization of rural administration.

A Constitutional Amendment Bill was approved by an overwhelming majority in a national referendum on Feb. 22, 1970. The Bill, submitted by President Senghor early in October 1969 and unanimously approved by the National Assembly on Dec. 8, 1969, provided for the creation of the post of Prime Minister who, while he was to be nominated or dismissed by the President, would be responsible to the National Assembly. It also empowered the President to sign, without counter-signature by Cabinet Ministers, orders concerning foreign policy, defence, the appointment of magistrates and the exercise of special powers.

On Feb. 26, the President appointed M. Abdou Diouf in terms of this Bill as the country's first Prime Minister since M. Mamadou Dia's unsuccessful coup in 1962.

MALI

Area: 465,000 sq. miles.
Population 1969: 4,929,000.
Capital: Bamako (286,000).
Official language: French.
Chief products: Rice, groundnuts, cotton, cattle, fish.

The French Sudan, part of French West Africa, became the independent Republic of Mali on Sept. 22, 1960, after the Sudanese Legislative Assembly had accepted that the Federation of Mali no longer existed.

The Federation of Mali comprising the two States of the French Sudan and Senegal came into official existence on April 4, 1959, as a "member-State of the [French] Community", in the words of the Malian Federal Assembly. The first announcement of the formation of the Federation had been made on Jan. 17, 1959; it was then to unite four of the Republics – Senegal, Sudan, Dahomey and Upper Volta – in what was formerly French West Africa. However, the two latter withdrew from the Federation before April 4, 1959. Having achieved independence within the French Community on June 20, 1960, under the leadership of M. Léopold Senghor, President of the Federal Assembly, the Federation effectively ceased to exist on Aug. 20, 1960, when the Senegalese Legislative Assembly proclaimed the independence of Senegal as a separate Republic. This decision was made after the Federal Government had taken measures which were alleged by the principal Senegalese leaders to constitute an attempted coup directed against Senegalese interests.

Elections held on March 6–8, 1959, in the French Sudan resulted in M. Modibo Keita's party, the *Union soudanaise*, which advocated a "federalist" policy, gaining all the seats in the National Assembly. The principal opponent in the elections was the local section of the *Parti du regroupement africain* led by M. Fily Dabo Sissoko and M. Hammadoun Dicko. M. Keita, who was Prime Minister of the Federation of Mali, was elected Prime Minister of the Sudan on April 16, 1959.

Immediately after the proclamation of independence, on Sept. 20, 1960, the Malian Assembly (formerly the Sudanese Legislative Assembly) conferred the prerogatives of Head of State on M. Keita.

On Oct. 1, 1962, M. Dicko and M. Sissoko were sentenced to death on charges of plotting to overthrow the regime and carrying out "anti-national activities"; these sentences were subsequently commuted on Oct. 8 to hard labour for life.

President Keita announced on Aug. 22, 1967, that the political bureau of the ruling *Union soudanaise* party had been dissolved and that the *Comité national de défense de la révolution* (CNDR) – another *Union soudanaise* party body – had taken full powers over all governmental and party organs as an interim measure. Foreign correspondents considered this move to be a result of political and economic difficulties – a split between the pro-French and pro-Chinese factions in the *Union soudanaise*, and the effects of the devaluation of the Mali franc on May 6, 1967.

"Modibo Keita's dictatorial regime", however, came to an end on Nov. 19, 1968, when it was announced that a National Liberation Committee (NLC), led by Lieutenant Moussa Traore, had assumed all political and administrative functions. It was also stated that the Army would remain in power until free elections had been held, President Keita being placed under arrest.

The coup followed widespread expressions of dissatisfaction which, over the previous two years, had resulted in a number of changes. The President had, on Jan. 17, 1968, dissolved the National Assembly, elected in 1964, and had himself taken over full powers because of the "hostility" shown to deputies in certain areas in connexion with austerity measures taken in August 1967.

A Provisional Government, headed by Captain Yoro Diakité as Prime Minister, was announced on Nov. 23, 1968. Early in December, the existing Constitution was abrogated and replaced by a Basic Law, in terms of which Lieutenant Traore assumed the functions of Head of State until the outcome of a proposed constitutional referendum.

No further move towards the formation of a civilian Government was made, however, apart from the decision to set up a consultative council, taken by the National Liberation Council on June 19, 1969, with the aim of obtaining the co-operation of the greatest number of representative persons in the planning of the economic and financial recovery of Mali. The economic situation improved considerably during 1969, partly as the result of the new regime's abandonment of socialist controls in agriculture and its liberalization of trade.

A plot allegedly aimed at restoring ex-President Keita's regime was foiled by forces loyal to the NLC on Aug. 12–13; sentences of various terms of imprisonment were passed on 25 military men accused of being involved in the plot on Dec. 14.

It was announced on Sept. 19, 1969, that Lieutenant Moussa Traore, chairman of the NLC, had assumed the functions of Head of both State and Government.

MAURITANIA

Area: 419,000 sq. miles.
Population 1970: 1,500,000.
Capital: Nouakchott (40,000).
Official languages: Arabic and French.
Chief products: Iron ore, cereals.

Mauritania, formerly part of French West Africa, became the independent Islamic Republic of Mauritania on Nov. 27–28, 1960, under the premiership of M. Mokhtar Ould Daddah. The Prime Minister's party (the *Parti du regroupement mauritanien*) had won all 40 seats in the Legislative Assembly on May 17, 1959, after the country had become an autonomous Republic within the French Community on Nov. 28, 1958.

Mauritania's application for membership of the United Nations was vetoed by the Soviet Union on Dec. 4, 1960, in view of the Western Powers' alleged discrimination against "certain countries" and their "repeated sabotage" of Mongolia's application for U.N. membership. However, admission to the United Nations was eventually approved by the General Assembly on Oct. 27, 1961, of both Mongolia and Mauritania.

Agreements signed on June 19, 1961, between France and Mauritania provided that the latter would remain outside the French Community. M. Daddah, the Prime Minister and acting Head of State, was in August 1961 elected President, being the only candidate, under a new Constitution establishing a presidential system of government.

President Daddah was re-elected on August 7, 1966, according to the official result by 96 per cent of the country's registered voters. Previously, on May 9, 1965, the President's party, then known as the Mauritanian People's Party, which had been the sole legal party since December 1961, had won all 40 seats in the National Assembly. The formation of a new opposition Party (calling itself *Front national démocratique* and later *Parti démocratique mauritanien*) was disallowed by the Government in August 1964.

Some political dissension was caused by the fact that, while the majority of the population were Moors, about 25 per cent were Africans living mainly in the south. Many officials and teachers were educated Africans who resented being largely excluded from holding key posts, and some of whom agitated for the establishment of a federal system.

In January 1966 a Government decree making the teaching of Arabic compulsory in all schools led to school strikes and clashes between African and Moorish pupils in the capital, Nouakchott, on Feb. 8–9, at least six people being reported killed. President Daddah announced on Feb. 15, 1966, that it would be forbidden from that date to talk of the existence of a "race problem" in Mauritania; he stated on March 7 that all those responsible for the disturbances had been arrested.

Africans were given greater representation in the Cabinet when on Feb. 1, 1968, the President increased the number of Ministries from eight to 13 and allocated five of them to Africans.

[For Moroccan claims to Mauritania's territory, see MOROCCO, page 198.]

ALGERIA

Area: 855,000 sq. miles.

Population 1969 (estimate): 13,349,000.

Capital: Algiers (943,000).

Other important towns: Oran (328,000), Constantine (254,000), Annaba (formerly Bône) (169,000).

Official languages: Arabic and French.

Chief products: Iron ore, oil, natural gas, phosphates, cement, vegetables, wine.

Algeria was declared an independent State on July 3, 1962, thus ending 133 years of French rule. Algiers had surrendered to a French force on July 5, 1830, and Algeria was annexed to France in February 1842. From 1881 the three northern departments of Algiers, Oran and Constantine formed an integral part of France. The Southern Territory of the Sahara, formerly a separate colony, became an integral part of Algeria on the attainment of independence.

The Algerian War

The Algerian Nationalist Movement

The two nationalist parties – the radical Movement for the Triumph of Democratic Liberties (MTLD), led by M. Messali Hadj, and the more moderate Democratic Union of the Algerian Manifesto (UDMA), led by M. Ferhat Abbas – were formed in Algeria after the Second World War of 1939–45.

A "Secret Organization" (OS) was formed in 1947 by a small group inside the MTLD, led by M. Ben Bella, to prepare for an armed rebellion against the French authorities; this movement was banned by the French in 1950, most of its leaders escaping to Cairo.

In March 1954 nine former members of the OS formed a Revolutionary Committee for Unity and Action (CRUA); during the next six months, five members of this Committee met in Berne (Switzerland) and divided Algeria into six *wilayas* (military zones), commanders being appointed for each, in preparation for the uprising of Nov. 1 [see below]. The nine men – subsequently referred to as the "historic leaders of the Algerian Revolution" – were M. Ben Bella, Dr. Hocine Aït Ahmed, M. Mohammed Boudiaf, M. Mohammed Khider, M. Rabah Bitat, M. Krim Belkacem, M. Mourad Didouche, M. Mostefa Ben Boulaïd and M. Larbi Ben M'hidi. The first five of these were subsequently captured by the French, M. Belkacem remained at liberty throughout the war, MM. Didouche and Boulaïd were killed in action and M. M'Hidi committed suicide in prison, according to official reports.

By August 1956, the only nationalist organizations remaining outside the National Liberation Front (FLN – the new title of CRUA) were the Communists and the left-wing section of the MTLD, the Algerian National Movement, led by M. Hadj. In August 1956, a secret FLN conference held in north-eastern Algeria adopted a socialist programme and elected a central committee of 34 members – the National Council of the Algerian Revolution (CNRA) – and a five-man Committee of Co-ordination and Execution (CCE) including M. M'hidi, M. Belkacem and M. Ben Khedda.

At a meeting in Cairo in 1957 the CCE was enlarged by the addition of 10 new members including M. Ferhat Abbas; this new committee formed the nucleus of the "Provisional Government of the Republic of Algeria" (GPRA) set up in Cairo in September 1958, under the leadership of M. Abbas.

On Sept. 28, 1959, following President de Gaulle's statement on self-determination for the Algerian peoples [see page 244], the GPRA issued a statement to the effect that it was prepared to open negotiations with France on the political and military conditions for a cease-fire and self-determination. At the same time, however, they emphasized that these conditions must include the withdrawal of the French forces from Algeria.

Negotiations between the French Government and the Provisional Government opened on May 20, 1961, and proceeded with several interruptions until March 18, 1962, when a cease-fire agreement between France and the GPRA was signed at Evian in France, together with a general declaration summarizing the agreements reached on the future of Algeria. The latter agreements included provision for a referendum on self-determination for the people of Algeria (to be held on July 1, 1962), and outlined the terms of Algerian independence.

Under the provisions concerning Franco-Algerian co-operation, Algeria guaranteed the interests of France and the rights acquired by individuals and organizations, while France, in exchange, undertook to provide technical, cultural and financial assistance to Algeria. Preferential treatment would be applied in certain spheres of trade, and Algeria would be part of the Franc Zone. In the *départements* of the Oases and Sahara the development of subsoil wealth would be carried on under Franco-Algerian co-operation, to be ensured by a technical body for co-operation which would include an equal number of French and Algerian representatives.

The military arrangements laid down in the agreements included the withdrawal of French troops from Algeria, and the leasing to France by Algeria of the naval base of Mers-el-Kébir and the air base of Bou-Sfer for a 15-year period. France was also granted the use of a number of other military areas required by her (including rocket and nuclear-testing installations in the Sahara).

The Evian Agreement also provided for the creation of an interim Provisional Executive; this was formed on March 28 under M. Abderrahman Farès, former president of the Algerian Assembly, who had been released from prison on March 19, where he had been held since November 1961.

On July 1, 1962, a referendum on the question "Do you wish Algeria to become an independent State co-operating with France under the conditions laid down by the declaration of March 19, 1962?" resulted in 91.2 per cent of the total registered electorate voting in favour.

The Algerian revolution began on Nov. 1, 1954, the most serious incident on that date being an armed insurrection in the Aurès mountains. The nationalist uprising spread on a considerable scale during the spring and summer of 1955 to new areas of north-eastern Algeria, while the Aurès mountains remained the main centre of the revolt.

The military situation of the French forces in Algeria deteriorated seriously between September 1955 and the spring of 1956, considerable sections of north-eastern Algeria passing entirely under nationalist control. In the department of Oran, rebel forces began operating on Oct. 1, 1955, and by May 1956 were largely in control of a sector adjoining the Moroccan border.

Between March and July 1956, the strength of the French forces was increased from 190,000 to 400,000; in view of the increased odds against them, the insurgents, who had been operating in bands up to 3,000 strong, split up into smaller units which carried on guerrilla action. The rebels also moved into hitherto peaceful areas, until by the spring of 1957 military operations were in progress across the whole of northern Algeria and along the line of the Saharan Atlas, and from July 1957 rebel activity was extended into the Sahara desert.

The situation improved from the French point of view during the summer and autumn of 1957; this continued, apart from a slight setback in the early months of 1958, until June 1958. At this date it was apparent that the rebels' own casualties, at their highest since the outbreak of the war, were imposing an intolerable strain on them and that they were reverting therefore to smaller organizational units, guerrilla tactics and the increased use of terrorism.

At the beginning of 1958 French military sources estimated the strength of the National Liberation Army (ALN) to be 30,000 "regulars" and 30,000 "reserves"; FLN figures stated that 100,000 men were under arms. French forces in Algeria during 1958 totalled 450,000 men.

Large-scale offensives were carried out by the French between December 1958 and February 1961; at the same time FLN terrorism gradually declined in intensity. Between February 1961 and the cease-fire in March 1962, the French did not engage in any major offensives as negotiations with the GPRA were in progress throughout this period. Military operations by the FLN were largely replaced by mass demonstrations during 1961.

At the time of the cease-fire French forces in Algeria consisted of slightly over 400,000 men. According to French estimates the Nationalists had 150,000 men inside Algeria and between 30,000 and 37,000 in Morocco and Tunisia.

European Resistance

Political agitation by extreme right-wing elements among the European population in Algeria became increasingly apparent from 1956 onwards, in opposition to the nationalist uprising.

On May 13–14, 1958, the military authorities supported by civilian leaders carried out a coup, setting up a Committee of Public Safety for Algeria and the Sahara which exercised powers independently of the French Government. The French settlers in Algeria considered that Algeria should remain part of France; following General de Gaulle's declaration on May 15 of his readiness "to assume the powers of the Republic" and of his understanding for their wishes, the French in Algiers, along with a large number of Moslems, demonstrated in favour of the General on May 16.

With the formation of a Government by General de Gaulle in France on June 1, 1958, the French settlers became more hopeful of a solution which would be in accord with their wishes for *"Algérie française"*. On June 13 General de Gaulle outlined his Government's task which was, *inter alia*, to pacify Algeria and to "make her one with France for ever". The role of the Committee of Public Safety progressively diminished and on Oct. 21, 1958, it was decided to transform this into an exclusively political body under the name of the Organization of Committees of Public Safety.

A new turn in events came on Sept. 16, 1959, when President de Gaulle undertook to grant the Algerian people a free choice between secession, complete integration with France and internal self-government in close association with France, within four years of the restoration of peace.

From the beginning of December 1959 onwards renewed outbursts of terrorism in Algiers and the surrounding countryside created growing anxiety and anger among the European population; this led to an insurrection which broke out in Algiers on Jan. 24, 1960, following a protest demonstration against President de Gaulle's Algerian policy, called by European extremist leaders who had played a prominent part in the 1958 coup. After the President had emphasized his Government's determination to restore order and not to modify its Algerian policy, the insurgents surrendered on Feb. 1.

During 1960 a number of new integrationist organizations, with the aim of maintaining *"Algérie française"*, were formed; further, on Sept. 14, 1960, General Salan, who, before his retirement, had been the French C.-in-C. and Delegate-General in Algeria, issued a statement in which, by implication, he attacked President de Gaulle's policy of self-determination for Algeria.

A referendum on a Bill outlining the future organization of public powers in Algeria, while awaiting self-determination, held on Jan. 8, 1961, resulted in the majority of the European electorate voting against the proposals. This was followed by the development of widespread "activist" terrorism directed against the supporters of General de Gaulle.

On April 22, 1961, a military uprising directed against the President's Algerian policy broke out under a "directorate" of four retired generals — Maurice Challe, Raoul Salan, Edmond Jouhaud and André Zeller — with the collaboration or collusion of a number of other officers. The revolt collapsed within four days because of the firm attitude of President de Gaulle and the French Government, strong popular opposition in France and the continued loyalty of the Army as a whole.

A final attempt to prevent a negotiated settlement being reached between the French and the Algerian nationalists was made by the *Organisation de l'Armée Secrète* (OAS) which violently resisted the policy of negotiation. The strategy of the OAS was based on the theory of "subversive warfare" worked out by the French Army as a result of its experiences in fighting the *Vietminh* in Vietnam and the National Liberation Front (FLN). The military leaders of the OAS were primarily concerned with bringing about the overthrow of President de Gaulle's regime in France, while the civilian leaders were more interested in defending the interests of the European community in Algeria. OAS terrorist activities in Algeria ended in June 1962, when the majority of the European population in Algeria realized that the Evian Agreement would have to be implemented.

Meanwhile mass emigration of Europeans from Algeria had begun, and by August 1962 over 800,000 (more than four-fifths) of the European population had left the country.

The withdrawal of French military forces, other than those at the bases of Mers-el-Kébir and Bou-Sfer and France's nuclear-testing grounds in the Sahara, was completed by June 15, 1964. The Sahara testing grounds were dismantled in 1966, upon completion of France's nuclear-testing grounds in the Pacific. The Mers-el-Kébir base was evacuated in January 1968, and that at Bou-Sfer in December 1970.

The Ben Bella Regime, 1962—65

In the first elections to be held after the achievement of independence, 81.5 per cent of the total electorate of 6,504,033 cast their vote for a single list of candidates for membership of the Constituent Assembly. The list had been chosen by the Political Bureau of the FLN, mostly from among its own supporters. [The Political Bureau consisted of M. Ben Bella, M. Khider, M. Boudiaf, Dr. Aït Ahmed, M. Bitat (all of whom had been released from prison on March 18, 1962), M. Saïd and M. Ben Allah.]

At the same time a referendum on whether the Assembly should have power to choose a Provisional Government, to legislate and to draw up a Constitution resulted in 99.6 per cent of the votes cast being in favour of such powers.

M. Ferhat Abbas was elected president of the new Assembly on Sept. 25, 1962, by 155 votes with 36 abstentions; after reading a message from M. Ben Khedda, who surrendered to the Assembly the powers of the GPRA, M. Abbas proclaimed "the Algerian Democratic and Popular Republic". On the following day M. Ben Bella was elected Prime Minister by 141 votes to 13 with 31 abstentions, while the new Government, drawn largely from M. Ben Bella's personal supporters, from former ALN staff officers and from former members of UDMA, was invested on Sept. 29.

M. Ben Bella's Government encountered opposition from three main sources: (a) the existing rival parties, for example, the Algerian People's Party (PPA) – formerly the Algerian National Movement (MNA) – led by M. Messali Hadj, and the Communist Party; (b) a new underground left-wing party, the Party of the Socialist Revolution (PRS); and (c) organizations affiliated to the FLN, notably the General Union of Algerian Workers (UGTA) and the FLN Federation of France. A number of measures were taken during November 1962 to suppress this opposition; the Communist Party was banned on Nov. 29, the official organ of the PPA – Le Cri du Peuple – was suppressed on Nov. 6, while the FLN Federation of France was officially dissolved by the Political Bureau on Nov. 20.

The Government was also faced with a serious economic crisis, arising out of the departure from Algeria of 80 per cent of the European population, including most technicians and skilled workers, and the concurrent transfer of large amounts of capital to France. These two facts were responsible for mass unemployment and the resultant rapid increase in Moslem emigration to France.

Emergency measures had to be adopted during the autumn of 1962 to overcome the acute difficulties which also faced the Government in the field of education, following the departure of the majority of the 25,000 teachers of French nationality out of a total of 27,000 school-teachers employed in 1961–62.

Agreements were signed in Paris on Aug. 28, 1962, defining the terms of French aid, on a large scale, to Algeria. Economic and military aid was also received from Arab, Western and Communist countries.

A draft Constitution, prepared by the Government, and approved by an FLN conference on July 31, 1963, laid down that the President, who would be nominated by the FLN and elected by universal suffrage, would be Head of State, leader of the Government and supreme Commander of the armed forces. He would appoint Ministers, promulgate laws and define and direct the country's policy. The National Assembly would be elected by universal suffrage, the candidates being nominated by the FLN. The Constitution also laid down that the FLN would carry out the objectives of the Algerian revolution and the building of socialism, define the aims of national policy and supervise the activities of the Government and the Assembly.

The submission of the Constitution to a party conference before being considered by the Constituent Assembly and the provisions of the Constitution were criticized by M. Ferhat Abbas who, as a result, announced his resignation from the Presidency of the Assembly on Aug. 14. M. Abbas was considered the leading spokesman of liberal opinion and was critical of the Government's nationalization policy and of its suppression of the Opposition.

The Assembly adopted the draft Constitution on Aug. 28 by 139 votes to 23 with eight abstentions and 23 deputies absent.

The Constitution was then submitted to a popular referendum; 5,287,229 votes were cast out of a total registered electorate of 6,391,818. Of these, 5,166,195 were in favour, 104,861 against, with 16,173 spoilt papers. In the Kabylie, the main stronghold of the Opposition, the referendum was largely boycotted.

M. Ben Bella, the sole candidate, was elected President of the Republic on Sept. 15 by 5,805,103 votes to 22,515. The new Cabinet was formed on Sept. 18, effectively increasing the number of the President's personal supporters in the Cabinet; Colonel Houari Boumedienne became First Deputy Premier and Minister of Defence.

Following the resignation of M. Bitat on the ground that, although a member of the Political Bureau, he had not been consulted about the above Cabinet changes, M. Ben Bella became the only representative in the Government of the "historic leaders of the Algerian Revolution" [see page 241]. Of the others, M. Khider had resigned his post as general secretary of the Political Bureau on April 17, 1963, because of "fundamental differences of opinion inside the Political Bureau on whether it was opportune to prepare for and hold a national congress of the FLN before the present [Constituent] Assembly's mandate expired". M. Boudiaf, the leader of the PRS [subsequently banned on Aug. 16], had been arrested by military police on June 21, on a charge of plotting against the State; Dr. Aït Ahmed, who was the Chief Opposition spokesman in the Assembly before his resignation from the latter on Sept. 7, had left Algiers for the Kabylie, while M. Krim Belkacem, who had resigned from the Assembly along with Dr. Ahmed, was living in voluntary exile in Switzerland.

A serious revolt began in the Kabylie on Sept. 29, 1963, when Dr. Aït Ahmed, addressing a meeting at Tizi-Ouzou organized by the "Front of Socialist Forces" (FFS) – a clandestine organization led by Dr. Ahmed, denounced President Ben Bella's regime as "Fascist" and "illegal" and called for a "decisive struggle" to overthrow it.

Kabyles are of pure Berber stock and speak a Berber language; the majority of Algerians are descended from the Arabs who overran North Africa in the seventh century and intermarried with the Berbers. M. Ben Khedda, M. Krim Belkacem and Dr. Aït Ahmed were Berbers, whereas M. Ben Bella's Government consisted almost entirely of Arabs. Apart from the communal issue, the Kabyles' grievances were primarily economic.

Dr. Ahmed was supported by Colonel Mohand Ou el Hadj (commander of the Kabylie, the rebels' main stronghold in the Algerian war). Following the occupation of various towns in the Kabylie by Government troops, with virtually no resistance from the rebels who wanted to avoid bloodshed, talks between the Government and the rebels culminated in an agreement between President Ben Bella and Colonel Mohand Ou el Hadj on Nov. 12. Under this all political prisoners would be released within a week; all officers who had been dismissed would be reinstated in their commands; and a Commission would be set up immediately to prepare for an FLN congress to be held within five months. M. Boudiaf, who had been accused of having connexions with an alleged opposition "maquis" in the Kabylie, was released on Nov. 16, as demanded by Dr. Ahmed on Oct. 4.

This agreement was not accepted by Dr. Ahmed and on Feb. 23, 1964, the FFS announced the resumption of "the struggle against President Ben Bella's regime of dictatorship and misery".

On June 30, 1964, Colonel Mohammed Chaabani entered into open rebellion from his headquarters at Biskra on the ground that Islam was "incompatible with socialism". By July 5, however, President Ben Bella claimed that 3,000 of the Colonel's men had come over to the loyalists and that the Colonel had taken to the hills with 100 of his supporters.

A "National Committee for Defence of the Revolution" (CNDR) was formed on July 6 by Dr. Ahmed, M. Boudiaf, Colonel Chaabani, M. Moussa Hassani and M. Mohammed Ben Ahmed; the Committee represented an alliance between left-wing Socialist and Islamic opponents of the Government – a fact which largely contributed to discredit the rebel leaders by suggesting that they were motivated by personal grievances rather than political principles, and to lose them popular support.

By the end of July the rebellion had collapsed; Colonel Chaabani was captured on July 8 and M. Ben Ahmed on July 13. M. Boudiaf took refuge in France, Dr. Ahmed was captured with a few supporters on Oct. 17, while M. Hassani surrendered voluntarily on Jan. 19, 1965. Colonel Chaabani was condemned to death on Sept. 2, 1964, by a Military Court and shot the following day. Of the rebel leaders only M. Dehylès remained at large in Algeria; the FFS was reduced to a few isolated bands in the Kabylie and did not constitute a serious danger.

The trial of Dr. Ahmed opened on April 7, 1965, before the Revolutionary Criminal Court. Five of his associates were tried with him, while M. Dehylès and six political exiles, including M. Boudiaf and M. Khider, were tried *in absentia*. Dr. Ahmed, M. Ben Ahmed and the seven men tried *in absentia* were sentenced to death on April 10; President Ben Bella, on April 12, commuted the sentences on Dr. Ahmed and M. Ben Ahmed to life imprisonment. [M. Khider was assassinated in Madrid on Jan. 3, 1967.]

On July 15, following a series of gestures which indicated President Ben Bella's desire for a reconciliation with his former opponents, it was announced that after discussions between the FLN and FFS, the latter had agreed to end its armed struggle against the regime.

Meanwhile at the first FLN Party congress to be held since independence on April 16—21, 1964, President Ben Bella had been unanimously elected to the new post of general secretary of the Party, while a central committee of 80 members was chosen, to elect a Political Bureau. Both these bodies included a number of former opponents of the Government, for example, Colonel Mohand Ou el Hadj, and a high proportion of officers.

General elections were held on Sept. 20, 1964, 5,164,846 out of the 5,177,631 votes cast being in favour of the single list of candidates.

Nationalization

A decree was issued on March 22, 1963, ordering all industrial, agricultural and commercial enterprises which were not being carried on normally to be handed over to workers' management committees; similar action was permitted against other enterprises which ceased to operate without a legitimate reason. All houses and flats which had not been occupied for two consecutive months since July 1, 1962, were declared vacant; this allowed local authorities to take possession of such property under an order of Sept. 7, 1962. Under the decree of March 22 much French-owned property was taken over; during talks between M. Ben Bella and M. Jean de Broglie (French Secretary of State for Algerian Affairs) on May 1—2, it was agreed that one-fifth of French financial aid to Algeria should be used to compensate Frenchmen whose land had been taken over.

On Sept. 15, 1963, President Ben Bella said that the Government would nationalize all the French settlers' land, as well as land owned by "traitors" and the principal industrial enterprises. The President stated on Oct. 1 that the settlers would be compensated for their crops.

Other nationalization measures taken during 1963 included: (1) The taking-over of road and air transport companies following the passage on July 25 of a Bill establishing a National Transport Office with a monopoly of transport facilities; (2) the nationalization on Sept. 20 of two of the leading Algiers hotels, followed by that of other hotels in different parts of the country; (3) the taking-over of the various enterprises including factories, flour-mills, shops, restaurants and cinemas between May and November 1963; (4) the nationalization of the tobacco and match industries on Nov. 4; and (5) that of the last three French-owned newspapers in Algeria – *Dépêche d'Algérie, Echo d'Oran, Dépêche de Constantine* – on Sept. 17.

M. Ben Bella stated on June 10, 1963, that the Government intended to establish a mixed economy containing both a socialist and a private sector.

The Boumedienne Regime, 1965–

The armed forces carried out a bloodless *coup d'état* in Algiers on June 19, 1965, under the command of Colonel Houari Boumedienne. President Ben Bella was arrested and removed to an unknown destination, and the Revolutionary Council took power immediately.

The major factor in deciding the date of the coup was a forthcoming Afro-Asian Conference; the Revolutionary Council, in the communiqué announcing its formation, made clear that the conspirators feared that this Conference would so enhance President Ben Bella's prestige as to make his removal impossible. A further factor precipitating the crisis was the military faction's alleged opposition to the agreement with the FFS [see above] and M. Ben Bella's other conciliatory gestures towards the Opposition.

Demonstrations in support of M. Ben Bella and against the Revolutionary Council occurred in Algiers between June 20 and 25; these were started by students and young people, with whom M. Bèn Bella was extremely popular, but joined by increasing numbers of adults. A number of demonstrators were shot dead in similar incidents in Annaba (formerly Bône) and Oran.

Opposition to the coup was believed to be strongest inside the UGTA – the national trade union federation, the FLN Youth and the *Union nationale des étudiants algériens*, each of which contained a large left-wing element.

The Algerian association of *ulema* [doctors of Moslem law], on the other hand, gave complete support to the Council; the emphasis laid on Algerian traditions in the Council's communiqué of June 19 was regarded as an indication that the Council would pursue a more strongly Islamic policy than M. Ben Bella. Among the leading opponents of M. Ben Bella's regime, however, only M. Bitat announced his support for the Revolutionary Council.

The membership of the Revolutionary Council, under the chairmanship of Colonel Boumedienne, announced on July 6, comprised the commanders of four of the five military regions, four Staff Officers, four former commanders of *wilayas* [see page 241], two security officers, nine civilians who had held military commands during the war and two other civilians. Eight out of the 26-member Council had held Cabinet posts under the previous regime.

The membership of the Cabinet, under Colonel Boumedienne (who also exercised the powers of a *de facto* Chief of Staff), was announced on July 10; this was essentially a broad-based civilian Government, including representatives of both left-wing and Islamic opinion as well as technical experts and comprising nine members of the outgoing Cabinet, three former Ministers and eight newcomers.

In November 1967 a group of Ministers, generally regarded as holding left-wing views and opposed to President Boumedienne's "autocratic" rule, were joined by Colonel Tahar Zbiri, Chief of the Army's General Staff, and other officers in demanding a meeting of the Revolutionary Council (which had not met since early 1967) and the election of a Constituent Assembly.

On Dec. 14–15 Colonel Zbiri and his supporters attempted to overthrow the Government but a month later most of the latter were under arrest and Colonel Zbiri sought political asylum in Tunisia.

A Revolutionary Court set up in Oran in November 1968 subsequently tried a large number of persons implicated in the attempted rising, passing death sentences on Colonel Zbiri (*in absentia*) and four others on July 23, 1969, as well as long prison sentences on other defendants.

Opposition to President Boumedienne's regime remained ineffective, largely because the various opposing groups remained divided and failed to obtain mass support. Of the various movements opposing President Boumedienne, the FFS was reconstituted in May 1966 by Dr. Aït Ahmed after he had escaped from prison, and the *Mouvement démocratique de renouveau algérien* (MDRA) was led by M. Krim Belkacem, then outside Algeria, who was later found assassinated in Frankfurt (Western Germany) in October 1970.

4. FORMER BELGIAN, ITALIAN OR SPANISH TERRITORIES

DEMOCRATIC REPUBLIC OF THE CONGO (Kinshasa)

Area: 905,000 sq. miles.
Population 1970: 21,638,000.
Capital: Kinshasa (1,404,000).
Other important towns: Lubumbashi (700,000), Kisangani (400,000).
Official language: French.
Chief products: Copper, manganese, cobalt, palm oil, rubber, coffee.

The former Belgian Congo attained independence as the Republic of the Congo on July 1, 1960, after agreement had been reached on the constitutional development of the territory at a round-table conference of Belgian and Congolese representatives in Brussels from Jan. 20 to Feb. 20, 1960.

The provisional Constitution of the new State, which was divided into six provinces – Katanga, Kasai, Léopoldville, Equator, Kivu and Eastern Province – was embodied in a Belgian Basic Law signed by King Baudouin of the Belgians on June 19, after being approved unanimously by the Belgian Chamber of Representatives and (with one abstention) by the Senate. The Law closely followed the main decisions of the Brussels Conference which were (*a*) that there should be a bicameral legislature consisting of a Chamber of Representatives, whose members would be elected by universal adult male suffrage, and a Senate, whose members would be designated by the Provincial Assemblies; (*b*) that authority would be divided between the Central Government and the Provinces; (*c*) that Provincial Assemblies and Provincial Governments should be set up, the latter consisting of a President and from five to 10 members elected by the respective Assembly from among its own members or from outside; and (*d*) that a treaty of friendship and co-operation with Belgium should be signed [which was done on June 29], and also co-operation agreements with the then Trust Territory of Ruanda-Urundi. The Basic Law also provided for an elected Head of State in the Republic, a question on which the Brussels Conference had been unable to make an agreed recommendation.

The Belgian Government's decision, announced on Jan. 13, 1959, to grant independence to the Congo in a series of gradual stages, followed a period of nationalist agitation among Africans in the Lower Congo — largely as a result of nationalist movements in other parts of Africa. The situation was aggravated by widespread unemployment and serious riots in Léopoldville on Jan. 4—5, 1959.

The Belgian Government's further proposals, announced on Oct. 16, 1959, for accelerated progress to independence failed to satisfy the extremist nationalist leaders; M. Patrice Lumumba, principal leader of the *Mouvement national congolais* (MNC), announced a boycott of the forthcoming elections in December 1959 and the launching of a "positive plan for immediate liberation of the Congo" on Oct. 29. When the police attempted to arrest M. Lumumba on charges arising out of his statements, serious riots followed in Stanleyville on Oct. 30—31.

Elections for the Chamber of Representatives (the Lower House in the future Congolese Parliament) were held on May 11—22, 1960; the six Provincial Assemblies were elected concurrently, and they in turn elected the members of the National Senate.

The extremist faction of the MNC, led by M. Lumumba, gained more seats than any other single party in both the Chamber of Representatives (41 out of a total of 137 seats) and the Senate (22 out of a total of 84 seats). In the Provincial Assemblies the Lumumba wing of the MNC was the only party to gain seats in all six provinces, many of which had been gained by purely local or tribal groups, such as the Conakat in Katanga. The remaining seats in the Chamber of Representatives were distributed among the *Parti national du progrès* (PNP) — 22, the *Parti solidaire africain* (PSA) — 13, the *Association des Bakongo* (Abako) — 12, the *Centre du regroupement africain* (Cerea) — 10, the moderate faction of the MNC led by M. Albert Kalonji — eight, and the Balubakat — seven, while 24 seats went to various other groups.

Following confused negotiations between the political parties and discussions with the Belgian Government, M. Lumumba, on June 23, 1960, formed a Government comprising representatives of virtually all political parties except the Kalonji wing of the MNC.

M. Joseph Kasavubu (the leader of the Abako) was elected President (Head of State) by Parliament on June 24, gaining 159 votes against 43 for the only other candidate, M. Jean Bolikango, leader of the *Parti de l'unité nationale africaine* (Puna).

A serious crisis arose in Katanga on June 24 where M. Moïse Tshombe, the leader of the Conakat, which with its allies held a majority in the Provincial Assembly, expressed his "grave concern" over the composition of the central Cabinet, alleging that M. Lumumba had failed to fulfil promises made to the Conakat.

The Civil War

On the night of July 5–6, 1960, mutiny broke out among the soldiers of the Congolese *Force Publique* at Thysville (south-west of Léopoldville) and in Camp Léopold II outside Léopoldville; it was understood that the men resented the existing officer system, under which the highest rank open to a Congolese soldier was that of warrant officer, and that they had serious grievances over Army pay and conditions. Despite immediate attempts by President Kasavubu and M. Lumumba to restore order among the mutineers and to satisfy their demands, it soon became apparent that the mutiny was turning into a general movement against Belgian and other European residents, while at the same time disorders spread to many parts of the country.

On July 7 Europeans began to flee from the Léopoldville area to the French Congo. With the aim of restoring law and order, and protecting European residents, the Belgian Government announced the next day (July 8) that Belgian troops would be sent to the Congo; these went into action against the Congolese mutineers in several places on July 10 and subsequently in many parts of the territory.

Developments took a new turn on July 11. When it was learnt that M. Lumumba had appealed to the United Nations for the help of military specialists to assist in the reorganization of the Congolese military forces, M. Moïse Tshombe late the same day announced Katanga's independence; he alleged that the Central Government's sole wish was "the disintegration of the whole military and civil machine, and the creation of a reign of terror which is driving out our Belgian collaborators", with the aim of replacing the latter by advisers "which it already seems to have recruited from the Communist countries".

The U.N. Security Council passed a resolution on July 14 authorizing the immediate dispatch of U.N. military forces to the Congo and requesting Belgium to withdraw her troops; the first U.N. troops arrived in Léopoldville on July 15, building up by July 28 to a force of over 10,000 with units in all provinces except Katanga. In response to the Security Council's decision, the Belgian Government promised ultimately to withdraw Belgian troops to their bases in the Congo but insisted that this could not be done until U.N. forces were in a position to ensure the safety of Europeans throughout the country. The Council then passed a second resolution on July 21, demanding the "speedy" withdrawal of Belgian troops and calling on all countries to respect the territorial integrity of the Congo Republic as established on July 1.

The Congolese Government had meanwhile announced on July 14 that it had broken off diplomatic relations with Belgium; it alleged that Belgium had "flagrantly violated the Treaty of Friendship . . . especially the clause stipulating that Belgian troops cannot intervene in Congolese territory except at the express request of the Congolese Government" and had violated Congolese territorial integrity "by the incitement of Katanga to secession". Further, on July 25 the Congolese Government denounced the still unratified Belgo-Congolese Treaty of June 29 on which Belgium based her right to retain her Congolese bases. On the other hand M. Tshombe insisted that the presence of Belgian troops in Katanga at his Government's request was essential for security and declared that his own forces would resist any attempt by U.N. troops to enter Katanga.

Dr. Dag Hammarskjöld, then U.N. Secretary-General, arrived in the Congo on July 28 and it was announced on July 30 that a "basic agreement" had been reached between himself and the Central Government on the position of the U.N. Force, and that a commission of Congolese Ministers had been set up to co-operate with the U.N. authorities.

Following the announcement on Aug. 2 by Dr. Hammarskjöld that the decision had been taken to move U.N. troops into Katanga and that Dr. Ralph Bunche, Dr. Hammarskjöld's personal representative in the Congo, would go to Elisabethville on Aug. 5 "to start negotiations to begin the withdrawal of Belgian troops to their bases as the first step . . . to the complete execution of the Security Council's resolution as far as Katanga is concerned", the Katanga Government stated on the next day (Aug. 3) that it had ordered the "general mobilization" of all its armed forces to resist the entry of U.N. troops into the province; at the same time M. Tshombe strongly reaffirmed his Government's intention to maintain the territory's independence. In view of the Katanga Government's stand, Dr. Hammarskjöld announced in Léopoldville on Aug. 5 that he had decided to postpone the despatch of U.N. troops to the province pending a further meeting of the Security Council, which was held on Aug. 8–9. In his report to the Security Council, Dr. Hammarskjöld, commenting on the Katanga problem, said: "The question is a constitutional one. . . . The problem for those resisting the U.N. Force in Katanga may be stated in these terms: 'Will U.N. participation in control of security in Katanga submit the province to the immediate control and authority of the Central Government against its wishes?' They consider this seriously to jeopardize their possibility of searching for constitutional solutions other than a strictly unitarian one. . . ." The Council adopted a resolution calling on Belgium to withdraw her troops from Katanga "immediately"; reaffirming that U.N. troops must enter Katanga; and reiterating that the U.N. Force must not in any way intervene in domestic Congolese affairs or disputes. On Aug. 12 Dr. Hammarskjöld arrived in Elisabethville (Katanga) for personal talks with M. Tshombe [who had been elected Head of State of Katanga by the Katangese Parliament on Aug. 8] on the deployment of U.N. forces in Katanga; these were concluded satisfactorily on the following day and the replacement of Belgian by U.N. troops begun.

Relations between Dr. Hammarskjöld and M. Lumumba deteriorated over the month following the above agreement; M. Lumumba alleged that Dr. Hammarskjöld's interpretation of the Security Council's resolution of Aug. 9 [see above] was "erroneous" and claimed that it was made clear by this resolution that the U.N. was not to act as a neutral body in the Congo, but had to "place all its resources at the disposal of my Government", and that the U.N. Force could therefore be used to subdue the "rebel government" of Katanga. The situation, which was exacerbated by the maltreatment of U.N. personnel by Congolese troops, led the Secretary-General to request another meeting of the Security Council to clarify his mandate; this was held on Aug. 21–22 but ended without any new resolution being adopted.

The most important developments following the Security Council meeting were the despatch of Central Government troops to Kasai for the subjugation of a secessionist "Etat Minier" in that province (which had been formally proclaimed by M. Albert Kalonji on Aug. 10) and the subsequent invasion of Katanga, and the receipt by M. Lumumba's Government from the Soviet Union of numbers of transport aircraft and lorries for military use.

At the fifth meeting of the Security Council on the Congo crisis held between Sept. 9 and Sept. 17, 1960, a Ceylonese-Tunisian resolution expressing support for the actions of Dr. Hammarskjöld was vetoed by the Soviet Union. An emergency session of the General Assembly, called at the request of the United States, opened on Sept. 17 and ended on Sept. 20 with the unopposed adoption of an Afro-Asian resolution approving Dr. Hammarskjöld's execution of U.N. policy in the Congo.

Meanwhile a constitutional crisis had arisen in the Congo following President Kasavubu's dismissal of M. Lumumba from office and the appointment of M. Joseph Ileo, president of the Senate, as Prime Minister on Sept. 5. Announcing this decision the President declared that M. Lumumba had been "put in place by the Belgians and was leading the country into civil war". M. Lumumba immediately claimed that he was still Prime Minister and that M. Kasavubu was a "traitor" and was no longer Head of State.

In this situation Colonel Joseph-Désiré Mobutu, Army Chief of Staff (who had previously appeared to be a supporter of M. Lumumba) announced on Sept. 14 that the Army was taking over supreme power and that all other political activity, including that of the two rival Governments of M. Ileo and M. Lumumba, would be suspended until Dec. 31, 1960. Colonel Mobutu subsequently appointed a "college of commissioners" to run the country's Government; its members were university graduates and students, of whom the senior was M. Justin-Marie Bomboko, who had served as Foreign Minister both in M. Lumumba's Cabinet and in that of M. Ileo.

Between the middle of September and the end of October 1960, events were characterized by the increasingly strained relations between the U.N. authorities and Colonel Mobutu on the one hand, and the U.N. authorities and M. Kasavubu on the other; this was accentuated by (a) the failure of attempts by the Colonel to arrest M. Lumumba, who remained in the Prime Minister's official residence under U.N. protection; (b) strong criticism of the behaviour of Congolese troops in Léopoldville by Mr. Rajeshwar Dayal, the Secretary-General's personal representative in the Congo; and (c) U.N. criticism of the Belgian advisers who were returning to work with the Central Government in the capital.

Growing hostility also developed between M. Tshombe and the U.N. authorities following the posting of U.N. troops to northern Katanga to maintain law and order in view of disturbances caused by anti-Tshombe Baluba tribesmen.

The whole Congolese situation, however, was radically changed by the capture of M. Lumumba by Colonel Mobutu's troops on Dec. 1 after he had escaped from Léopoldville on Nov. 27 with the aim of reaching a group of his supporters under the leadership of M. Antoine Gizenga, General Victor Lundula and M. Bernard Salumu, who had established a Lumumbist centre of power at Stanleyville, capital of Eastern Province.

Following the transfer of M. Lumumba from the Thysville prison to Katanga during January 1961, it was announced by the Katangese Minister of the Interior, M. Godefroid Munongo, that M. Lumumba had been assassinated by villagers near Kolwezi (210 miles north-west of Elisabethville). M. Munongo said that the villagers had acted "somewhat precipitately" but "excusably"; that they had "rid the Congo and the world of a problem which menaced humanity"; and that they would receive the reward offered for M. Lumumba's recapture.

The U.N. Security Council met immediately following this announcement and on Feb. 20 adopted a resolution authorizing the U.N. to use force in the Congo if necessary to prevent civil war; urging the immediate withdrawal of all Belgian and other foreign military and para-military advisers; and calling for an investigation into M. Lumumba's death. This resolution was subsequently approved by the General Assembly at its resumed 15th session from March 7 to April 22, 1961.

According to the report of the U.N. commission investigating M. Lumumba's death (published on Nov. 14, 1961) it was "most likely" that the former Prime Minister had been shot, with two companions, by a Belgian officer in the presence of M. Tshombe and other Katangese leaders – but M. Tshombe immediately described the report as "completely false".

Shortly before M. Lumumba's death, President Kasavubu had issued, on Feb. 9, 1961, a decree establishing a central Congolese Government under the premiership of M. Joseph Ileo, and at the same time dissolving the College of Commissioners. [Colonel Mobutu had previously, on Jan. 22, been named by the President as C.-in-C. of the Congolese National Army.]

Several attempts to reconcile the various political factions in the Congo were made over the next six months.

A Congolese round-table conference was held at Tananarive (Madagascar) on March 8–12, 1961; the participants included President Kasavubu, three anti-Lumumbists – M. Ileo, M. Tshombe and M. Kalonji, M. Cléophas Kamitatu, head of the Léopoldville provincial government, and delegates from Léopoldville and Equator provinces, Katanga and the "Etat Minier". Although invited, three Lumumbist leaders – M. Antoine Gizenga, head of the Lumumbist regime at Stanleyville, M. Anicet Kashamura and General Victor Lundula – did not attend. Agreement was reached at this conference that the existing Republic of the Congo should be replaced by a Confederation of Congolese States under the Presidency of M. Kasavubu.

A further conference was held from April 24 to May 27 at Coquilhatville, again with no Lumumbist representatives; after bitterly denouncing President Kasavubu for accepting the Security Council resolution of Feb. 20, President Tshombe walked out of the conference and was subsequently arrested. On his release from detention and return to Katanga on June 25, M. Tshombe repudiated agreements signed by him to reunite Katanga with the rest of the Congo.

The central Congolese Government reconvened on July 25 after almost a year had passed since their last meeting; deputies and senators were present from all parts of the Congo except Katanga. On Aug. 1 it was announced that M. Ileo had formally tendered his Government's resignation and that President Kasavubu had asked M. Cyrille Adoula, the Minister of the Interior in the outgoing Cabinet, to form an administration; the membership of this, announced on Aug. 3, included representatives of all leading Congolese parties (except those in Katanga), both Lumumbist and anti-Lumumbist.

Subsequently, on Aug. 6, it was announced in Elisabethville that it had been decided to send Katangese representatives to the central Parliament; this did not, however, imply any renunciation of Katanga's "actual position or acquired rights".

On Aug. 15, Dr. Hammarskjöld confirmed that the new Government was recognized by the U.N. as the sole legal Government of the Congo.

The overall situation in the Congo provinces, in the autumn of 1961 was as follows: (a) The provinces of Léopoldville and Equator were under the control of the central Government; (b) the Eastern Province was under the control of M. Gizenga's Lumumbist administration in Stanleyville; (c) two administrations were functioning in Kasai – M. Kalonji's "Etat Minier", which co-operated with President Kasavubu, and an anti-Lumumbist provincial administration at Luluabourg which, however, exercised largely nominal authority in an area of predominantly Lumumbist sympathies; (d) most of Katanga province was controlled by President Tshombe's regime in Elisabethville, but Lumumbists had established themselves in northern Katanga and set up a "province" of Lualaba; (e) Kivu Province was without any effective administration, Lumumbist control of that province being purely nominal.

For the next eighteen months the situation in Katanga remained extremely confused despite the participation of Katangese delegates in the central Government.

After the reported intention of central Government troops to invade Katanga, U.N. forces took control of Katanga on Sept. 13, 1961, "in order to prevent civil war"; several days of confused fighting between the U.N. forces and Katangans, still led by Europeans, followed. A cease-fire protocol, however, was signed by the two sides on Oct. 13, virtually restoring the status quo of Sept. 12.

On Nov. 13, the Security Council met "to consider the situation prevailing in the province of Katanga, caused by the lawless acts of mercenaries". A resolution was adopted on Nov. 24 declaring full support for the central Congolese Government, authorizing the use of U.N. forces "if necessary" to apprehend all "foreign mercenaries and hostile elements" and demanding that all secessionist activities in Katanga should cease forthwith. Further, on Dec. 1, the U.N. Secretariat issued a report stating that unless M. Tshombe gained control over his military forces the U.N. would use force against them; this was followed during the next few days by numerous clashes between the two sides. Fighting continued despite the signing by both sides, at Kitona, on Dec. 21, 1961, of a cease-fire agreement, in which M. Tshombe declared that he accepted the application of the Basic Law of May 19, 1960, and recognized the indissoluble unity of the Republic of the Congo, President Kasavubu as Head of State and the authority of the central Government over all parts of the Republic.

On Oct. 9, 1962, an increasing military build-up in Katanga was reported by the U.N. representative in the Congo, Mr. Robert Gardiner; during November the U.N. repeatedly accused Katanga of taking offensive action. Matters came to a head on Dec. 27, when M. Tshombe alleged that the U.N. were planning to arrest him and his Ministers "so as to paralyse the country and plunge it into chaos if the U.N. decided to apply military measures". In reply a U.N. spokesman emphatically denied that there was any intention to arrest M. Tshombe. Later the same evening several incidents occurred in Elisabethville which eventually led to strong military action by the U.N. forces; after heavy fighting the U.N. troops were in complete control of Elisabethville on Dec. 29, and took the towns of Kipushi and Kamina on the next day, whereupon it was announced that the "defensive action" had been concluded.

By Jan. 9, M. Tshombe no longer had any effective power in Elisabethville; on Jan. 15, 1963, he issued a statement in Kolwezi, declaring that he was ready to end the secession of Katanga and to return to Elisabethville to supervise methods of applying U Thant's "Plan of National Reconciliation." [U Thant had succeeded Dr. Hammarskjöld as U.N. Secretary-General on Nov. 3, 1961, after the latter had been killed in an air crash on Sept. 17 while on his way to Elisabethville.]

This plan, which had been accepted in principle by M. Adoula and M. Tshombe in August 1962, embodied the following proposals: (1) A new Federal Constitution; (2) a new law for the division of revenue between the central and provincial Governments; (3) the rapid integration and unification of the entire Congolese army; (4) representation abroad by the central Government only; (5) the reconstitution of the central Government to provide representation for all political and provincial groups; and (6) a general amnesty for political prisoners.

Two other secessionist movements in the Congo had previously ended during 1962 – those of M. Antoine Gizenga in Stanleyville and of M. Albert Kalonji in South Kasai.

Following clashes between Gizenga supporters and Congolese troops under General Victor Lundula, U Thant ordered U.N. forces "to restore and maintain order in Stanleyville and to avert civil war there", while on the same day (Jan. 13) M. Adoula ordered the arrest of M. Gizenga. On Jan. 14 the last of M. Gizenga's bodyguard surrendered to General Lundula; M. Gizenga was flown to Léopoldville on Jan. 20 and taken into preventive custody.

The "Etat Minier" in South Kasai ceased to exist on Sept. 30, 1962, when all leaders of M. Kalonji's gendarmerie pledged their allegiance to the central Government; M. Kalonji had himself pledged his loyalty to the central Government on Sept. 9, promising to work with it for a United Congo Federation.

Continued Unrest, 1963–65

A major Cabinet reorganization in Léopoldville on April 17, 1963, resulted in what was described as a "Government of Reconciliation" by the inclusion of a greater number of Lumumbist as well as of Conakat and Balubakat Ministers.

Legislation was passed on June 25, creating a new province of East Katanga formed by uniting all South Katanga with parts of North Katanga, including the district of Baudouinville on the shores of Lake Tanganyika; the former province of Katanga was thus split into three – North and East Katanga and Lualaba. [The creation of North Katanga had been proclaimed on July 11, 1962, it being an area mainly inhabited by anti-Tshombe Balubas; Lualaba, embracing the western part of the original South Katanga, was brought into being on May 28, 1963.]

During the period March – May 1963 considerable unrest continued in various parts of the Congo, notably in Katanga, involving much loss of life. However, in a report to the U.N. General Assembly on May 12, U Thant stated that the U.N. Forces in the Congo would be reduced from 19,000 men at its peak, to 6,700 by Oct. 1, 1963. Total U.N. losses in the Congo from July 1960 to Jan. 6, 1963, were given as 127 killed and 133 wounded.

Referring to "a dangerous crisis during which anarchy has installed itself among us", President Kasavubu announced on Aug. 27, 1963, that he would call Parliament to meet in extraordinary session as a Constituent Assembly. When the two Houses of Parliament met in mid-September no agreement was reached on the form which the meeting of such a Constituent Assembly should take. Thereupon the President dissolved the central Parliament on Sept. 29; two days later he announced that he had granted the Government full legislative powers, that a special Government-appointed commission would draft a Constitution within 100 days after its first meeting and that the draft would then be submitted to a referendum.

Developments during 1964 were largely influenced by the activities of the National Liberation Committee (NLC) in Brazzaville (French Congo) which was led by followers of M. Antoine Gizenga, headed by M. Christophe Gbenye, the former president of the Lumumbist faction of the MNC and leader of the Opposition in the Congolese central Parliament.

The central Parliament, whose mandate expired on June 30, 1964, in terms of the Basic Law of 1960, was suspended by President Kasavubu on March 2, 1964. The House was without a quorum as at least 15 members had defected to the NLC and between 30 and 40 others had left Léopoldville for the interior and feared arrest if they returned.

The Committee appointed to draft a new Constitution had advanced sufficiently for the Government to publish a statement on March 13 showing that the draft made the following principal provisions: (a) full executive powers would be given to the President; (b) the powers of the Prime Minister and Parliament would be drastically limited; and (c) the President and Cabinet Ministers could be dismissed only on conviction of high treason, violation of the Constitution or corruption.

In view of the impending constitutional changes and the threat to the unity of the country by uprisings in several provinces [see below] a regrouping of political parties took place during June as follows: (a) the *Front commun national,* an alliance of moderate left-wing parties opposed to M. Adoula and comprising 13 parties including the MNC; (b) the *Rassemblement des démocrates congolais* (Radeco) formed in September 1963 out of about 50 small political groupings and which elected M. Adoula as its President on June 14, 1964; and (c) the *Comité démocratique africain,* formed through the merger of President Kasavubu's party, Abako, with several smaller parties.

M. Adoula resigned on June 30 (the date on which the U.N. forces in the Congo were withdrawn) at the end of his term of office but was asked at once by the President to head a caretaker Government for an indefinite period, until the appointment of a transitional Government, which would prepare for national elections. At the same time the President officially dissolved Parliament.

M. Tshombe had meanwhile been preparing his return to the Congo, after over a year abroad in Paris and Madrid; he announced on June 24 in Madrid that he was going to Léopoldville "at the invitation of the central Government" and that they would all work together to achieve "effective and immediate reconciliation and liberation of the country from misery and anarchy". On July 6, President Kasavubu officially invited M. Tshombe, who had arrived in Léopoldville on June 26, to form a Cabinet; this was sworn in on July 10, most of its members being relatively unknown. The referendum on the new Constitution ended on the same day (July 10) and was reported to have resulted in approval by 92 per cent of the voters; the Constitution was promulgated early in August.

Meanwhile the country was faced by serious and widespread rebellion organized by the NLC in various parts of the country.

The rebels were most successful in Kwilu, Central Kivu, Maniéma and North Katanga. Acts of terrorism in Kwilu ascribed to followers of M. Pierre Mulele, who had been a member of M. Lumumba's Cabinet and the "ambassador" in Cairo for M. Gizenga's Government, were first reported in December 1963, and little progress was made against the rebels by the central Government. Unrest was first reported in Kivu on April 20, 1964, after the Provincial President had been attacked by rebels at Bukavu, the provincial capital, led by M. Gaston Soumialot, who was stated to have his headquarters at Bujumbura (Burundi).

In North Katanga and Maniéma difficulties first arose during January 1964 when the Provincial President, M. Jason Sendwe, announced that all police at Manono had been disarmed after an attempted mutiny, and warned the population against the "communism which Messrs. Gizenga and Gbenye wish to impose on the Congo". The first widespread insurrection occurred on May 27 when followers of M. Mulele took control of Albertville, the provincial capital, and Kongolo; a Congolese Army unit regained control of Albertville on May 30. A second rebellion, however, on June 19 was successful, all forms of government ceasing in Albertville and M. Sendwe being assassinated. On July 24 M. Soumialot, who had arrived in Albertville on June 24, announced the formation of a "provisional Government" of the "National Liberation Committee (Eastern Section)" with himself as President and Minister of Defence. Rebel forces commanded by "Colonel" Nicolas Olenga occupied the town and airport of Stanleyville (Upper Congo) on Aug. 4–5, 1964. On Aug. 6 M. Soumialot announced that he was the "head of the Revolutionary Government of the Eastern Congo", declaring: "I am the new Lumumba". Earlier Lumumbist attempts to seize power in Stanleyville had been effectively suppressed by forces loyal to the Adoula Government. The formation of a "People's Republic of the Congo" was announced in Stanleyville on Sept. 7, with M. Christophe Gbenye as "Prime Minister" and M. Soumialot as "Defence Minister".

The Tshombe Government took several measures to counteract the effect of the rebels; these included the creation of a "pacification council" announced on July 15, 1964, and talks between M. Tshombe and representatives of the NLC, including M. Mulele, in Bujumbura on July 24. During the period August – November 1964 the central Government succeeded in most areas of the country in containing the NLC rebellion. The nature of the fighting was such, however, that the International Committee of the Red Cross appealed on Sept. 18 to all combatants in Congo to observe the humanitarian principles of the Geneva Conventions.

The military operations of the Congolese Government against the insurgents were greatly helped by a supply of U.S. aircraft and the arrival of a few hundred white mercenaries recruited mainly in Southern Africa. Unsuccessful appeals for help were also made to several African countries and to the U.N.

Following several appeals to the OAU to consider the situation in the Congo, made by the Congo and other African States, an extraordinary session of the OAU Council of Ministers held on Sept. 5–10 adopted a compromise resolution which *inter alia* appealed to "all those now fighting in the Congo to cease hostilities"; urged all Congolese political leaders to seek, by all appropriate means, to restore and consolidate national reconciliation; established a 10-man Commission with the object of (*a*) assisting the Congolese Government to achieve national reconciliation of all political parties, and (*b*) bringing about normal relations between the Congo and its neighbours; and appealed "strongly to all Powers at present intervening in the internal affairs of the Congo" to cease their interference.

A new development in the situation followed the announcement by M. Gbenye in Stanleyville on Oct. 29 that since the Belgians were aiding the Government forces his regime could no longer "guarantee Belgian subjects and their property". On the same day, the rebel commander, General Nicolas Olenga, ordered all whites in the Stanleyville area to be placed under house arrest. Negotiations between the rebels, the U.S.A., the U.N., Belgium and the OAU during the next three weeks failed to lead to any agreement over the fate of the hostages. On Nov. 20, M. Tshombe stated in a letter to the U.S. Ambassador in Léopoldville that his Government had decided to authorize the Belgian Government "to send an adequate rescue force to accomplish the humanitarian purpose of evacuating civilians held as hostages by the rebels and to authorize the American Government to furnish the necessary transport for this humanitarian mission".

On Nov. 24, a Belgian paratroop battalion landed at Stanleyville airport and moved into the city, rescuing 220 white hostages; a further 30 had been killed by the rebels immediately before the soldiers' arrival on the scene. A second rescue operation, involving 211 white hostages, was carried out by the Belgians at Paulis the next day. International reaction to these operations ranged from outright condemnation in Moscow, Peking, Belgrade and many African capitals via qualified acceptance in a number of other African capitals to approval in Western countries.

The immediate developments following this incident were varied.

The OAU Congo Conciliation Committee [see above] met in Nairobi on Nov. 27–28, 1964, to consider the situation and adopted a resolution condemning Britain [who had given Belgium permission to use Ascension Island as a base for the rescue operations], Belgium and the U.S.A. for "foreign military intervention in the Congo".

The U.N. Security Council adopted a resolution on Dec. 30, 1964, which requested all States to refrain from or to cease intervening in the internal affairs of the Congo, and appealed for an immediate cease-fire in the fighting which had continued after the Stanleyville incident. Shortly after the Stanleyville action most of the rebel leaders fled to the Sudan; according to a statement by M. Thomas R. Kanza, "Foreign Minister" of the "Congolese People's Republic", in Nairobi on Nov. 27, they included M. Gbenye, M. Soumialot, General Olenga and M. Pierre Mulele.

During the period February – May 1965 the central Government succeeded in consolidating its position both by the victories of Government troops over the rebels, who lost control of almost all towns following the cessation of military aid from abroad and whose leadership was divided, and also by gaining an absolute majority of seats in the general elections held from March 18 to April 30 for a new Chamber of Deputies of 166 members.

In the general elections there were two principal political alignments; (a) the National Congolese Convention (CONACO) formed on Feb. 3, 1965, with M. Tshombe as National President and claiming to have the

support of "an overwhelming majority of Congolese politicians", and
(b) the Alliance of Congolese Nationalist Movements (MNC–Lumumba) formed on Feb. 19, 1965, by the amalgamation of all Lumumbist
parties.

The result of the voting – in which neither women nor Europeans
could participate – showed that by May 22, CONACO had gained 86 seats
against 39 for all other parties.

A conference held in Elisabethville from May 14–18, attended by
M. Tshombe, the 72 newly-elected deputies in the central and provincial Legislatures and 89 Katangese tribal chiefs, decided in favour of the
reunification of East and North Katanga and Lualaba provinces.

M. Tshombe's Fall from Power

Fresh elections held on Aug. 22, 1965, in the three provinces of Kwilu,
Kivu-Central and Cuvette-Centrale – where the previous elections were
annulled by the Léopoldville Court of Appeal – resulted in a setback for
CONACO. Although this party held 106 out of the 166 seats in the
Chamber of Deputies, which opened on Sept. 20, observers thought that
M. Tshombe could rely on only 85 of the deputies. The movement which
progressively weakened CONACO was led by Mr. Victor Nendaka, who on
Oct. 1 announced the formation of the Congolese Democratic Front
(CDF) in opposition to CONACO and with the aim of demanding the
formation of a Government of national union. The CDF asked President
Kasavubu on Oct. 8 to dismiss M. Tshombe's Government; the President
did so on Oct. 12, giving the following reasons: (a) the mission with which
they had been entrusted in July 1964 had been completed; (b) the
Government had not, of its own accord and as required by the Constitution, resigned after the assembly of the new Parliament; and (c) the
composition of the Government conformed neither with constitutional
norms, election results nor the requirements of the country's political
equilibrium.

Later the same day (Oct. 12) it was announced that M. Evariste Kimba,
"Foreign Minister" under the Tshombe regime in Katanga, had accepted
the President's invitation to form a new Government. [M. Kimba's
party – the Balubakat – was a founder-member of the CDF and therefore
he was assured of the support of M. Nendaka and his followers.] M. Kimba
stated that he would endeavour to form a Government of national union;
however, the final list of members issued on Oct. 18–19 did not include

any members of CONACO who had been ordered by M. Tshombe to follow the latter's example of refusing to take part in the Government.

In the meantime, fighting continued against the rebels in the northern and eastern regions of the Congo; the Government forces occupied most of the remaining urban areas still in rebel hands, while a substantial number of armed rebels were reported to be still in control of large areas of the bush and most of the villages – but the rebel leaders had left the Congo and were divided into several factions.

During August and September the Governments of both the U.A.R. – who had previously given military aid to the rebels – and the Sudan took action against Congolese rebel leaders staying in their territories.

General Mobutu assumes Absolute Power

President Kasavubu was deposed without bloodshed on Nov. 25, 1965, by General Joseph-Désiré Mobutu, C.-in-C. of the Congolese National Army, who himself assumed the Presidency. At the same time General Mobutu issued a proclamation by which he appointed Colonel Léonard Mulamba as Prime Minister and charged him with forming a Cabinet of 21 Ministers, drawing one from each of the provinces; this proclamation also stated that the coup had been decided upon the previous day at a meeting of high-ranking officers "in view of the impotence of M. Kimba's Government".

M. Tshombe immediately sent his congratulations to General Mobutu on the measures taken by him "to restore order in the Congo" while both Houses of Parliament approved General Mobutu's investiture as President by acclamation on Nov. 25. Colonel Mulamba's Government received a vote of confidence on Nov. 28 in Parliament by 256 votes with two abstentions, 40 deputies being absent. The regime also obtained the support of the MNC-Lumumba, led by M. Antoine Kiwewa, on Dec. 21. [M. Tshombe, however, left the Congo late in December 1965.]

On Dec. 1, President Mobutu announced that "to ensure the recovery of the country" he had assumed power to rule by decree and this would have the force of law unless Parliament voted to reverse a decree; however, on March 7, 1966, the President declared that Parliament would not be allowed to debate any laws which he might decree. The President assumed further personal powers when he issued a decree on March 22 transferring those of the Legislature to himself; certain powers were restored to Parliament, however, on Sept. 15, 1966.

A provincial reorganization was announced on April 6, 1966, resulting in the country being divided into 12 provinces instead of the 21 established in 1962–63. The new provinces were: Central Congo, Bandundu, Equator, Uele, Kibali-Ituri, Upper Congo, North Kivu, South Kivu, South Katanga, North Katanga, East Kasai and West Kasai. As from June 30, several towns whose names were of European origin would be renamed as follows, the old names being in brackets: Kinshasa (Léopoldville), Lubumbashi (Elisabethville), Kisangani (Stanleyville), Mbandaka (Coquilhatville), Bandundu (Banningville) and Isiro (Paulis).

President Mobutu overcomes Internal Resistance –
Trial and Death of M. Tshombe

Immediately after his resumption of power, President Mobutu had declared that the struggle against the rebels would be continued until the uprising was "utterly strangled by military means". Rebel leaders in exile emphasized their determination to continue the fight and condemned the regime of General Mobutu. Civil unrest continued to be reported from many parts of the country.

It was announced on May 30, 1966, that a plot to overthrow General Mobutu and to replace him by a Provisional Committee had been foiled during the previous night and that its four instigators had been arrested; these were named as M. Kimba, M. Jérôme Anany (Minister of Defence in M. Adoula's last Cabinet in 1964), M. Alexandre Matiamba (a Minister in the first Adoula Cabinet in 1961) and Senator Emmanuel Bamba (a former Minister of Finance and a close collaborator of ex-President Kasavubu). The four men were tried in open court on May 31 by a special military tribunal; having been found guilty and sentenced to death, they were hung on June 2 in Léopoldville in the presence of the C.-in-C. of the Army, General Louis Bobozo, and a crowd variously estimated at between 80,000 and 300,000.

A mutiny by about 2,500 Katangese gendarmes, supported by some white mercenaries, broke out in Kisangani on July 23; this was reported to be due to discontent and complaints of not having been paid for three months. President Mobutu assumed military and civilian control in Kinshasa on the following day and sent the Prime Minister to Kisangani for talks with the mutineers; the President also ordered an investigation into the problem of payment of Katangese gendarmes. No settlement was reached with the mutineers, however, and fighting between them and troops loyal to General Mobutu occurred between July 28 and Aug. 1. It was alleged by the Congolese Press Agency on July 28 that the mutiny was part of an overall plan to restore M. Tshombe to power in the Congo. Government troops did not regain control of Kisangani until Sept. 25, after two days of hand-to-hand fighting. The mutineers, who had fled into the bush, surrendered unconditionally on Oct. 4 following an appeal by the President to do so.

Two other incidents, allegedly to help restore M. Tshombe to power, occurred during September.

On Sept. 22, M. Thierry de Bonnay, a Belgian citizen, and 11 other persons were committed for trial in Paris on charges of enlisting soldiers on French soil on behalf of a foreign Government; it had been stated by a French police spokesman on Sept. 20 that inquiries seemed to confirm that M. Tshombe had approved of the formation of a mercenary force. Although M. Tshombe denied this at first, he subsequently declared on Sept. 23 that he himself had disclosed to the French Government the training of these men in France. A charge of high treason was officially preferred against him on Sept. 28 in the Congo.

Following a Congolese allegation on Sept. 19 that a large force of mercenaries recruited by M. Tshombe was concentrated at Vila Luso in Angola, near the border with Katanga, anti-Portuguese riots broke out in Kinshasa, and it was announced on Oct. 5 that diplomatic relations with Portugal had been broken off. The Congolese Government also lodged a complaint with the U.N. Security Council, which unanimously adopted on Oct. 14 a resolution requesting the Portuguese Government "not to permit foreign mercenaries to use Angola as a base for operations aimed at interference in the Congo's internal affairs" and calling upon all States to desist from such interference.

The trial *in absentia* of M. Tshombe on a charge of high treason opened before a special military tribunal on March 6, 1967; the six leaders of the Kisangani mutiny were tried at the same time. On March 13, after 10 minutes' deliberation, the Court passed sentence of death against M. Tshombe and ordered the confiscation of all his assets. Lieut.-Colonel Ferdinand Tshimpola, leader of the regiment of gendarmes which mutinied in Kisangani, and Capt. Kalonda Mwanda, of the same regiment, were also sentenced to death, while three other men were sentenced to 20 years' imprisonment and one was acquitted.

On June 30, 1967, M. Tshombe arrived at Boufarik military airport near Algiers after the British-owned and piloted aircraft in which he was travelling on a charter-flight between Ibiza and Palma (Majorca) had been diverted from its course. Along with the other occupants of the aircraft, M. Tshombe was immediately detained by Algerian security officials. A request for the extradition of M. Tshombe to the Congo, made by the Congolese Government on July 2, was examined by the Algerian Supreme Court on July 19; the Court announced on July 21 that it had recommended that M. Tshombe should be extradited, but no such action was taken by the Algerian Government, and M. Tshombe died of heart failure in Algiers on June 29, 1969.

Further Consolidation of President Mobutu's Powers

On Oct. 26, 1966, President Mobutu announced that he had dismissed General Mulamba from his post as Prime Minister and had himself taken over the premiership; Radio Kinshasa explained the measure as "a step towards a presidential regime". The President's position was strengthened further when, under a decree signed on Oct. 31, 1966, he assumed powers to annul decisions taken by the provincial authorities whenever he considered them to be against the public interest.

A number of far-reaching measures were announced on Nov. 25, 1966, by the President, who forecast the creation of a "unitary and decentralized State". These measures included (*a*) the establishment of a single national insurance company (Sonas) to replace all existing private companies; (*b*) the introduction of a balanced budget in 1967; (*c*) a reduction in the number of provinces from 12 to eight during January 1967; (*d*) the restoration of the right to strike [strikes had been banned since Feb. 16, 1966]; and (*e*) the transfer to Kinshasa of all head-offices of foreign companies by Jan. 1, 1967.

New governors were sworn in by President Mobutu on Jan. 3, 1967, for the eight new provinces – Bandundu, the Central Congo, East Kasai, the Eastern Province (combining the former Upper Congo, Uele and Kibali-Ituri), Equator, a reunited Katanga, Kivu and West Kasai. The posts of vice-governors and provincial Ministers were abolished, and the provincial assemblies were reduced to provincial councils with purely advisory powers.

A referendum was held on June 4–16, 1967, on a draft "Revolutionary" Constitution which (i) ended the mandate of the existing bicameral legislature and replaced it by a unicameral legislature to be elected in 1968; (ii) instituted a unitary State under a presidential regime with the President ruling by decree until the 1968 elections; and (iii) restricted the number of political parties to two. The President proclaimed the new Constitution on June 24, announcing that it had been approved by 97.8 per cent of the registered electorate who had taken part, all men and women over 18 being entitled to vote. Previously on April 17, the creation of President Mobutu's own political party, the *Mouvement populaire de la révolution* (MPR), had been announced. The role of the sole permitted Opposition party, as provided for in the Constitution, was expressly denied by President Mobutu to two existing parties, one of which was the MNC–Lumumba.

The Mercenaries' Action of 1967

On July 5, 1967, action described by President Mobutu as "imperialist aggression" was started by a small commando of white mercenaries landing from the air at Kisangani, while at Bukavu (formerly Costermansville) a group of Europeans attacked the Congolese National Army (CNA).

At Kisangani the commando, surrounded by the CNA, held several hundred persons as hostages until, on July 13–15, they allowed these hostages to be evacuated in two Red Cross and one U.S. aircraft, and the remaining mercenaries withdrew with 40 – 50 white civilians. On Aug. 9 this commando under Major Jean Schramme captured Bukavu and held it for several weeks against attacks by the CNA. After intervention by the OAU the International Red Cross agreed early in October to supervise the evacuation of mercenaries from Bukavu and also the removal of some 950 Katangese gendarmes with their wives and children. Before this could be carried out, however, the CNA recaptured Bukavu on Nov. 4 and the mercenaries and Katangese withdrew to Rwanda. President Mobutu thereupon demanded their extradition from Rwanda. Meanwhile another group of mercenaries entering the Congo from Angola on Nov. 2, had been repulsed by the CNA by Nov. 5.

After President Mobutu had agreed to the evacuation of the Katangese from Rwanda to Zambia and had also offered them an amnesty, which was accepted by most of them, the Katangese returned to the Congo after Nov. 17.

The fate of the remaining mercenaries was the subject of protracted negotiations, but on April 24–25, 1968, they were flown to Europe – on the understanding that they would not take up arms again in Africa, a pledge to this effect having been signed by them on Nov. 17, 1967.

Meanwhile the country was recovering from the widespread anarchy caused by the "Mulelist" rebellion, which had begun in 1963 and declined after the middle of 1965. While many thousands of rebel fighters had subsequently withdrawn to inaccessible areas in the bush, many of these surrendered to Government forces in 1967–68. The loss of life caused by this rebellion had been estimated as at least 9,000, and probably many more, killed, including about 180 Roman Catholic missionaries.

271

Internal developments, 1968–70

In view of the great improvement in the internal situation President Mobutu signed a decree, on Aug. 29, 1968, for the release of all political prisoners. As a result of this, M. Pierre Mulele, who had been living in exile in Congo (Brazzaville), arrived in Kinshasa accompanied by M. Bomboko. However, on Oct. 2, President Mobutu announced that M. Mulele would be tried as a "war criminal", as the amnesty applied only to "political prisoners" and "not to war criminals". A military tribunal, set up by President Mobutu on Oct. 7, sentenced M. Mulele to death the following day, and he was executed on Oct. 9. A deputation headed by the Foreign Minister of the Congo (Brazzaville) had previously gone to Kinshasa on Oct. 3 to protest against M. Mulele's arrest; the Foreign Minister had stated that his Government had received solemn guarantees from Kinshasa before it had allowed M. Mulele to contact the Congo (Kinshasa) Embassy in Brazzaville with a view to returning home. Following the execution of M. Mulele, the Brazzaville Government announced the breaking-off of diplomatic relations with Kinshasa. [These were subsequently resumed on June 16, 1970. See PEOPLE'S REPUBLIC OF THE CONGO, page 232.]

Cabinet Changes –
Re-election of President Mobutu – New National Assembly

In the most sweeping Cabinet re-organization since the accession to power of President Mobutu, nine Cabinet Ministers and 10 Deputy Ministers lost their posts on Aug. 1, 1969; the number of members in the Government was reduced from 42 to 30. A National Security Council of eight members – the President, the Ministers for Foreign Affairs, Internal Affairs, Defence and Justice, the C.-in-C. of the Army, the Inspector-General of Police and the Security Chief – had been established on July 25 "to assist the Head of State in ensuring the internal and external security of the State". On June 12, 1969, the MPR announced that it was "unnecessary to speak of the existence or creation of a second political party other than the MPR".

On Nov. 1, 1970, President Mobutu was, in terms of the 1968 Constitution, re-elected for a three-year term. He had been nominated as the sole presidential candidate by the MPR on May 23, 1970, and according to the official announcement of the result on Nov. 5 he obtained practically all votes cast.

A new National Assembly of 420 members, all nominated by the MPR's political bureau on Sept. 19, was elected early in November, the Ministry of the Interior announcing on Nov. 17 that these candidates had obtained 98.34 per cent of the 9,854,417 votes cast. The new Assembly amended the Constitution on Dec. 7 so that the Congo officially became a one-party State, as proposed by the MPR on May 23.

On the same day President Mobutu reorganized his Cabinet, retaining the Defence portfolio for himself, and entrusting the Foreign Affairs Ministry to M. Edouard Bulundwe, in succession to M. Adoula. The President also announced an amnesty for all Congolese who had been guilty of acts against the security of the State between 1960 and 1970.

Relations with Belgium — Agreement on
Compensation for Nationalized Mining Assets

The Congo's relations with Belgium, the former colonial Power, which had been strained to breaking-point on many occasions since 1960, improved greatly during President Mobutu's regime.

The most contentious issue affecting these relations was that of the Congolese assets of the *Union Minière du Haut Katanga,* engaged in the mining of copper, cobalt and other minerals.

On Dec. 31, 1966, the Congolese Government decided that these assets should be taken over by a new Congolese company, the *Société Générale Congolaise des Minerais* (*Gécomin*), with a Congolese Government shareholding of 60 per cent; in May 1968, however, the Government became the sole shareholder of *Gécomin*. After protracted negotiations, agreement was reached on Sept. 25, 1969, on compensation to be paid to the *Union Minière* for its former assets in the form of six per cent of the value of all minerals produced by *Gécomin* during 15 years within the framework of a 25-year technical co-operation agreement.

BURUNDI

Area: 10,747 sq. miles.
Population 1969 (estimate): 3,475,000.
Capital: Bujumbura (70,000).
Official languages: French and Kirundi.
Chief products: Coffee, cotton.

The Belgian-administered U.N. Trust Territory of Ruanda-Urundi achieved independence as two separate States on July 1, 1962; the southern part — Urundi — became the Kingdom of Burundi under the rule of Mwami (King) Mwambutsa IV, and the northern part — Ruanda — became the Republic of Rwanda [see page 275]. The establishment of the two States followed the failure of attempts under U.N. auspices to bring about an agreement for the creation of a single independent country comprising both halves of the Territory. [Ruanda and Urundi had both been part of German East Africa before 1918, and had thereafter been administered by Belgium as a League of Nations Mandate.]

A National Council for Urundi had been established on Oct. 19, 1960, after communal elections, held in July 1960, had resulted in the Bahutu parties [see RWANDA, page 276] winning 2,154 out of the 2,873 seats. In general elections held on Sept. 18, 1961, the *Uprona* (National Union and Progress) party gained 58 seats out of 64; the remaining six seats went to the *Front commun*, comprising the coalition which had formed the Urundi Government since the communal elections in 1960.

The subsequent political developments in Burundi were marked by a struggle between the traditional rulers of the country — the Batutsi — and the leaders of the Bahutu, who formed the majority of the people.

Ganwa (Prince) Louis Rwagasore, eldest son of the Mwami of Burundi and leader of *Uprona*, which he had founded in 1958, took office as Prime Minister on Sept. 29, 1961, but was assassinated on Oct. 13. According to a report by a U.N. Commission published on Jan. 30, 1962, this crime appeared to be, firstly, the result of a plot organized by the Prince's enemies in the *Front commun*, particularly members of the Christian Democratic Party and, secondly, "one more episode in a long series of crimes marking the course of age-old rivalry" between the two leading clans of the Batutsi tribe, those of Mwami Mwambutsa and Chief Barranyanka.

Arising out of this murder a total of six persons were sentenced to death, viz. a Greek who confessed having shot the Prince and who was executed on June 30, 1962, and five others, including a former Minister of the Interior and the founder of the Christian Democratic Party, all publicly executed on Jan. 15, 1963.

M. André Muhirwa, the Prince's brother-in-law, was elected by the Assembly on Oct. 20 to succeed him as Prime Minister and continued in this office until he resigned in June 1963. M. Pierre Ngendandumwe then became Prime Minister and, apart from the period April 1, 1964, to January 1965, when M. Albin Nyamoya replaced him, remained in this post until he also was assassinated on Jan. 15, 1965, four days after his reappointment. This assassination was again attributed to political motives, several arrests being made, including that of M. Nyamoya.

On Oct. 18–19, 1965, an attempted coup was carried out by a

group of Army and gendarmerie officers and some political leaders. The revolt was suppressed and the rebels were subsequently executed after summary trial. This marked the climax to a period of political unrest which followed the closing of the Chinese Embassy by the new Government headed by M. Joseph Bamina on Jan. 29, 1965, and general elections on May 10, 1965, in which the ruling *Uprona* party maintained its hold in the National Assembly. However, the *Parti du peuple,* an Opposition party based principally on Bahutu support, won a strong minority of the seats. The Bahutu element of the Opposition in particular criticized not only the powers of the Mwami but also the under-representation of the Bahutu in the Government and the Public Service. In mid-September 1965 the Mwami appointed M. Léopold Biha, a Tutsi, as Prime Minister; this appointment, regarded as a conciliatory move by the King, did not satisfy the Bahutu progressive circles who were anti-monarchical and pro-Chinese.

The son of Mwami Mwambutsa, Prince Charles Ndizeye, announced on July 8, 1966, that he had assumed the position of Head of State in place of his father; that he had demanded the resignation of M. Léopold Biha's Cabinet; and that he had suspended the Constitution. The Mwami learnt of this action in Geneva, having lived in Europe since the attempted coup of 1965, and on July 9 accused his son of treason. Captain Michel Micombero was appointed Prime Minister on July 11 and the Prince was crowned as Mwami Ntari V on Sept. 1.

On Nov. 29, 1966, Captain Micombero deposed Mwami Ntari, and declared himself President of the Republic of Burundi. He dissolved the existing Government and appointed a "provisional revolutionary committee". The *Uprona* party central executive approved, on Dec. 2, proposals to establish a presidential regime and a one-party State.

President Micombero announced on Oct. 8, 1969, that an attempt to overthrow his Government had been foiled in September; the alleged plotters were subsequently tried and executed.

RWANDA

Area: 10,169 sq. miles.
Population 1969 (estimate): 3,500,000.
Capital: Kigali (25,000).
Official languages: French and Kinyarwanda.
Chief products: Coffee, tin ore.

Formerly the northern part of the Belgian Trust Territory of Ruanda—

Urundi, Rwanda became an independent Republic on July 1, 1962, after two years of self-government marked by considerable tension which followed tribal disorders in November 1959. [See BURUNDI for details of early history.]

The first communal elections, held in July 1960, resulted in a victory for the Bahutu tribe over the dominant Batutsi tribe, the Party of Bahutu Emancipation (*Parmehutu*) winning 70 per cent of the 3,126 seats and the allied Association for the Promotion of the Masses (*Aprosoma*) six per cent; the main Batutsi party, the Ruandese National Union (*Unar*), obtained 17 per cent of the seats and the remainder went to the Ruandese Democratic Rally (*Rader*). The Ruanda National Council, established on Oct. 19, 1960, and comprising 35 Bahutu, 12 Batutsi and one Batwa pygmy, elected M. Joseph Gitera Habyarimana (candidate of the *Parmehutu* and *Aprosoma* parties) as its president, and M. Grégoire Kayibanda (national president of the *Parmehutu*) as head of the Ruanda Provisional Government.

At a meeting on Jan. 29, 1961, attended by over 3,000 African burgomasters and councillors, it was decided to depose Mwami (King) Kigeri V of Ruanda, who had left for Europe in mid-1960 and had been forbidden by the Belgian authorities to return, and to proclaim Ruanda a Republic, whilst recognizing "provisional" U.N. trusteeship over the Territory. The meeting elected a Legislative Assembly in which all 44 seats went to the Bahutu parties (40 to *Parmehutu* and four to *Aprosoma*). The new Assembly elected, as President of Ruanda, M. Dominique Mbonyumutwa who, in his turn, appointed M. Kayibanda as Prime Minister; M. Habyarimana was elected President of the Legislative Assembly.

General elections were held on Sept. 25, 1961, resulting in victory for *Parmehutu*, now a Republican Democratic movement, which won 35 out of the 44 seats in the Assembly. Two seats went to *Aprosoma*, seven to *Unar*, which supported the former King, whilst *Rader* failed to win a seat. A referendum on the future of the monarchy, held on the same date, resulted in a majority vote in favour of a Republic. The abolition of the monarchy was formally announced on Oct. 2, 1961, and on Oct. 26 the Assembly elected M. Kayibanda as President of the Republic, combining the duties of Head of State and of Government.

Between 1960 and 1964 up to 200,000 Watutsi – who had been feudal overlords over the Bahutu peasants – left the country for the Congo, Uganda, Burundi and Tanganyika, but many of them made attempts to invade Rwanda with the intention of restoring the monarchy. As a result of a raid by some 500 Watutsi from Burundi in December 1963 the Bahutu population turned on the remaining Watutsi in Rwanda so that in January 1964 large-scale massacres of thousands of people were reported; accusations of genocide were made against the Rwanda Government, *inter alia* by two officials of U.N. agencies, and the Government of Burundi alleged on Feb. 7 that as many as 15,000 Watutsi had been killed in Rwanda. These accusations were refuted by the Government of Rwanda, which claimed that the death toll was less than 1,000. At the end of August 1966, however, the two Governments joined with the Congo (Kinshasa) in signing a mutual security pact involving *inter alia* provisions for the protection of refugees. After some Watutsi refugees were again reported to have "disturbed the peace of Rwanda" early in November 1966, the Congolese Government acted as mediator between Burundi and Rwanda, and relations between these two countries improved after the establishment of a Republic in Burundi on Nov. 29, 1966.

President Kayibanda was re-elected as the sole candidate for the presidency in October 1965 and October 1969; the *Parmehutu* party was returned to the National Assembly with an absolute majority on each of these dates.

LIBYA

Area: 810,000 sq. miles.
Population 1969 (estimate): 1,875,000.
Capital: Beida (to replace Tripoli and Benghazi).
Other important towns: Tripoli (380,000), Benghazi (299,000).
Official language: Arabic.
Chief products: Oil, groundnuts.

Libya was formally proclaimed independent on Dec. 24, 1951; formerly a possession of the Ottoman Empire and ceded to Italy by Turkey under the Treaty of Ouchy (October 1912), the country had been provisionally placed under British and French administration after World War II (i.e. the two territories of Cyrenaica and Tripolitania under British and the Fezzan under French administration).

A resolution of the U.N. General Assembly of Nov. 21, 1949, laid down that Libya should become an independent State before Jan. 1, 1952, whilst on Dec. 3, 1950, the Libyan Constituent Assembly adopted a resolution formally proclaiming Mohamed Sayed Idris el-Senussi, Emir of

Cyrenaica, as King of Libya and declaring that Libya should be an independent and sovereign State.

Federation, 1951–63

The principal provisions of the Constitution, unanimously approved by the Constitutional Assembly on Oct. 7, 1951, were that the country would be officially known as the United Kingdom of Libya consisting of the three above territories and that it would be a hereditary monarchy with a federal form of Government. The bicameral legislature would consist of a nominated Senate of 24 members, equally distributed amongst the three provinces, and an elected House of Representatives, on a basis of one deputy for every 20,000 inhabitants.

The first general elections by adult male suffrage were held on Feb. 19, 1952. Most candidates ran as Independents, but it was reported that a strong majority of those returned would support the Government of Mr. Mahmoud Bey Muntasser, formed on Dec. 25, 1951, and the federal system. The only organized party contesting the elections was the National Congress Party, the principal Opposition group; winning eight seats, it drew its support almost entirely from the towns of Tripolitania.

During the period under review a succession of leaders headed the Libyan Government, the members of which included Cyrenaican, Tripolitanian and Fezzani Ministers. Mr. Mahmoud Bey Muntasser tendered his resignation on Feb. 15, 1954, and was followed by Mr. Mohammed Saquizly (head of the Royal Cabinet); his Government resigned on April 8, however, in protest against a judgment by the Libyan Supreme Court which set aside a royal decree dissolving the Legislative Council of Tripolitania. Mr. Mustapha Ben Halim, the new incumbent, remained in office until May 25, 1957, when he tendered his resignation to the King for reasons of ill-health and "internal and external obstacles" to his Government's policy. After general elections were held, during the following Government's period in office on Jan. 17, 1960, certain Cabinet changes under Prime Minister Abdul Majid Kobar were announced on Feb. 6 on a purely personal basis, as no party system existed.

A new Cabinet headed by Mohammed bin-Othman Al-Said was sworn in by King Idris on Oct. 17, 1960, following the resignation of Mr. Abdul Majid Kobar's Government, and this Government was extensively reorganized by royal decree on May 4, 1961, and Oct. 15, 1962.

Relations with Foreign Countries, 1954–63

On Nov. 13, 1954, the Libyan Government informed the French authorities that it did not propose to renew a provisional agreement,

278

concluded in December 1951 and due to expire on Dec. 31, 1954, under which France had been permitted to maintain 400 troops and an air base in the Fezzan. During a debate in the French National Assembly on Dec. 6, 1954, the State Secretary for Foreign Affairs announced that France had informed the Libyan Government that she could not accept the Libyan demand for the evacuation of French troops and that she could not modify the existing situation until a permanent agreement had been concluded. With this aim in view negotiations between the two countries were opened on Dec. 31, 1954, in Paris and continued in Benghazi from Jan. 28, 1955.

Under the political agreement announced in Paris and Tripoli on Aug. 11, 1955, French troops would evacuate Fezzan within 12 months of the ratification of the treaty, whilst France would retain the right to reactivate the bases handed over to the Libyan authorities under the agreement, in the event of war, and would retain at all times landing and transit facilities at these bases. The first contingent of French troops left the Fezzan on Nov. 30, 1955; at the same time it was announced that the remainder would be withdrawn by July 1, 1956.

On Oct. 2, 1956, an agreement between Italy and Libya settling a number of problems outstanding since the end of the Second World War was signed in Rome.

During this period Libya received aid in various forms from Western countries. It was announced on Nov. 16, 1955, that the British and United States Governments, in response to a Libyan Government request, had decided to supply arms. Further announcements were made on April 7, 1956, and July 3, 1956, respectively, to the effect that the United States and Britain had agreed to increase their military and financial assistance to Libya. In March 1956 it had been reported that Libya had rejected a Soviet offer of economic aid. Further British assistance was announced on May 20, 1958 – involving financial and military aid – and on Nov. 23, 1961, in forming a Libyan Navy.

Unification, 1963–69

On April 2, 1963, Dr. Mohieddine Fekini, who had been appointed Premier of Libya in succession to Mr. Mohammed bin-Othman Al-Said on March 20, 1963, announced that the new Government intended to introduce legislation under which Libya would be turned from a federal into a unitary State, with the aim of securing economies and ensuring administrative efficiency. A Bill to this effect was presented to Parliament on April

15 with the following provisions: the franchise was conferred on women; in future the King would nominate all 24 members of the Senate, previously composed of 12 nominated and 12 elected members, which remained the Upper House of the Legislature; the country would be divided into 10 administrative units instead of being a federal State of three provinces; the administrative councils in the provinces would be abolished and executive powers throughout Libya would be exercised by the Council of Ministers.

Libya became a unitary state by royal proclamation on April 27, following the unanimous approval of the above proposals by Parliament and the three provincial legislative assemblies. The 10 administrative districts would each be headed by a Government-appointed administrator assisted by local advisory councils for certain matters including education, health, labour, communications and agriculture.

On Jan. 22, 1964, Mr. Mahmoud Bey Muntasser, Libya's first Premier after independence, was appointed Prime Minister in succession to Dr. Fekini who had resigned; no reason was given for this resignation but it was believed to have been connected with recent student disturbances in Benghazi and Tripoli.

The Prime Minister announced on March 9, 1964, that his Government had asked Britain and the United States to enter into negotiations on the future of their bases in Libya; this decision followed a speech on Feb. 22 by President Nasser of Egypt in which he called for the closing of British and American bases on Libyan territory. On the next day (Feb. 23) the Libyan Government had issued a statement that it had "no intention of renewing or extending" the military agreements with Britain and the United States, which it had been "compelled to conclude because of special circumstances". On March 16, the Prime Minister expanded his statement of March 9, declaring that the negotiations would be "for the termination of the treaties, the liquidation of the bases and the fixing of an evacuation date"; a resolution to this effect was unanimously approved by the Chamber of Deputies immediately afterwards. Negotiations on the Anglo-Libyan Treaty of Alliance of 1953 started on April 20, and by March 31, 1966, the partial withdrawal of British troops had been accomplished.

The Libyan Parliament was dissolved by King Idris on Feb. 13, 1965, in preparation for new general elections, following protests over the barring of some Opposition candidates from standing for the elections held on Oct. 10–11, 1964. Membership of the Lower House had been increased from 55 to 103 seats (on the basis of one deputy to 20,000 voters) after a census in August 1964 had shown the population to be just over

1,500,000. There were no political parties, each candidate pledging his loyalty to the King and the country and his determination to represent his constituents to the best of his ability. The new elections were held on May 8, 33 out of 103 members being returned unopposed; prior to this Mr. Mahmoud Bey Muntasser had resigned for health reasons and had been succeeded by the Foreign Minister, Mr. Husain Maziq.

As an Arab country, Libya reacted to the Middle East War of 1967 by taking measures against Britain and the United States, all oil exports being temporarily suspended on June 6; they were resumed following an Arab summit conference in Khartoum in August 1967. The Government officially requested the British and United States Governments to "liquidate" their military bases in Libya and to withdraw their troops from the country "as soon as possible".

Republic, 1969–

On Sept. 1, 1969, King Idris was deposed in a bloodless military coup carried out by a group of young officers. The Heir Apparent, Crown Prince Hassan al Rida, announced his voluntary abdication and expressed his support for the new regime. Tripoli Radio announced the formation of a Revolutionary Council exercising all executive and legislative powers and the setting up of a Libyan Arab Republic. The Revolutionary Council's first communiqué, broadcast from Tripoli on Sept. 1, stated *inter alia* that all legislative institutions of the former regime were abolished and all M.P.s dismissed, that the Council was the only authority responsible for the affairs of the Republic and that it would build up a "revolutionary and undoctrinal socialist State".

The formation of a Republican Government comprising two Army officers and seven civilians, and responsible to the Revolutionary Council, was announced on Sept. 8; this was headed by Dr. Mahmoud Soliman al Maghrabi.

Apart from the identity of the chairman, Colonel Moamer al Kadhafi, the membership of the Revolutionary Council – consisting of 12 officers – was not made public until Jan. 10, 1970.

The Council published the new Republican Constitution on Dec. 11, 1969; this described Libya as a "free democratic Republic" and stated that the Council, "the highest authority in the Libyan Arab Republic", would have the prerogatives of appointing the Council of Ministers (the Cabinet), signing and modifying treaties and declaring war. No mention was made of the establishment of a Parliament, nor of any other form of elected or representative assembly.

A new Cabinet was announced on Jan. 16, 1970; headed by Colonel Kadhafi who replaced Dr. Maghrabi as Premier, this included four other officers who were also members of the Revolutionary Council and eight civilians. Following a Cabinet reorganization on Sept. 16, 1970, the number of officers was increased to a total of eight.

A special military court established by the Revolutionary Command Council in December 1969 pronounced sentences of life imprisonment on Aug. 7, 1970, on Colonel Adam al Hawaz and Colonel Moussa Ahmad [the two officers in the first Republican Cabinet, see above] on charges of having plotted to kill Colonel Kadhafi in December 1969.

On Sept. 19, 1969, Dr. Maghrabi had announced that agreements governing foreign air bases in Libya would not be renewed at the expiration of the existing agreements permitting the use of such bases. Talks on the future of the two remaining British bases in Libya were held on Dec. 8–13, 1969, between the two countries; an agreement was concluded for the evacuation of all British forces and equipment from Libya to begin on Dec. 14 and to be completed by March 31, 1970. The installations at the two bases would be handed over to the Libyan authorities. Similar negotiations were held on Dec. 15–23 with the United States, resulting in an agreement being reached for the withdrawal of all American forces and equipment from the one U.S. air base in Libya by June 30, 1970. Further action against foreigners had been taken on Sept. 21, 1969, with the publishing of a decree barring all foreign businessmen from operating in Libya and laying down that all business concerns in the country would have to be wholly Libyan-owned.

On July 21, 1970, Colonel Kadhafi announced that his Government had decreed the confiscation of all assets in Libya owned by Italians. Italian protests that the Libyan Government's action violated the Italo-Libyan treaty of 1956 (which laid down that "no claim may be lodged as regards the property of Italian citizens in Libya") and the U.N. resolution of 1950 (which declared that "the property, rights and interests of Italian citizens in Libya will be respected provided they have been lawfully acquired") were rejected by the Libyan authorities; Colonel Kadhafi reiterated his attacks on "Italian colonialism" on Sept. 1, 1970, and during the next few months most of the 19,000 Italians in Libya returned to Italy, the Italian Government having made special provision for compensation for their losses.

SOMALIA

Area: 246,000 sq. miles.
Population 1969 (estimate): 2,730,000.
Capital: Mogadishu (200,000).
Official languages: Arabic, English, Italian.
Chief products: Livestock, sugar cane.

The Republic of Somalia, consisting of the former British Somaliland and the former Trust Territory of Somalia, became independent on July 1, 1960; on the same day Mr. Aden Abdullah Osman, president of the Somalia (Trust Territory) Legislative Assembly, was elected provisional President of the Republic at a joint meeting of representatives of the two former territories.

British Somaliland, which had been connected with the United Kingdom for about 130 years, had been a Protectorate since 1887. In general elections held on Feb. 17, 1960, the ruling National United Front suffered a major defeat by the Somali National League, winning only one seat compared with the 20 seats gained by the League. The remaining 12 seats went to the United Somali Party. All parties called for early independence and the unification of all Somali territories. [Somalis also lived in parts of Kenya, Ethiopia, and French Somaliland in addition to British Somaliland and Somalia.]

Somalia, an Italian colony from 1889, was occupied by British and Commonwealth forces in World War II and subsequently, in 1951, placed under U.N. trusteeship, with Italy as the administering power. On March 4–8, 1959, the first general elections held under universal suffrage for men and women resulted in the Somalia Youth League, the Government party led by Seyyid Abdullah Issa, winning 83 out of the 90 seats in a new Legislative Assembly, 61 out of the 83 being uncontested. Five seats went to the Independent Constitutional Somali Party and the remaining two to the Liberal Somali Youth Party. The opposition parties' reluctance to contest the elections was based on complaints that Government officials had allegedly interfered with party affairs.

From Parliamentary Democracy to Military Rule, 1960–70

Agreement was reached on the unification of British Somaliland and Somalia at meetings on April 16–24, 1960, between Somali representatives from both territories. The Republic would be unitary, democratic and parliamentary; the Legislative Assembly of Somalia and the Legislative

Council of British Somaliland would form themselves into a National Assembly on the achievement of independence. At the London constitutional conference on the future of British Somaliland, held on May 2–12, 1960, agreement was reached on the achievement of independence by the Protectorate on June 26, 1960, in order to enable the territory to unite with Somalia (Trust Territory) on July 1, 1960.

On July 12, 1960, Dr. Abdelrashid Ali Shermarke, a member of the former Somalia Legislative Assembly, was nominated Prime Minister of the Republic by the President; his Cabinet, announced on the following day, consisted of nine Ministers from Somalia (Trust Territory) and four from British Somaliland.

The Constitution for the Republic was approved by a large overall majority in a national referendum on June 20, 1961; however, a small majority against the Constitution was registered in the former British Somaliland.

The first national elections since independence, held on March 30, 1964, under a system of proportional representation, resulted in the Somali Youth League gaining an absolute majority of 69 seats in the 123-seat Assembly. The remaining seats were distributed amongst 11 Parties, the two strongest being the Somali National Congress (22) and the left-wing Somali Democratic Union (11).

A new Government under Mr. Abdirizak Hadji Hussein as Prime Minister and consisting exclusively of members of the Somali Youth League was sworn in on June 14, 1964, after Dr. Shermarke's resignation earlier that month. This Government was defeated on its first confidence vote on July 13, Mr. Hussein being regarded as pro-Western. Despite calls for the reappointment of Dr. Shermarke, the President again entrusted Mr. Hussein with the formation of a Government, which was announced on Aug. 31.

On June 10, 1967, Dr. Shermarke was elected President of the Republic by the National Assembly in a secret ballot, which gave him 73 votes against 50 for President Osman. This was an unexpected result, because the ruling Somali Youth League with 95 seats in the Assembly had nominated President Osman and the main Opposition party, the Somali National Congress, had pledged its unconditional support for him. President Shermarke appointed Mr. Mohammed Ibrahim Egal (Premier of British Somaliland before independence) as Prime Minister on July 6, 1967.

In the general elections held on March 25, 1969, Mr. Egal's party, the Somali Youth League, returned to power with 73 out of a total of 124 seats compared with 93 seats before the dissolution. 68 political parties or groupings contested the elections in addition to the Somali Youth League; 19 parties gained one seat each, whilst the party of the former Prime Minister, Mr. Hussein, gained only two seats.

On Oct. 15, 1969, President Shermarke was assassinated by a member of the police force, who was subsequently, on Oct. 8, 1970, sentenced to death. Sheikh Mukhtar Mohammed Hussein, President of the National Assembly, became acting President of the Republic, and all political activities were banned. On Oct. 20 the Central Committee of the Somali Youth League nominated Hadji Musa Boghor, said to be the wealthiest trader in Somalia, for the post of President.

However, the following day Army commanders supported by the police seized power without meeting any opposition; they dissolved the National Assembly, suspended the Constitution, arrested all the members of the Cabinet and declared a state of emergency. It was stated that this action had been taken in order to "fight against the corruption of the ruling classes" which had "led to the assassination of President Shermarke". General Mohammed Siyad Barreh (C.-in-C. of the Armed Forces) was named as chairman of a 25-member Revolutionary Council; the Prime Minister, Mr. Egal, who had been widely criticized in connexion with alleged irregularities during the elections of March 25, 1969, was placed under arrest by the Council.

It was announced on Oct. 22 that a new Constitution had been drafted under which the Revolutionary Council would elect a new President. The Council decided on the same date to abolish the Supreme Court, to prohibit all political parties, to close down three Government-owned newspapers and to change the country's name to "Somali Democratic Republic". It also announced that it would make every effort to achieve the unification of the Somali people.

In a decree published on Oct. 29 the Council assumed (as from Oct. 21) the powers of the President, the National Assembly, the Government and the Supreme Court. Two weeks later, on Nov. 15, General Siyad Barreh announced that a new Constitution was being prepared and would be submitted to a referendum.

On April 27, 1970, it was officially announced that a "counter-revolutionary plot" had been foiled and that the several persons arrested included Major-General Jama Ali Korshel, who was dismissed from his post as First Vice-Chairman and member of the Revolutionary Council, and charged with high treason.

The nationalization of certain large foreign-owned firms in Somalia, including banks and oil companies, was announced by Major-General

Siyad Barreh on May 7, 1970; this decision affected mainly Italian interests.

Disputes with Neighbouring States

The main problem facing Somalia during the period since the declaration of independence has been the question of Somali territorial claims on French Somaliland and parts of Kenya and Ethiopia. Aspirations towards a "Greater Somalia" were embodied in the Republic's Constitution and all political groupings, both in power and in opposition, support the reunion of Somali peoples wherever they may live.

Kenya

The dispute with Kenya arose prior to that country's independence. On March 18, 1963, diplomatic relations were broken with the United Kingdom by Somalia, because of the British decision to create a seventh Kenyan region from part of the Northern Frontier district, "thus failing to recognize the wish expressed by the people of the Northern Frontier District to secede from Kenya and unite with the Somali Republic". In reply to this action by the Republic, Mr. Edward Heath, then the British Lord Privy Seal, said in the House of Commons on March 25, 1963, that the creation of a seventh region was "designed to give Kenya's Somalis a greater opportunity for the expression of their racial and religious identity". He continued: "The Somali Government apparently takes the view that this decision is final. [It] has been informed that the decision is not a final determination."

On April 14, 1963, Dr. Shermarke, Prime Minister of Somalia, reaffirmed the territorial claim over the Northern Frontier district. Discussions between representatives of Britain and the Somali Republic, held on Aug. 25–28, 1963, were unsuccessful in that the British Government, though legally responsible for Kenya until independence, declined to make any decision on the dispute over the North-Eastern Region of Kenya.

Unrest in this region continued throughout the period 1963–67; an agreement was signed on Sept. 13, 1967, by the Governments of Kenya and Somalia during meetings of the OAU Assembly, by which they undertook to end the fighting in the border areas of their two territories and resume normal relations. A memorandum of agreement was signed in Arusha (Tanzania) on Oct. 28, 1967, by President Kenyatta of Kenya and the Prime Minister of Somalia, Mr. Egal, implementing the OAU agreement. On Jan. 5, 1968, diplomatic relations between Somalia and the United Kingdom were re-established whilst President Kenyatta announced on Jan. 31, 1968, the immediate establishment of diplomatic relations between Kenya and Somalia.

Prior to the proclamation of Somali independence, the Ethiopian Government announced on June 5, 1960, that the British-Ethiopian agreement of 1954 [see ETHIOPIA, page 44] which gave British Somaliland tribesmen the right to graze their cattle in the Haud area of Ogaden (Ethiopia) would automatically become invalid when the Protectorate achieved independence on June 26, 1960. The disagreement between Somalia and Ethiopia erupted at the beginning of 1964; clashes occurred at many different places along the 900-mile border both on Somali and Ethiopian territory. Not all the fighting involved armed forces of Somalia, being in part due to the activities of insurrectionist Somali bands in the Ethiopian province of Ogaden under the leadership of Mukhtal Taher, the self-styled "Prime Minister" of a "liberation Government" set up in the province. Appeals for the peaceful settlement of their differences were made to the two Governments by U Thant on Feb. 9, and by the Dar-es-Salaam conference of OAU Foreign Ministers on Feb. 14, 1964. A cease-fire, for which the OAU conference had called, officially became effective at noon on Feb. 16 after President Ibrahim Abboud of the Sudan had advised the Emperor of Ethiopia that the Somali Government had accepted the cease-fire proposal.

However, the cease-fire was breached several times during March 1964; a conference held at the invitation of the Sudanese Government opened on March 25 to settle the dispute. Agreement was reached on March 30 by the Somali and Ethiopian Foreign Ministers to undertake to solve the dispute peacefully, to maintain a cease-fire and to complete the withdrawal of military forces from the border for distances from six to nine miles between April 1 and 6. On Sept. 22, in an agreement published simultaneously in Addis Ababa and Mogadishu, Ethiopia and Somalia agreed to "eliminate all forms of tension" between themselves.

Relations with Communist Countries

The Somali Republic was one of the first countries in Africa to conclude aid and trade agreements with Communist countries.

In November 1963 the Somali Government concluded an agreement with the Soviet Union on military aid worth $30,000,000 for the Somali Army, and at the same time the Somali Parliament ratified the country's first trade agreement with Communist China.

Somalia was also among the first African States to establish diplomatic relations with Eastern Germany (April 1970) and North Vietnam (June 1970).

EQUATORIAL GUINEA

Area: 10,935 sq. miles.
Population 1969 (estimate): 286,000.
Capital: Santa Isabel (38,000).
Official language: Spanish.
Chief products: Coffee, cocoa, timber.

Equatorial Guinea, consisting of the island province of Fernando Poo and the mainland province of Rio Muni, achieved independence on Oct. 12, 1968, after 110 years of Spanish rule in Fernando Poo and 68 years in Rio Muni.

Presidential elections held on Sept. 22, 1968, resulted in no candidate receiving an absolute majority; in the second ballot on Sept. 29 the successful candidate was Señor Francisco Macias Nguema, then Deputy Premier, sponsored by the Popular Idea of Equatorial Guinea Party (IPGE) and dissident members of the Movement for National Unity of Equatorial Guinea (MUNGE) and the National Liberation Movement of Equatorial Guinea (Monalige). Elections were held on Sept. 22 for the 35 seats in the National Assembly and for seats on the provincial councils. Señor Macias announced his Government on Oct. 10, a coalition of the three main nationalist parties, who were united in their desire for total independence with the severance of all links with Spain and for the continued federation of Fernando Poo and Rio Muni. The *Unión Bubi*, a party representing the main ethnic group of the island of Fernando Poo, the Bubis, advocated separation of Fernando Poo and Rio Muni, however, and the retention of autonomous status for Fernando Poo with possible later independence.

The country had had a degree of autonomy since Jan. 1, 1964, with an elected Assembly and a Government council, members of the latter being elected by the Assembly and approved by the Commissioner-General representing the Spanish Government.

The draft Constitution which had been approved in a national referendum held on Aug. 11, 1968, established the independence of Equatorial Guinea as a unitary state with a presidential system of Government, and provided for a bicameral legislature, comprising an Assembly of 35 members and a Council of the Republic with six members equally representative of both Rio Muni and Fernando Poo, and universal adult suffrage.

In February 1969, a dispute arose with Spain over a demand made by

President Macias that the Spanish armed forces stationed in Equatorial Guinea should be withdrawn.

On March 5, a number of high-ranking political leaders were arrested after an unsuccessful coup against President Macias. Señor Atanasio Ndongo Miyone, Foreign Minister of Equatorial Guinea and alleged leader of the coup, was reported to have tried to persuade the President, on March 4, to discontinue his broadcasts which – Señor Ndongo claimed – were inciting the people to attack whites. The attempted coup followed on President Macias' refusal to meet this request. According to a message on March 6 from the British Consul in Santa Isabel, and to refugees reaching Spain, there was "virtual anarchy" in Equatorial Guinea. President Macias declared on March 8 that all remaining Spaniards were free to leave the country; two days later on March 10 he warned youth gangs that they should desist from terrorizing Europeans, and on March 13 he was reported to have assured Spanish nationals wishing to remain in Equatorial Guinea that they would be safe.

By March 28 all Spanish forces had been withdrawn from Rio Muni together with all civilians who wished to leave, and their evacuation from Fernando Poo was complete by April 5. The number of Spanish settlers remaining was probably no more than 600 in Fernando Poo and about 80 in Rio Muni.

Despite the dispute with Spain in March, an agreement on economic and commercial co-operation was signed with that country in Bata (Rio Muni) on May 20, 1969. Further agreements on Spanish technical and cultural aid were signed in November 1969.

I. AFRICAN STATES' MEMBERSHIP OF ORGANIZATIONS

	OAU	Commonwealth	Communauté	OCAM	Conseil de l'Entente	Defence Pact with France	Associate of E.E.C.	Arab League	Maghreb Consultative Committee	East African Community	Central African Customs & Economic Union (UDEAC)	West African Customs Union (UDEAO)	Organization of Riparian States of River Senegal
Algeria	X							X	X				
Botswana	X	X											
Burundi	X												
Cameroon	X		X	X		X	X				X		
Central African Republic	X		X	X		X	X				X		
Chad	X			X		X	X				X		
Congo Democratic Republic (Kinshasa)	X			X			X						
Congo People's Republic (Brazzaville)	X		X	X			X				X		
Dahomey	X			X	X		X						
Equatorial Guinea	X											X	
Ethiopia	X												
Gabon	X		X	X		X	X				X		
Gambia	X	X											
Ghana	X	X											
Guinea	X												
Ivory Coast	X			X	X	X	X					X	X
Kenya	X	X					O			X			

Lesotho

Liberia

Libya

Malagasy Republic

Malawi

Mali

Mauritania

Mauritius

Morocco

Niger

Nigeria

Rhodesia

Rwanda

Senegal

Sierra Leone

Somalia

South Africa

Sudan

Swaziland

Tanzania

Togo

Tunisia

Uganda

United Arab Republic

Upper Volta

Zambia

O   As member of East African Community

II. MEMBERSHIP OF UNITED NATIONS AND ITS AGENCIES

	UN	IAEA	ILO	FAO	UNESCO	WHO	BANK	IFC	IDA	FUND	ICAO	UPU	ITU	WMO	IMCO	GATT
Algeria	×	×	×	×	×	×	×		×	×	×	×	×	×	×	
Botswana	×			×			×		×	×		×	×	×		×
Burundi	×		×	×	×	×	×		×	×	×	×	×	×		×
Cameroon	×	×	×	×	×	×	×		×	×	×	×	×	×	×	×
Central African Republic	×		×	×	×	×	×		×	×	×	×	×	×		×
Chad	×		×	×	×	×	×	×	×	×	×	×	×	×		
Congo, Democratic Republic (Kinshasa)	×	×	×	×	×	×	×		×	×	×	×	×	×		
Congo, People's Republic (Brazzaville)	×		×	×	×	×	×		×	×	×	×	×	×		×
Dahomey	×			×		×	×		×	×		×	×			
Equatorial Guinea	×		×	×	×	×	×		×	×		×	×	×		×
Ethiopia	×	×	×	×	×	×	×	×	×	×	×	×	×		×	
Gabon	×	×	×	×	×	×	×	×	×	×	×	×	×	×		×
Gambia	×			×			×		×	×		×	×			
Ghana	×	×	×	×	×	×	×	×	×	×	×	×	×	×		×
Guinea	×		×	×	×	×	×		×	×	×	×	×	×		
Ivory Coast	×	×	×	×	×	×	×	×	×	×	×	×	×	×	×	×
Kenya	×	×	×	×	×	×	×	×	×	×	×	×	×	×	×	×
Lesotho	×		×	×	×	×	×		×	×		×	×			
Liberia	×	×	×	×	×	×	×	×	×	×	×	×	×		×	×
Libya	×	×	×	×	×	×	×	×	×	×	×	×	×	×	×	×

	Col 1	Col 2	Col 3	Col 4	Col 5	Col 6	Col 7	Col 8	Col 9	Col 10	Col 11	Col 12	Col 13
Malagasy Republic	X	X	X	X	X	X	X	X	X	X	X	X	X
Malawi	X	X	X	X	X	X	X	X	X	X	X	X	X
Mali	X		X	X	X	X	X	X	X	X	X	X	
Mauritania	X	X	X	X	X	X	X	X	X	X	X	X	X
Mauritius	X	X	X	X	X	X	X	X	X	X	X	X	X
Morocco	X	X	X	X	X	X	X	X	X	X	X	X	X
Niger	X	X	X	X	X	X	X	X	X	X	X	X	X
Nigeria	X	X	X	X	X	X	X	X	X	X	X	X	X
Rhodesia	X	X			A		X	X	X	X	X		
Rwanda	X	X	X	X	X	X	X	X	X	X	X	X	X
Senegal	X	X	X	X	X	X	X	X	X	X	X	X	X
Sierra Leone	X	X	X	X	X	X	X	X	X	X	X	X	X
Somalia	X	X	X	X	X	X	X	X	X	X	X	X	
South Africa	X	X		X		X	X	X	X	X	X	X	X
Sudan	X	X	X	X	X	X	X	X	X	X	X	X	
Swaziland	X												
Tanzania	X	X	X	X	X	X	X	X	X	X	X	X	X
Togo	X	X	X	X	X	X	X	X	X	X	X	X	X
Tunisia	X	X	X	X	X	X	X	X	X	X	X	X	P
Uganda	X	X	X	X	X	X	X	X	X	X	X	X	X
United Arab Republic	X	X	X	X	X	X	X	X	X	X	X	X	X
Upper Volta	X	X	X	X	X	X	X	X	X	X	X		
Zambia	X	X	X	X	X	X	X	X	X	X	X	X	X

A Associate member
P Provisionally acceded

293

III. POLITICAL STRUCTURE
OF AFRICAN STATES

	MONARCHY	REPUBLIC	PRESIDENTIAL REGIME	PARLIAMENTARY DEMOCRACY	UNITARY STATE	FEDERATION	MILITARY REGIME	ONE-PARTY STATE
Algeria		X	X		X		X	
Botswana		X	X		X			
Burundi		X	X		X		X	X Uprona Party
Cameroon		X	X			X (Two States)		X Union nationale camerounaise
Central African Republic		X	X		X		X	X Mouvement d'évolution sociale d'Afrique noire
Chad		X	X		X			X Parti progressiste tchadien
Congo, Democratic Republic (Kinshasa)		X	X		X		X	X Mouvement populaire de la révolution
Congo, People's Republic (Brazzaville)		X	X		X		X	X Parti des travailleurs congolais
Dahomey		X	X		X		X	
Equatorial Guinea		X	X		X			
Ethiopia	X		X		X			
Gabon		X	X		X			X Parti démocratique gabonaise
Gambia		X	X		X			
Ghana		X		X	X			
Guinea		X	X		X			X Parti démocratique de Guinée
Ivory Coast		X	X		X			X Parti démocratique de la Côte d'Ivoire

Country					One-party state (party)
Kenya		X		X	X Kenya African National Union (Constitution suspended)
Lesotho	X		X		
Liberia		X	X	X	X True Whig Party
Libya		X	X	X	
Malagasy Republic		X	X	X	
Malawi		X	X	X	X Malawi Congress Party
Mali		X	X		
Mauritania		X	X		X Mauritanian People's Party
Mauritius	X	X	X	X	
Morocco	X		X		
Niger		X	X		X Parti progressiste nigérien
Nigeria		X	X	X (12 States)	
Rhodesia		X	X	X	
Rwanda		X	X		X Parmehutu
Senegal		X	X		
Sierra Leone	X	X	X		
Somalia		X	X		
South Africa	X	X			
Sudan	X	X			
Swaziland		X			
Tanzania				X (a) Mainland (b) Zanzibar	X (a) Tanganyika African National Union (b) Afro-Shirazi Party
Togo		X			X Rassemblement du peuple togolais
Tunisia		X	X	X	
Uganda		X	X	X	
United Arab Republic		X	X	X	X Arab Socialist Union
Upper Volta		X	X	X	X Union démocratique voltaïque
Zambia		X	X		

IV. GROSS NATIONAL PRODUCT (GNP)
(per head in U.S. dollars)

	Below 50	50-99	100-149	150-249	250-650
Algeria				220	
Botswana		60			
Burundi		50			
Cameroon			110		
Central African Republic			110		
Chad		70			
Congo (Brazzaville)			120		
Congo (Kinshasa)		60			
Dahomey		80			
Equatorial Guinea		60			
Ethiopia		60			
Gabon					400
Gambia		90			
Ghana				230	
Guinea		80			
Ivory Coast				220	
Kenya		90			
Lesotho		60			
Liberia				210	
Libya					640
Malagasy Republic		90			
Malawi		50			
Mali		60			
Mauritania			130		
Mauritius				210	
Morocco				170	
Niger		80			
Nigeria		80			
Rhodesia				210	
Rwanda	40				
Senegal				210	
Sierra Leone				150	
Somalia		50			
South Africa					550
Sudan			100		
Swaziland					290
Tanzania		80			
Togo			100		
Tunisia				200	
Uganda			100		
United Arab Republic				160	
Upper Volta		50			
Zambia				180	

[The Statesman's Year-Book, 1970–71]

V.   DEPENDENT TERRITORIES IN AFRICA

COUNTRY	AREA (Square miles)	POPULATION
Portuguese Provinces		
Angola	481,000	5,200,000 (250,000 whites)
Cape Verde Islands	1,600	220,000
Mozambique	298,000	6,950,000 (70,000 whites)
Portuguese Guinea	14,000	580,000
São Tomé & Principe Islands	372	64,000
French Possessions		
Comoro Islands	838	210,000
French Territory of the Afars and Issas (French Somaliland)	9,000	81,000
Reúnion	970	387,000
Spanish Territories		
Spanish Sahara	103,000	48,000
Spanish North Africa (Ceuta and Melilla)	Ceuta 7.6 Melilla 4.8	Ceuta 75,000 Melilla 90,000
British Dependencies		
Seychelles	160	46,000
St. Helena	47	4,700
Territory Administered by South Africa		
South West Africa	318,000	610,000 (73,464 whites)

SUBJECT INDEX

Aburi Agreement, 1967, 111
Abyssinia
  see Ethiopia
Algeria, 240-52
  Arab Countries, other, relations with, 82, 191, 198-9, 202, 205
  Democratic Republic of the Congo (Kinshasa), 269-70
  "Historic Leaders of the Revolution", 241, 247
  Rhodesia, 181
  "Algérie Française", 244
Anglo-Egyptian Condominium of the Sudan
  see Sudan
Anglo-Egyptian Treaty, 1936, 62
Angola, 269
Ansar Moslems, 84, 87
Anya Nya, 82, 87
Apartheid (South Africa), 7, 50-61, 162
  Lusaka Declaration, 42
  Lusaka Manifesto, 12-14
Apartheid – South African Legislation, 50-61
  Bantu Authorities Act, 1951, 54, 58
  Bantu Education Act, 1952, 56
  Coloured Representative Council Act, 1964, 59
  Group Areas Act, 1950, 53-4
  Native Representation Act, 1936, 57

Native (Urban Areas) Consolidation Act, 1945, 52-3
Pass Laws, 51, 55, 60
Population Registration Act, 1950, 55
Promotion of Bantu Self-Government Act, 1959, 54
Separate Representation of Voters Act, 1951, 58; 1956, 58-9
South African Indian Council Act, 1968, 60
Arab-Israeli Conflict, 70, 72-4
  Arab Countries, policy, 47, 86, 281
  Arab League, resolutions, 32, 33
Arab Liberation Front for Eritrea (Ethiopia), 47
"Arab Socialism", 68-70, 74-5, 203
Army of Liberation (Morocco), 190, 191, 197
Arusha Convention, 1968, 40-1; 1969, 41
Arusha Declaration, 1967, 124
Aswan High Dam, 75-7

Bantustans, 54
Banwell Commission, 1965, 165
Barotseland, 154
Basutoland
  see Lesotho
Bechuanaland
  see Botswana

International Control Commission (Tangier Zone), 189-90
Iraq, 70
Italian Somaliland, 44
  see also Somalia
Italy
  Arab Countries, relations with, 44, 76, 282, 286
  Arms to South Africa, 42
  Zambia, 157, 158-60
Ivory Coast, 222-4
  African Countries, other, relations with, 6-7, 100, 207
  French Community, The, 27-8
  West African Monetary Union, 19

Japan, 42, 182-3

Kamerun
  see Cameroon, Federal Republic of — Cameroon, Republic of
Kampala Conference, 1967, 12
Kariba Dam
  Rhodesian territory, 158
  Zambian territory, 159
Katanga, 254-61, 262-3, 266, 268, 271
Kenya, 129-35
  Arab Countries, relations with, 82, 286-7
  Arms to South Africa, 7
  Conferences of African States, 10-12, 15
Khartoum Conference, 1970, 15
Kinshasa, Declaration of, 1967, 11

League of Arab States
  see Arab League
League of Nations, 44, 46
  Mandated territories, 88, 120, 209-10, 212, 274
Lesotho, 27, 41, 163-4
Liberation Front of the Somali Coast (Territory of the Afars and Issas), 6
Liberation Movements
  Algeria, 241-5
  Conferences of African States, resolutions, 10-15
  Organization of African Unity, resolutions, 5-6
Libya, 277-82
  Arab Countries, other, relations with, 33-4, 72, 200
  Arab-Israeli Conflict, 34
  Rhodesia, 176
"Lost Counties" Problem (Uganda), 126
Lower Congo
  see Democratic Republic of the Congo (Kinshasa)
Lumpa Church, 156
Lusaka Declaration, 1970, 41-2
Lusaka Manifesto, 1969, 12-14

Madagascar
  see Malagasy Republic
Maghreb, The, 40
Maghreb Permanent Consultative Committee, 18
Malagasy Republic, 35, 214-5
Malawi, 151-3
  Conferences of African States, 10, 11, 15
  Rhodesia, 181, 183
Mali, 19, 181, 237-9
Mali Federation
  see Mali
      Senegal
Mauritania, 239-40
  French Community, The, 27-8
  Morocco, 198
  Rhodesia, 181
  West African Monetary Union, 19
Melilla, 197
Mercenaries
  Democratic Republic of the Congo (Kinshasa), 260, 264, 269, 271
  Guinea, 208
  Nigeria, 115
Middle Congo
  see People's Republic of the Congo (Brazzaville)
Mining and Industrial Development Corporation (Zambia), 158
Monckton Commission, 1960, 144-6
Moroccan Workers' Union, 191-2, 194
Mozambique, 8, 15, 177, 187

Nairobi Conference, 1966, 10
Namibia
  see South West Africa
Nationalization
  Algeria, 247, 249-50
  Democratic Republic of the Congo (Kinshasa), 270
  Ghana, 98, 102
  Guinea, 206-8
  Ivory Coast, 223
  Libya, 282
  Morocco, 194, 196
  People's Republic of the Congo (Brazzaville), 228
  Somalia, 286
  Sudan, 86
  Tanzania, 122, 124
  Tunisia, 203-4
  Uganda, 128-9
  United Arab Republic, 67, 74-6
  Zambia, 155, 158
National Liberation Army (Algeria), 243, 246
Native Representative Council (South Africa), 57-8
Netherlands, The, 38, 76, 164
New Zealand, 181, 183

Niger, 18, 19, 28, 207, 218-9
Nigeria, 104-17
  Cameroon, Federal Republic of, 211-2
  Organization of African Unity, resolutions, 6-7
  Northern Cameroon
    see Cameroon, Federal Republic of –
    Southern Cameroons
    Nigeria
Northern Rhodesia, 135-51
  see also Zambia
Nyasaland, 135-51
  see also Malawi

OAS
  see *Organisation de l'armée secrète*
OAU
  see Organization of African Unity
OCAM
  see Common African, Malagasy and Mauritian Organization
Organisation commune africaine et malgache
  see Common African, Malagasy and Mauritian Organization
Organisation commune africaine, malgache et mauricienne
  see Common African, Malagasy and Mauritian Organization
Organisation de l'armée secrète (Algeria), 245
Organisation des Etats riverains du fleuve Sénégal
  see Organization of Riparian States of the River Senegal
Organization of African Unity, 1-8, 11, 42
  Lusaka Manifesto, 14
  Peace negotiations
    Biafra, 116
    Democratic Republic of the Congo (Kinshasa), 264-5, 271
    Ghana, 100
    Somalia, 287
  Rhodesia, 180-1
Organization of Committees of Public Safety
  see Committee of Public Safety for Algeria and the Sahara
Organization of Riparian States of the River Senegal, 19-20
Ottawa Agreement, 1932, 175
Ouchy, Treaty of, 1912, 277

PAIGC
  see *Partido africano de independência da Guiné e do Cabo Verde*
Partido africano de independência da Guiné e do Cabo Verde (Portuguese Guinea), 6

People's Republic of the Congo (Brazzaville), 225-33
  Conferences of African States, 10-11, 15
  Democratic Republic of the Congo (Kinshasa), 272
  Organization of African Unity, resolution, 11
  Rhodesia, 181
People's Republic of the Congo (Stanleyville), 264-5
Portugal
  African Countries, relations with, 208, 269
  Dar-es-Salaam Conference, resolution, 12
  Decolonization, 6, 42
  Lusaka Manifesto, 14
  Organization of African Unity, resolution, 7
  Rhodesia, 176, 182-3, 186
Portuguese Territories, 6, 7, 15, 42, 115, 177, 187, 224, 269

Refugees
  Country of Origin
    Algeria, 249, 251
    Dahomey, 100
    Democratic Republic of the Congo (Kinshasa), 254, 265, 271
    Equatorial Guinea, 289
    Ghana, 100
    Guinea, 208
    Ivory Coast, 100, 223
    Niger, 100, 219
    Nigeria, 115
    Rwanda, 276-7
    Sudan, 81-2
    Togo, 214
    Upper Volta, 100
  Nairobi Conference, resolution, 10
  Organization of African Unity, resolutions, 5-7
Republic of South Africa Constitution Act, 1961, 50
Réunion, 27, 35
Rhodesia, 22, 27, 172-88
  African Organizations, resolutions, 11-15
  Decolonization, 7
  Zambia, 157, 158-60
  see also Southern Rhodesia
Rio de Oro
  see Spanish Sahara
Rio Muni
  see Equatorial Guinea
Rodrigues
  see Mauritius
Rome, Treaty of, 1958, 34, 37, 39

304

Togoland
  see Togo
Tomlinson Report
  see Commission on the Socio-Econom-
    ic Development of the Bantu Areas
Tredgold Commission, 1957, 142
Tunisia, 39-40, 41, 199-205
Turkey, 68

UAM
  see *Union africaine et malgache*
UAMCE
  see *Union africaine et malgache de co-
    opération économique*
U.A.R.
  see United Arab Republic
Ubangi-Shari
  see Central African Republic
Uccialli, Treaty of, 1889, 44
UDEAC
  see Central African Customs Union
UDEAO
  see West African Customs Union
UDI (Rhodesia)
  see Unilateral Declaration of Independ-
    ence
UEAC
  see *Union des états de l'Afrique cen-
    trale*
Uganda, 125-9
  Arab Countries, relations with, 44, 82
  Conferences of African States, 11-12,
    15
  Kenya, 132-3
U.N.
  see United Nations
Unilateral Declaration of Independence
  (Rhodesia), 171-4, 175-8, 182
Union africaine et malgache, 8
*Union africaine et malgache de coopéra-
  tion économique,* 8
Union des états de l'Afrique centrale, 17
*Union douanière des états d'Afrique oc-
  cidentale*
  see West African Customs Union
Union Minière du Haut Katanga (Demo-
  cratic Republic of the Congo), 12,
  273
Union of Arab States, 68
United Arab Republic, 61-77
  Arab Countries, other, relations with,
    33-4, 47, 81-2, 280
  Democratic Republic of the Congo
    (Kinshasa), 267
  Rhodesia, 181
United Kingdom
  African Countries, relations with,

88-90, 95, 98, 100, 114, 116-7, 120,
    129, 131, 132, 154, 156, 159-60,
    164, 165, 209,265
  Arab Countries, relations with, 44, 46,
    61-2, 72-3, 74, 76, 79, 277, 280-1,
    282, 283, 286, 287
  Arms to South Africa, 7, 42
  Central African Federation of Rhode-
    sia and Nyasaland, 135-7, 140,
    144-50
  Commonwealth, The, 21-3
  Decolonization, 42
  Organization of African Unity, 7
  Rhodesia, 11-13, 22, 168, 169,
    170-87
  South Africa, 49
United Nations
  Democratic Republic of the Congo
    (Kinshasa), 254-60, 261, 263-4
  Guinea, 208
  Nigeria, 117
  South Africa, 7, 14
United Nations – General Assembly,
    Resolutions
  Democratic Republic of the Congo
    (Kinshasa), 256, 258
  Ethiopia, 46
  Ghana, 90
  Libya, 277, 282
  Lusaka Manifesto, 14
  Morocco, 198
  Rhodesia, 176
United Nations – Security Council, Res-
    olutions
  Arab-Israeli War, 1967, 73
  Democratic Republic of the Congo
    (Kinshasa), 254, 256, 258, 260, 265,
    269
  Rhodesia, 176, 178, 182-3, 187
United States of America
  African Countries, relations with, 47,
    99-100, 122, 123, 131, 132, 159,
    233, 256, 264-5, 271
  Arab Countries, relations with, 73, 76,
    79, 199, 279, 280-1, 282
  Arms to South Africa, 42
  Decolonization, 41-2
  Lusaka Manifesto, 15
  Rhodesia, 172, 177, 182-3, 187
Unlawful Organizations Act, 1960
  (South Africa), 61
Upper Volta, 219-21
  African Countries, other, relations
    with, 207, 237
  French Community, The, 28
  West African Monetary Union, 19
U.S.S.R.
  see Soviet Union

305

INDEX OF
POLITICAL PARTIES:
PAST AND PRESENT

308

310

INDEX OF
SELECTED NAMES

314